AMERICAN DIPLOMACY

The Twentieth Century

AMERICAN DIPLOMACY

The Twentieth Century

ROBERT H. FERRELL
INDIANA UNIVERSITY

W · W · NORTON & COMPANY
New York · London

The text of this book is composed in Janson, with display type set in Bulmer. Composition by Vail-Ballou Press. Manufacturing by The Maple-Vail Book Group.

Library of Congress Cataloging-in-Publication Data

Ferrell, Robert H.
American diplomacy.

Includes index.
1. United States—Foreign relations—20th century.
I. Title.
E744.F48 1987 327.73 87-7667

ISBN 0-393-95609-1

W. W. Norton & Company, Inc., 500 Fifth Avenue, New York, N.Y. 10110
W. W. Norton & Company Ltd., 37 Great Russell Street, London WC1B 3NU

1 2 3 4 5 6 7 8 9 0

For LILA *and* CAROLYN

Acknowledgments

Material in this book has appeared in three previous editions of a full American diplomatic history. Thoroughly revised and updated, it now reappears as a diplomatic history of twentieth-century America.

Over the years I have benefited from readings of chapters and from conversations with scholars representing several generations, and for their assistance I am deeply grateful. Some of these individuals helped make the history recorded in these pages. Charles Seymour attended the Paris Peace Conference of 1919 as a member of the advisory group known as the Inquiry. Samuel Flagg Bemis was aboard the steamer *Sussex* in 1916 when a German submarine torpedoed it in the English Channel. Bemis saw the wake of the torpedo, and his testimony together with that of a few other passengers confirmed that the ship was sunk by a submarine, rather than a British mine as the German government contended. On the basis of this testimony President Woodrow Wilson sent a virtual ultimatum to Germany, which led to war the next year.

Among others who have read portions of the book, F. Lee Benns, Hajo Holborn, and Bernard F. Nordmann provided useful comments. I have likewise enjoyed much conversation with Julius W. Pratt and with Dexter Perkins, himself a member of the delegation at the Peace Conference.

My generation regarded American diplomacy in the twentieth century as centering on the approach, course, and sequels of World War II, and for this era I have had assistance from friends too numerous to mention. Similarly from the first postwar generation. And now from a second. In those two latter generations—third and fourth since World War I—have been many Indiana doctoral students, now teaching in American colleges and universities. They are Democrats and Republicans and independents, traditionalists and revisionists, realists and idealists, but none is a doctrinaire, every one worth listening to.

This time around a special thanks to Patrick O'Meara who explained South Africa, and to David MacIsaac who knows about warheads and carriers; to John M. Hollingsworth who updated the maps; and especially to Deborah Malmud, Debra Makay, Steven Forman, and James L. Mairs—fine people as well as wonderful editors.

R.H.F.

Contents

Illustrations

Maps

Preface

This book is thorough in its coverage of diplomatic events from 1898 to the present day. It organizes the diplomatic history of our century through eras of change rather than through arbitrary periods described by the presidential succession; America's foreign relations in this century overlap the neat categories of presidential administrations. It stresses the nuclear age, the dangerous period that began with the explosion of a plutonium test device near Los Alamos early on the morning of July 16, 1945. Since that time diplomacy has changed dramatically and assumed a new, awesome importance, having now to mediate the nuclear arms race. Over the years the arms race has oscillated between the development of warheads and carriers, and has been marked by a single point of stability, what one might describe as a truism, namely, that anything American science might produce is reproduced by the Soviet Union within a period of four to six years. The race has become far more complex because of what Secretary of State John Foster Dulles described in an ugly word as "proliferation." Arms secrets, if such there ever were, have passed gradually to other nations.

As it must, the book ends with the great diplomatic challenge of our time: the need for nuclear nations, especially the United States and the Soviet Union, to engage in arms control beyond the beginnings set out in the SALT-I and SALT-II agreements. The enormous danger of the present era is the continuing inability of nations, principally the superpowers, to arrange an end—either immediate or by stages—to the insanity of overkill. It is increasingly clear that whatever the diplomacy of the moment, whether deterrence or détente, the dire peril for the world, not just the U.S. and the USSR, is that in any crisis, not to mention war, command and control of weapons will break down. The danger of our time is a nuclear war that will open not like World War II, owing its origins to the aggressive designs of a dictator, but like World War I, through a series of automatic, unthinking, undesired, and local decisions.

Considering the danger of our very special age there is, surely, a need for education. The American people, and other peoples, will have to learn the requirements of contemporary diplomacy. But to what use? Education was the vain hope of eighteenth-century philosophers and nineteteeth-century liberal reformers, and in the twentieth century the best-educated country in Europe, Germany, adopted a foreign policy full of error, precipitating the world into its present difficult position.

One thing is certain, that foreign relations have become the central problem of the great republic of the new world.

AMERICAN DIPLOMACY

The Twentieth Century

☆ 1 ☆

The Tradition

In the wars of the European powers in matters relating to themselves we have never taken any part, nor does it comport with our policy so to do. It is only when our rights are invaded or seriously menaced that we resent injuries or make preparation for our defense.

—President James Monroe, State of the Union Address, December 2, 1823

For two centuries and more, American diplomacy has sought to represent the interests of the United States to the peoples and governments of friendly nations and to protect those interests from adversaries, and almost of necessity the result was a diplomatic tradition, which took the form of a set of principles. The early diplomats and their successors often pondered the remarkable way in which the thirteen colonies with barely three million inhabitants became a nation. They did their best to draw on the wisdom of their time, to bring it into a form easily remembered and followed. By the era of the Spanish-American War at the end of the nineteenth century, basic principles supported the country's diplomatic tradition. The war of 1898 then raised up a popular diplomatic and military course, imperialism, that almost became an accepted principle. After an exhilarating decade or so, judgment prevailed, and Americans gave it up, at least in its most obnoxious form, which was the taking of territory outside the continental United States.

1. *Independence*

The first requisite of Americans once they had declared their independence was to maintain it—and so over the next fifty years, until the time of the Monroe Doctrine, the diplomacy of the United States dealt with independence. Such a policy aim might seem odd today when the United States is one of the two most powerful nations in the world. But in the late eighteenth and early nineteenth centuries, when the American republic was a small if growing power, well below the stature of France, Russia, Austria, and Prussia on the Continent, not to mention the former mother country, Great Britain, independence could not be taken for granted.

The vigilance with which the early diplomats sought to ensure independence has rightfully become a source of pride to later generations. The customs of the eighteenth and early nineteenth centuries were conducive neither to the birth nor growth of new nations conceived in liberty and dedicated to such absurd propositions as that all peoples are created equal and endowed by their Creator with certain unalienable rights. The Spanish statesman Alberoni, a later writer observed, cut and gnawed at states and kingdoms as if they were Dutch cheese. The American Revolution occurred in the time of Prussia's Frederick the Great, who as a young man had composed a long dissertation refuting Machiavelli's principles of power politics and who spent the rest of his life exercising those very principles. In the eighteenth and early nineteenth centuries there was no United Nations to which small powers might go to denounce a great power. It was the genius of America's first diplomats in this unemotional age that they realized the nature of their international opposition—which included all the powers of the day, not excepting France—and adroitly maneuvered their country's case through the snares and traps of Europe's diplomatic coalitions until they irrevocably had secured national independence.

America's ally in Europe until the year 1800, and presumed friend thereafter, France, was not least in the roster of diplomatic opponents. American diplomats well understood that the French monarchy intervened in the Revolution in 1778 for the major purpose of humbling its ancient enemy, Britain. The problem of the early diplomats during and after the Revolution was to watch the changing power balance in Europe so as to discern, before events passed beyond recall, when France's interests no longer corresponded with those of the United States. In a dark moment the French, whether under the monarchy, Convention, Directory, Consulate, or the regime of Napoleon I, would not have hesitated to abandon the Americans.

The initial occasion when the Americans came to distrust the French arose toward the end of the American Revolution. The Americans never could have won that conflict without the help of French munitions and arms; Saratoga in 1777 was a victory achieved with French gunpowder, and at Yorktown in 1781 more Frenchmen were present than Americans. Yet in a secret treaty concluded with Spain during the war the French had indirectly pledged American independence to the achievement of an aim of the Spanish monarchy, the capture of Gibraltar from the British. Since in their 1778 alliance with France the Americans had promised to make no separate peace, they apparently would have to wait until Gibraltar, the great "pile of rocks," passed to Spain before concluding a peace. Just before Yorktown the French foreign minister, Charles Gravier Comte de Vergennes, contemplated peace on the basis of the war map of the moment which would have excluded the Americans from New York, Charleston, and Savannah, not to mention Maine and much of the Great Lakes country. The French minister to the United States, the Chevalier de la Luzerne, was managing (so he claimed in a letter to Vergennes) the election of Robert R. Livingston as secretary for foreign affairs to the Congress, and Livingston was concerting with La Luzerne the instructions to the American negotiators then in Paris; surely with the approval of the French minister, possibly under his direction, Congress through Livingston instructed the American peace commissioners appointed in June 1781 to do nothing without the advice and consent of the French court. It seemed in 1781 as if the French government, having done some good things for the Americans, if for a purpose European in nature, was at least ready to employ with the new American nation the techniques of the Spaniard Alberoni.

Perhaps out of suspicion of France's motives, at this juncture John Jay, John Adams, and Benjamin Franklin began to negotiate behind the back of the French foreign minister, contrary to their instructions and to the letter of the alliance of 1778. They signed with a British representative on November 30, 1782, a "preliminary treaty" which in everything but name was a final treaty. After the Franco-American victory at Yorktown, Vergennes appears to have ceased contemplating an American peace on the basis of the war map. It may be that Jay and Adams became unnecessarily alarmed in their belief that Vergennes was about to take advantage of the United States. The Americans could not be sure. They knew the habits of the French monarchy, the continuingly dissolute and unpredictable nature of court life at Versailles, the backstairs tradition of European diplomacy. If Franklin later claimed that Adams had become unduly suspicious, and wrote in 1784 to Livingston that his fellow commissioner was "always an honest man, often a wise one, but sometimes in some things, absolutely out of his senses," he carefully allowed himself to be drawn into the separate negotiation with the Briton Richard Oswald, and may even have initiated it. Whatever the misinterpretation of French motives, if there was such, the commissioners' independent diplomacy proved a stroke of genius. Vergennes, France's foreign minister, seemed not to have been too saddened by the result. In a perfunctory way he protested a breach of faith by the American commissioners, but he had obtained for France the humbling of Britain, which was his main purpose. He gave Franklin another loan, which that insouciant philosopher asked for in the same breath as he apolo-

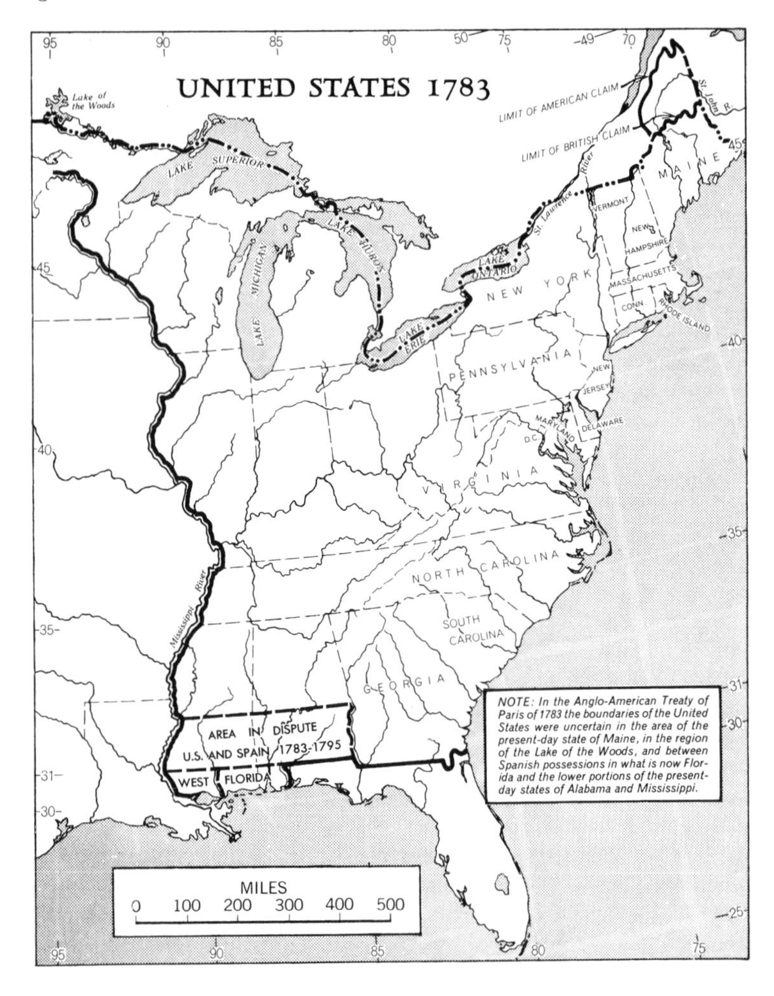

gized for his own and his countrymen's lack of propriety. Vergennes immediately set about disentangling himself from the now-inconvenient Spanish, who clearly were not going to obtain Gibraltar: the British, a short time before, had repulsed a combined Franco-Spanish fleet and lifted the siege of the fortress.

In this first and totally successful confrontation between American diplomats and the old world, one may conclude with a recent scholar that: "The peacemaking began as an encounter between innocence and guile, but the Americans rapidly acquired a measure of sophistication sufficient for the task at hand. Neophytes in the arts of secret diplomacy at the start, they were the peers of their Old World counterparts at the finish."

In later years the problem of French interests versus American arose again, and it is instructive how each time the statesmen of the new world repulsed any possible French challenge to independence. It was a curious situation when after the revolution of 1789, France, the second new nation, appeared as a threat to the United States, the first. The changes of regime in France seemed only to make the French more willing to abridge the rights of Americans. In the 1790s a succession of French ministers to the United States sought to enlist part of the American populace against the other, all in the interest of France in Europe or—as was the case in the late 1790s—France in the new world. All thought they could subvert the American government as easily as France was subverting Holland, that they could turn the United States into a client nation as easily as the Grand Nation acquired Naples. One French minister had analyzed Thomas Jefferson, secretary of state from 1790 to 1793 and the leader of a gathering and supposedly pro-French political party, in a way which the French government might better have remembered: "Jefferson, I say, is American and, by that title, cannot be sincerely our friend. An American is the born enemy of all European peoples." Least of all did the minister follow his own analysis, and like the great majority of his countrymen he continued to think that the Jeffersonians essentially were democrats of the French persuasion. Only after the errant minister had departed, and France and the United States had come into open hostilities during the undeclared war between the American and French navies of 1797–1798, did French diplomats sense that even if their country had numerous vocal supporters in the United States they would not be able to pursue with the Americans the techniques that worked in Europe.

During those same years the French minister, Talleyrand, was conceiving a scheme to recreate the North American empire lost many years before, in 1763, after the Seven Years War. He wished to obtain Louisiana, which had passed from France to Spain in the peace settlement of 1763, and to conquer Canada from Britain, both territories to support the sugar islands of Guadeloupe and Santo Domingo. As an unwilling resident of the United States in 1795–1796 during the Reign of Terror in France, Talleyrand had sensed the vitality of the American republic. He knew that if France were to recreate the new world empire of Louis XIV he would have to move quickly before the Americans themselves took up the western territories. The only result of this scheme—and a wonderful result for Americans—was the Louisiana Purchase, caused by the accession of Louisiana to France just at a time when the young first consul, Napoleon, thirty-four years old, was bursting with his own plans for Europe and could not restrain himself long enough to create an empire across the Atlantic. The 1803 sale of Louisiana to America was no mark of French friendship for the United States but the fortuitous result of a train of events which, but for the old world ambitions of Napoleon, would have drastically constricted American territorial expansion and might have extinguished American independence.

The government of the United States was well aware of the enmity of Napoleon during the long years of European war, which began in 1803 and ended in the emperor's final defeat and banishment to the South Atlantic island of St. Helena in 1815. Both the Jefferson and Madison administrations knew that the French, with or without an alliance with the United States, would look after their own interests. The Federalists tried to make out a case against Jefferson, claiming the president to be "the lackey" of the French emperor. They contended that the Jeffersonian embargo of American trade with the European belligerents (1807–1809) reinforced Napoleon's continental system—his closing of Europe to British trade—at the moment of its greatest extension. The Federalists sent Jefferson innumerable accusatory letters, among which was a missive dated from Boston, March 4, 1808:

> To His Excellents & Supreme French Majesty
> Thomas the First
> Slave of Napoleon
> Cowardly Emperour
> Enclosed receive as true statement of the feelings
> of your Subjects and after due reflection if
> you have not remorse of conscience Thou has none.
> Thy Friend
> Anti-Bonaparte

The president endorsed this letter "Anon. Blackguard." Another communication (endorsed "ribaldry") came from New York on August 25, 1808:

> Thomas Jefferson
> You are the damdest
> dog that God put life into
> God dam you.

But no one found the slightest trace of evidence supporting the canard of a secret alliance between Jefferson and "his master." When Jefferson put into effect the embargo it was not because the measure aided Napoleon; it was because the opposing belligerent systems of France and Britain had so entrapped American neutral commerce that common sense advised a stop to that commerce.

What of Britain, as compared to France? Was there not more of a threat to independence from the British? Such was the case, except that the threat differed from that presented by France. The truth was that once the American colonies had been lost, the British accepted them for lost. No one much wished them back in the British empire. In a famous phrase uttered upon receipt of news of Saratoga, William Pitt the elder lamented that America "was, indeed, the fountain of our wealth, the nerve of our strength, the nursery and basis of our naval power." To modern-day students any easy solution to this complaint would have been reconquest. The idea enjoyed little support in London in the years after the end of the Revolution. The threat Britain posed to American independence was less obvious than that posed by the French. Before the imperialism of the latter nineteenth century, colonies had as their chief justification the advantage of trade. Their duty was to take manufactures of the mother country and send back raw materials and hard money. After Yorktown the British government decided that the American Revolution was a fairly minor political convulsion and that independence could not change the facts of economic life which bound the United States to the trade of England. The scornful British attitude toward American independence in the years through 1815 arose from this belief, which the commerce of those years amply supported. The credit of the American government, inaugurated under the federal Constitution in 1789, rested upon its trade with England.

Britain's supercilious belief in the economic dependence of the United States eventually produced the War of 1812, the conflict which Americans fought ostensibly over the trading rights of neutrals and against the impressment of its seamen but actually for the assertion of economic independence. The British government had refused to respect the rights of American citizens.

The diplomacy leading to the War of 1812 showed something less than the care which earlier had marked American foreign relations. President James Madison and his secretary of state, James Monroe, succumbed to the occasion of British high seas authoritarianism. But the "chapter of accidents," as Jefferson liked to describe the good fortune that often had worked for him and his country, continued to work for the good of the United States. Upon sending the peace treaty with Britain, the Treaty of Ghent, to the Senate in 1815, President Madison said that it was "highly honorable to the nation, and terminates, with peculiar felicity, a campaign signalized by the most brilliant successes." The war in fact had been a series of almost unmitigated American military disasters, ended only by victory in the Battle of New Orleans, which occurred after the Treaty of Ghent was signed. But Americans quickly forgot the spectacle of the burning of their capital city, of President Madison fleeing across the Potomac in a small boat, of the incomparable Dolley Madison scurrying out of the Executive Mansion after securing the portrait of George Washington, of British general Robert Ross helping his soldiers pile furniture outside the mansion preparatory to setting the place on fire. They remembered instead "The Star-Spangled Banner," composed shortly thereafter.

The success of American independence over the long span of years by careful diplomacy, if during one short span by sheer luck, received its ultimate testimony in President Monroe's message of 1823.

2. *Freedom of Commerce*

The War of 1812 was fought to secure not only independence but also the second of the foreign policy principles of the United States: freedom of commerce. The protection and increase of commerce was an end of American diplomacy second only to independence.

Freedom of commerce was essential to the growth of the American nation and its rise to a position of world power. During the initial years of American independence the country had few industries and depended on the export of foodstuffs and naval stores to gain the currency needed to import manufactured goods. American vessels also earned hard currency by carrying much of Europe's colonial and coastal trade.

Because of the essential importance of trade, and in recognition that merchants and sea captains and crews suffered from enough natural dangers to deserve assistance against human restrictions, the American government zealously moved to protect its citizens' commerce in peace and war. In peacetime the nations of Europe disliked having American vessels "horning in" on their own trade, whether between ports on the Continent or between European and colonial ports. But the largest troubles came in wartime. And war was the common condition of Europe during the early years of independence. The wars of the French Revolution and Napoleon began in 1793 and continued until 1815, with the exception of 1802–1803. In 1776 and 1784 Congress therefore carefully set out treaty plans with provisions for neutral, that is, American, trading rights in wartime. The hope was to incorporate these ideal articles in a series of bilateral commercial treaties with the important maritime powers, and thereby establish commercial rights in advance of a war.

The campaign to establish the American view of neutral trading rights in wartime proved extremely difficult. The American government won the agreement of some of the lesser nations to the idea that goods carried on free (neutral) ships can be traded without impingement; the right to trade between two or more ports of a belligerent (to pick up either the coastal carrying trade or the trade between colonies and mother country); a tight definition of contraband that excluded foodstuffs and naval stores; and—this was the peculiar contribution of the treaty plan of 1784—a definition of blockaded ports as those at which vessels seeking to enter would find themselves in imminent danger. France had agreed to American neutral rights in 1778, and treaties followed with the Netherlands (1782), Sweden (1783), Prussia (1785), and Spain (1795). All that was necessary was for the British government to adhere to American ideas of neutrality, but the British refused.

In Jay's Treaty of 1794, the first treaty of commerce between the United States and Britain, the London ministry refused to do anything more than admit that the royal navy's captures might be subject to compensation. Discouraged, the Americans toward the end of the eighteenth century proved willing to negotiate similarly restricted treaties with other countries, including France. The youthful diplomat John Quincy Adams renegotiated the commercial treaty with Prussia in 1799. Then Napoleon, in the treaty of September 1800 ending the French alliance, decided to reaffirm America's neutral rights according to the plans of 1776 and 1784 in hope of support in raising a league of armed neutrals against his enemy, Britain. French recognition, though, was one thing, and respect for those rights another.

During the wars of the French Revolution and Napoleon, not merely the British government but also the French government was glad to find excuses to confiscate American ships. The British restricted American commerce partly to prevent aid to the French but often to hurt a commercial rival. (The American merchant marine was second in size in the world only to the merchant marine of Britain.) The French seized American ships and goods so as to sell them and obtain money to prosecute the European war. Not until the peace concluded in 1815 was the problem of neutral rights abated by the elimination of major war from Europe. The world war of 1914–1918 reopened the whole issue, and the British government in 1915 reprinted the publicist James Stephen's pamphlet of 1805, *War in Disguise; Or, the Frauds of the Neutral Flags.*

America was concerned with the commercial rights of neutrals because it depended so heavily on trade. During the first decades of independence, Americans tried to establish a large commerce with a country other than Britain. There was some hope that the French might prove interested in filling the trade gap left by the exclusion of the United States from the British imperial system. But the French were not interested in this American problem, except during wartime, and then the British did their best to impede trade with the French. The Spanish colonies might have been another place where Americans could trade, but the Bourbon rulers of Spain tried as long as possible to continue the mercantilist restrictions which had made Spain great in the sixteenth century and then contributed to her long decline; and when the Spanish colonial trade did open up during the

Spanish revolt against French domination which began on May 2, 1808—the famous *Dos de Mayo*, Spain's Fourth of July—the British managed to get most of the trade.

The Americans meanwhile sought a trade with China. The year after the end of the Revolution the *Empress of China*, a merchantman in which Robert Morris of Philadelphia, the financier of the Revolution, possessed an interest, sailed to Canton and became the first American vessel to trade in a Chinese port. The China trade was a modest success, sometimes a huge success for an individual voyage. In addition to the tea, cotton goods, and silks brought by the returning vessels the merchants of the era graced the drawing rooms of their houses with scrolls and vases and bric-a-brac. As a substitute for trade with Britain, though, the China business was a failure.

Freedom of commerce on the Mississippi River and its tributaries was another important American concern during these years. It would be difficult to conceive of a water system more important than the Mississippi. The diplomacy of the United States on the Mississippi question was the more contentious because coupled with an almost instinctive understanding of the need for access to the great waterway went a weak diplomatic position. In the years after the American Revolution the Spanish controlled the river by virtue of their possession of Louisiana. The only argument the United States could raise to support its aim of unrestricted commerce on the river was that colonial land grants had reached to the Mississippi as a result of the treaty between Britain and Spain that had ended the Seven Years War in 1763, and that this same treaty had given Britain and the colonists the right of navigation. The Spanish properly remarked that the subsequent war between Spain and Britain, which began in 1779, had canceled the navigation of the Mississippi and even the boundaries of 1763. Moreover, throughout the American Revolution the Spanish had not recognized American independence. Congress sent John Jay to Spain with the hope that he could obtain recognition, a loan, and confirmation of American rights on the Mississippi. It is worth noting that Jay's belief in the importance of the Mississippi question proved stronger than that of Congress, which body in 1781, perhaps under French influence, instructed Jay that if necessary he might offer a forbearance of navigation from the thirty-first parallel south to the Gulf of Mexico in return for Spain's recognition of independence and an alliance. Jay wisely made his offer to the Spanish court conditional upon immediate acceptance, and when the Spanish did not take up this proposition he withdrew it.

The treaty of peace between the United States and Britain ending the Revolution granted the U.S. navigation of the Mississippi. The Americans noticed uneasily that the British said nothing about rights on the Mississippi in their separate treaty of peace with Spain.

Jay, as secretary for foreign affairs from 1784 to 1789, almost made a mistake over the Mississippi question. In 1786 he proposed an amendment to his instructions by Congress, to permit him to offer the Spanish minister, Diego de Gardoqui, a forbearance of navigation for twenty-five or thirty years. In a closely argued speech before Congress the secretary sought to show that the advantages of trade with Spain to be derived under the treaty he proposed to sign—not to mention the prestige to the United States from a treaty with so great a power as Spain—would compensate for the forbearance of a right which, if looked at closely, was no right at all but a hope. This hope, he believed, could not be realized in the foreseeable future, given the huge territory which Americans would have to settle before the navigation of the Mississippi could become lucrative.

What Jay overlooked, easterner that he was, was that fifty thousand American settlers had passed over the mountains during the first year after the peace treaty of 1783, turning a theoretical question into an economic necessity. These settlers had produced their first small crops of grain and tobacco in 1785 and wished to send this produce down the river to New Orleans. It was far easier to send goods downriver from Pittsburgh and thence by ocean vessel from New Orleans to Philadelphia than to use the axle-breaking trails across Pennsylvania from Pittsburgh to Philadelphia. The vote on Jay's request for congressional authorization was seven states for and five against, Delaware abstaining. The margin was too close, and Jay abandoned his ill-considered project. As a result the constitutional convention in 1787 wrote the two-thirds rule for treaties into the Constitution. At last the United States achieved an agreement with Spain in Pinckney's Treaty of 1795, which granted America free navigation of the Mississippi, the right to deposit goods at New Orleans, and which settled as the Spanish-American boundary the thirty-first parallel. The end of the Mississippi question came of course with the "retrocession" of Louisiana from Spain to France in 1800, and the subsequent purchase of the huge region by the United States in 1803.

3. *The Monroe Doctrine*

The Monroe Doctrine of 1823 eventually became the most honored principle of American foreign policy, but strangely enough it was not considered of large importance at the time. It was not taken seriously outside the United States, and to Monroe himself it was little more than an expedient required by the diplomatic situation of the moment. Little further was heard from it until President James K. Polk's first annual message to Congress in 1845. Interested in the fate of California and Oregon, then in dispute with, respectively, Mexico and Britain, Polk announced that Monroe's principles were "our settled policy, that no future European colony or dominion shall, with our consent, be planted or established on any part of the North American continent." Polk's emphasis upon North America, one should add, was unique with him. The doctrine of 1823 did not receive its name of Monroe Doctrine until 1852. Not until 1895 did an American president, Grover Cleveland, invoke it in the form originally announced by Monroe, i.e., as applicable to the entire Western Hemisphere, and only in the twentieth century did it obtain recognition from the nations of the world.

Monroe's famous message to Congress assuredly did not contain much that was original. Throughout the latter eighteenth century there had been a feeling in America that the new world possessed institutions and a culture different from the old, and Thomas Paine in his *Common Sense* easily had obtained agreement when he wrote that "It is the true interest of America to steer clear of European contentions, which she never can do, while, by her dependence on Britain, she is made the make-weight in the scale of British politics." John Adams along with other revolutionary patriots urged the same course, and later wrote, "we should separate ourselves, as far as possible and as long as possible, from all European politics and wars." The principle of nonentanglement broke down in 1778 because of the need for help against Britain, but the uneasiness of association with France became manifest in the peace negotiations. At one point in the negotiations in Paris occurred the conversation between Adams and the British emissary Richard Oswald, in which the latter said that "You are afraid of being made the tools of the powers of Europe." Replied Adams: "Indeed I am. It is obvious that all the powers of Europe will be continually maneuvering with us, to work us into their real or imaginary balances of power. They will all wish to make of us a make-weight candle, while they are weighing out their pounds."

Instances of this feeling that America should stay clear of European politics occurred time and again in the early diplomacy of the United States, one being Washington's neutrality proclamation of 1793 at the outset of the wars of the French Revolution. In his Farewell Address of 1796 there was the sensible inquiry, "Why, by interweaving our destiny with that of any part of Europe, entangle our peace and prosperity in the toils of European ambition, rivalship, interest, humor or caprice?" President Jefferson in his inaugural address of 1801 struck the familiar note: "peace, commerce and honest friendship with all nations, entangling alliances with none." Events in Europe after the Napoleonic wars called forth a restatement of this tradition of American detachment.

The course of European politics after Waterloo led to the Monroe Doctrine. The powers of the Continent had managed by the most profound exertions to defeat Napoleon, and the narrowness of their victory had impressed upon all of them the importance of maintaining their wartime coalition during the first uneasy years of peace.

The powers commenced their conservative politics with the peace conference, the Congress of Vienna. The keynote of that conference in 1814–1815 was "legitimacy," a word advanced by Talleyrand, who had insinuated himself into the allied counsels to save his own country from further territorial spoilation. France now was back under the rule of a Bourbon, Louis XVIII. The Vienna conferees hoped to recreate the politics and borders of the Continent as in 1792, just before the French Revolution had turned outward. Leaders of the great powers believed that, partly by thinking so and partly by judicious use of force, they could remove themselves and their nations from the nineteenth century back into the eighteenth, to the era when thrones and altars had not begun to shake and fall. They had waited a long time to reconstruct Europe on its prerevolutionary foundations and now were determined to do it.

What would be the guarantees of the peace settlement? By the Treaty of Chaumont of March 1814, formally renewed in the Treaty of Paris of November 1815, Austria, Russia, Prussia, and Britain bound themselves to the future convocation of diplomatic congresses for the preservation of peace and the status quo. This was the "concert of Europe," the Quadruple Alliance (and after the formal entry of France in 1818, the Quintuple Alliance).

The Quadruple Alliance worked for a few years and then fell apart. At the outset the allies displayed little disagreement over postwar policy. The victory over Napoleon had been so narrow. But as the years went by the differences arose. Britain especially found its interests departing from those of the nations of the Continent. The problem was that the keeping of peace soon became not so much a question of subduing the rivalries of rulers as one of quieting the unrest of liberals. The latter were threatening their reactionary sovereigns with revolution. A series of disturbances commenced in Piedmont, Naples, Greece, and Spain. Accustomed to virtual independence during the war years, the provinces of Spain in the new world once more revolted and declared their independence. The British government under Lord Liverpool was no friend of revolution or liberalism, but its foreign secretary, Castlereagh, thought that the general policing of Europe was beyond the scope and ability of the concert of Europe and also contrary to British interests. The principal European statesman, Prince Klemens von Metternich of Austria, disagreed. Metternich wished to hold down the lid on revolutionary disturbances. At Troppau in 1820 the statesmen of Austria, Russia, and Prussia, with British dissent, agreed that

> States which have undergone a change of government due to revolution, the results of which threaten other states, ipso facto cease to be members of the European Alliance and remain excluded from it until their situation gives guaranties for legal order and stability. . . . If, owing to such alterations,

immediate danger threatens other states, the powers bind themselves, by peaceful means, or if need be by arms, to bring back the guilty State into the bosom of the Great Alliance.

By the time a new conference opened in Verona in 1822 the British had become alarmed, and at Verona they duly separated themselves from their European allies.

Verona was the turning point of reaction in Europe and the immediate European event which inspired the Monroe Doctrine. The task of Metternich at Verona was a large one, putting down revolutions from the Near East to the Andes. The conference appeared adequate for the work at hand. Present were two emperors, three kings, three reigning grand dukes, a cardinal, a viceroy, three foreign secretaries, twenty ambassadors, and twelve ministers. The forces of reaction in Europe, facing the forces of revolution, seemingly would have no difficulty. At this juncture the British government moved out of the European concert of powers, and in the course of this exit the new British foreign secretary, George Canning, who had replaced Castlereagh, sought to concert his policy with that of the United States and unintentionally prompted President Monroe to announce the doctrine of 1823.

Canning moved specifically to restrain the French, who had sent their army into Spain to restore that nation to its monarch, Ferdinand VII. Canning feared that the French would act to restore the Spanish colonies to Ferdinand VII. In his determination to prevent this, Canning approached the American minister in London, Richard Rush, on August 16, 1823, and on August 20 sent "unofficial and confidential" terms on which the United States and Britain could concert their policy toward any possible French intervention in the new world. "Nothing could be more gratifying to me," he wrote, "than to join with you in such a work, and I am persuaded, there has seldom, in the history of the world, occurred an opportunity when so small an effort of two friendly governments might produce so unequivocal a good and prevent such extensive calamities."

President Monroe believed that there was some danger of intervention by France in the new world. He had before him the examples of Spain, Naples, and Piedmont, where the continental allies had snuffed out revolutions. He knew there was talk of an invasion of Latin America. His secretary of state, John Quincy Adams, sensed that there was never serious danger of a French expedition, and it was Adams who urged Monroe and the cabinet to seize the occasion and make a unilateral statement of American principle. Upon Monroe's suggestion the statement was placed in the annual message to Congress in December 1823. The resultant doctrine contained the following three essential points: noncolonization, "hands off" the new world, and American abstention from the quarrels of Europe.

Noncolonization came from Adams's experience with Russian designs along the Pacific coast. The tsar in a mood of impetuosity had announced in 1821 that Russia possessed sovereignty to Pacific coast territory and waters from Alaska south to the fifty-first parallel. This was an extension southward of the tsar's dominions, and Secretary Adams, in a plucky note to the Russian minister in Washington in the summer of 1823, announced the idea of noncolonization, that "we should contest the right of Russia to *any* territorial establishment on this continent, and that we should assume distinctly the principle that the American continents are no longer subjects for any new European colonial establishments." As repeated in the Monroe Doctrine, this rule stated that "the American continents, by the free and independent condition which they have assumed and maintain, are henceforth not to be considered as subjects for future colonization by any European powers."

The second idea of the doctrine, hands off the new world, appeared in Monroe's message of 1823 as follows: "We owe it, therefore, to candor and to the amicable relations existing between the United States and those powers [of Europe] to declare that we should consider any attempt on their part to extend their system to any portion of this hemisphere as dangerous to our peace and safety."

In regard to abstention, the third idea, the president remarked that "In the wars of the European powers in matters relating to themselves we have never taken any part, nor does it comport with our policy so to do."

The Birth of the Monroe Doctrine; painting by Clyde O. Deland. Left to right: John Quincy Adams, W. H. Crawford, William Wirt, President Monroe, John C. Calhoun, Daniel D. Tompkins, and an unidentified man.

Such was the doctrine announced by President Monroe. As mentioned, the president did not consider it a large and special pronouncement but a prudent diplomatic move called forth by the state of European politics in the year 1823. He well knew that the British government would take care of its enforcement.

As for the European reaction to the doctrine, it was, quite naturally, one of surprise and disgust. If Lafayette in a typical remark of esteem for Americans thought the doctrine "the best little bit of paper that God had ever permitted any man to give to the World," the men who directed European affairs believed that the United States was taking credit for a British policy and doing so in an officious way. The powers found Monroe's principles monstrous, haughty, blustering, and arrogant. Metternich wrote the tsar that the new American act was another revolt, more unprovoked than and fully as audacious as the American Revolution. It was an "indecent declaration," which cast "blame and scorn on the institutions of Europe most worthy of respect, on the principles of its greatest sovereigns, on the whole of those measures" necessary for preservation of society in the old world. The tsarist government agreed, and informed the Russian minister in Washington that "the document in question . . . merits only the most profound contempt."

The doctrine thereupon passed into history and slumbered until the turn of the twentieth century when, under Grover Cleveland and Theodore Roosevelt, the European powers came to realize that the principle of President Monroe was worthy of respect.

4. *Continental Expansion*

With the Louisiana Purchase of 1803 a spirit of expansion took hold of almost the entire nation. The purchase brought about a feeling of what the Democratic party journalist John L. O'Sullivan in 1845 called "manifest destiny." Florida, Texas, New Mexico, California; Canada to the north; Mexico, Cuba and the other Caribbean islands, the Isthmus, South America to Tierra del Fuego: a wild view opened to imaginative diplomacy!

The full sweep of American ambition was not visible to the statesmen who presided over the affairs of the republic into the latter 1820s. Monroe and John Quincy Adams both felt that turmoil was not good for the Western Hemisphere. Oddly Adams, with his tradition of Federalism—he had become a Republican only in 1808—saw more boldy than Monroe. It was Secretary of State Adams instead of the president who in the summer of 1818 talked the Spanish minister, Luis de Onís y Gonzales, into running the border between Spanish and American western possessions on out to the Pacific coast along the forty-second parallel. This act of vision on the part of Adams, at

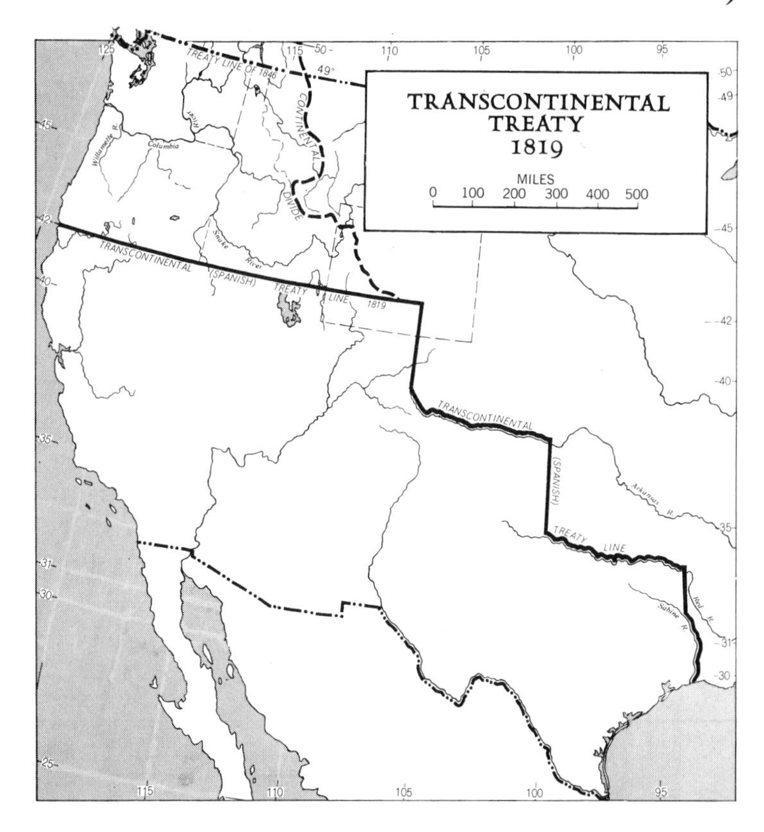

the time he was negotiating the cession of Florida from Spain, is difficult to explain. But one fact was certain about those first years after the War of 1812, namely, that the Monroe administration had little interest in Texas. Adams talked about Texas in the negotiation with Onís. Adams again saw farther than Monroe and would have pressed for a boundary west of the Sabine River (the present-day boundary between the states of Louisiana and Texas) if the president and cabinet would have supported him. Not only did they refuse to do so, but cabinet members communicated their refusal to the French minister and to Onís. Adams, in February 1819, carefully asked the opinion of General Andrew Jackson about getting Texas from Onís, and even that champion of the West said that what Adams was getting, Florida and a continental boundary with Spain, was worth much more than Texas.

Within a few years the fat was in the fire, and Adams for the rest of his life would have to defend his "failure" to obtain Texas in 1819. Adams, like Monroe, had not anticipated what was going to happen in Texas. Beginning in 1821 with the colonization projects of Stephen A. Austin, Texas filled with American settlers. Manifest destiny was plainly visible by the middle of the 1820s, when American secretaries of state began to propose the purchase of the territory from Mexico with arguments which were as sincere as they were ingenious. A lull followed in the Texas agitation while the Lone Star Republic achieved and then maintained its independence, until President John Tyler in 1844 placed annexation before Congress as an issue suitable for passage by a joint resolution of both houses rather than a two-thirds vote of the Senate. Tyler signed the resolution on March 1, 1845.

A little more than a year later the Mexican government obliged President Polk by engaging the troops of General Zachary (Old Zack) Taylor along the Rio Grande, and the war was on. The war aroused considerable opposition within the United States. At last in 1848 Polk got the nation out of the war in a way which struck some of his supporters as irregular but which he had the good judgment to see was sensible and even appropriate. He had disavowed his own representative accompanying the army of General Winfield Scott, the chief clerk of the State Department, Nicholas P. Trist; but when Trist then negotiated the Treaty of Guadalupe Hidalgo, which gave Polk everything he had asked for, the president submitted the treaty to the Senate, which accepted it.

Was the Mexican War a war of aggression? Not technically, for the Mexican troops attacked first. As Polk put it in his war message, it was war "by the act of Mexico herself." Perhaps the president provoked the Mexicans by sending Taylor's troops down into a disputed area between the Nueces River and the Rio Grande. The result of the war—of "President Polk's war," said many people including Congressman Abraham Lincoln of Illinois—was an imperial domain similar to that of the Louisiana Purchase. This domain together with the Gadsden Purchase of 1853 and the Alaska Purchase of 1867 rounded off the continental territory of the United States as we know it today.

In the 1840s and 1850s manifest destiny was not merely continental but turned outward in a series of expansive projects. The Clayton-Bulwer Treaty arranged for a future isthmian canal in Central America. Commodore Matthew C. Perry opened trade with Japan. Meanwhile the United States had begun diplomacy with China with the Cushing Treaty of 1844.

The Civil War and its diplomatic aftermath brought American territorial expansion to a close. On the field of battle the Union armies preserved rather than advanced American nationality and manifest destiny. In the foreign ministries of Europe, especially London and Paris, ministers of the United States pursued the essentially negative task of reminding Europeans that the South under Jefferson Davis had not made a nation. A postscript to the Civil War was the expul-

General Scott's entrance into Mexico City. Note the figure in front of the *Vinoteria* (left foreground) about to throw a paving brick.

sion of French troops from Mexico, in which the diplomacy of Secretary of State William H. Seward was reinforced by the presence of American troops on the Mexican border.

The era ended with Secretary Seward's Alaska Purchase of 1867 and the Geneva arbitration of 1872. The purchase of Alaska was as fortuitous as the purchase of Louisiana, and its critics as strenuous ("Walrussia," "Seward's Folly," "Andy Johnson's polar bear garden"). Even Seward did not altogether understand what he had done, though like Jefferson he knew that he had made a noble bargain. The full value of the purchase would not become evident until well into the twentieth century. Alaska marked the end of American territorial ambitions for at least a generation. The United States government then turned to the consolidation of its international position in the Washington Treaty of 1871, and the ensuing Geneva arbitration, wherein Britain admitted culpability for the escape of the *Alabama* and other Confederate cruisers built in British shipyards during the Civil War.

The award of 1872 was a fitting end to the era. The American judge in 1872, Charles Francis Adams, the son of John Quincy Adams, realized that in accepting an arbitral award the British were making a formal apology in which the *Alabama* was only the nominal issue. The British were apologizing for a century of miscalculations and mistakes and at last welcoming the United States as a full-fledged member of the family of nations—indeed, of the small circle of great powers. With his fellow arbitrators Adams listened to the arguments in a little room in a building almost in the shadow of John Calvin's old church, and the setting may well have reminded him of his country's predestination.

5. *Toward Imperialism*

But 1872 ushered in a period of quiescence in American foreign affairs. Issues of foreign relations fell from sight. Officials in Washington occasionally raised them, but only for purposes which smacked of domestic politics. "I have sometimes been inclined to think," Senator George F. Hoar of Massachusetts once remarked about this inward-looking era, "that when you saw uncommon activity in our grave, reverend, and somewhat sleepy Committee on Foreign Relations . . . it was circumstantial evidence, not that there was any great trouble as to our foreign relations, but that a presidential election was at hand."

It was not until the mid-1880s, when notions of Darwinian thought entered into American consciousness, that opinion began to change. The intellectual justification for the new manifest destiny of course traced back many years before, to the year 1859, just before the American Civil War, when Charles Darwin published his *On the Origin of Species,* which referred in its subtitle to *The Preservation of Favored Races in the Struggle for Life.* Its vocabulary included "natural selection," "survival of the fittest," and "struggle for existence." Darwin had been talking about pigeons, but there seemed no reason why his theories should not apply to human beings. Whatever the gap between Darwinian theories and their application by eager publicists who never read the scientist's words except at fourth or fifth hand, politics and diplomacy thenceforth had to live with the notion that life was a struggle in which the fittest survived. From this notion was derived a corollary, that success is an indication of fitness—that survival is, of necessity, fitness—and the secondary corollary that a nation which achieved the ordinary measurements of a great power (large military establishment, economic strength, population) was by this fact a fit nation, a chosen nation, qualified to instruct other and less successful nations in the facts of life. This, to be sure, was an erroneous doctrine. Survival, as anyone who observes the results of war can attest, does not always mean survival of the fittest: the fittest young men are those who go to war and are killed or wounded fighting the fittest young men of the other side. The political Darwinists also forgot or overlooked the phenomenon of mutual aid, to which people owe much of their survival and achievement: by helping each other the members of the human race have risen to wealth and to such security as they have. And the survival-of-the-fittest enthusiasts forgot that the cause of progress was not the struggle of individual against individual but the struggle of individuals against their environment. In the heat of the Darwinian dialectic these subtleties were lost from view. In the United States of the late nineteenth century, even those persons who rejected biological evolution often accepted without demur the necessity of the struggle of person against person, nation against nation; many individuals cheerfully confused the Christian religion with such beliefs and concluded that the American people, a successful people (and therefore a fit people), were a chosen people, God's anointed.

There thus seemed no reason to doubt the destiny of the United States. Americans basked in their own excellence. Even Darwin seemed to have fallen under the spell of American success and in his 1871 work *The Descent of Man* wrote, "There is apparently much truth in the belief that the wonderful progress of the United States, as well as the character of the people, are the results of natural selection; the more energetic, restless, and courageous men from all parts of Europe having emigrated during the last ten or twelve generations to that great country . . ."

The greatest exponent of the new manifest American destiny, Theodore Roosevelt, the individual who more than any other was the leader of American territorial expansion at the turn of the century, was as certain of the Darwinian truths as if he had discovered them himself. "TR" was verily a mirror to the Darwinian prejudices of his age. Here was an activist manifestation of the idea of survival of the fittest. "I preach to you . . . my countrymen," he was saying in 1899, "that our country calls not for the life of ease but for the life of strenuous endeavor." And again:

> The timid man, the lazy man, the man who distrusts his country, the over-civilized man, who has lost the great fighting, masterful virtues, the ignorant man, and the man of dull mind, whose soul is incapable of feeling the mighty lift that thrills "stern men with empire in their brains"—all these, of course, shrink from seeing the nation undertake its new duties.

It was under the impulse of this new sense of manifest destiny, of Darwinism, that there came an important development for American diplomacy in the 1880s and 1890s: the rejuvenation of the American navy. The appearance of the new navy at the end of the nineteenth century had a notable effect on diplomacy. It increased American stature abroad, making easier the tasks of the republic's diplomats. It also increased the belligerence of public opinion; Americans were proud of their navy, and it was no small factor in the outbreak of the war with Spain in 1898.

After the Civil War, in the late 1860s and throughout the 1870s, the U.S. navy had been an almost insignificant force. It was during this saddening era that a warship in the American fleet, the U.S.S. *Tallapoosa*, sailing on the Hudson River, was run down by a coal barge.

Then in 1883 there was an appropriation for several new ships, and this was followed by the naval act of 1890, which provided for first-class—that is, high seas—battleships and the construction of such later famous vessels as the U.S.S. *Oregon*.

The navy was building, and the appropriation of 1890 was passing through Congress, when a book appeared by Captain Alfred Thayer Mahan, *The Influence of Sea Power upon History*, which in its effect upon history was as important as that other fateful nineteenth-century opus, *On the Origin of Species*.

The Influence of Sea Power upon History contained a message of extreme clarity, easily understandable to hasty readers who needed only to peruse the first and final chapters and not wade through the book's technical middle sections. Mahan taught that naval power was the key to national greatness. He said that nations may rise or decline but never stand still, that expansion was essential, that to support expansion a government must have access to accumulated wealth, that a large and flourishing foreign commerce was the best means of accumulating wealth, that a navy was necessary to secure and ensure foreign commerce, and that a navy required colonies for coaling stations. Mahan had generalized his theories from the rise of England and the British navy, and *The Influence of Sea Power upon History* dealt with the history of English sea power from 1660 to 1783. He put into a coherent philosophy the strategic principles which the British admiralty had been pursuing almost blindly for over two hundred years. In the year 1890 the world power of Britain had not yet been challenged and stood at its zenith; Mahan's message about its origins and progress was the more convincing because of this fact. Without command of the seas, Mahan argued, no nation could attain the fullest measure of internal well-being, or the greatest influence in world affairs.

While the works of Darwin and Mahan were proclaiming the virtues of conflict and power, a series of opportunities arose that helped prepare the United States for conflict. The first of these was over the Samoan Islands, an archipelago set down obscurely in the South Pacific, so remote that even today many Americans could not tell the location of the Samoas within thousands of miles. And yet Secretaries of State Thomas F. Bayard (1885–1889) and James G. Blaine (1889–1892) made the Samoas into an issue with Imperial Germany, and forced first a condominium—a joint three-nation ownership—in 1889 including Britain, and a decade later a partition into German and American Samoa.

The second of the opportunities to focus American imperial ambition came with the revolution in the Hawaiian Islands in January 1893, an affair which in its background and immediate cause was more local than imperial. The revolutionists dearly desired annexation to the United States, and only the chance changing of administrations in Washington, from the imperial ideas of Benjamin Harrison (1889–1893) to the "little America" beliefs of Grover Cleveland (whose

Captain Alfred Thayer Mahan.

second nonconsecutive term began in March 1893), prevented annexation at that moment. Later, in the midst of the Spanish-American War, the Hawaiians entered the American empire by joint resolution of Congress, as a "war measure."

The third and fourth issues of the time that raised the possibility of imperial tasks were both over events in Latin America—the *Baltimore* affair of 1891, and the Venzuelan affair of 1895. In the former, a mob attacked unarmed American sailors on leave in the city of Valparaiso. The American government eventually—and properly, considering the provocation—demanded redress, and the Chilean government abjectly gave in, although not before an admirable naval commander, Robley D. (Fighting Bob) Evans, opposed a concentration of Chilean torpedo boats in Valparaiso harbor. In the Venezuelan affair, the most important expression of American overseas power prior to the war of 1898, the Cleveland administration told the British government (which was supporting an enlargement of the territory of British Guiana, at the expense of Venezuela) that the Monroe Doctrine was in force; Cleveland invoked the doctrine, for the first time since its announcement seventy-two years before. Succeeding generations of historians of the United States would read with near-incredulity the high point of the lecture that Secretary of State Richard Olney read to the British over Venezuela:

> Today the United States is practically sovereign on this continent, and its fiat is law upon the subjects to which it confines its interposition. Why? It is not because of the pure friendship or good will felt for it. It is not simply by reason of its high character as a civilized state, nor because wisdom and jus-

> tice and equity are the invariable characteristics of the dealings of the United States. It is because, in addition to all other grounds, its infinite resources combined with its isolated position render it master of the situation and practically invulnerable as against any or all other powers.

Olney's adversary, Lord Salisbury, with some annoyance pointed out that the occasion was hardly worth the words bestowed upon it. Upon reading Olney's message, Lord Salisbury

> made courteous expression of his thanks, and expressed regret and surprise that it had been considered necessary to present so far-reaching and important a principle and such wide and profound policies of international action in relation to a subject so comparatively small.

The occasion was more important than Salisbury thought because of what it meant for the future. After 1895 he and his successors would be extremely careful with the proud Americans and the proudest of all American doctrines.

Then, at last, came the war with Spain, with its remote causes probably the new feeling of manifest destiny inspired by the Darwinian ideology, the existence of a new navy eager to demonstrate its prowess, and the sudden opportunities of the time that gave the American eagle a chance to stretch its wings. The precipitating cause of the war, to be sure, was the inhumanity of Spanish policy in Cuba, which cried out for intervention.

ADDITIONAL READING

Samuel Flagg Bemis, *The Diplomacy of the American Revolution* (New York, 1935), remains the best single volume on its subject. An excellent general account of the war of 1775–1783 is John Richard Alden, *The American Revolution* (New York, 1954), in the New American Nation series. Lawrence S. Kaplan, *Colonies into Nation* (New York, 1972), in the American Diplomatic History series, covers colonial problems with Britain from the end of the Seven Years War and then the diplomacy of the United States down to the inauguration of Jefferson. The revolutionary era onward appears in Paul A. Varg, *Foreign Policies of the Founding Fathers* (East Lansing, Mich., 1964), and Richard B. Morris, *Seven Who Shaped Our Destiny* (New York, 1973)—the latter volume covering Franklin, Washington, John Adams, Jefferson, Jay, Madison, and Hamilton. For its special subject see James H. Hutson, *John Adams and the Diplomacy of the American Revolution* (Lexington, Ky., 1980). A stirring account of the diplomacy ending the war is by Richard B. Morris, *The Peacemakers* (New York, 1965).

For troubles of maintaining independence during the 1790s see Alexander De Conde, *Entangling Alliance* (Durham, N.C., 1958), together with the same author's *The Quasi-War* (New York, 1966); Lawrence S. Kaplan, *Jefferson and France* (New Haven, Conn., 1967); Harry Ammon, *The Genet Mission* (New

York, 1973); Albert Hall Bowman, *The Struggle for Neutrality* (Knoxville, 1974); and William Stinchcombe, *The XYZ Affair* (Westport, Conn., 1981). Harry L. Coles, *The War of 1812* (Chicago, 1965), shows the intense nationalism of that conflict.

For freedom of commerce as it affected relations with Britain there is Samuel Flagg Bemis, *Jay's Treaty* (rev. ed., New Haven, Conn., 1962); Jerald A. Combs, *The Jay Treaty* (Berkeley, 1970); Bradford Perkins, *The First Rapprochement* (Philadelphia, 1955), and the same author's *Prologue to War* (Berkeley, 1961); and Reginald Horsman, *The Causes of the War of 1812* (Philadelphia, 1962). Trade with the Far East is in John King Fairbank, *Trade and Diplomacy on the China Coast* (Cambridge, Mass., 1953), and Foster Rhea Dulles, *Yankees and Samurai* (New York, 1965). For the Louisiana Purchase see the classic account in the second volume of Henry Adams, *History of the United States during the Administrations of Jefferson and Madison* (9 vols., New York, 1889–1891), together with Alexander De Conde, *This Affair of Louisiana* (New York, 1976).

The historian of the Monroe Doctrine, the late Dexter Perkins, published three detailed volumes and abridged them in *A History of the Monroe Doctrine* (2d ed., Boston, 1955). A more recent account is Ernest R. May, *The Making of the Monroe Doctrine* (Cambridge, Mass., 1975). General books on the period are George Dangerfield, *The Era of Good Feelings* (New York, 1952), and the same author's *The Awakening of American Nationalism* (New York, 1965), the latter a volume in the New American Nation series. For their subjects see Samuel Flagg Bemis, *John Quincy Adams and the Foundations of American Foreign Policy* (New York, 1949); Bradford Perkins, *Castlereagh and Adams* (Berkeley, 1964); and Harry Ammon, *James Monroe* (New York, 1971).

Continental expansion is in Philip C. Brooks, *Diplomacy and the Borderlands* (Berkeley, 1939); Norman A. Graebner, *Empire on the Pacific* (New York, 1955), which sees concrete objectives, such as the Pacific ports, as more important than philosophical notions like manifest destiny; Samuel Flagg Bemis, *John Quincy Adams and the Union* (New York, 1956); Glyndon G. Van Deusen, *The Jacksonian Era* (New York, 1959), a volume in the New American Nation series; Otis A. Singletary, *The Mexican War* (Chicago, 1960), in the Chicago History of American Civilization series; Frederick Merk, *Manifest Destiny and Mission in American History* (New York, 1963); William A. Goetzmann, *When the Eagle Screamed* (New York, 1966), in the America in Crisis series; David M. Pletcher, *The Diplomacy of Annexation* (Columbia, Mo., 1973), definitive; and Ronald J. Jensen, *The Alaska Purchase and Russian-American Relations* (Seattle, 1975).

Imperialism appears in Ernest R. May, *Imperial Democracy* (New York, 1961), and the same author's *American Imperialism* (New York, 1968); David M. Pletcher, *The Awkward Years* (Columbia, Mo., 1961); Walter La Feber, *The New Empire* (Ithaca, N.Y., 1963); David Healy, *US Expansionism* (Madison, 1970); Milton Plesur, *America's Outward Thrust* (De Kalb, Ill., 1971); Charles S. Campbell, *The Transformation of American Foreign Relations* (New York, 1976), in the New American Nation series; Robert L. Beisner, *From the Old Diplomacy to the New* (2d ed., Arlington Heights, Ill., 1986); and Joyce Goldberg, *The Baltimore Affair* (Lincoln, Nebr., 1986).

☆ 2 ☆

War with Spain

There may be an explosion any day in Cuba which would settle a great many things.

—Senator Henry Cabot Lodge to Henry White, January 1898

In a military sense the Spanish-American War was one of the least impressive conflicts of the nineteenth century. The war boiled up suddenly in the springtime of 1898. For most Americans it was an exhilarating experience, sensational, not dangerous. The outcome was never in doubt. The antagonist, Spain, had a population of eighteen million compared with the seventy-five million people in the United States. Captain Alfred Thayer Mahan, in Europe when the war started, was asked how long it would last, and he answered, "About three months." By the end of the summer the fighting was over, won by the small but new and efficient American navy against the antiquated seagoing contraptions that passed for the navy of Spain. In the peace that followed the Spanish relinquished the remnants of a once grand empire: Cuba, Puerto Rico, Guam, the Philippine Islands. The war had no visible effect upon the large questions of international politics, especially the European balance of power which at the moment was gaining the attention of the world's statesmen. The Spanish-American War was a ripple on the surface of world affairs, and by the time the peace conference assembled in Paris in October 1898, relations between the United States and Spain were again almost cordial. Perhaps the Spanish realized, although they could not admit it, that if the United States had not taken their colonies, some other power would have.

Behind this summer turmoil of 1898, however, there was a deeper than military meaning, which makes the war of interest to the student of diplomatic history. The war suddenly brought into focus the ideas which had been generating in the minds of Americans in the 1880s and 1890s—ideas which, once the weariness and near-exhaustion of the Civil War disappeared, had fired the imagination of the American people. Several years before the war of 1898, the American nation had begun to look outward and exert its influence abroad. This new attitude was not merely a matter of interest in Latin America, for there was interest also in Samoa, an island group far beyond the bounds of the Western Hemisphere as conceived in the Monroe Doctrine of 1823. American interest in Samoa indicated that the United States was a world power, and when during the war with Spain an opportunity was presented to take more territory outside the Western Hemisphere, the United States did not hesitate. The meaning of the Spanish-American War lay in its appeal to the emotions of the new manifest destiny. The war focused these emotions and attached them to new and widely dispersed territories.

1. *Cuba*

Cuba was the precipitating cause of the war. The Ever-Faithful Isle, as it was known because of its loyalty to Spain during the Latin-American revolutionary period, had in the mid-nineteenth century begun to acquire feelings of nationalism. Cuban nationalism produced open warfare for a decade beginning in 1868. This long and savage guerrilla conflict between Spanish military forces and the revolutionaries was confined chiefly to the wild and unsettled eastern end of the island and did not afflict the rich and populous western half which includes Havana. The war of 1868–1878 was led by the revolutionary general Máximo Gómez, a Santo Domingan who seems to have acted under the revolutionary ardor which possessed so many Latin Americans during the period of liberation; for while the era of Bolívar and San Martín had long since passed, in Gómez there still burned the revolutionary fire. It is possible that during the insurrection of 1868–1878 most Cubans did not desire liberation. Perhaps Gómez did not secure enough assistance from Cuban expatriates in the United States. The American government and people in the years after their own Civil War were too weary of warfare and too busy with their own concerns to assist the Cuban revolutionists. The revolt spent itself on February 10, 1878, and the Pact of Zanjón was signed, by which the insurgent Cubans received amnesty and the island was granted the same system of government enjoyed by Puerto Rico. It developed later that in the weariness and confusion which attended the end of the war neither side had known, when the pact was signed, the nature of the government enjoyed by Puerto Rico.

Had the United States wished to intervene in Cuba during this insurrection, there had been at least one opportunity. This was the famous *Virginius* episode of 1873, when Spanish authorities seized the ship *Virginius* and took it into Santiago. Captured on the high seas far beyond Cuban territorial waters, the ship, although flying the American flag, was obviously on a filibustering expedition. The crew and passengers, despite their American-sounding names, were of a strongly Cuban countenance. They were all able-bodied males and had no legitimate business which they could claim to be pursuing so close to the insurrectionary island of Cuba. After a short trial the Spanish decided to shoot these men as pirates, and fifty-three were killed before a British captain sailed in with a warship and stopped the executions. The *Virginius* affair would have offered an excuse for American action, had the United States in 1873 wished to start a quarrel with Spain. But there was no American willingness to invade and take Cuba. Perhaps the coincidence of the *Virginius* incident with a domestic economic crisis, the panic of 1873, had some part in the general American desire to avoid war. Instead the State Department under Hamilton Fish bided its time, inquired into the circumstances of the case, and ascertained that the ship was falsely flying the American flag. The British minister in Madrid helped persuade the Spanish government to agree to a settlement. The secretary of state obtained a Spanish apology and indemnity for the dubious American citizens killed.

The revolution of 1868–1878 came to an end with the Pact of Zanjón, and there followed a period until 1895—when a new revolt broke out—during which there was peace and something approaching prosperity in Cuba. One of the most important causes of American concern over the island, the continuing existence there of the institution of human slavery, was eliminated when Spain abolished slavery in the colony in 1886 after a gradual emancipation. Meanwhile the sugar plantations expanded and began to flourish under the beneficent terms of the McKinley Tariff of 1890, which provided for reciprocity agreements. Spain and the United States arranged in 1891, in return for Spanish concessions, for free entrance of Cuban sugar into the United States. Unfortunately, a new American tariff act of 1894 ended the reciprocity. This act followed the business panic of 1893, and the general business stagnation of the mid-1890s together with the new and unfavorable American tariff almost ruined the Cuban economy. The island again was ready for revolt.

At the beginning of the second Cuban revolution in 1895, few individuals in the United States were willing to go to war to liberate Cuba from Spain. American economic interests, about $50,000,000 in Cuban property and $100,000,000 annually in trade, were not large enough to generate enthusiasm for the revolution. Then came the election of 1896, when the United States, for one of the few times in its history, seemed to be dividing politically along economic lines, the poor against the rich. Once that vision had dissolved, the nation concentrated its energies on bettering business conditions, which had stagnated after the panic of 1893. Only after the presidential election did the business cycle at last begin to move upward, after four long and grinding years of depression, and in the United States there was little eagerness to risk this gain in the uncertainties of a foreign war.

The Cubans by this time had turned their revolution against Spain into a ferocious contest, and to Americans it seemed evident that the rebels because of their wanton acts deserved no sympathy, though they constantly sought it. They were pursuing a scorched-earth policy, burning crops and destroying food in the hope of either forcing the Spanish government to grant independence or forcing the United States to intervene for independence. These tactics infuriated President Cleveland, who privately referred to the revolutionaries as "rascally Cubans." From his successor after March 1897, President William McKinley, there was more sympathy, but McKinley was determined not to be involved: the Republican administration was a business-oriented administration, devoted to the welfare of the American industrialist and businessmen, and in 1897 and early 1898 shunned war. The Cuban tactics of destruction had no effect on the policy of the United States and little effect upon the Spanish government, which in 1896 had sent over a new captain-general, Valeriano Weyler.

General Weyler undertook a rigorous policy of forcing the population in the disaffected Cuban provinces into concentration camps, separating the people from the revolutionaries, and thereby identifying the latter. His arrival in Cuba marked a turning point in American sentiment toward the Cuban revolution. Before Weyler adopted his policy of herding the Cubans to concentration camps, the government of the United States had stood against intervention. American hesitation over Cuba stemmed, as was mentioned, from dislike of the destructive tactics of the Cuban revolutionaries. It came also, one should add, from the problem of disposing of the island once Americans should intervene and expel the Spanish. Most Americans believed that the Cubans, many of whom were illiterate, could not govern themselves. Nor could the island be annexed and brought into the American union. Annexation would have precipitated grave difficulties because of the mixed racial composition of the Cuban population. But Americans could not overlook the miseries of General Weyler's camps. Weyler appears to have been a man of decent intentions who was a victim of the inefficiency of Spanish colonial administration. It was easy to bring the people into the camps, but the subsequent duty of feeding them and watching over sanitation was too much for Spanish bureaucracy. Cuba by late 1897 was in a tragic plight. Perhaps as many as 200,000 Cubans died in the camps. And errors of Spanish administration had been compounded by the actions of the Cuban revolutionaries, who in hope of increasing the general misery of the island took measures to prevent the feeding of the *reconcentrados*.

Americans were shocked by what was going on so close to their shores and there began to be talk of intervention. This was at once encouraged by the famous newspaper circulation war in New York City between the New York *Journal*, owned by William Randolph Hearst, and the *World*, owned by Joseph Pulitzer. These two newspapers took advantage of every little change in American-Spanish relations to increase their circulation. They stopped at nothing to blow up the trouble in Cuba into a crisis of major proportions. As E. L. Godkin, a more staid and gentlemanly contemporary of Hearst and Pulitzer, said at the time, and without much exaggeration, "Nothing so disgraceful as the behavior of these two newspapers . . . has ever been known in the history of journalism."

Perhaps Godkin was exercised over the way in which jingoist newspapers exploited the issue of sex—which at that time was a subject not unknown but usually unmentioned in respectable circles. The Hearst papers had taken interest in the plight of a young Cuban girl, Evangelina Cisneros, who allegedly had been jailed for defending her honor against a Spanish officer. Asked what to do about the Cuban Girl Martyr, the chief of the Hearst papers reportedly had said, "Enlist the women of America!" This his underlings did with a vengeance. Mrs. Jefferson Davis, widow of the Confederate president, signed an appeal to the Queen Regent of Spain to "give Evangelina Cisneros to the women of America to save her from a fate worse than death." Mrs. Julia Ward Howe signed an appeal to Pope Leo XIII. A general petition obtained twenty thousand women's signatures. Among them were Mrs. Mark Hanna; Mrs. John Sherman, the wife of the secretary of state; and Mrs. Nancy McKinley, the mother of the president. Alarmed, the Spanish minister denied the Hearst press's version of the Cisneros story, which only made matters worse. Whereupon a Hearst reporter went to Havana and rescued Miss Cisneros, who was spirited off to the capital of liberty in the north. The New York *Journal* then was able to announce in a banner headline, "An American Newspaper Accomplishes in a Single Stroke What the Best Efforts of Diplomacy Failed Utterly to Bring About in Many Months." In New York City, Miss Cisneros was feted with an immense reception in Madison Square Garden. A week later there was another reception in Washington. The Cuban Girl Martyr was introduced to the president by Mrs. John A. Logan, widow of the Civil War general.

Meanwhile a similarly unfortunate incident involving women passengers aboard the American steamer *Olivette* had occurred. A dispatch from Havana by Richard Harding Davis was published in the Hearst *Journal* under the headline of "Does Our Flag Protect Women?" The story related that when the ship was about to sail it was boarded by Spanish police officers for the purpose of searching the persons of three young Cuban women, one of whom was supposed to be carrying insurgent dispatches. The account was illustrated with a pencil drawing by Frederic Remington, the artist of Indians and the American West, also in the Hearst employ, showing the bestial Spanish soldiery going about their search while the young lady in question stood nude before them in the cabin. War, the *Journal* remarked, "is a dreadful thing, but there are things more dreadful than even war, and one of them is dishonor." Alas for the dishonor revealed by this journalistic coup, for it all attached to the New York *Journal*. Queried by its arch-rival, the Pulitzer *World*, the Hearst paper confessed a sin of omission, namely, that the searching aboard the *Olivette* had been carried out by a police matron in the privacy of a stateroom while the officers walked the deck outside. Remington's pencil, it turned out, had been guided by his imagination.

The trouble in Cuba following 1895 and the yellow journalism of Hearst, Pulitzer, and similar editors provided the circumstances for the outbreak of the Spanish-American War. But the famous episode of the Dupuy de Lôme letter (February 9, 1898) and especially the sinking of the battleship *Maine* in Havana harbor on February 15, 1898 precipitated the war.

The letter was written to a friend in Cuba by the Spanish minister in the United States, Enrique Dupuy de Lôme. The circumstances surrounding its composition were altogether understandable. All diplomats are by the nature of their work repressed individuals—they know and feel so much more than they dare say officially that there is a temptation to confide intimate thoughts to friends. The Spanish minister by the autumn of 1897 was receiving increasing advices about Cuba from American government officials, and he may be excused for finding some of them impertinent. The result was an undiplomatic private letter. Señor Dupuy de Lôme did not like the tone of President McKinley's state of the union address in December 1897 and wrote to his friend in Cuba, "Besides the ingrained and inevitable coarseness with which it repeated all that the press and public opinion in Spain have said about Weyler, it once more shows what McKinley is, weak and a bidder for the admiration of the crowd, besides being a common politician who tries to leave a door open behind himself while keeping on good terms with the jingoes of his party." One can only imagine Dupuy de Lôme's embarrassment when he learned that this letter had fallen into the hands of the Cuban revolutionaries, who had given it to Hearst and the New York *Journal*. He hastily resigned his post.

The minister had said of McKinley what many Americans believed and published daily in their own newspapers, but a foreign diplomat must be discreet. McKinley had in truth seemed to many of his countrymen preeminently a politician, the more so when compared to the courageous Grover Cleveland. As McKinley talked in meaningless generalities while desire for intervention in Cuba mounted, Theodore Roosevelt found him with "no more backbone than a chocolate eclair." A current joke went, "Why is McKinley's mind like a bed?" (Answer: "Because it has to be made up for him every time he wants to use it.") But the truth or falsity of Dupuy de Lôme's opinions was no issue in 1898, and the Spanish minister inflamed the American people against Spain when he repeated the popular wisdom.

Almost immediately following this *faux pas* occurred the *Maine* disaster. The battleship was in Havana harbor on the not very convincing pretext of a courtesy visit. Probably the reason for the *Maine*'s visit was that the McKinley administration feared not to have a ship in Havana should trouble break out and American citizens ask for protection. It was risky to send a ship to Havana during the revolutionary chaos, but McKinley was almost forced to protect his countrymen when Americans by the latter 1890s were becoming so sensitive to their rights and position in the world. He did not reckon how desperate the Cuban situation was.

The *Maine* on the evening of February 15, 1898, sank at its moorings after a terrific explosion. Of 350 officers and men aboard, 252 were dead or missing and 14 died afterward. A naval court of inquiry in 1898 found in favor of an external explosion touching off the magazines. When the vessel was raised in 1911 an inward buckling of its plates was evident, and a second court of inquiry then reported, as had the first court, that "the injuries to the bottom of the *Maine* . . . were caused by the explosion of a low form of explosive exterior to the ship." The hulk was towed out to sea in 1912 and sunk in 600 fathoms of water. No one to this day has discovered who or what in 1898 blew up the *Maine*. One can say only that the vessel's destruction greatly benefited the Cuban revolutionaries, already distinguished by the abandon with which they conducted their guerrilla actions against the Spanish. The sinking of the *Maine*, as few other events could have done, precipitated the United States entry into the revolutionary struggle against Spain.

The American people and Washington officials were at first incredulous and then deeply angered. Years afterward the watchman in the White House remembered McKinley pacing the floor in the first shock of the news, murmuring "The *Maine* blown up! The *Maine* blown up!" Hearst's New York *Journal* emblazoned for its readers, THE WARSHIP MAINE WAS SPLIT IN TWO BY AN ENEMY'S SECRET INFERNAL MACHINE. "Remember the *Maine*," became a national watchword:

> Ye who made war that your ships
> Should lay to at the beck of no nation,
> Make war now on murder, that slips
> The leash of her hounds of damnation;
> Ye who remembered the Alamo,
> Remember the *Maine!*

The battleship *Maine*, entering Havana harbor, and after the explosion.

In a Broadway bar a man raised his glass and said solemnly, "Gentlemen, remember the *Maine!*" Through the streets of American cities went the cry, "Remember the *Maine!* To hell with Spain!"

After this disaster at Havana, it is doubtful if McKinley or anyone else could have checked the course of events. It seemed as if everything conspired for war. A Republican senator from Vermont, Redfield Proctor, believed to be on good terms with McKinley, visited Cuba and upon return made a speech in the Senate favoring intervention. The speech was all the more effective because of the unemotional tone:

> I have endeavored to state in not intemperate mood what I saw and heard, and to make no argument thereon, but leave everyone to draw his own conclusions. To me the strongest appeal is not the barbarity practiced by Weyler nor the loss of the *Maine*, if our worst fears [that is, that the Spanish sank the vessel] should prove true, terrible as are both of these incidents, but the spectacle of a million and a half of people, the entire native population of Cuba, struggling for freedom and deliverance from the worst misgovernment of which I ever had knowledge.

When Congress on March 28 received the report of the naval board of inquiry into the *Maine* sinking, it was one more inspiration to action. If the board did not fix responsibility for the sinking, finding evidence only of "the explosion of a submarine mine," the latter conclusion was all the supporters of war needed.

All the while the Spanish could not bring themselves to solve the Cuban problem in a way that would suit the Americans. The United States government in reality wanted three things from the Spanish: revocation of the concentration camp order; an armistice effective until October 1; and the independence of Cuba if in the mind of President McKinley such a course should prove necessary. The Madrid government agreed to the first demand on April 5. On April 9 it decided to grant an immediate armistice. The sticking point proved to be Cuban independence. To grant it outright or to place the determination of such a matter in the hands of an American president was difficult if not impossible for a sovereign nation, especially after the belligerent tone of American public statements about the sinking of the *Maine*. A new Spanish minister in Washington, replacing Dupuy de Lôme, said flatly that independence was impossible. Though he spoke without authorization, he accurately reflected the view of his government.

And so, given this situation, what was McKinley to do? Historians have differed in their answers to this question, and the usual conclusion has been that the president of the United States in 1898 lacked courage. It is not difficult to trace McKinley's actions through the years and to say that he seldom had shown himself to be a forthright leader of men. One of his friends late in March saw him break down in tears, crying like a boy of thirteen, the friend said. The president confessed that he hadn't slept more than three hours a night, he thought, during the past two weeks. There he sat, on a large, crimson brocade lounge, resting his head on his hands, a grown man, veteran of the Civil War, president of his country, pouring out his

$50,000 REWARD.—WHO DESTROYED THE MAINE?—$50,000 REWARD.

EDITION FOR GREATER NEW YORK

NEW YORK JOURNAL

AND ADVERTISER.

The Journal will give $50,000 for information, furnished to it exclusively, that will convict the person or persons who sank the Maine.

NEW YORK, THURSDAY, FEBRUARY 17, 1898.—16 PAGES. PRICE ONE CENT

DESTRUCTION OF THE WAR SHIP MAINE WAS THE WORK OF AN ENEMY.

$50,000!

$50,000 REWARD!

For the Detection of the Perpetrator of the Maine Outrage!

Assistant Secretary Roosevelt Convinced the Explosion of the War Ship Was Not an Accident.

The Journal Offers $50,000 Reward for the Conviction of the Criminals Who Sent 258 American Sailors to Their Death. Naval Officers Unanimous That the Ship Was Destroyed on Purpose.

$50,000!

$50,000 REWARD!

For the Detection of the Perpetrator of the Maine Outrage!

Hearst's New York *Journal* blames the Spanish.

distress privately while a White House musicale was going on in an adjoining room. He said that Congress was trying to shove him into war. This was the period when the belligerent Theodore Roosevelt, coming away from a visit to the White House, angrily asked of some reporters at the gate: "Do you know what that white-livered cur up there has done? He has prepared *two* messages, one for war and one for peace, and doesn't know which one to send in!"

But is it not too easy a judgment to say that McKinley proved weak in 1898? Actually he was turning every which way in his efforts to preserve peace. Congress, especially the Senate, was thundering for war. Popular feeling throughout the country was demanding it. If the president's friends, religious leaders and businessmen, did not want war, almost everyone else did. Senator Proctor had joined them. Secretary of War Russell A. Alger was saying, "Congress will declare war in spite of him. He'll get run over and the party with him." In McKinley's mind surely was the situation, only a few years before, of Grover Cleveland, who in his second term had defied the silverites in his party, only to lose control of the Democrats, who stampeded to William Jennings Bryan. The Spanish meanwhile were not meeting all the American demands. When McKinley was preparing a message to Congress, with almost evident desperation (White House visitors of the time saw the manner in which his face had become lined, how rapidly he was aging under the strain), word came in from the American minister in Madrid, General Stewart L. Woodford, of Spain's capitulation over the issue of an armistice. After momentarily sensing that peace was at hand, the president then realized that there was no decision on Cuban independence.

The harassed McKinley could have negotiated some more, but in the minds of his closest political supporters he already had delayed too long. When on Wednesday, April 6, a presidential message was scheduled to go up to Congress, a crowd of ten thousand people had jammed the corridors and galleries of the Capitol. A telegram then had arrived from Havana that without further delay the lives of Americans in Cuba might be in danger. He put off the message. His advisers protested, but the president, raising his hand, refused. "I will not do it," he said. "I will not send in that message today; I will not do such a thing if it will endanger the life of an American citizen in Cuba."

On Monday, April 11, he could wait no longer. When on that day he submitted a message to Congress, remarking that body's "solemn responsibility," he said that he had "exhausted every effort to relieve the intolerable condition of affairs which is at our doors. Prepared to execute every obligation imposed upon me by the Constitution and the law, I await your action." To this message he tacked two small paragraphs announcing the Spanish proclamation of an armistice in Cuba.

The outcome could not be in question. A congressional joint resolution demanded the independence of Cuba, empowered the president to force Spain's withdrawal, and disclaimed any intention by the United States of exercising "sovereignty, jurisdiction, or control" over Cuba. This latter clause, the Teller Amendment, passed Congress without a dissenting vote. McKinley signed the joint resolution on April 20 and dispatched a three-day ultimatum to Spain. Word that the Madrid government had broken diplomatic relations arrived the next day. On April 25 he signed a joint resolution declaring war. Two days earlier, after authorization from Congress, he had called for 125,000 volunteers.

2. *The Course of the War*

During the Spanish-American War there was scarcely a military campaign worthy of the name. The war began in late April and ended with an armistice on August 12. During this time Commodore George B. Dewey blew up ten old Spanish ships in Manila Bay (May 1), and a minuscule Spanish squadron was sunk near the harbor of Santiago de Cuba (July 3). American land forces under General William R. Shafter accepted the surrender of Santiago after skirmishes and some sharp fighting, and in the Far East General Wesley Merritt on August 14, unaware of the armistice signed in Washington two days earlier, took Manila after a token resistance by the Spanish forces to keep out the insurgent Filipinos. With this, and including the virtually unopposed campaign by General Nelson A. Miles in Puerto Rico, the war came to an abrupt end. The result had never been in doubt. The military operations on some occasions became so ludicrous that Mr. Dooley, the mythical Chicago Irishman created by Finley Peter Dunne, could remark, apropos General Miles's Puerto Rican expedition, that it was "Gin'ral Miles' gran' picnic an' moonlight excursion . . . 'Tis no comfort in bein' a cow'rd," he added, "whin ye think iv them br-rave la-ads facin' death be suffication in bokays an' dyin' iv waltzin' with th' pretty girls iv Porther Ricky."

Annexation of the Hawaiian Islands came at last during the Spanish-American War. Acquisition of these islands had been urged in the United States for several reasons. There was a moral argument: the islands had been begging for annexation and had placed themselves in danger, for Spain might attack them. There was another argument to the effect that Hawaii should be annexed as a war measure—the islands were necessary for prosecution of the war. This contention broke down on at least two counts, namely that the war was practically over after the sinking of the Spanish squadron at Santiago on July 3 (Hawaii was annexed on July 7), and that Hawaii was a less advantageous stopping place for ships en route to the Far East to support Dewey in the Philippines than was another harbor which the United States already owned, Kiska in the Aleutian Islands. Kiska was a far more commodious harbor than Honolulu, and the Kiska route was several hundred miles shorter than that via Hawaii. Moreover, Kiska was closer to being a halfway point to the Philippines than was Honolulu. A number of ships in the American navy could not carry sufficient coal for the Honolulu-to-Manila run. The northern route also was more healthful for transporting soldiers. But there was a real point in a third contention for annexing Hawaii—that the Hawaiians should be annexed to facilitate the future defense of the United States. The defense argument, unlike the war-measure argument and the moral argument, was sound in 1898, before the era of air power made American possession of the Hawaiian chain even more important. The war lent urgency to the defense argument, and the McKinley administration, to play safe with a still doubtful Congress, submitted the proposal for annexation of Hawaii in the form of a joint resolution requiring only a majority vote.

Grover Cleveland, retired in Princeton, remained adamant to the end, and inquired of his friend Olney, "Did you ever see such a preposterous thing as this Hawaiian business?" Cleveland in January 1898 had said that annexation of islands in the Pacific was "a perversion of our national mission. The mission of our nation is to build up and make a greater country out of what we have, instead of annexing islands." His anti-imperialism certainly suggested one way of resolving doubts over annexation. Perhaps, however, there could have been a middle position between that of Cleveland—taking no islands at all—and the decision of the McKinley administration to annex both the Hawaiian Islands and the Philippine Islands. Perhaps Hawaii would have been enough new territory.

The most fateful territorial acquisition of the Spanish-American War was the taking of the Philippines, after Dewey had sunk the Spanish squadron. Annexation of the Philippines was of large importance to the future of American diplomacy. It projected the United States far into the Western Pacific, and so close to Japan and China—two future trouble spots of the world—that American interests, once established in the Philippines, were almost bound to become involved and probably hurt in Far Eastern rivalries quite as remote from the American national interest as had been the European rivalries against which President Washington once had counseled. The British admiral P. H. Colomb, writing in the *North American Review* for October 1898, showed with remarkable prescience what might happen to the United States because of annexation of the Philippines. Taking the islands, the admiral stated, meant that America was "for the first time giving hostages to fortune, and taking a place in the world that will entail on her sacrifices and difficulties of which she has not yet dreamed. . . . with outlying territories, especially islands, a comparatively weak power has facilities for wounding her without being wounded in return." This move into the Far East has seemed in retrospect very unwise. Perhaps, on the other hand, it was only the working out of American destiny, and could not have been humanly avoided. The victor of Manila Bay, surveying his triumph over the Spanish fleet, declared that "If I were a religious man, and I hope I am, I should say that the hand of God was in it." Of this, more later; here is the place and time to recount the administrative intrigue by which the United States became prepared in 1898 to take the Philippines, once war had started over Cuba.

The intrigue was such a natural expression of Theodore Roosevelt's exuberance that perhaps there was no intrigue at all. Roosevelt was assistant secretary of the navy, having been placed in that post (according to "Boss" Platt of New York, who put him there) because "Theodore" could "probably do less harm to the [Republican Party] organization as Assistant Secretary of the Navy than in any other office that can be named." Roosevelt bent his energies to developing the fighting readiness of the new battleships and cruisers which in the last decade or so had been coming off the ways of American shipyards. It was obvious to him that a war with Spain was imminent, and he took it upon himself to prepare the American Asiatic squadron. By some string-pulling he arranged the appointment of his friend, Commodore Dewey, to command it.

Nor was this the only Rooseveltian maneuver, for there was the famous occasion on February 25, 1898, when Secretary Long went home for an afternoon rest and left Roosevelt as acting secretary of the navy. TR broke loose in the department that afternoon, moved ships around as if they were yachts, and among other things ordered Dewey, at last in the Far East at Hong Kong, to coal his ships and prepare for offensive operations in the Philippines in the event of war. Dewey was not to allow the Spanish squadron to leave the islands, for fear it might somehow find its way to the American west coast and ravage Seattle and San Francisco.

It is difficult to take seriously the fear that the Spanish ships in Manila could endanger the American Pacific coast. One might have thought, too, that when Secretary Long returned from his afternoon rest he could have countermanded his assistant secretary's orders and perhaps demanded Roosevelt's resignation. Nothing happened; Roosevelt stayed at the department, and when war came, Dewey was ready. After the Spanish squadron had been destroyed the commodore requested army troops to the number of 5,000 to invest Manila. The war department sent 11,000 and Manila was taken.

The investiture of Manila went off without a hitch, except for some friction that developed between Dewey and the commander of a German naval squadron then in Manila harbor. This friction was later interpreted as endangering peace between the United States and Germany. The Germans had originally blundered by sending to Manila a vice admiral in charge of a squadron slightly stronger than Dewey's, and during the summer there had been trouble over the blockade regulations which, Dewey claimed, the Germans violated.

WELL, I HARDLY KNOW WHICH TO TAKE FIRST!

There was hardly any doubt that Uncle Sam's appetite for territory was large. But, then, the bill of fare offered a great deal.

Dewey at Manila told Admiral Otto von Diederichs's flag lieutenant that if Germany wished war she could have it. He also told some newspapermen that he had a plan to engage, if necessary, the German fleet. When Dewey on August 13 was preparing to bombard Manila in support of General Merritt's troops, the squadrons of France, Germany, and England, then in harbor, eagerly jockeyed for position to observe the firing. In the course of the positioning, the Germans managed to get to the left of Dewey's ships, the French were behind the Germans, and the British in an ungentlemanly maneuver sailed into position immediately in front of the Germans. The German admiral had to move his flagship from its moorings to get a better view of the hostilities. Later the story arose that the German squadron had threatened Dewey's operations, and that the British moved in between the Germans and Dewey to protect the American commodore. But there was never danger of war with Germany. Dewey later asked Frederick Palmer, who ghosted his *Autobiography*, to omit these contretemps from the record.

The Spanish-American War had no serious repercussions upon the European balance of power, for none of the European powers other than Spain became involved in it. Likewise, so far as concerned the two combatants, the war did not permanently impair their good relations—at the peace conference there appeared little enmity between American and Spanish negotiators.

The summer of hostilities in 1898 did mark a notable consolidation of American nationalism. The war gave to the entire American people a vague feeling of danger, of risky adventure, and all but remnants of those political passions between North and South which had grown out of the Civil War and reconstruction disappeared in the comradeship of a national war. The events of the Civil War era had by this time slipped far into history. "The youngest boy who could have carried arms at Gettysburg," Paul H. Buck has written, "was a man of fifty when the century closed. . . . By far the greater portion of the generation which had listened with awe while the guns boomed in Virginia and the ships of war steamed on the Mississippi slept in silent graves in which the issues for which they had contended were buried with them. The old had given way to the new." McKinley during a speech at Atlanta in 1898 affirmed the care of Confederate graves to be a national duty. When the president appointed four temporary major generals, he diplomatically chose two ex-Confederate generals, Joseph ("Fighting Joe") Wheeler and Fitzhugh Lee. Fitzhugh Lee, nephew of Robert E. Lee, already had come to public attention in performing his duties as consul general at Havana at the time the *Maine* was sunk. Fighting Joe Wheeler went to Cuba and took part in the surrender of the island. During the campaign before Santiago there occurred the rather humorous incident when General Wheeler at one point in a battle cried, "The Yankees are running! Dammit! I mean the Spaniards!" The nation, both North and South, fought together in the Spanish-American War, and this to all American patriots was a heartwarming scene.

There were many touching evidences of this new national unity, but perhaps no event was more poignant than the demonstration that occurred when on May 20, 1898, the Sixth Massachusetts Regiment marched through Baltimore on its way to camp. In 1861 the regiment had been stoned by hostile mobs as it marched to defend Washington. The Massachusetts men in their uniforms of blue with the gallant new leggings, broad-brimmed campaign hats slouched over their faces, pennants flying, marched through the streets in 1898 with the regimental band playing "Dixie." Senator Lodge, having journeyed up from the capital to see the parade, wept unashamedly. "It was 'roses, roses all the way,' " he afterward remembered, "—flags, cheers, excited crowds. Tears were in my eyes. I never felt so moved in my life. The war of 1861 was over at last and the great country for which so many men died was one again."

3. *The Paris Peace Conference of 1898*

The Spanish ambassador at Paris on July 19, 1898, requested the French foreign minister, Théophile Delcassé, to mediate between Spain and the United States. This the foreign minister did through his ambassador in Washington, Jules Cambon, and Cambon on August 12 signed an armistice on behalf of the Spanish. According to its terms a peace conference was to assemble in Paris not later than October 1. President McKinley appointed five peace commissioners: the chairman of the Senate committee on foreign relations, Senator Cushman K. Davis; the next ranking Republican member, Senator William P. Frye; the leading minority member of the foreign relations committee, Senator George Gray; Secretary of State William R. Day (who on September 30 yielded his secretaryship to John Hay); and Whitelaw Reid, publisher of the New York *Tribune.* Curiously there was some question over the propriety of McKinley's appointments, because the three senators, so the contemporary argument ran, would have to vote on their own handiwork after returning from Paris. The politically astute McKinley ignored such pleas and set a precedent which Woodrow Wilson twenty years later might well have followed at the peace conference of 1919.

Upon arrival in Paris the commission was treated to an elaborate luncheon given by Delcassé at the Quai d'Orsay Palace, September 29, 1898: oysters, lake trout, beef, cutlets Sévigné d'ivoire, duck, partridges, ham, salads, artichokes au champagne, ices (Russian style), fruits, French wines. During the deliberations which followed—the conference lasted two months and two days—the peace commissioners meeting in a large room of the French foreign office had constant access to an anteroom containing a well-stocked larder. In view of the paucity of diplomatic business before the conference, this may explain why its sessions took so long. There were only two unsettled questions, namely the Cuban debt (should the United States assume it?), and the Philippines (should the islands be annexed?). The American commissioners refused to assume the $400,000,000 Cuban debt. As for the Philippines, there was little to discuss, because the question would have to be settled in Washington.

Until Dewey encountered the Spanish squadron the Philippines meant little to the American people. McKinley himself said afterward, "When we received the cable from Admiral Dewey telling of the taking of the Philippines I looked up their location on the globe. I could not have told where those darned islands were within 2,000 miles!" As debate grew in volume over disposition of the Philippines, Mr. Dooley remarked to his good friend Mr. Hennessy that " 'tis not more thin two months since ye larned whether they were islands or canned goods. . . . Suppose ye was standin' at th' corner iv State Sthreet an' Archey R-road, wud ye know what car to take to get to th' Ph'lippeens? If yer son Packy was to ask ye where th' Ph'lippeens is, cud ye give him anny good idea whether they was in Rooshia or jus' west iv th' thracks?" But the governing fact of the Philippine question was that the United States had taken possession of Manila. Hennessy had begun the above colloquy by remarking that "I know what I'd do if I was Mack. I'd hist a flag over th' Ph'lippeens, an' I'd take in th' whole lot iv thim." After protests from Dooley he still was saying "Hang on to thim. What we've got we must hold." Hennessy captured the essence of the Philippine argument, for possession was nine-tenths of the decision.

Taking the islands was easier for the McKinley administration when American businessmen began to see in the Philippines a steppingstone to the China trade. Markets in China, as we shall see in the next chapter, had long intrigued American businessmen. The new sense of manifest destiny had stemmed in part from the feelings of the American business community that the domestic market of the United States was saturated, and that expansion of foreign trade was the only hope of further developing the American economy. Businessmen, down to the beginning of hostilities with Spain, had opposed war, believing that a war could only harm the economy. A war's effects, business leaders maintained, would perhaps include derangement of the currency and a revival of the free-silver agitation. They suspected that most of the jingoes were free-silverites. "Free Silver and Free Cuba," so Senator Lodge believed, would be the Democratic Party's campaign slogan in the election of 1900. With the taking of Manila, business fears began to evaporate. Business pressures to keep the Philippines in anticipation of the China trade converged upon Washington at the same time that retention of the islands was attracting popular support throughout the country. The railway magnate James J. Hill declared that whoever controlled the trade of the Orient held the world's purse strings. The Philippines, according to another business figure, were the key to the Orient. Senator Lodge argued that Manila was the great prize and "the thing which will give us the eastern trade."

The China trade was, one should add parenthetically, a mirage. It has never met the high expectations Americans have had of it. In 1898 the mirage was more important than reality, especially after the nation had just emerged from the difficult economic era of the mid-1890s.

There was no chance of the United States taking part of the Philippine Islands—say Luzon with Manila. It was a case of all the islands or none. General Merritt went to Paris from Manila to give his views to the peace commissioners, and while he at first indicated that Luzon might be held alone, under further questioning he admitted that Manila was prosperous only because it was the capital of the archipelago. Militarily, too, there could be little advantage, and positive disadvantage, in allowing the other islands to pass under control of some power other than the United States.

If the United States refused to take the islands, they would probably have passed to one of the European powers, perhaps Germany (Japan and England were also interested). Germany made an agreement with Spain, after Spain's armistice with the United States and before the assembling of the Paris peace conference, in which it was stipulated that Spain would resist any demands of the Americans for the Caroline Islands, if such demands were made, and that after the peace settlement these islands would be sold to Germany.

President McKinley is reported by many people who saw him at the time to have been much worried about the fate of the Philippines. What, he asked casual visitors to the White House, could he do with the islands? At one juncture he said that "If old Dewey had just sailed away when he smashed that Spanish fleet, what a lot of trouble he would have saved us." Old Dewey had not sailed away, and popular opinion in the United States had risen to such heights of adulation over the hero of Manila Bay that the commodore could not have departed from the scene of his triumph even if the national interest dictated it.

A religious factor, albeit one based on something of a misunderstanding, exerted a considerable influence in the American decision to take the Philippines. American Protestants looked to the islands as an area to be Christianized. President McKinley, a devout Methodist who instituted hymn singing in the White House each Sunday evening during his years of office, was much concerned over the religious needs of the Filipinos. Mrs. McKinley, according to one White

House visitor, "talked ten to the minute about converting the Igorrotes. . . . Anyhow she wants you and Alice to pray for the Igorrotes." Actually, of course, the Philippine Islands were the single flourishing outpost of Christianity in the Far East, for most of the Filipinos were Catholics, having been converted by the Spanish some centuries before the Spanish-American War. American Catholics found the religious argument for retention of the islands difficult to follow. Nonetheless it was of importance.

Having made up his mind, somehow or other, and reinforced his opinions by a speaking trip through large areas of the Middle West where he received ovations after such words and phrases as *destiny*, *duty*, *humanity*, and *the hand of the Almighty God*, McKinley sent word to the American peace commissioners in Paris. The Spanish commissioners had no recourse except, after a month and more of stalling, to acquiesce.

The terms of the Treaty of Paris, signed on December 10, 1898, were cession of the Philippine Islands, Puerto Rico, and Guam. The latter island, 3,300 miles west of Honolulu, was well situated as a naval station en route to the Philippine Islands, and the decision to retain the Philippines led logically to inclusion of Guam in the peace settlement of 1898. The United States paid $20,000,000 for the Philippines. Spain surrendered all claim to Cuba and agreed to assume the Cuban debt.

There was a small crisis in getting the treaty through the Senate, for until the end of debate the issue lay in doubt and the vote on February 6, 1899, was close, 57 to 27, one vote above the necessary two-thirds majority. William Jennings Bryan, who had felt some of the martial spirit during the war and volunteered as a colonel of cavalry, greatly assisted the McKinley administration in urging the treaty upon some of the reluctant Democratic senators. It was said that the non-Republican senators (Democrats, Populists, and some independents) who voted for the treaty were partly converted by the counsel of Bryan, personally given during a hurried trip to Washington. In the end, some further arguments seem to have been offered to one or two wavering senators. The Democratic Senator Gray, who as a peace commissioner had strongly opposed taking the Philippines, voted for the treaty in the Senate and shortly thereafter received a federal judgeship from the Republican McKinley. One should add that the McKinley administration could have waited if necessary until March 4, 1899, and the admission of a sufficient number of recently elected Republican senators to approve the treaty.

But the importance of the Spanish-American War in the history of American diplomacy does not lie in the closeness of the vote on the treaty, for that could have been favorably changed a month later. Nor does it lie in the relation of the war to the diplomacies of the

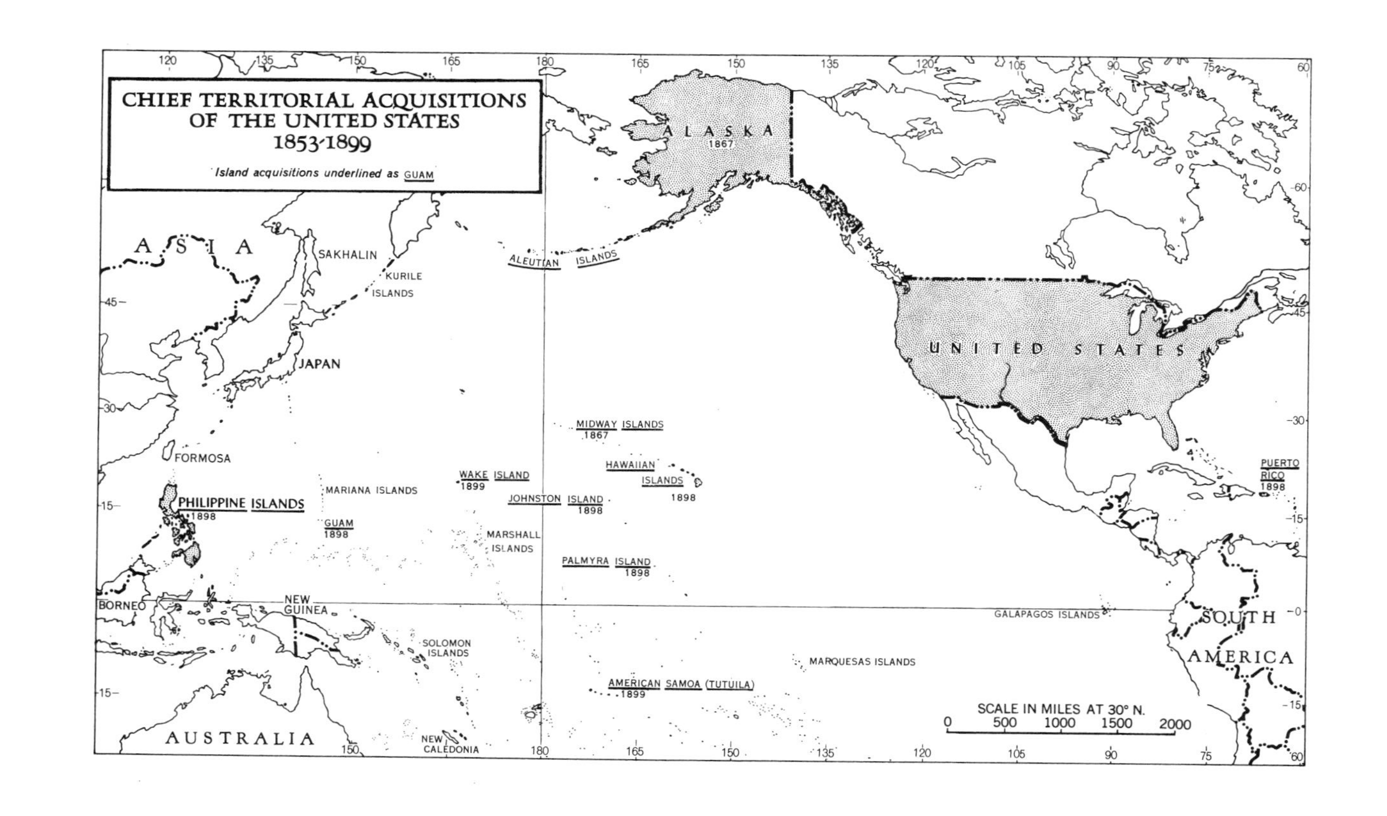
CHIEF TERRITORIAL ACQUISITIONS
OF THE UNITED STATES
1853-1899
Island acquisitions underlined as GUAM
ASIA
SAKHALIN
KURILE ISLANDS
JAPAN
FORMOSA
PHILIPPINE ISLANDS
1898
MARIANA ISLANDS
GUAM
1898
WAKE ISLAND
1899
MARSHALL ISLANDS
BORNEO
NEW GUINEA
SOLOMON ISLANDS
NEW CALEDONIA
AUSTRALIA
ALEUTIAN ISLANDS
ALASKA
1867
MIDWAY ISLANDS
1867
HAWAIIAN ISLANDS
1898
JOHNSTON ISLAND
1898
PALMYRA ISLAND
1898
AMERICAN SAMOA (TUTUILA)
1899
MARQUESAS ISLANDS
UNITED STATES
PUERTO RICO
1898
GALAPAGOS ISLANDS
SOUTH AMERICA
SCALE IN MILES AT 30° N.
0 500 1000 1500 2000

European powers, who by 1898 were pursuing the rivalries which led to the World War in 1914. The powers did not believe their vital interests challenged by the war, and Germany, while wistful about the disposition of the Philippines, was content with receiving the Caroline and Palau Islands and the Mariana Islands with the exception of Guam. Nor did the new status of Cuba, an American protectorate, affect greatly the course of American history. The importance of the Spanish-American War for the diplomatic history of the United States lies in its appeal to the new sentiment of manifest destiny, its lending of substance and a feeling of achievement to what hitherto had been largely dreams and hopes. America in 1898 "emerged" as a world power, to use the verb of the day. The experience was thrilling. At the moment few foresaw how acquisition of the Philippine Islands had committed the United States in the far Pacific, and that in subsequent years with the rise of Japan to world power there would come difficulties that eventually, forty-three years after 1898, would lead the country into a first-class Asian war.

ADDITIONAL READING

Several books cover the war, among them H. Wayne Morgan, *America's Road to Empire* (New York, 1965), in the America in Crisis series. A book of pictures and text is Frank Freidel, *The Splendid Little War* (Boston, 1958). The best account of the war, army and navy and diplomatic, is David F. Trask, *The War with Spain* (New York, 1981), in the Macmillan Wars of the United States series. Graham A. Cosmas, *An Army for Empire* (Columbia, Mo., 1971) describes the army's difficulties. A recent and interesting account is G. J. A. O'Toole, *The Spanish War* (New York, 1984). Special studies of interest are Richard H. Bradford, *The Virginius Affair* (Boulder, 1980); and on naval problems in 1898, John Edward Weems, *The Fate of the Maine* (New York, 1958); Ronald Spector, *Admiral of the New Empire* (Baton Rouge, 1975), on Dewey; and Hyman Rickover, *How the Battleship Maine was Destroyed* (Washington, D.C., 1976). (See also the listings after Chapter 1.)

The president of the United States has his accounting by Margaret Leech, *In the Days of McKinley* (New York, 1959), a "life and times," and H. Wayne Morgan, *William McKinley and His America* (Syracuse, N.Y., 1963). Other biographies are Tyler Dennett, *John Hay* (New York, 1933); Kenton J. Clymer, *John Hay* (Ann Arbor, 1975); and John Braeman, *Albert J. Beveridge* (Chicago, 1971). W. A. Swanberg, *Citizen Hearst* (New York, 1961), was denied the Pulitzer prize because of a committee opinion that the prize should be only for biographies of individuals worthy of emulation. See also Swanberg's *Pulitzer* (New York, 1967).

Mr. Dooley's witty disgust with American imperialism is in Finley Peter Dunne, *Mr. Dooley: In Peace and in War* (Boston, 1898), and Elmer Ellis, ed., *Mr. Dooley at His Best* (New York, 1938). Robert L. Beisner, *Twelve Against Empire* (Chicago, 1968), and Frank Freidel's essay in *Dissent in Three American*

Wars (Cambridge, Mass., 1970), cover the Spanish-American War. The distinguished Swedish scholar, Goeran Rystad, in *Ambiguous Imperialism* (Stockholm, 1975), shows the peculiar mixture of politics and imperialism in the presidential election of 1900.

Paul H. Buck, *The Road to Reunion: 1865–1900* (Boston, 1937), sets out a signal result of the war, the consolidation of American nationalism.

☆ 3 ☆

The Far East, 1899–1921

Wherever man oppresses man
  Beneath Thy liberal sun,
O Lord be there, Thine arm laid bare,
  Thy righteous will be done.
—Protestant hymn, verse by John Hay

1. *The Open-Door Notes*

By the end of the nineteenth century the westernization of the Orient, despite some initial resistance, had proceeded rather far. The Japanese took over Western culture wholesale, in many cases jettisoning their heritage of centuries in favor of the latest Western nicknack. One westernized Japanese destroyed a precious collection of Japanese prints to fill his house with cheap Western art. As for the Chinese, they at first proved more resistant to Western ways, but by the end of the century there was scarcely a locality in China, hinterland or coast, where the influence of the Western world had not reached.

It was perhaps coincidental that the disruptive effect of westernization in China was accompanied by a decline in vigor of the Manchu dynasty. The Manchus had begun their reign with considerable prestige and power in the mid-seventeenth century, but after two hundred years the Taiping rebellion, together with disorders by the so-called Nien Fei bandits, who ravaged large parts of the country, had shaken the Dragon Throne to its foundations. The authority of Peking was tenuous in the extreme by the end of the nineteenth century, and it was obvious to all intelligent observers that the Manchu empire was breaking up, that a chaotic situation was arising not unlike that of

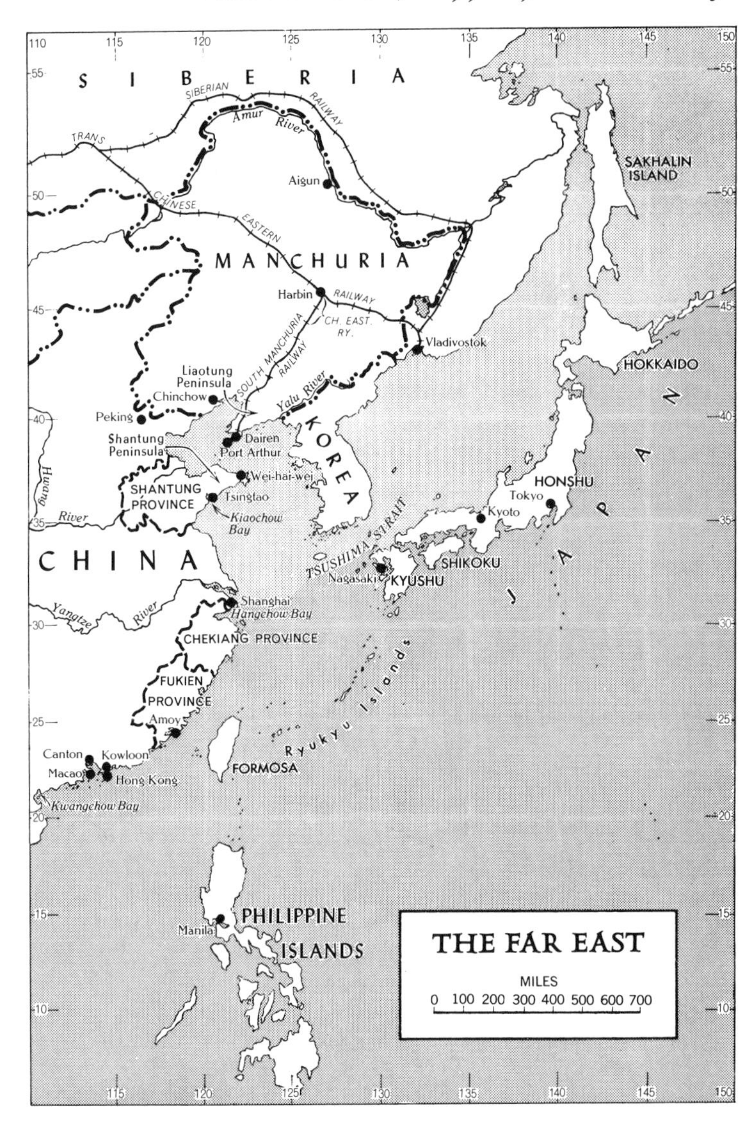

India at the beginning of the eighteenth century. As in India, an opportunity presented itself to Western powers. But whereas in India only British power was able to take great advantage of the weakness of the native dynasty, in China in the 1890s all the major powers of Europe sought to take part of the spoils.

The first move was by the Russians, and their greed was quickly matched by that of the other nations. After the Japanese had defeated the Chinese in a war in 1894–1895, demonstrating to the world the weakness of the Manchu regime, the tsarist government concluded in June 1896 the Li-Lobanov Treaty providing the right to construct a railway across Manchuria—the Chinese Eastern Railway—as a shortcut for the Trans-Siberian route to Vladivostok. Moves by the other powers followed at once. When two German missionaries were murdered by Chinese bandits in the Shantung peninsula in November 1897, the Germans in early March 1898 extracted a convention giving them a 99-year lease on Kiaochow bay and its port of Tsingtao, together with economic rights in Shantung. Three weeks later the Russians undertook to procure a 25-year lease of the southern part of the Liaotung peninsula including Talienwan (Dairen) and Port Arthur, with the right to construct a railroad from Harbin in the north to the newly leased ports (this railroad, at first a feeder of the Chinese Eastern, became known after the Japanese acquired it in 1905 as the South Manchuria Railway). The British in a strategic counter took a 99-year lease of Kowloon opposite Hong Kong and a lease on Wei-hai-wei on the Shantung peninsula "for so long a period as Port Arthur shall remain in the occupation of Russia." Meanwhile they had obtained other privileges from China, along with a pledge not to alienate to a foreign power any of the Yangtze Valley. The French obtained Kwangchow Bay in South China. Japan obtained rights in Fukien province opposite Formosa. Only the Italians, seeking in 1899 a naval station in Chekiang province, were successfully rebuffed.

The United States was at first oblivious to the impending chaos in China and to the probability that the Western nations would cut up the decrepit Manchu empire, although the turn of events in China coincided with the Spanish-American War and the somewhat fortuitous acquisition of the Philippine Islands, by which the United States became a Far Eastern power. The British government in March 1898 had suggested a joint Anglo-American approach to the other Western powers interested in China, calculated to avoid a partition of the Chinese empire and a parceling-out of its trade among the partitioners. Because of the imminent war with Spain, President McKinley failed to heed the British request. Again, in January 1899, the British ambassador in Washington made an inquiry of the state department, suggesting the cooperation of London and Washington in the Far East. Once more the American government evinced no interest.

At this point came a personal intervention which always has intrigued students of American diplomacy. The Far Eastern adviser of Secretary of State Hay was William W. Rockhill, an "old China hand" intensely devoted to the welfare of the Chinese people. He feared that a partition of the Manchu empire would only mean further exploitation for the already downtrodden Chinese population. Rockhill was visited in the summer of 1899 by a friend from China, another old China hand, a Britisher named Alfred E. Hippisley. The latter suggested that in view of the concession-hunting in China the time was ripe for an American diplomatic move in favor of China, an attempt to obtain adherence by the powers of Europe to a commercial policy of the "open door" in China. The extraordinary nature of Hippisley's proposal becomes manifest when one realizes that Great Britain already had attempted twice to obtain the cooperation of the United States in promoting the open-door policy in China. Could it be that the British foreign office, wise in the ways of diplomacy, had undertaken to influence American policy through an intermediary?

Actually there appears to have been nothing untoward or devious about the connection of this policy with the Britisher, Hippisley, for the latter was a genuine friend of the Chinese people, as was his American confidant Rockhill. Hippisley had long been an official of the Imperial Chinese Maritime Customs Service, a British-administered organization but one distinct in interests, responsibility, and outlook from the foreign office. Hippisley by 1899 was second in charge of the customs service, was doubtless concerned over the service's control of tariffs in the new spheres of interest of the Western powers, and for this reason alone had justification for seeking through Rockhill an American move to protect the open door and generally China's control over trade throughout the empire. Moreover, both he and Rockhill were students of Chinese history and culture, and they, for this reason too, were interested in a pro-Chinese diplomatic move by the United States. Hippisley had long been a Sinologue, and Rockhill was one of the world's authorities on Tibet. There was thus an easy explanation of why Hippisley proposed the open door to Rockhill and why the latter responded by forwarding Hippisley's proposition to Secretary of State Hay. The two men naturally would talk in terms of the threatened closing of the China market, which would attract the American people, rather than presenting an argument purely in terms of China's welfare or of China's control over customs.

Hippisley, as is well known, drew up a memorandum on the open door. His friend Rockhill revised this analysis for presentation to President McKinley and afterward put the substance of the revised memorandum in the form of diplomatic notes which, with minor changes, were adopted by Secretary Hay and sent out to Berlin, St. Petersburg, London, Paris, Rome, and Tokyo on September 6 and November 17, 1899. This was the first open-door note, containing the following three points:

First. The recognition that no power will in any way interfere with any treaty port or any vested interest within any leased territory or within any so-called "sphere of interest" it may have in China.

Second. That the Chinese treaty tariff of the time being shall apply to all merchandise landed or shipped to all such ports as are within said "sphere of interest" (unless they be "free ports"), no matter to what nationality it may belong, and that duties so leviable shall be collected by the Chinese Government.

Third. That it [each power] will levy no higher harbor dues on vessels of another nationality frequenting any port in such "sphere" than shall be levied on vessels of its own nationality, and no higher railroad charges over lines built, controlled, or operated within its "sphere" on merchandise belonging to citizens or subjects of other nationalities transported through such "sphere" than shall be levied on similar merchandise belonging to its own nationals transported over equal distances.

The note could by no stretch of the imagination be described as epoch-making. The traditional American commercial policy toward China during the nineteenth century had been a policy of free competition among the powers for trade—in other words, a policy of the open door in regard to China. There had not hitherto, it is true, been an effort to line up the other powers to favor this policy. The open door, as traditionally interpreted, had been a unilateral policy of the United States, contained only in treaties with China. But sooner or later it would have been elaborated in diplomatic intercourse with the nations interested in Chinese trade. To make multilateral this doctrine of fair trade in China was perhaps no more than a logical development of a traditional American policy. The first open-door note contemplated free commercial intercourse under the Chinese treaty tariff of five percent—within the spheres of interest of the various powers. It did not contemplate abolition of the spheres of interest, although Hay's adviser Rockhill, to be sure, thought that by providing for collection of duties by the Chinese he had taken a stand in favor of protecting Chinese sovereignty within the spheres.

It was in the year 1900 that Hay made a second open-door effort, one far more important than the initiative of the previous year, and much different. An outbreak of antiforeign agitation in China, the Boxer Rebellion, had required an expedition by an international force of 19,000 troops—including an American contingent—to rescue the besieged legations in Peking. On July 3, 1900, when it was uncertain whether the besieged legations in Peking would be saved, and when it seemed likely that after taking Peking the troops of the powers would engage in a grand division of Chinese territory, Hay made the bold and—in view of the conditions under which he made it—imaginative move of sending a circular note to the powers favoring the territorial integrity of China. This second open-door note, unlike its predecessor, was a novel statement of American policy. In the note of 1900 the secretary of state advanced to ground quite different from that covered by his note of the year before. In some ways the two open-door notes should not be coupled, for the second note in its stipulations regarding Chinese territorial integrity contradicted the note of September–November 1899. The first note had stipulated commercial freedom for all nations within any of the spheres of interest. In his second open-door note Hay announced that American policy sought to "preserve Chinese territorial and administrative entity," that is, that the United States was taking a stand against the further partitioning of China.

The second note, like the first, expressed the views of Hay's adviser Rockhill (and of his adviser, Hippisley), but neither Hippisley nor Rockhill nor Hay dreamed that the open-door policy would be more than a temporary buttress to Far Eastern peace. They did not envision that their diplomacy of the moment, "a kind of *modus vivendi*" as Rockhill described the first open-door note, would become a cardinal doctrine of twentieth-century American policy in the Orient. As the twentieth century advanced and Japan became ever more powerful in the Far East, threatening the integrity of China in numerous ways and on various occasions, American diplomacy tended to distort the sense of the second Hay open-door note. The idea of preserving Chinese territorial and administrative entity, in itself a somewhat ambitious policy, gave way almost unconsciously to the idea of downright guarantee of Chinese territory. There had never been a contractual guarantee of Chinese territory by the United States. But by 1941 the American public was virtually convinced that this was traditional American policy.

2. *Rooseveltian Diplomacy, 1900–1909*

The year 1900 was certainly a signal year in modern Chinese history, what with the suppression of the Boxer Rebellion by the troops of the powers, and their forceful occupation of Peking. The nations imposed upon China a large claim for damages in the form of an indemnity of $333,000,000, distributed among Britain, France, Germany, Italy, Austria-Hungary, the United States, and Japan. The United States, after accepting $4,000,000 to satisfy private claims, eventually remitted the remaining payments for the purpose of training Chinese students in America. The other nations kept the indemnities due them. Thus the new century opened, but in 1900, it seems safe to say, the shape of the future was still uncertain. Settlement of the Boxer Rebellion seemed to quiet affairs in the Orient—for good, so many Americans and Europeans hoped.

In the year 1900 it was Russia, not Japan, which appeared to be the problem of the Orient. Although Japan had defeated China in 1894–1895 in an exhibition of military prowess that boded ill for the future, when the powers had reached Peking and there was looting by some of the troops of the European nations the Japanese soldiers were well-behaved. In 1900 the Russians, far more than the Japanese, seemed the nation to watch. Russia had participated in a triple

American infantry moving up to the gate at Peking, during the Boxer Rebellion.

intervention along with Germany and France to thwart Japan in 1895, after the Japanese had won the war against China. At that time the tsarist government had insisted that Japan not take the southernmost part of Manchuria, the Liaotung peninsula, including a port on its tip which controlled the approaches to Peking. Faced with the intervention of three European powers, the Japanese in 1895 diplomatically withdrew their claims to Liaotung. The next year the Russians began moving into northern Manchuria under an agreement with the Chinese. By the time of the Boxer Rebellion Russia was ready to occupy Manchuria, including all of the Liaotung peninsula, the territory denied to Japan in 1895. Russia also was showing considerable interest in Korea.

Theodore Roosevelt, upon succeeding the assassinated McKinley in the presidency, was thoroughly distrustful of the activities of tsarist Russia in the Orient. After the Boxer Rebellion, when trouble began to increase between Russia and Japan and war loomed, TR was happy to say that in case of a Russo-Japanese war he hoped Japan would win. The Russians were attempting to close Manchuria to foreign trade, on the theory that Manchuria was no longer a part of China. This was contrary to the idea of the open door, and other Americans also hoped that if Russia and Japan went to war, Japan would win and open Manchuria to trade.

Japan severed diplomatic relations with Russia on February 6, 1904, after pressing the Russians to agree over a partition of Korea, and growing discouraged at the delay and evasion and the continuing expansion of Russian power in the Far East. Two days later Japan suddenly attacked the tsarist fleet at Port Arthur, and declared war two days after hostilities began. Japanese troops invested Russian positions in Manchuria, giving no heed to the neutrality of Chinese soil, and in a matter of a few months, albeit with expenditure of over

100,000 Japanese lives, the island empire had bested one of the most ancient of European nations. The last hope of the Russians was the thirty-two ships of the Baltic fleet, sent on a long voyage through the Mediterranean (the most powerful units went around Africa) and the Indian Ocean to the Far East, only to be annihilated by Japan's Admiral Togo in Tsushima strait.

What happened during the Russo-Japanese War of 1904–1905 was one of the surprises of the twentieth century—the abject defeat of Russia, the emergence of Japan as one of the first-class military powers of the world. Although they had disliked the Russians, the Americans had not bargained for this development. Japan, by defeating Russia, unsettled the entire Far East in a way that no event had done before, and the vulnerability of the Philippines began to appear as a major problem for the United States. The Americans, perhaps, had only themselves to blame for this turn of affairs. They had for decades been doing their best to avoid any breakup of Japan similar to that of China, and in pursuing this purpose had done much to bolster Japan's military capabilities. American military assistance had begun with Perry's gift of one cannon from the *Saratoga.* The commodore had recommended to the navy department that two more be sent, for gifts, he said, would on some future occasion be "returned a hundredfold." The Japanese mission to the United States in 1860 had received a hundred muskets, four howitzers, shells and shell-filling machines. The United States sold three war vessels to Japan in 1863 and delivered them in 1865. Annapolis was opened to Japanese students in 1868. By contributing a number of political advisers to the Japanese government in the latter nineteenth century, the United States further helped to make Japan a strong naval power. Mahan himself said that his writings had been more fully translated into Japanese than into any other language. But in the war of 1904–1905 the Japanese had suddenly exhibited the results of this American tuition in a new and startling and not altogether pleasant manner.

After initial requests from the belligerents, President Roosevelt undertook to mediate the war in the summer of 1905, and this task he performed with his usual aplomb, bringing his work of peace to a suitable end in the Treaty of Portsmouth, signed by Japan and Russia at Portsmouth, New Hampshire, on September 5, 1905. By this treaty Japan acquired the South Manchuria Railway, the Liaotung peninsula under guise of a leasehold, and the southern half of Sakhalin Island. Russia acknowledged Japan's paramount interest in Korea.

The Portsmouth Treaty, narrowly considered, was a diplomatic accomplishment of the first order, and the American president eventually received the Nobel Peace Prize for his work in 1905. Unfortunately, in its long-term effects on American policy the treaty was hardly a triumph—indeed it was a disaster—for in reality it increased the American-Japanese political antagonism that would plague

Theodore Roosevelt at Portsmouth, with (left to right) Witte, Rosen, Komura, and Takahira.

American relations with the Far East during the first half of the twentieth century. Policy could no longer placidly continue in the nineteenth-century pattern of trade-Christianity-civilization. The Portsmouth Treaty, it is true, was probably the best treaty that either Russia or Japan could have obtained in the summer of 1905. The Russians were exhausted and the tsarist regime faced the first stirrings of the revolution that would engulf it in 1917. The Japanese were in equally bad straits, for their credit abroad was such as to dictate a speedy end to the war. Japanese finances had long been precarious, and the burden of further war in 1905 was almost too much to endure. The Japanese representatives at Portsmouth should have been satisfied with the peace treaty, and they were pleased, but they had failed to get an indemnity from Russia and obtained only half of Sakhalin. The government in Tokyo diplomatically allowed popular disappointment to focus on the American president who had mediated the peace, rather than the Japanese envoys who had signed it. Anti-American riots broke out in Tokyo, mobs burned four American churches, the United States embassy was placed under guard, and in subsequent years—as the Japanese spread further into Manchuria, taking advantage of Western weakness or preoccupation elsewhere—the rift in American-Japanese relations widened into a chasm.

In the uneasy years after the outbreak of the Russo-Japanese War there followed three special agreements by which Japan and the United States sought to allay their mutual suspicions and somehow recreate the friendly atmosphere that had prevailed in an earlier era: the Taft-Katsura Agreement (1905), the Root-Takahira Agreement (1908), and the Lansing-Ishii Agreement (1917). Unfortunately each agreement produced disagreement and became a milestone in the antagonism developing between the United States and Japan. Each was accompanied by complicating arrangements or proposed arrangements: the so-called Gentlemen's Agreement concerning immigration, the Knox neutralization scheme, the China consortium, the Twenty-One Demands.

The Taft-Katsura Agreement, an "agreed memorandum" between Secretary of War William Howard Taft and the Japanese premier, Taro Katsura, dated July 29, 1905, marked the initial effort of President Roosevelt to reach a harmonious arrangement with the Japanese government. It was obvious to Roosevelt that Japan was the coming power in the Orient, and since the United States had acquired the Philippines, islands which lay at Japan's doorstep, it was prudent to placate the owners of the house. Placation meant giving away, in effect, an old edifice which lay close to the house, the kingdom of Korea. According to the Taft-Katsura Agreement, which supposedly bound only the administration then in power at Washington (though it is difficult to imagine how such an agreement could bind merely a single administration), the United States recognized Japan's dominant position in Korea, and the Japanese disavowed "any aggressive designs whatever" on the Philippines.

No sooner was this memorandum drawn and the Portsmouth Treaty signed than trouble appeared with Japan, in an unexpected quarter—the segregating of Japanese schoolchildren together with Chinese and Koreans in the San Francisco schools. The immigration of the Chinese to California in the years after the discovery of gold and during construction of the transcontinental railroad became in time an exceedingly sore point in California and eventually forced an exclusion act through Congress in 1882. It was easy to exclude the Chinese, for the Chinese government was unable to do much more than protest such an act by the Americans. In the case of the Japanese, in the years after the Russo-Japanese War when the Japanese government was feeling its power and able to protest with vigor and effect, to take discriminating measures was far more dangerous. Yet in 1906, just a year after signature of the Portsmouth Treaty, the issue of Japanese immigration to California arose in this singularly ugly form.

The action of the San Francisco school board was precipitous and undiplomatic in the extreme and raised a storm in Japan. The whole issue of Japanese immigration to California suddenly came into the open, and the utmost diplomacy had to be exercised with the Californians, and with the Japanese, before the matter was settled by the Gentlemen's Agreement in 1907–1908. According to this agreement in the form of a series of diplomatic notes, Japan would not allow laborers to obtain visas to the mainland of the United States, and thus halted the immigration which was causing so much trouble in

California. The San Francisco school board, under its president—an erstwhile bassoon player under indictment for fraud—rescinded its rule.

Trouble again arose in California in 1913 when the legislature took under consideration a bill making it impossible for Japanese to own or lease land for agricultural purposes. President Woodrow Wilson was reduced to sending Secretary of State William Jennings Bryan to California in April 1913 to plead with the governor and the legislature. The discriminatory legislation as finally passed was so ingeniously worded as to sound less offensive than it was. Without directly affronting Japan or violating the letter of America's treaty obligations, it barred Japanese from owning agricultural land. The Californians later in 1920 passed an act refusing to Japanese the right to lease agricultural land. Over a dozen states during the early 1920s followed California's example.

The increase of Japanese power in the Orient and the necessity of concluding an agreement for protection of the Philippines dissipated the Roosevelt administration's original friendliness for Japan. Relations between the two nations had not been improved by the San Francisco school controversy. Roosevelt in 1907 conceived the idea of sending the American battleship fleet around the world, stopping at Oriental ports en route, in the hope that a display of American power would impress the Japanese. This was a typical Rooseveltian move in its feeling for display and show of force, and TR later boasted in his *Autobiography* that it was "the most important service that I rendered to peace." This boast may have been true. Probably the battleship fleet did impress the Japanese people with the growing strength of America.

Meanwhile the Root-Takahira Agreement had been concluded on November 30, 1908, an agreement over which there has always been a controversy, for no one has ever established the precise meaning of this accord concluded by Secretary of State Elihu Root and the Japanese ambassador in Washington, Kogoro Takahira. In the exchange of notes between the two statesmen it was declared that the two governments wished to maintain the status quo in the region of the Pacific Ocean, together with the open door in China, and that each would respect the territories of the other and support "by all pacific means at their disposal the independence and integrity of China and the principle of equal opportunity." This seemed to indicate that the United States would not challenge Japan's newly created position in Manchuria; the peaceful promises by Japan in turn pointed to another guarantee of the Philippines, together with Hawaii and Alaska. The Japanese doubtless considered the Root-Takahira Agreement a complement to their new position evidenced in the Anglo-Japanese Alliance of 1902, the Portsmouth Treaty, and agreements of 1907 with France and Russia. Secretary Root hoped and later affirmed that the

Elihu Root negotiated an agreement with Japan in 1908.

agreement would ensure the open door in Manchuria rather than any special Japanese-fashion "status quo." There was no meeting of minds in the curious Root-Takahira Agreement, stemming as it did from the multiplying uncertainties and frictions of American-Japanese relations. It was one more attempt to find some formula that might make for better feeling between Washington and Tokyo.

3. *The Far East and the First World War*

The Far East, as we have seen, was in ferment in the years after the turn of the century, with the decline of Manchu strength in China coinciding with the rising power of Japan. And these disturbing factors were joined by a third complication, the embroilments of Russia in the Far East. The Russo-Japanese War had been an illustration of the novel difficulties in Asia.

The entire Far Eastern situation was enormously complicated by the developing antagonisms of Europe. Russia's diplomacy in the East, to name but one example, was closely linked to the deepening international crisis on the Continent. The alignments of the First World War were forming. The Triple Alliance of Germany, Austria-Hungary, and Italy soon would face the Triple Entente of Great Britain, France, and Russia. Far Eastern politics became the backyard of European politics. The German kaiser William II had striven for some time to interest his cousin, Tsar Nicholas II, in Far Eastern territory, to turn the attention of the tsar from Europe. "Willy" and "Nicky," as they signed their personal correspondence, had encouraged each other with the titles of Admiral of the Atlantic (Willy) and Admiral of the Pacific (Nicky). Insofar as Nicky took Willy seriously, and there is some evidence that he did, the ultimate result of these imperial pleasantries was the defeat of Russia by Japan and a weakening of the Franco-Russian alliance in Europe. It was, one should add, a somewhat mixed victory, for it meant too the weakening of the monarchical principle in Russia, which in due time had repercussions for European monarchs, as the kaiser would learn.

The quest of Great Britain for alliances and friendships in the years before the First World War—conclusion of the Anglo-Japanese Alliance of 1902, and after it the rapprochement with France of 1904 and the Anglo-Russian Entente of 1907—also had its effects in the Far East. The Anglo-Japanese Alliance enlisted Japanese support of British interests in Asia and gave Britain a freer hand in Europe. The alliance was directed also, and this was Japan's *quid pro quo*, against Russia, for it promised that should Japan engage in a war with another power (that is, Russia) and that power be joined by a third power (that is, France, in accord with the Franco-Russian Alliance of 1894), then Britain would enter the war on the side of Japan. In effect this arrangement gave Japan assurance that in a war with Russia there would be no intervention by France.

This is not the place to set down in detail the Far Eastern ramifications of European politics; what mattered for American diplomacy was that after the Treaty of Portsmouth a new international arrangement took effect in the Far East, in large part a result of European political developments: Russia in 1907 concluded the entente with Britain, France had done so in 1904, and because of the already existing Franco-Russian and Anglo-Japanese alliances Japan therefore came to an agreement with Russia (Japan, Russia, France, and Britain would side against Germany in 1914). The Russo-Japanese rapprochement that took place during the years 1907–1910 was, of course, at the expense of China. Russia and Japan formally divided Manchuria into two spheres of interest, its southern part to Japan, its northern to Russia.

In view of this new alliance structure, any intervention by the United States in Far Eastern politics was likely to affect directly the European balance of power. Here was a new problem for American diplomacy in the Far East. But one must doubt whether the individuals who directed American policy after the era of Theodore Roosevelt really appreciated it. They knew that there had been a traditional American policy in the Far East, and that the rise of Japanese power had made that policy difficult. They saw the troubles in China, the crumbling of the Manchu empire which in 1911–1912 brought disintegration of the dynasty and proclamation of a republic. They had no sense of the connection of Far Eastern and European diplomacy. In the years between 1900 and 1914, and especially in the era 1905–1914, any sort of American diplomacy in the Orient without knowledge of the factors and forces governing European international relations would have been foolish, or dangerous, or both.

Theodore Roosevelt had sensed the problems of American policy and he sought to placate Japan in the agreements of 1905 and 1908, but his successor President Taft unfortunately forgot the power equation in the Far East. Taft was a constitutional lawyer, and together with his secretary of state, Philander C. Knox, also a lawyer, he endeavored to promote American trade with China through legalistic maneuvering of a sort which would not have brought results in the nineteenth century, to say nothing of the twentieth. The two blunders of the Taft administration, and they were blunders, were the attempted neutralization of the existing Manchurian railways, sponsored by Secretary Knox, and the effort of the administration to promote a China consortium for developing Manchuria.

The Knox neutralization scheme was one of the most foolish proposals ever made by an American diplomat. The secretary of state was secure in his ignorance of Manchurian realities, that is, of the new friendship of Japan and Russia in Manchuria. He attempted through Britain, France, Germany, Japan, and Russia to obtain for China an international loan of sufficient size to enable that government to buy up all the foreign railways in China, including Manchuria, and thereby "neutralize" the roads by retiring foreign capital. As an alternative he suggested construction under neutral administration of a north-south railway through Manchuria from Aigun to Chinchow. He overlooked the fact that the railroads of China, particularly Manchuria, had always been a prime means of foreign intervention, and that Russia's Chinese Eastern Railway in northern Manchuria and Japan's South Manchuria Railway were the thread on which these two nations had strung their interests in Manchuria. To ask those countries to neutralize their railway concessions was to ask retirement from an area over which wars had been fought in 1894–1895 and 1904–1905. The American secretary of state had made a preposterous suggestion. The European powers accepted the Knox proposal in principle, but would do nothing more. Japan argued in reply to Knox that his suggestion was at variance with the peace of Portsmouth and arrangements for concessions in Manchuria made with China at the end of that conflict. The Russians, after perfunctorily expressing enthusiasm for the open door and equal opportunity in Manchuria—as the Japanese had also done—contended that Knox's proposal was against their interests and refused to accept it. As a result of the neutralization scheme, Japan and Russia concluded a new agreement in July 1910 strengthening their agreement of 1907.

Undaunted, Knox set out to force American capital into a new international consortium which was organizing to finance currency reform and industrial development in Manchuria. The United States went to the length of sending a special message from President Taft to the prince regent of China, begging the latter to look with favor upon American entrance into the consortium. The matter dragged on, and China was plunged into the revolution of 1911–1912, precipitated by foreign demands for concessions. The Americans finally were admitted to the consortium, but Wall Street financiers were reluctant to take part and demanded explicit government support. When Wilson became president in March 1913, he refused to support the consortium and allowed American bankers to leave what they had never wished to enter in the first place.

By the time of the Wilson administration, the American diplomatic position in the Far East had deteriorated to a grievous state, and with the outbreak of the First World War in 1914 the American government was beset with problems of neutrality. Little energy remained for Far Eastern matters. Neither the United States nor the European nations could do anything against the shameless demands made by Japan upon China in 1915. The Twenty-One Demands, as they were called, contained several conditions which if accepted by the Chinese would have brought that hapless nation directly under the control of Tokyo. The United States protested on May 11, 1915, that it would not recognize any situation forced upon China by Japan. Luckily the crisis passed when the Japanese decided not to force their most rigorous demands upon the Chinese.

But in 1917, when the United States entered World War I, there came another opportunity for the Japanese, this time to obtain a concession directly from the Americans. France and Britain were sending missions to the United States in the spring of 1917, to arrange the policy and details of American participation in the European conflict, and the Japanese sent a special envoy, Viscount Kikujiro Ishii, but not on the same sort of mission the European governments were undertaking. Ishii was instructed to secure from the American government a recognition of Japan's position in Asia. Unblushingly performing his embassy, he threatened that Japan might go over to the side of Germany and abandon the Allies. He told Secretary of State Robert Lansing that Germany three times had sought to persuade Japan to forsake the Allied cause, and the hint was altogether obvious. The Lansing-Ishii Agreement was concluded on November 2, 1917, in this difficult atmosphere.

The agreement between Secretary of State Lansing and the special Japanese ambassador was if anything more ambiguous than the Root-Takahira Agreement of nine years before. "The governments of the United States and Japan," it stipulated, "recognize that territorial propinquity creates special relations between countries, and, consequently the government of the United States recognizes that Japan has special interests in China, particularly in the part to which her possessions are contiguous. The territorial sovereignty of China, nevertheless, remains unimpaired . . ." Lansing always maintained that he had only recognized the "special interests" of Japan in China, interests of an economic nature created by geographical propinquity and contiguity. The Japanese translated the phrase "special interests" as "paramount interests," and refused to consider them as limited to economic concerns. Later Ishii wrote in his *Diplomatic Commentaries* that he and Secretary Lansing were only "performing the role of photographers, as it were, of a condition," namely, Japan's paramount situation in the Far East. "Even though Americans may destroy the print because it is not to their liking," Ishii added, "the negative will remain. And even if the negative also be destroyed, does not the substance of the picture remain?"

What could one conclude about all these perplexities of American-Japanese relations? Certainly there could be no doubt about Japanese intentions in Eastern Asia when in the year 1919 the peace conference for the First World War met in Paris. The Japanese by this time, not content with a sphere of interest in Manchuria and virtual hegemony over China, had made an effort to separate Siberia from Russia. Japan had sent over seventy thousand troops into Siberia, nominally to assist in the protection of Allied war materials stored at Vladivostok. The supposed purpose of sending these Japanese troops, together with contingents from other nations including the United States (the United States contingent in Siberia never numbered more than nine thousand), Britain, Serbia, Italy, and Rumania, had been to hold these stores against the Bolsheviks, who had taken over the Russian government in November 1917 and soon thereafter made a separate peace with the Germans. There was also, one should add, another purpose of the Allied troops in Siberia, namely to facilitate the exit from Russia of thousands of Czechs, former enemy prisoners freed by withdrawal of Russia from the war, who wished to pass over the Trans-Siberian Railway and take ship from Vladivostok to Europe, there to fight on the Allied side against Austria-Hungary to achieve an independent Czechoslovakia. A third purpose for Allied intervention in Siberia, set forth by the United States, was to assist the Russians with self-government or self-defense. But it was the hope of the Japanese to intrigue with Russian factional leaders and assist to power a pro-Japanese regime which someday might place Siberia under Japanese sovereignty. The Japanese war ministry defied the foreign office and forced Japan's diplomats at home or abroad to defend the actions of the military. Eventually the Japanese government went back under civil control. Meanwhile the United States and the other allies withdrew their troops. Japanese troops left Siberia in October 1922.

At the Paris Peace Conference of 1919 there was, in addition to such difficulties with the Japanese, the problem of Shantung, the formerly German sphere of interest in China. If the Allied leaders at Paris had not recognized Japan's right to economic and other concessions in Shantung, the Japanese delegation would have retired from Paris. "They are not bluffers," Wilson told one of his assistants in

1919, "and they will go home unless we give them what they should not have." When a recognition of Japanese interests in Shantung was written into the Versailles Treaty, the president accepted it, realizing sadly that it "was the best that could be had out of a dirty past." The Chinese, who had assisted the Allies in Europe, were outraged with the result.

Other advantages accrued to Japan at the Paris Peace Conference, for in addition to Shantung the Japanese were confirmed in their control over the former German Pacific islands north of the equator. Japan had taken the islands at the outset of the war, under a secret arrangement with Great Britain whereby the British took the German islands south of the equator. By the peace settlement of 1919 the islands went to Japan as a mandate, a special colonial trust, of the new League of Nations. The Japanese were supposed to administer these former German possessions for the benefit of the inhabitants thereof, but in fact the islands became Japan's private property and were fortified contrary to League rules for mandated territories.

The peace conference of 1919 marked generally a triumph for Japan. The island empire was included as one of the five great powers represented on the Council of Ten (to which each of the powers sent two delegates). This marked a large addition to Japanese prestige, for the council was designed to serve as a sort of executive body for the peace conference. Later, when the council gave way to the Big Four—private meetings of the leaders of Britain, France, the United States, and Italy—and the Big Three (Italy withdrawing), the Japanese received a careful explanation from President Wilson's adviser, Colonel Edward M. House, who assured one of the chief delegates from Tokyo, Baron Makino, "that the work of the Four will be submitted to him before its final adoption and that then the Big Four will be expanded into the Big Five."

Japan, it is true, did lose face at the conference when Makino in the last session of the League of Nations Commission, the committee for drafting the League Covenant, raised the issue of racial equality and asked for a statement in the preamble of the Covenant, then in final draft, of "the principle of equality of nations and the just treatment of their nationals . . . as a fundamental basis of future international relations in the new world organization." Under unbearable pressure from Prime Minister William M. Hughes of Australia, the British delegate at the commission meeting, Lord Robert Cecil, refused to admit the principle of racial equality. In the voting that followed the British and American delegations abstained, which was equivalent to voting against the Japanese proposal. This was an unpleasant pill for the Japanese representative at Paris, but the gains to Japan at the conference were otherwise so impressive and gratifying that the Japanese in 1919 could well feel that, racially equal or not, they had achieved a large and important place in the world family of nations, including perhaps an unassailable position in the affairs of the Far East.

This latter notion was not the view of the great powers of the West, in particular Britain and the United States, who at length reorganized the affairs of the Orient according to their desires, for a time, at the Washington Naval Conference of 1921–1922—which will be dealt with in chapter 7.

Suffice to close this present chapter by remarking the transfer at the end of the First World War of the bulk of the American fleet from Atlantic to Pacific. There it remained as a counterpoise to the Japanese navy during the increasingly critical relations between the United States and Japan in the 1920s and 1930s. This transfer symbolized the end of an era in American relations with Europe, the period during which Americans feared Europe more than Asia, and the beginning of a new outlook on world affairs in which the security of the United States vis-à-vis Japan began to occupy the calculations of American strategists, military and diplomatic.

ADDITIONAL READING

A. Whitney Griswold, *The Far Eastern Policy of the United States* (New York, 1938), is still helpful for American relations from the turn of the century until the First World War, after which its sources thin out. Griswold's beautifully written book influenced a generation of students and teachers. For more up-to-date accounts see Akira Irye, *Across the Pacific* (New York, 1967); Ernest R. May and James C. Thomson, Jr., eds., *American-East Asia Relations* (Cambridge, Mass., 1972); and Robert A. Hart, *The Eccentric Tradition* (New York, 1976).

Warren I. Cohen, *America's Response to China* (New York, 1971), and Thomas H. Etzold, ed., *Aspects of Sino-American Relations since 1784* (New York, 1978), are general treatments of American relations with the most populous country in the world. Korean-American relations have not inspired many books, but were of importance, if only for their effect on Sino-Japanese affairs, and Yur-Bok Lee, *Diplomatic Relations between the United States and Korea* (New York, 1970), considers the early years. For Japan see William L. Neumann, *America Encounters Japan* (Baltimore, 1963); Charles E. Neu, *Troubled Encounter* (New York, 1975), a volume in the America in Crisis series; Eugene P. Trani, *The Treaty of Portsmouth* (Lexington, Ky., 1969); and Akira Irye, *Pacific Estrangement* (Cambridge, Mass., 1972). Robert A. Hart, *The Great White Fleet* (Boston, 1965), is a stirring account of the voyage around the world. Hart discovered that among other items taken round the world were five dozen pianos. The ships carried so much gear that they were low in the water, and before any action it might have been necessary to throw the pianos overboard. See also Richard D. Challener, *Admirals, Generals, and American Foreign Policy* (Princeton, 1973). Intervention in Siberia has inspired a large literature, notably

George F. Kennan's prize-winning *Russia Leaves the War* (Princeton, 1956) and *The Decision to Intervene* (1958), together with Robert J. Maddox, *The Unknown War with Russia* (San Rafael, California, 1977).

For biographies see Paul A. Varg, *Open Door Diplomat: The Life of W. W. Rockhill* (Urbana, Ill., 1952), a fascinating account of the high-strung, strange, yet likable scholar-diplomat; and Noel H. Pugach, *Paul S. Reinsch* (Millwood, N.Y., 1979), the American minister during the Wilson period. Presidential and other figures for this era appear in suggestions for additional reading after Chapters 2, 5, and 6.

☆ 4 ☆

Colossus of the North

There is a homely adage which runs, "Speak softly and carry a big stick; you will go far."

—Vice President Theodore Roosevelt, September 2, 1901

The relations of the United States with Latin America compare in one respect to relations with the Far East, namely that—as in Asia—there have been two major periods of policy. The first of these, which might well be described as the era of intervention, ran roughly from the time of the Spanish-American War down to the entrance of the United States into the First World War in 1917. In the initial period the United States wrested Cuba from Spain, then in 1903 allowed the Panamanians to revolt from Colombia and cede a canal zone. Afterward came the series of interventions—Dominican Republic in 1905, Nicaragua in 1911, Haiti in 1915, Mexico in 1913–1917. When a crisis occurred with Germany, it seemed wise policy to abandon intervention in Mexican politics, and the American army pulled out of northern Mexico in February 1917. Victory in World War I removed the need for protection of the canal approaches in the Caribbean, and after the decade of the 1920s had passed mostly in inaction, the United States in the 1930s recognized the need for a new policy toward the Latin republics and put it into effect, beginning with the Montevideo Conference of 1933, the policy of the good neighbor, which was the liquidation of protective imperialism.

1. *Cuba*

We've seen that the deplorable situation in Cuba led in the early spring of 1898 to American intervention in that island. It is testimony to American good will and an early interest in the twentieth-century notion of national self-determination—Cuba for the Cubans—that even before intervention the Congress of the United States opted, through the Teller Amendment, against taking Cuba as a territorial appendage (to use a nineteenth-century imperialist phrase). The nations of Europe, observing the passage through Congress of the resolutions favoring intervention in Cuba, must have wondered if the Teller Amendment to these resolutions meant what it said. They must also have thought it strange that the Americans carried out their resolve in the following few years.

The resolutions favoring intervention, approved by the president on April 20, 1898, sounded familiar enough to Americans who liked the phrases of liberty, and to Europeans who saw only the phrases of double-dealing. The resolves declared, "the people of Cuba are, and of right ought to be, free and independent," demanded that Spain "at once relinquish its authority and government in the Island of Cuba and withdraw its land and naval forces from Cuba and Cuban waters," and—much like a latter-day resolution concerning Vietnam—empowered the president to use the forces of the United States to back up this demand. Senator Henry M. Teller of Colorado thereupon had added the famous declaration: "That the United States hereby disclaims any disposition or intention to exercise sovereignty, jurisdiction, or control over said Island except for the pacification thereof, and asserts its determination, when that is accomplished, to leave the government and control of the Island to its people."

President William McKinley, who had said that he would have no jingo nonsense during his administration, was a bit slow to put the Teller Amendment into effect, and in his annual message of 1899, a portion of which he devoted to Cuban matters, he may even have sought to put the Cuban case in such a way that his countrymen would contemplate going back on their promise of Cuban independence. Or it may have been just his way of stating facts in a resounding manner. The president remarked that the United States had "assumed before the world a grave responsibility for the future good government of Cuba." Good enough. The new Cuba, he added, "must needs be bound to us by ties of singular intimacy and strength if its enduring welfare is to be assured." Perhaps not so good. But it was not long before McKinley was taking measures to patch up the machinery of government in the once Ever-Faithful Isle. In 1899 he appointed General Leonard Wood as military governor, and Wood began a series of political, social, and medical reforms which bade fair to transform Cuba from the sinkhole it had become under Spanish rule. Wood remained in office only until 1902, when he moved on to other imperialist tasks under guidance of his new commander in chief in the White House, his onetime lieutenant colonel of the Rough Riders. Under Wood's agency and that of his successors, the

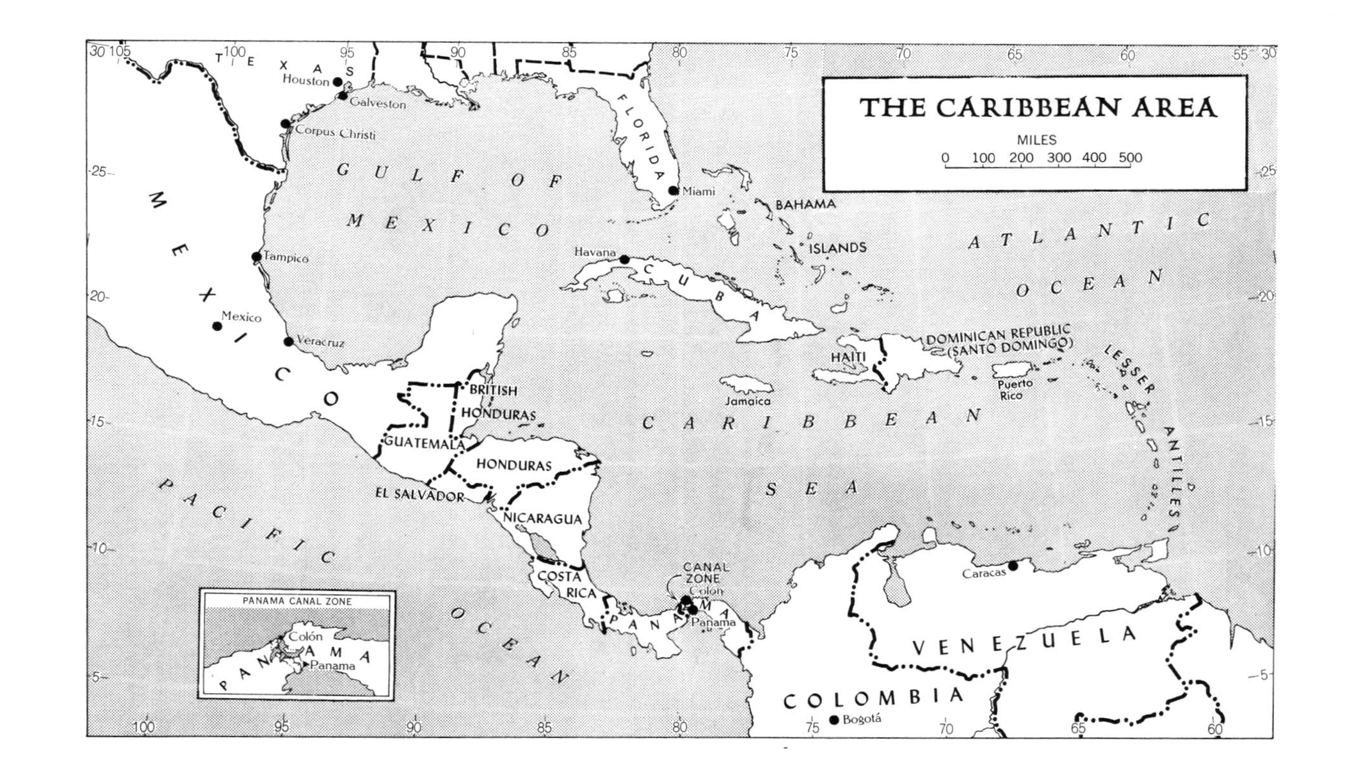
THE CARIBBEAN AREA
MILES
0 100 200 300 400 500
TEXAS
Houston
Galveston
Corpus Christi
FLORIDA
Miami
GULF OF MEXICO
MEXICO
Tampico
Mexico
Veracruz
BAHAMA ISLANDS
Havana
CUBA
ATLANTIC OCEAN
DOMINICAN REPUBLIC
(SANTO DOMINGO)
HAITI
Puerto Rico
LESSER ANTILLES
Jamaica
CARIBBEAN SEA
BRITISH HONDURAS
GUATEMALA
HONDURAS
EL SALVADOR
NICARAGUA
COSTA RICA
PANAMA
CANAL ZONE
Colon
Panama
PACIFIC OCEAN
Caracas
VENEZUELA
COLOMBIA
Bogotá
PANAMA CANAL ZONE
Colón
Panama

Americans cleaned up Cuba, as they long had wished to do, and made sure that their measures would have a modest permanency.

The Cuban constitution was taking shape in 1901–1902, and at Secretary of War Elihu Root's request Senator Orville H. Platt of Connecticut inserted provisos in the 1901 army appropriation bill. Root wanted these timely points included in the Cuban constitution, and the Cubans were not happy about this. General Wood wrote to Root, with considerable acumen, that it might be best to force the Platt Amendment upon them, so that the politicos could report to their constituents that they had signed under duress. This stratagem produced an appendix to the Cuban constitution containing the Platt Amendment. The amendment also was embodied in a treaty of May 22, 1903, between Cuba and the United States, which remained in force until replaced by another treaty in 1934.

According to the Platt Amendment, the Cuban government could not enter any treaty impairing Cuban independence; it could not contract a public debt in excess of ordinary revenues; the United States might intervene to preserve independence and maintain law and order; and Cuba agreed to allow the United States Navy to develop coaling stations such as Guantánamo Bay (still held).

Cuba under American tutelage was not a perfect example of a wayward colony brought to salvation. The Cuban sugar crop enjoyed special arrangements in the American market. Investment in the island by citizens of the United States went up from an estimated $50,000,000 at the time of the Spanish-American War to more than $200,000,000 by 1911, and more than $500,000,000 by 1920. Americans such as the young Norman Davis—later to serve as undersecretary of state during the Harding administration and as ambassador-at-large during the administrations of the Democratic Roosevelt—went down to Cuba and learned Spanish and flourished in such pursuits as banking and insurance. Havana changed from seedy elegance to the hustle-bustle of a big town turning into a city. The Morro Castle became a tourist attraction and symbol of a political system gone forever. The Cubans nonetheless chafed at their instruction in democracy and the American proscription of the practice of revolution. The United States government intervened frequently, taking over the Cuban government in 1906–1909, until in the late 1920s the temper of nationalism became too high. Then the *norteamericanos* backed away from such policies, turning to the civilities of the good neighbor, whatever that phrase meant in future years when the Cubans found themselves under regimes so difficult that they may have wished for the reappearance of American marines.

Perhaps the trouble was that Americans felt themselves superior to Cubans, and despite the many well-intentioned efforts at reform they failed to win support of the people of Cuba. One does not have to look far to find corroboration of this theory. American diplomats, spending a few years in Cuba prior to passing on to some more prestigious assignment, looked upon the Cubans as children capable of a behavior not in vogue on the mainland north of the Rio Grande. It may be that America's attempted serious reforms in Cuba could not stick because the purpose behind them was not right.

2. *"I Took the Canal Zone"*

In setting out the interventions of the United States government in Latin America, interventions which for the most part made sense at the time, even if they do not seem noble to a later generation, it is embarrassing to relate one major mistake in the actions of Washington officials, the intervention in Panama in 1903 to obtain the Panama Canal zone. Here was a highly undiplomatic and totally unnecessary act which has been an embarrassment ever since and will require many years before Latin Americans will forget it. President Theodore Roosevelt had tired of the slowness of the Colombian senate in consenting to a canal zone for the United States in the Colombian province of Panama. He protected a revolution which broke out in Panama in 1903 by recognizing within three days the new Panamanian regime, with which he soon signed a treaty giving rights to the United States for constructing a canal. This was a totally unnecessary affair, because Roosevelt could either have paid the price desired by the Colombians or could have obtained a canal site across Central America through Nicaragua. TR was in too much of a hurry to build a canal. He was too much moved by the obvious need of the United States after 1898 for a canal, which was rooted in the increasing demand for cheap ocean transportation between the United States's east and west coasts, the hurried voyage of the *Oregon* around Cape Horn in 1898 to join the fleet off Santiago de Cuba, the existence after the Spanish-American War of the new Pacific possessions of the United States. One might charitably say that Roosevelt moved before he thought things out, although more probably he never thought things out but simply moved. The intervention in Panama thereupon became the greatest blunder made by the American government among its Latin neighbors from the beginning of relations down to the present day.

The setting of the stage for the Panama drama began with some moves of American diplomacy prior to the coup of November 1903. Initially the United States had to arrange with Great Britain to revise the terms of the Clayton-Bulwer Treaty of 1850, which had debarred either nation from exclusive rights in any canal built across the isthmus of Panama and required neutralization of such a canal under international auspices. An arrangement was duly secured in the so-called second Hay-Pauncefote Treaty, concluded on November 18,

1901, by Secretary of State John Hay and the British ambassador in Washington, Sir Julian Pauncefote. The first Hay-Pauncefote Treaty, signed on February 5, 1900, had come to grief because it did not provide for American fortification of the proposed canal; the second treaty, by providing for the abrogation of the Clayton-Bulwer Treaty, and by making the United States the sole guarantor of the neutrality of the canal, implicitly allowed its fortification by the American government.

There then was the question of routes: Nicaragua or Panama. Much sentiment favored cutting the canal through Nicaragua instead of Panama, but in 1902 the Panama route became practically certain. For one thing, important individuals in Washington, including President Roosevelt, became convinced that the Panama route was easier and better. For another, the Panama route was financially the more attractive. The New Panama Canal Company, a French company which owned the rights to the route, reduced its price for selling out to the United States to a competitive figure. This company was the successor of the concern which, under direction of the builder of the Suez Canal, Ferdinand de Lesseps, had gone bankrupt in 1888 after squandering $400,000,000 on a Panama canal, which the old company had left only about two-fifths finished. The New Panama Canal Company had been asking $109,141,500 for its rights (the United States then having to pay for the remaining construction), until an American commission estimated that the construction cost of the Nicaragua route was $189,864,062, only $45,630,704 more than the remaining construction cost of the Panama route. The New Company was pricing its route out of the competition.

Thereupon the New Company came down to $40,000,000 for its rights, which gave the Panama route an anticipated total cost (rights plus remaining construction) cheaper by $5,630,704 than the cost of the route through Nicaragua. After this financial de-escalation, Congress passed the Spooner Act, which became law on June 28, 1902, stipulating that the canal should be constructed in Panama and the New Company receive its $40,000,000, provided an agreement could be made with Colombia. But if such an agreement could not be made, the United States, the act stated, should come to an arrangement with Nicaragua and construct the canal there. Secretary of State Hay on January 22, 1903, concluded a treaty with the Colombian chargé in Washington, Dr. Tomás Herrán, providing for $10,000,000 to Colombia and $250,000 annually as rental, the rental to begin in nine years. The United States was to receive a 99-year lease of the canal zone, subject to renewal.

At this point the Colombian senate refused to ratify the treaty, because of the indefinite nature of the lease and a stipulation for mixed American-Colombian courts in the canal zone. The senators also knew that President Sanclementi's government in 1900 had used a legislative decree to extend the franchise of the New Panama Canal Company, due to run out in 1904, by six more years. After passage in the United States of the Spooner Act, authorizing $40,000,000 to the New Company, it seemed a false economy to have extended the franchise. The idea occurred to the Colombian senate that if a court of Colombian law were to find the extension by legislative decree unconstitutional, it would be possible to take all the money by waiting an extra year to 1904. In Washington, Secretary Hay was incensed. He described the Colombian senators as "greedy little anthropoids."

President Roosevelt was deeply angered at what he considered highway robbery. "Make it as strong as you can to Beaupré [A. M. Beaupré, the American minister to Colombia]," TR wrote Secretary Hay. "Those contemptible little creatures in Bogotá ought to understand how much they are jeopardizing things and imperiling their own future." On August 17, 1903, he said that "we may have to give a lesson to those jack rabbits." On September 15 he referred to the Colombians as "foolish and homicidal corruptionists." On October 5 he said it might be well "to warn these cat-rabbits that great though our patience has been, it can be exhausted." The president was ready to welcome any turn of events in Panama that would take matters out of the hands of the Colombians. Because the New Panama Canal Company was as interested as the president in this matter, albeit for different reasons (the $40,000,000), it is understandable how word of the president's humor reached the ears of officers of the canal company, and the latter gentlemen wasted no time in seizing their opportunity. They were seconded in their enthusiasm, quite understandably, by the inhabitants of Panama, who feared that the delay of the Colombian senate might lead the United States to choose the alternate waterway in Nicaragua and destroy the prospect, which otherwise would be excellent, for a boom in the Panamanian economy.

The company's initiative was prosecuted by two important agents. One was a French soldier of fortune who had formerly been de Lesseps' chief engineer, Philippe Bunau-Varilla. The other was the lawyer for the New Panama Canal Company, William Nelson Cromwell of the New York firm of Sullivan and Cromwell. Working together, they managed to engineer a revolution in Panama and ease the way in Washington, if such easing were needed, for American recognition of the revolutionaries. Bunau-Varilla had come from France in 1901 to launch his campaign for the Panama route. As he later described his activities, which met with such great success, "fortune smiled" upon him for the next years, and "At every turn of my steps it seemed as if I were accompanied by a protecting divinity. Every time I was in need of a man he appeared, of an event it took place." At the crucial point in the whole affair, he operated from Room 1162 in the old Waldorf-Astoria in New York, which, he later wrote, "deserves to be considered as the cradle of the Panama Republic." There he put together the constitution of the state and readied a declaration of independence; his wife stitched the new national flag. The flag looked very much like that of the United States, but with yellow instead of white for the background and two suns instead of stars. Preparatory to events, he readied for himself a commission as Panama's first minister to the United States. Meanwhile the lawyer Cromwell was busy in Washington instructing members of the Senate about the plight of the suffering Panamanians.

When the revolution came off in Panama on November 3, 1903, it was hardly unexpected, and everything occurred with complete success, thanks in part to the arrival the day before of the U.S.S. *Nashville* at Colón on the Caribbean side of the isthmus. The presence of the American vessel lent substance to the hope of the revolutionists on the Pacific side, in Panama City, for American support. The *Nashville* did not prevent the Colombians from landing 474 troops at Colón to suppress the uprising. Happily, railroad officials on the spot (the railroad was owned by the New Panama Canal Company) failed to make any transportation available so that the troops could cross the isthmus to Panama City. The captain of the *Nashville* then negotiated with the commander of the Colombian troops and persuaded him to re-embark his men and leave the port. The revolution duly broke out in Panama City at about six o'clock on the evening of November 3, and it was over almost as soon as it began. Except for a brief shelling by a Colombian gunboat, which killed a man who was in bed and mortally wounded a donkey in the slaughterhouse, there was no violence. Bunau-Varilla's henchman Dr. Manuel Amador Guerrero, the new president of the republic, paid off the soldiers who supported the revolution at a rate allegedly of $35,000 and $30,000 for two generals, from $6,000 to $10,000 each for the lesser officers, and $50 apiece for the men. Amador made a speech and complimented his countrymen: "The world is astounded at our heroism! Yesterday we were but the slaves of Colombia; today we are free. . . . President Roosevelt has made good. . . . Free sons of Panama, I salute you! Long live the Republic of Panama! Long live President Roosevelt! Long live the American Government!"

The United States recognized the new regime on November 6, an interval between revolution and recognition which was then considered appallingly short. Fifteen days after the revolution, on November 18, 1903, Secretary Hay and Minister Bunau-Varilla made a treaty granting to the United States in perpetuity the use and control of a canal zone ten miles wide across the isthmus of Panama. The treaty gave the United States "all the rights, power and authority within the zone . . . which the United States would possess and exercise if it were the sovereign of the territory." The American government agreed to pay $10,000,000 and an annual fee of $250,000, the same arrangement offered in the Hay-Herrán Treaty with Colombia, beginning nine years after exchange of ratifications which occurred in 1904. "The United States," according to the first article of this treaty, "guarantees and will maintain the independence of the Republic of Panama." This article made Panama a protectorate, which ended only with a treaty between Panama and the United States signed March 2, 1936, ratified in 1939.

A question never answered about the Panama affair is "Who received the $40,000,000?" According to his own statement, Bunau-Varilla held $115,000 worth of stock in the New Panama Canal Company. Cromwell presumably had holdings, or at the least was working for someone for his legal fee, which turned out to be $832,449. To this day it has not been revealed how the $40,000,000 was distributed. The United States government paid the money to J. P. Morgan and Company, which disbursed it.

American policy, as stated at the outset of this discussion, blundered in the business at Panama in 1903, producing an obvious farce of a revolution, a black mark on the record of the United States in Latin America. The United States easily could have constructed a canal through Nicaragua, where the canal would have been much closer to the United States and saved time and trouble on coast-to-coast shipping. Of if President Roosevelt had been firm with the senators of Colombia, threatening to take his canal business to Nicaragua, they perhaps would have accepted his offer of $10,000,000. If Roosevelt had to have the Panama route, it would have been better if he had paid whatever price was desired in Colombia.

Building the Panama Canal. This photo shows progress being made at Bas Obispo, August 1907.

TR received a large volume of public criticism over the Panama affair, and his sensitivity to it led to a semihumorous situation one day during a cabinet meeting. The president had turned to his attorney general, Philander C. Knox, and said: "I think, Mr. Attorney-General, that it will be just as well for you to give us a formal legal opinion sustaining my action in this whole matter." The attorney general looked quizzically at the president and said, with a smile: "No, Mr. President, if I were you I would not have any taint of legality about it."

After leaving office Roosevelt compounded the Panamanian imbroglio in a speech in 1911 at the University of California by asserting:

> I am interested in the Panama Canal because I started it. If I had followed traditional conservative methods, I should have submitted a dignified State paper of probably ten hundred pages to the Congress and debate would have been going on yet. But I took the Canal Zone, and let Congress debate, and while the debate goes on the canal does also.

This was all Colombia needed. Bogotá turned in a bill for indemnity. In 1914, the year the canal opened, the Democratic Wilson administration came close to paying it—so close that Roosevelt had to enlist his friend Henry Cabot Lodge to block the appropriation in the Senate. After TR's death, and apparently inspired by prospects of oil concessions in Colombia, the United States in 1921 paid $25,000,000 in what might be described as hush money.

Nor was paying off the Colombians the end of the Panama trouble—the United States later had to pay off the Panamanians. At the outset the relations between the government of the United States and the sovereign new nation of Panama were uncomplicated and, one might say, direct. When the first American minister to Panama wished to tell President Amador what to do he summoned the president to the legation. Over the years this arrangement changed. The basic agreement of 1903 over the canal had to be changed, too. Renegotiation of the treaty in 1936 raised the annual rental from $250,000 to $430,000. The rent went up to $1,930,000 in 1955. The Panamanians that year had asked for $5,000,000. Forgotten were the huzzas for President Roosevelt. Panamanian students commemorated the anniversary of the signing of the Hay–Bunau-Varilla Treaty as a day of mourning, and not least of the ceremonies was the burning in effigy of the French author, whose memory was not cherished in the land of which he had been so fond. Serious trouble occurred in 1964 when American high school students at the Balboa High School within the canal zone raised an American flag, in defiance of an agreement that within the zone both the United States and Panamanian flags should appear side by side. In the ensuing riots twenty-one Panamanians and four American soldiers were killed and some 350 persons injured. Once tempers cooled, the result was another move by the Panamians to renegotiate the canal treaty.

Negotiations for a new canal treaty actually began in 1965, the year after the riots, but it took a dozen years for tempers to cool and wisdom to prevail in a new arrangement, signed in 1977 and ratified six months later. The canal meanwhile often became a point of high contention. The head of the Panamanian government in 1973, General Omar Torrijos, persuaded the United Nations Security Council to meet in Panama City, and then maneuvered the United States into vetoing a resolution calling for fulfillment of Panama's "just demands." Secretary of State Henry Kissinger and the Panamanian foreign minister agreed to a set of principles in 1974, but could get no further. In the American presidential primaries of 1976 Ronald Reagan, a contender for the Republican nomination (which eventually went to the then president, Gerald R. Ford), made the canal a central issue: "We bought it, we paid for it, it's ours and we're going to keep it!" President James E. Carter, the victor in the 1976 election, finally managed a solution.

The State Department cannily arranged two treaties. The first gave Panama $10,000,000 a year plus a sum up to a similar amount from any surplus operating revenues, and provided joint U.S.-Panamanian control over the canal until noon, Panama time, December 31, 1999, when the canal would pass to Panama. The second, called the Neutrality Treaty, defined American rights to defend the canal after that remote year. Both treaties caused a great deal of trouble in Panama and the United States. In Panama it was essential to give the impression that the treaties absolutely forbade any future American intervention. Everything was nearly lost by Carter's national security adviser, Zbigniew Brzezinski, when at a meeting with senators he was asked how the United States proposed to ensure that after 1999 the canal would remain open under all circumstances, and what would happen if Panama should simply declare the canal "closed for repairs." His answer was that, "according to the provisions of the Neutrality Treaty, we will move in and close down the Panamanian government for repairs." It was a closed meeting, and the comment fortunately did not become public. In the United States the situation was equally delicate. All the opinion polls registered that the American public was against the treaties. Carter and officials of his administration nonetheless believed an arrangement was necessary and spent six months attempting to convince the Senate, which was where the important votes were. The treaties passed in March and April 1978, by identical margins of 68–32. A shift of two votes would have meant defeat.

3. *The Corollary*

The third interference of the United States in the Caribbean–Central American area was in the Dominican Republic in 1905, and it gave rise to the famous Roosevelt Corollary to the Monroe Doctrine. But before setting out the manner in which President Roosevelt chose to solve the woes of the Dominican government, one must relate the so-called Venezuelan affair of the winter of 1902–1903; for this attempted European intervention in the New World led through a tortuous process to Roosevelt's corollary.

It may be that good behavior by a great country toward a small one breeds contempt, that the altruism which moved President Grover Cleveland and Secretary of State Richard Olney to protect Venezuela in 1895 was in the longer view of things a mistake; the government of Venezuela, so suddenly protected, may have come to believe that it could play fast and loose with European nations and then hide behind the Monroe Doctrine. At the turn of the twentieth century, the dictator of Venezuela was a rascal named Cipriano Castro, who without much effort had managed to create for his country a large bonded debt. In the name of his country he also refused to pay. The problem of the foreign bondholders was to get their money, and in sheer desperation the British and German and Italian governments sent gunboats to Venezuela in December 1902, sank three of Castro's gunboats, blockaded five ports and the mouths of the Orinoco River, and threatened to put troops ashore.

What would the United States do for its erstwhile ward, the government of Venezuela, now so cruelly attacked? Theodore Roosevelt a year or so before, while still vice president, had remarked in a letter to his German friend and tennis companion, Baron Speck von Sternburg, that if one of the little Latin American nations misbehaved the best procedure would be to spank it. Obviously, no notion of a Roosevelt Corollary had crossed his mind. When the bond crisis occurred in Venezuela, Roosevelt, now president, seems to have changed his mind. Years later, during the First World War, Roosevelt testified that he indeed had sent Admiral Dewey and the United States fleet into the vicinity of Puerto Rico and had been willing to use force to throw the Germans out of Venezuela in case they went into it. As TR recalled in 1916:

> I speedily became convinced that Germany was the . . . really formidable party, in the transaction. . . . I became convinced that England would not back Germany in the event of a clash over the matter between Germany and the United States, but would remain neutral. . . . I also became convinced that Germany intended to seize some Venezuelan harbor and turn it into a strongly fortified place of arms, on the model of Kiaochow, with a view to exercising some measure of control over the future Isthmian Canal, and over

South American affairs generally. . . . Germany declined to agree to arbitrate . . . and declined to say that she would not take possession of Venezuelan territory, merely saying that such possession would be "temporary"—which might mean anything. I finally decided that no useful purpose would be served by further delay, and I took action accordingly. I assembled our battle fleet, under Admiral Dewey, near Porto Rico, for "maneuvres," with instructions that the fleet should be kept in hand and in fighting trim, and should be ready to sail at an hour's notice. . . .

I saw the [German] Ambassador, and explained that in view of the presence of the German squadron on the Venezuelan coast I could not permit longer delay in answering my request for an arbitration, and that I could not acquiesce in any seizure of Venezuelan territory. The Ambassador responded that his Government could not agree to arbitrate, and that there was no intention to take "permanent" possession of Venezuelan territory. I answered that Kiaochow was not a "permanent" possession of Germany's—that . . . I did not intend to have another Kiaochow, held by similar tenure, on the approach to the Isthmian Canal. The Ambassador repeated that his Government would not agree to arbitrate. I then asked him to inform his Government that if no notification for arbitration came during the next ten days I would be obliged to order Dewey to take his fleet to the Venezuelan coast and see that the German forces did not take possession of any territory. He expressed very grave concern and asked me if I realized the serious consequences that would follow such action; consequences so serious to both countries that he dreaded to give them a name. I answered that I had thoroughly counted the cost before I decided on the step, and asked him to look at the map, as a glance would show him that there was no spot in the world where Germany in the event of conflict with the United States would be at a greater disadvantage than in the Caribbean sea.

A week later the Ambassador came to see me, talked pleasantly on several subjects, and rose to go. I asked him if he had any answer to make from his Government to my request, and when he said no, I informed him that in such event it was useless to wait as long as I had intended, and that Dewey would be ordered to sail twenty-four hours in advance of the time I had set. He expressed deep apprehension, and said that his Government would not arbitrate. However, less than twenty-four hours before the time I had appointed for calling the order to Dewey, the Ambassador notified me that His Imperial Majesty the German Emperor had directed him to request me to undertake arbitration myself.

How correct was this account? Recalling his anger against the Germans, Roosevelt may have been thinking more about his current—1915–1916—feelings about the Germans. Controversy at once arose over his version of the affair, and some well-known scholars such as Dexter Perkins, the historian of the Monroe Doctrine, have believed that Roosevelt made up the crisis out of whole cloth. A more recent writer, the late Howard K. Beale, in a volume entitled *Theodore Roosevelt and the Rise of America to World Power* (1956) devoted forty exhaustive pages to the problem, with explanatory notes, and concluded that Roosevelt's memory in 1915–1916 was essentially correct: that there had been a crisis thirteen years earlier with Germany over Venezuela, and that the president had forced the Germans into line. Beale concluded, "it seems certain that the substance of the story was not an invention of war years and that only the color and tones were heightened in the account recorded in 1916."

Whatever the proportions of the crisis in showing what an American president did, or an ex-president thought he had done, to preserve his country's hegemony in the Caribbean, the Venezuelan affair has interest for the historian because it led into an important diplomacy with the Dominican Republic and resulted in the Roosevelt Corollary to the Monroe Doctrine. After the European intervention in Venezuela, and Roosevelt's intervention of whatever sort, the president had arranged with Castro and the intervening governments to send the bond dispute to arbitration. The disputants appealed to a three-man tribunal chosen by the tsar of Russia from the panel established by the First Hague Peace Conference of 1899 (the latter conference had met in the Dutch capital to consider ways to world peace and included twenty-six nations, among them the United States; for the conference, see Chapter 5). The tribunal decided on February 22, 1904, that Venezuela should pay its debtors and that—this was the rub of the judgment—payment should be first to the nations which had engaged in the naval demonstration. The tribunal's decision put a premium on force in the collection of debts. Several of the Latin American governments, especially in Central America and the Caribbean, were now wide open, so to speak, to foreign naval demonstrations and perhaps even foreign occupations. No American president at the turn of the twentieth century, observing the fiscal chaos south of the United States, could have ignored the danger. TR thereupon produced a policy, applied first to the Dominican Republic, which became known perhaps inappropriately as the Roosevelt Corollary to the Monroe Doctrine.

The corollary was no sudden announcement. Roosevelt allowed an official of the State Department to remark in February 1904, at the time of the Hague decision, that the ruling put a premium on violence. In May 1904 he arranged for Secretary of War Root to read to a public assemblage a presidential letter in which Roosevelt made a statement almost identical to his later message to Congress in December 1904, the message which became known as the Roosevelt Corollary. He was not willing to make his letter to Root a formal pronouncement, to the extent of communicating it to Congress, until he won the presidential election in November. Then came the formal statement of December 6:

> Chronic wrongdoing, or an impotence which results in a general loosening of the ties of civilized society, may in America, as elsewhere, ultimately require intervention by some civilized nation, and in the Western Hemisphere the adherence of the United States to the Monroe Doctrine may force the United

States, however reluctantly, in flagrant cases of such wrongdoing or impotence, to the exercise of an international police power.

The President explained himself further in a message to the Senate on February 15, 1905:

The United States . . . under the Monroe doctrine . . . can not see any European power seize and permanently occupy the territory of one of these republics; and yet such seizure of territory, disguised or undisguised, may eventually offer the only way in which the power in question can collect any debts, unless there is interference on the part of the United States.

As for the little country to which he then applied the corollary, the Dominican Republic, that nation was in a saddening state. At the end of the 1860s President Grant had wished to annex the country, and President Baez had been willing. Fortunately for the United States, Senator Sumner's opposition had made annexation impossible, and revolution overtook President Baez. But that was not the end of things, for Baez was a patriot if compared to one of his successors, President Ulises Heureaux (who remarked on one occasion that he did not care what history might say about his presidency, because he would not be there to read it). Heureaux's presidency was a national disaster, and his assassination in 1899 left the country in dire straits. The Dominican Republic went from bad to worse—"to hell in a hack," to use a contemporary expression—until President Roosevelt announced the corollary in 1904.

The president of the United States intervened to prevent intervention by foreign governments seeking to protect their bondholders. Roosevelt wished to ensure the rights of all bondholders. But there were interesting sides to the question. The Dominicans had gotten deeply into debt with the citizens of quite a few nations: France, Belgium, Italy, Great Britain, Germany, the United States, the Netherlands, Mexico, Spain, Sweden, and Norway. It was hard to say how much information the purchasers of Dominican bonds possessed when they acquired their paper pledges. Presumably some individuals knew very well what they were getting, or might get, and were out to profit by whatever international crisis might arise. Other investors were what Americans would have described as suckers. French peasants apparently bought the bonds in belief that they were buying securities of the Dominican religious order. Whatever the deception, the holders of the New World's Dominican bonds soon were willing to have their governments intervene. After February 1904, the European bondholders were especially anxious for forcible intervention, since such a course in Venezuela had produced preferential treatment through the ruling of the Hague tribunal. The French, Belgian, and Italian bondholders managed to arrange for payments

Theodore Roosevelt, "The World's Constable," protecting the Latin American nations from Europe.

on their bonds beginning November 1, 1904. Not to be outmaneuvered, an organization representing American and British capital, known piquantly as the San Domingo Improvement Company, in an ungentlemanly maneuver got hold of the Dominican customs house at Puerto Plata. It was, then, an impossible situation.

Presidential action from Washington was accompanied by some confusion, but eventually everything worked out. Roosevelt took over all the Dominican customs houses. He sought first to do this by executive agreement, perhaps feeling that if he tried a treaty the delay for debate in the Senate would create only more confusion in a situation already filled with it. He may also have believed that his election in 1904 allowed him a certain freedom in foreign affairs. When the text of the proposed executive agreement reached Washington, there was an obvious resentment in the Senate, and Roosevelt changed the form of agreement to a treaty. When sentiment in the Senate then turned clearly against the treaty, he reluctantly arranged that the treaty not come up for a vote. The president managed a financial *modus vivendi* in the Dominican Republic for two years, 1905–1907, a retired American colonel acting as collector of customs, at the end of which time the Senate consented to the treaty.

The results in the Dominican Republic meanwhile were heartening to everyone but revolutionists. Roosevelt in September 1905 penned what Dexter Perkins has described as "an engaging note" to the secretary of the navy:

As for the Santo Domingo matter, tell Admiral Bradford to stop any revolution. I intend to keep the island in the *statu quo* until the Senate has had time to act on the treaty, and I shall treat any revolutionary movement as an effort to upset the *modus vivendi*. That this is ethically right, I am dead sure, even though there may be some technical or red tape difficulty.

Under the *modus vivendi* and subsequent treaty the Dominican Republic received more money from customs, after service on the debt, than had come in altogether under Dominican collection prior to 1905.

Money, the student of history might conclude, was the root of more evil in the Dominican Republic than met Roosevelt's eye. He disposed of one evil, financial insolvency, only to create a situation far worse than a few slow-paying bonds. The financial intervention of 1905 led to an American military occupation in 1916 under auspices of the navy, which continued until 1924, with a provisional republic established two years before the navy departed. A member of the marine-trained Dominican constabulary, Rafael Leonidas Trujillo y Molina, thereupon took charge of the republic, and turned it into a dictatorship. Trujillo was assassinated in 1961, and since then the Dominican Republic has led an uneasy political existence, which included a short-lived American intervention in 1965.

4. *Nicaragua*

President Theodore Roosevelt must have hoped that his contribution to the Monroe Doctrine would settle things in Latin America. It did settle them, for a few years, but even in the Dominican Republic the arrangement eventually came apart. Roosevelt's successor President William Howard Taft had to confront trouble in Nicaragua where the dictator-president, General José Santos Zelaya, tried to cancel the United States–Nicaragua Concession, a mining property owned by a Pittsburgh corporation, the principal American property in Nicaragua, so that he could sell it again for better terms. Reportedly Zelaya planned secret advances to Japan for a canal treaty. The dictator was also trying to pull apart a treaty settlement which Presidents Porfirio Díaz of Mexico and Roosevelt of the United States had persuaded the republics of Central America to conclude among themselves. According to this 1907 agreement they promised to submit all their disputes to arbitration and, generally, not go to war with each other or foment revolutions in each other's territories. Understandably, the United States had little love for the Nicaraguan dictator. When a revolution against him broke out in 1909, Zelaya executed two American citizens, professional dynamiters, for laying mines in the San Juan River in support of the revolutionists (the

Americans held commissions in the revolutionary army and considered themselves prisoners of war). President Taft broke diplomatic relations, and the dictator was overthrown.

Nicaragua thereupon became a ward of the United States. The individual who had been secretary of the American concession in Nicaragua, Adolfo Díaz, rose to power, and his administration on June 6, 1911, signed a treaty, the Knox-Castrillo Convention, with Secretary of State Knox, TR's erstwhile attorney general. The treaty was identical with another treaty signed by the United States in 1911 with Honduras. Knox would have liked to deal the same way with Guatemala. The Senate rejected the Nicaraguan and Honduran treaties, but in Nicaragua the New York bankers whom Secretary Knox had enlisted to set aright the finances of that country went ahead anyway and with the help of the State Department set up a financial regulation which lasted until 1914. A substitute then was arranged for the Knox-Castrillo Convention which had failed in the Senate. This Bryan-Chamorro Treaty, signed by Secretary of State William Jennings Bryan and the Nicaraguan minister in Washington, Emiliano Chamorro, in 1914 (ratified in 1916), provided that the United States should have perpetual and exclusive right to construct a canal through Nicaragua, together with a 99-year lease on Great and Little Corn Islands in the Caribbean and a 99-year right to establish a naval base on the Gulf of Fonseca, both the lease and right subject to renewal for another 99-year period. Which is to say that the lease and right if renewed could run to the year 2114. In return the United States gave Nicaragua $3,000,000.

An instance of imperialism? Students of American diplomacy should notice the name of the American negotiator, Secretary Bryan, an anti-imperialist. All of which brings to mind the story about Bryan's theory, at one time put forth, that no man in the United States ought to possess a sum of more than $100,000. The story has it that Bryan in later years made a killing in Florida real estate, and became a millionaire, and that when asked about his theory of the $100,000 limit he replied with a twinkle in his eye that times had changed.

In Nicaragua during the Taft era the government of President Díaz sorely needed support, and Taft in 1912 brought in at Díaz's request a "legation guard" of marines, and except for a brief trial withdrawal in 1925, which did not work, the marines stayed until 1933.

In the latter 1920s, beginning in 1925, a Nicaraguan revolution threatened serious trouble for the United States, and critics of American policy in Latin America still frequently cite the actions of the American government at that time as a horrible example of imperialism. In point of fact the politics of Nicaragua in 1925–1928 were rather confusing, even to Nicaraguans, and the behavior of the Colossus of the North proved remarkably impartial if slightly imperial.

The trouble came in 1925 when President Coolidge determined to pull out the marines. A Nicaraguan election had brought to power President Carlos Solórzano, who was a coalition candidate—a promising innovation in Nicaraguan politics, meaning that Solórzano represented both the Liberals and the Conservatives, the country's two traditional factions. The new president pleaded with Coolidge to keep the marines in Nicaragua long enough for his regime to train a constabulary to replace them, and Coolidge went along with this proposition, agreeing to withdraw the marines—by this time there were only about a hundred of them—on August 1, 1925. The American president kept his word. Three weeks after the marines left, the revolution broke out: the Second Nicaraguan Revolution, one might describe it in terms of American involvement, the First having occurred during the expulsion of Zelaya and installation of Zelaya's successor Díaz.

The trouble with the Second Revolution, to be brief, was that Solórzano apparently received $30,000 from the strong man of Nicaraguan politics, General Chamorro (of the Bryan-Chamorro Treaty). Chamorro then sent Solórzano to California and expelled Vice President Juan Sacasa, who went to Washington. Chamorro took over the country through a series of fast constitutional shuffles. In the course of these shuffles he violated the spirit of a Central American treaty of 1923, concluded in Washington, which forbade dubious successions to presidencies. Chamorro soon was president, by hook and crook. He was fortunate enough to take office at a time when the Nicaraguan treasury was full—hence the ease with which he could dispense $30,000 to Solórzano.

The grand question became what the United States would do. Apart from the embarrassment of Chamorro's violation of the United States-sponsored treaty of 1923, the question was the more embarrassing because Chamorro was saying publicly that the American government could not do a thing to get him out of office. The American minister in Managua received the intelligence that Chamorro in conversation had said, "To Hell with the United States, with the State Department, and with its diplomatic representative here!"

The American government began to put pressure on General Chamorro, and the result was a long involvement which went far beyond what anyone in Washington had intended when Chamorro first took possession of his tiny little country of approximately 700,000 people, 72 percent of whom were illiterate, and with whom the United States's nationals had invested only a few millions of dollars, nothing at all compared with investments in Cuba and Mexico, less than in any other Latin American country except Paraguay. The American minister went home on leave in 1926 and his chargé d'affaires, Lawrence Dennis, a young man with an authoritarian disposition, pressed Chamorro unmercifully to resign, which Chamorro eventually did after emptying the Nicaraguan treasury. The United States's old friend

Díaz became president. Solórzano's vice president, Sacasa, thereupon appeared back on the scene, having come from Washington via Mexico City, where he seems to have received certain promises of support. Sacasa appointed José Moncada as his chief general, and Moncada proved a better chieftain than Díaz's generals. President Coolidge and Secretary of State Frank B. Kellogg began to find themselves in the middle of a tornado of public opinion, with Senator William E. Borah of Idaho, the chairman of the foreign relations committee, trumpeting his criticisms up and down the land. Coolidge in the spring of 1927 appointed Henry L. Stimson to go down to Nicaragua and clean up the situation, bringing peace so that the United States could get its marines out (once Sacasa raised the flag of revolution the marines had returned and, after trying to declare areas of the country off limits to revolutionists, were in danger of getting shot at from both sides). Stimson arranged the Peace of Tipitapa, at a locality of that name, and the resultant marine-supervised elections in 1928 gave the presidency to Moncada, who soon was appreciating United States help almost as fervently as had his predecessor Díaz.

For a while under Moncada's presidency the marines sought to eliminate a dissident of the new regime, General Augusto César Sandino, a Nicaraguan Robin Hood who considered President Coolidge the sheriff of Nottingham. Sandino was accustomed to leave chits with fellow Nicaraguans from whom he had requisitioned supplies, which stated that "The Honorable Calvin Coolidge, President of the United States of North America, will pay the bearer $———," inserting the amount of the levied goods. A force of 5,480 marines and the marine-trained *Guardia Nacional* sought to catch Sandino, without result. Finally the Nicaraguan army betrayed him during a truce in 1934 and shot him.

When the marines left Nicaragua in 1933, the general in charge of the *Guardia*, by the name of Anastasio Somoza, took over the country, and he and his descendants ruled Nicaragua until 1979, when revolutionists who called themselves Sandinistas took over and aligned their country against the United States.

As we see it now, the Nicaraguan intervention from 1911 to 1933 was a mismanaged affair, not because it did too much in Nicaragua but because it did not do enough. The United States interfered barely enough to keep the elected government in power and the finances in order, and not enough to regenerate Nicaragua. The intervention aroused the animosity of some Nicaraguans, of other Latin American governments such as Mexico, and of many well-intentioned American citizens, such as Senator Borah, who thought that what looked like imperialism was imperialism. At this point, having lost support of these bodies of public opinion anyway, the United States government might well have become more thorough in its actions in Nicaragua.

5. *Haiti*

Another intervention in the Caribbean region—following upon the Cuban, Panamanian, and Dominican affairs, and the occupation of Nicaragua—occurred in Haiti in 1915.

The problem of Haiti was in part that of too many revolutions. Haitians by 1915 had endured a long history of revolts. In the late eighteenth century a revolution had broken out against the French, led by Toussaint l'Ouverture. An ever more saddening series of forcible changes of regime followed, until by the early twentieth century Haiti was sunk in political ineptitude. Between 1911 and 1915 the presidency of Haiti was occupied by a bewildering series of statesmen, two of whom met personal misfortune in office: Cincinnatus Leconte (blown up with the presidential palace) and Tancrède Auguste (died presumably by poison).

The Haitian problem was partly the government's defaulting on foreign-held bonds. The French and German governments in March 1914 proposed a joint customs receivership with the United States. President Vilbrun Guillaume Sam, coming to power in March 1915, faced a huge (for Haiti) debt of about $24,000,000, part of which was owed to American financial interests and much of the remainder to Europeans.

There also was a danger that foreign nations might use Haiti as a place for establishing a naval base, perhaps to threaten the Panama Canal. Years later, after the United States had taken care of Haiti, former secretary of state Robert Lansing was to tell darkly of German sailors having landed in secret at Port-au-Prince, only to withdraw suddenly on the eve of the outbreak of war in Europe.

The United States bided its time. In 1908 Albert Shaw, editor of the *Review of Reviews*, inquired of Secretary of State Elihu Root whether, since the American government had established control over Cuba, Panama, and the Dominican Republic, Root could not "invent a way to put Haiti under bonds." Root answered, "for any positive step . . . we must wait for the 'psychological moment.' "

The moment did not occur until President Sam created a crisis and expired therefrom.

Sam's end was nothing if not violent. His predecessor in the presidential chair, Théodore, had a friend named Dr. Rosalvo Bobo, who as soon as Sam became president traveled into the Haitian wilds, there to raise a revolt. Thereupon Sam seized 170 alleged partisans of Bobo, in and around Port-au-Prince. An attack on the palace on the night of July 26, 1915, persuaded President Sam to massacre almost all of his prisoners, 167 of them. Two days later, on July 28, the enraged populace of Port-au-Prince rose up. Sam sought asylum in the French legation. The mob invaded the legation, found the president hiding in a bathroom, and threw him out into the street.

The mob then cut him into small pieces and paraded these trophies around the capital city. At this juncture President Wilson instructed the marines to land, and the U.S.S. *Washington*, flagship of Rear Admiral Caperton, dropped anchor in Port-au-Prince that very afternoon. Before nightfall the marines occupied the town.

The marines governed the republic for several years. The United States government simply took over the country. Marine control was so obvious that former assistant secretary of the navy Franklin D. Roosevelt, running for the vice presidency in 1920, and alluding to the Dominican Republic as well as Haiti, could remark concerning his government experience that "One of my jobs was to look after a couple little republics that our navy is running." Young FDR also took credit in 1920 for writing the Haitian constitution, put into force in 1918; he described it as "a pretty good constitution, too." Secretary of the Interior Franklin K. Lane, knowing that his colleague Secretary of the Navy Josephus Daniels was queasy about the marines' work, was accustomed to rise at cabinet meetings of the Wilson administration and with mock seriousness proclaim to Daniels: "Hail the King of Haiti." The marines arranged for ratification of the 1918 constitution with a considerable artistry, and the vote came out 69,377 Haitians in favor, 355 against. Major General Smedley D. (Old Gimlet Eye) Butler liked to brag about his road-building program which had resulted in many miles of highway in a very short time and at remarkably little cost. He usually did not add that the Haitian government under his supervision had forced the natives into working for nothing, rather like the ancient French custom of the *corvée*. When the Haitians rose in revolt, Butler put them down. No wonder it was with difficulty that the marines found a Haitian willing to be president, in succession to President Sam. President Philippe Sudre Dartiguenave, elected in August 1915, signed a treaty on September 16 under which the Haitian republic became a protectorate of the United States. The treaty contained articles similar to those of the Platt Amendment for Cuba and was not terminated until 1934 when the marines left. Customs control continued in modified form until 1941.

Marine control, as mentioned, was roughly efficient. In 1917, Assistant Secretary Roosevelt paid a ceremonial visit to President Dartiguenave, and a symbolic incident occurred when the president of Haiti started to climb into his official limousine ahead of the United States assistant secretary. General Butler seized President Dartiguenave's coat collar and commenced to pull him back, but Roosevelt stepped aside and insisted that the Haitian should take precedence.

If the constitution along with the marines helped make Haiti a more orderly place for a short time, in subsequent years Haiti's political problems continued. Perhaps the cause of the more recent trouble was that the American government under President Franklin D. Roosevelt concluded the agreement with the Haitian government under which the marines withdrew, and fiscal supervision ended a few years later, allowing full sovereignty. After the American withdrawal the Haitian government deteriorated and set new lows for rapacity and rascality under the regime of President Dr. François (Papa Doc) Duvalier. Duvalier died in 1971 and was succeeded by his nineteen-year-old son, Jean-Claude, known as Baby Doc, who carried on his father's repressive policies. He was ousted in 1986, replaced by an interim government with a three-man ruling council. Haiti's prospects brightened, and if anything became almost too bright, for politics seemed to have no bounds. In advance of October 1986 elections for delegates to a constitutional assembly, dozens of political parties arose. A presidential election scheduled for November 1987 produced one hundred presidential candidates. The United States kept its hands off these latest confusions, leaving everything up to Haiti's three million voters. The exactions of the Duvaliers had left Haiti easily the poorest country in the Western Hemisphere, and quite possibly in the world. But for the moment Haiti enjoyed democracy.

6. *The Mexican Intervention*

The greatest of all the American interventions was the effort of President Woodrow Wilson in 1913–1917 to move Mexican politics in the direction he deemed proper—so the Mexicans would "elect good men" and protect American lives and property. The latter was no idle concern, for American holdings in Mexico, large and small, amounted to approximately one billion dollars.

For the United States the troubles with Mexico began shortly after the collapse of the regime of President Porfirio Díaz, who was ruler of the country from 1876 until 1911. Under General Díaz the nation had settled down and become prosperous, with many of its economic resources being exploited by foreign companies, particularly American. What with all the turmoil elsewhere in Latin America at the turn of the century, Díaz seemed a man whom Americans could trust. His regime appeared so wonderfully solid, its achievements so remarkable. One may therefore excuse Secretary of State Root when upon visiting in Mexico City in 1907 he offered a fulsome tribute to the Mexican president:

> No one lives to-day who I would rather see than President Díaz. If I were a poet I would write sophistry; if I were a musician I would compose triumphal marches; if I were a Mexican I should feel that the steadfast loyalty of a lifetime could not be too much in return for the blessings that he had brought to my country. As I am neither poet, musician, nor Mexican, but only an

American who loves justice and liberty and hopes to see their reign among mankind progress and strengthen and become perpetual, I look to Porfirio Díaz, the President of Mexico, as one of the great men to be held up for the hero worship of mankind.

Unfortunately for Root's enthusiasm, Díaz was growing old, his control over the government slipping, at the very moment when Root was singing these singular praises. An increasing Mexican nationalism, popular unwillingness to tolerate all the favors bestowed upon foreign capitalists, led at last to the president's retirement to Europe, where he died a poor man—he had not governed Mexico for his personal gain but for the good, as he saw it, of his country.

During the few years of his exile in Paris, Díaz liked to relate to admirers that at a crucial moment when rioters were in front of the presidential palace he had suffered from an infernal toothache, which prevented him from exercising a clarity of judgment sufficient to put the rioters down by force.

Whatever the reason for Díaz's departure, it was certainly true that when he left for Europe a grand political confusion settled upon Mexico. At first the government passed into the hands of Francisco I. Madero, who was no match for the animosities and intrigues which swirled down on the City of Mexico. Madero usually has been described as a dreamer. Perhaps also he was crazy. A small man, only five feet four inches in height, Madero had begun his adult life as a gentleman farmer but soon turned his attention to other pursuits, including spiritualism and homeopathic medicine as well as politics. One evening while waiting upon a patient, sitting in a darkened room, he had found himself doodling on a pad of paper, and psychic forces began to move the pencil which inscribed in firm letters, "Love God above all things and thy neighbor as thyself." Madero experimented with spirit writing under more controlled conditions, and the same message recurred, together with other messages. Gradually he got in touch with the great minds of the past who helped him overcome his indifferent literary talents and he began to write excellent essays. He began also to believe that he was a chosen instrument to regenerate Mexico, Latin America, perhaps the world. This was the man who at first took over the presidency from Díaz. At one meeting with the American ambassador, Henry Lane Wilson, the president of Mexico placed a third chair in the circle and announced to the ambassador that a friend was sitting there. The friend was invisible, Madero explained, but there nonetheless.

It was not unexpected that this visionary would run into trouble, and so Madero did, in the person of his principal military commander, General Victoriano Huerta. The latter was a full-blooded Indian whose two hallmarks were an incongruous pair of spectacles and a brandy bottle near at hand. Huerta's drunkenness was soon to

General Victoriano Huerta, 1915.

bring his demise while in exile in the United States, where in 1916 he succumbed to cirrhosis of the liver. But in early February 1913 he evicted Madero from the presidential palace and after a quick constitutional arrangement assumed the presidency.

The general then murdered Madero, together with Vice President Jase Pino Suarez. Huerta had sworn on a scapulary of the Virgin of Guadalupe, likewise on a medal of the Sacred Heart of Jesus, also by the memory of his mother who once had worn these holy images, that he would permit no harm to come to Señor Madero. Having made these commitments, he then visited the American ambassador, H. L. Wilson, and asked what he should do with Madero. Huerta suggested either exiling him or putting him in a lunatic asylum. Wilson replied that Huerta "ought to do that which was best for the peace of the country." This was, to use a later expression, open-ended advice. And so it happened that when an armed guard was transferring the ex-president and ex-vice president to a penitentiary at 2:00 A.M. the two men were shot, on the trivial claim that they were trying to escape. In actual fact this was a favorite Latin American way of execution.

The crisis in Mexico City occurred on February 9–18, 1913, the "tragic ten days" of Mexican history, and it caught the government of the United States in an uneasy position, for the Democrats and Woodrow Wilson were coming into Washington, Taft and the Republicans leaving the government. There was no American policy toward the events in Mexico until Wilson took office on March 4.

The new president had pronounced views on the Mexican situation. "I will not," he said privately, "recognize a government of butchers." He recalled H. L. Wilson and refused to appoint a successor. He laid down a policy on March 11, 1913, in regard to recognition of regimes in Latin America, declaring that recognition was "possible only when supported at every turn by the orderly processes of just government based upon law, not upon arbitrary or irregular force. We hold, as I am sure all thoughtful leaders of republican government everywhere hold, that just government rests always upon the consent of the governed, and that there can be no freedom without order based upon law and upon the public conscience and approval. We shall look to make these principles the basis of mutual intercourse, respect, and helpfulness between our sister republics and ourselves."

This new Wilsonian pronouncement, one should explain, stood in opposition to the recognition policy of the United States since the time when Thomas Jefferson was secretary of state. Jefferson had established the practice that any government in control of its territory and people—a government *de facto*—was a government *de jure* so far as concerned the United States, to be recognized as soon as decently possible. Wilson was undertaking to pass upon the legality of governments in Latin America, and presumably an illegal government would be for him, and his successors in office he doubtlessly hoped, an immoral government which it would be impossible to recognize. The Wilsonian theory for Latin America lasted until Secretary of State Henry L. Stimson revoked it on September 17, 1930, and went back to the practice of Jefferson. An exception to this rule of recognition was the Central American republics, which in the peace settlement of 1907 had sought, among other measures, to invoke a special recognition policy among themselves. These states, ridden by revolts and interventions across their several borders, had written out a code of proper revolutionary behavior, which even went to the length of stipulating what officials in a given government could and could not, by revolution, take office in a new regime. The treaty of 1907 was redrawn in 1923, and the United States, although not a signatory of the treaty of 1923, adhered to its specified recognition policy and followed the dictates of the treaty during revolts in Nicaragua in 1925, in Guatemala in 1930, and in El Salvador in 1931. The Central American States themselves abandoned their agreement in 1934, at which time the United States reverted, for this area of the Western Hemisphere, to its general recognition policy in Latin America as laid down in 1930—which, as mentioned, superseded Wilson's policy of 1913, returning American practice to that of Jefferson's time.

The president in 1913 refused to recognize Huerta the murderer, and he made his policy toward Mexico into a general policy toward all of Latin America, nonrecognition of any government which subverted the liberties of its people. This policy he hoped would freeze out the new dictator in Mexico City. It certainly would have done so in any of the smaller Central American states, but Mexico, as events turned out, was too large a state to handle in this way.

Huerta on October 10, 1913, threw 110 members of the Mexican chamber of deputies into prison and inaugurated a full-fledged military dictatorship. At this point President Wilson was still unwilling to interfere with open force in Mexico, though he was willing to use all diplomatic pressures. In a famous speech at Mobile, Alabama, on October 27, 1913, he declared that the United States "will never again seek one additional foot of territory by conquest." Having set out his position he employed diplomacy for the next months to oust the Mexican general from power. He obtained the support of the British in this venture, promising to Sir William Tyrrell, the representative of the British foreign secretary Sir Edward Grey, "I am going to teach the South American republics to elect good men" and that the United States would work to establish a government in Mexico under which foreign contracts and concessions would be safe. The British had been friendly to Huerta because they thought he would protect foreign investment, rather than undertake a series of social reforms as Madero had been threatening to do. But the British, when Wilson duly approached them, agreed not to give additional support.

Then came the Tampico incident, on April 9, 1914, when a boatload of American sailors landed at that port from an American ship and by error entered a restricted area without permission from the local authorities. The sailors were arrested, and afterward the local commander, a Huertista, upon learning of the incident, released the Americans and sent off an apology to Rear Admiral Henry T. Mayo, commanding the American squadron in the vicinity. The affair might have ended there, but, perhaps in memory of the *Baltimore* incident of over twenty years before, the admiral demanded a 21-gun salute to the American flag. President Wilson, upon learning of the affair, and willing to make trouble for Huerta, backed him up.

Wilson on April 18, 1914, issued an ultimatum to Huerta to salute the American flag or take the consequences. Then, when the American government learned that a German steamer was scheduled to arrive at Veracruz with a load of ammunition for Huerta, Rear Admiral Frank F. Fletcher was ordered to occupy that port forcibly. Marines and sailors went ashore on April 21 and soon occupied the town, at a cost of 19 American dead and 47 wounded, the Mexicans losing at least two hundred killed and another three hundred wounded. A difficult situation had arisen, because Wilson had not prepared the American public for this eventuality, and indeed the entire decline of American-Mexican relations had not been understood by the American people. To make matters worse, the followers of Huerta's enemy and rival in Mexico, the revolutionary commander Venustiano (Don Venus) Carranza, who was in the field against Huerta, condemned the occupation of Veracruz as wholeheartedly as did the Huertistas who controlled the town. The Americans left on November 23, 1914. The adjournment of the incident was obscured by the fall from power of Huerta and the occupation of Mexico City by Carranza in August, and by the beginning of the First World War in Europe that same month.

Huerta had caused plenty of trouble, and Wilson was glad to be rid of him. Publicly he had condemned the wily Mexican and now had forced the general's retirement from the president's palace in Mexico City. Privately Wilson had a "sneaking admiration" for his opponent and confessed to finding Huerta "a diverting brute . . . so false, so sly, so full of bravado, yet so courageous . . . seldom sober and always impossible yet what an indomitable fighter for his country." Huerta on his part never seems to have viewed President Wilson as anything more than the Puritan of the North.

The new government in Mexico City, headed by Carranza, soon showed a singular incompetence, in fair part because of the personality of its president. Don Venus was a dull, uninspiring man, of slender intellectual ability, every bit as rigid as the Puritan of the North. His countenance, peering from behind an impressive gray beard, commanded neither the love nor hate of fellow Mexicans. He was a conservative, middle-class liberal, hardly fitted to cope with the almost exploding revolutionary sentiment within his country which rapidly was moving from political to economic and social goals. Nor could Carranza understand the purposes of the United States, any more than those of his countrymen. The United States had helped his regime into power by weakening the government of Huerta. But he easily convinced himself that the United States, which had not officially recognized his government, was trying to do him in, evidently believing the quip of one of his predecessors, Díaz, who once had lamented about "Poor Mexico, so far from God and so near the United States."

What was President Wilson to do? The president of the United States, who had tried so hard to teach Mexico to elect good men, had received Carranza for his trouble. And unfortunately, a split now occurred in the forces of President Carranza—the succession, one recalls, had been Díaz, Madero, Huerta, Carranza—and there appeared the formidable figure of Doroteo Arango, or Pancho Villa, a wild and woolly character who could submit to control by no one, least of all a staid individual like Carranza, whose government he set out to pull down. In the year 1915 fighting between the troops of Carranza and Villa swayed back and forth inconclusively, while the United States was busy worrying about conditions on the high seas because of the European war. The *Lusitania* was torpedoed in May 1915, and the crisis with Germany over its sinking lasted through much of the summer. But in 1916 American attention came back to Mexico, and

Pancho Villa and his generals. Left to right: Fierro, Villa, Ortega, Medina.

for a while the major problem of American foreign policy appeared not to be the fighting in Europe but the troubles south of the border.

Villa, to arouse an American intervention in Mexico and (so he hoped) discredit Carranza, met a Mexican Northwestern train at Santa Ysabel on January 11, 1916, carrying 17 young American college graduates who had just come into Mexico from California under a safe conduct from Carranza to open a mine. Villa killed 16 of them on the spot. When this gesture failed to bring results, he made a desperate raid into American territory at Columbus, New Mexico, on March 9, 1916, burning the town and killing 17 Americans. The United States government rose in wrath and President Wilson sent Brigadier General John J. Pershing across the border six days later, with 6,600 troops. The expedition penetrated more than 300 miles into Mexico in search of the errant Villa. On June 18, 1916, when the situation had worsened—that is, when Villa was nowhere to be found—Wilson called out for protection of the border virtually the entire National Guard, some 150,000 men.

For the remainder of the year tension was considerable, although the meeting of a commission of Mexicans and Americans managed to neutralize the affair during the touchy period preceding Wilson's re-election in the autumn of 1916. Then the imminence of American involvement in the European war made advisable a withdrawal of the punitive expedition. The withdrawal was completed on February 5, 1917, and a chapter of American-Mexican relations was finished. The United States extended *de jure* recognition by sending Ambassador Henry P. Fletcher to Mexico City on March 3, a month before the declaration of war against Germany.

It was probably unwise of Wilson to interfere in Mexico, even to the extent of withdrawing the American ambassador as he did in March 1913. In the case of smaller Latin republics such policy held hope of success, and perhaps in the nineteenth century it was not so difficult to coerce larger nations such as Mexico. But by the early twentieth century the time had passed for such action, for the nationalism of peoples everywhere in Latin America had risen to a point where the United States could not undertake drastic measures without raising local hatred and ill-feeling to a point where they not merely made the immediate measures useless but continued for years thereafter. After the Wilson intervention, it took nearly a generation before American relations with Mexico were placed on a solid foundation.

What may one conclude about the era of American intervention in Latin America? Was it a period when the Colossus of the North loosed its power without stint or limit, and drastically—and erroneously—infringed on the sovereignty of many of the states south of the border? In Central America and the Caribbean, only El Salvador together with Guatemala, Costa Rica, and Honduras (the latter three nations controlled, some people said, by the United Fruit Company) remained without benefit of direct American guidance. President William Howard Taft in a well-intentioned phrase had said that his administration's policy was one of "substituting dollars for bullets," and gave credibility to the accusation of "dollar diplomacy," unfortunately alliterative in all the major Western languages. Critics of American foreign policy usually have had a double tactic: they first have denounced dollar diplomacy, and then have turned to the accusation that the United States practiced imperialism in Latin America just like the imperialism of France, Britain, and Germany in Africa and Asia.

This argument, that in the era after the turn of the century the United States simply stepped on the Latin American governments closest to its borders, overlooks the perhaps naive but nonetheless sincere belief of many citizens of the republic of North America that their government was helping its smaller sister republics. More important, it overlooks the strategic reason for most of the interventions: the closeness of the Central American and Caribbean countries to the Panama Canal. It may be that the Mexican intervention could not properly be considered under this latter justification, but one could say that Mexico geographically, right next to the United States, was all the more a concern of the government in Washington. Humanitarian impulse and military strategy should have answered the critics of American policy in Latin America after the Spanish-American War of 1898. And if the critics did not find such contentions convincing, they might have observed that when the security of the canal approaches was assured, after the world war of 1914–1918, the United States gave up its interventions and became a good neighbor.

ADDITIONAL READING

For early twentieth-century Latin American policy the general books are many—notably Dexter Perkins, *A History of the Monroe Doctrine* (rev. ed., Boston, 1963). Also Arthur P. Whitaker, *The United States and South America: The Northern Republics* (Cambridge, Mass., 1948), and the same author's *The United States and Argentina* (Cambridge, Mass., 1954); Julius W. Pratt, *Challenge and Rejection* (New York, 1967); Dana G. Munro, *Intervention and Dollar Diplomacy in the Caribbean: 1900–1921* (Princeton, 1964), and its sequel, *The United States and the Caribbean Republics: 1921–1933* (Princeton, 1974); Richard D. Challener, *Admirals, Generals, and American Foreign Policy* (Princeton, 1973); Lester D. Langley, *Struggle for the American Mediterranean* (Athens, Ga., 1976), and the same author's *The Banana Wars* (Lexington, Ky., 1983).

For special subjects see David F. Healy, *The United States in Cuba* (Madison, 1963), and Lester D. Langley, *The Cuban Policy of the United States* (New York, 1968). The background and construction of the Panama Canal are in David McCullough, *The Path between the Seas* (New York, 1977), an absorbing book, and Walter LaFeber, *The Panama Canal* (New York, 1978), occasioned by the canal treaties during the Carter administration. The Dominican Republic's checkered relations with the United States at the turn of the century, including the second Venezuelan crisis of 1902–1903 and the Roosevelt Corollary, appear in Howard K. Beale, *Theodore Roosevelt and the Rise of America to World Power* (Baltimore, 1956). The first Nicaragua occupation is in Munro's *Intervention and Dollar Diplomacy in the Caribbean*. The second has consideration, in all its oddly colored detail, in William Kamman, *A Search for Stability* (Notre Dame, Ind., 1968). Neil Macaulay, *The Sandino Affair* (Chicago, 1967), relates the activities of the Robin Hood of Nicaragua. Haiti's background of chaos is in David F. Healy, *Gunboat Diplomacy in the Wilson Era* (Madison, 1976).

Mexican-American relations have produced a large literature. A general treatment is in Arthur S. Link, *Woodrow Wilson and the Progressive Era* (New York, 1954), a volume in the New American Nation series. Studies of merit are Charles C. Cumberland, *Mexican Revolution: Genesis under Madero* (Austin, 1952), and *The Constitutionalist Years* (1972); Barbara W. Tuchman, *The Zimmermann Telegram* (New York, 1958); Robert E. Quirk, *The Mexican Revolution* (Bloomington, Ind., 1960), campaigning and diplomacy in the revolution's first era, and *An Affair of Honor: Woodrow Wilson and the Occupation of Veracruz*

(Lexington, Ky., 1962); Kenneth H. Grieb, *The United States and Huerta* (Lincoln, Nebr., 1969); Robert F. Smith, *The United States and Revolutionary Nationalism in Mexico* (Chicago, 1972); and Mark T. Gilderhus, *Diplomacy and Revolution* (Tucson, 1977).

Biographical references appear in suggestions for additional reading after Chapters 2, 5, and 6.

☆ 5 ☆

World Power

"We're a gr-reat people," said Mr. Hennessy earnestly. "We ar-re," said Mr. Dooley, "We ar-re that. An' th' best iv it is, we know we ar-re."

—Finley Peter Dunne

There is no more instructive chapter in the history of American foreign policy than the era from the Spanish War (1898) down to the beginning, in Europe, of the First World War (1914). This was the time when the United States came at last to full appreciation of its power in the world but not, alas, to an understanding of what its power should mean in terms of responsibility for the peace of Europe. The tragedy of American foreign policy in the crucial decade and a half before the outbreak of the war of 1914–1918 was that when American power had become evident to the nations of the world, and to the American people, the United States proved unwilling to use that power in the place where it most needed application: Europe. Alfred Thayer Mahan has been credited with a dictum regarding American policy for that heady era—in the Far East cooperation, in Europe abstention, in Latin America dominance. The ringing nouns misled readers into believing that they were hearing something novel, and the last word, dominance, seemed to prove that they were. The difficulty with this logic was that it offered nothing more for the most important of the three areas of the world, Europe, than countless American commentators and officials had been offering since the beginning of the republic. At the turn of the twentieth century the Far East was in a state of confusion which would last for decades. Latin America, for all of its future importance and its then pressing importance as the location of the Panama Canal, was not to be an amphitheater of world politics during the lifetimes of Americans living in the years before the First World War, nor indeed during at least the first half of the twentieth century. But Europe was to explode in 1914, and the four subsequent years of savage warfare tore apart European civilization as people hitherto had known it. Neither Europe nor the world could ever be the same again.

And so, with the United States abstaining, the Old World continued its blundering way toward war. One cannot say that the American failure of policy was responsible for what Europe did in 1914, for Europeans were responsible for that. Nor can one say that Americans consciously, with clear understanding of the alternatives, made a decision in 1898–1914 to stay out of European affairs. Many Americans never thought about foreign policy, and even among the leaders of the American government there was much more thought about the domestic problems of the United States, which then seemed to almost everyone the serious problems. Sometimes the important decisions are not decisions at all, and this was the way that the United States in the main stayed out of the affairs of Europe when, as we now see, the nation should have entered on the side of democracy and peace, with all the force, diplomatic and military, it could bring to bear.

I. *Imperial Years*

Theodore Roosevelt was central to American policy in the prewar years. For Theodore, "TR," he of the right fist pounding into the cupped left hand, the quivering eyeglasses, the shaking mustache, and the flashing teeth, this caricature of action incarnate, "pure act" as Henry Adams once said in recalling that quality which medieval theologians attributed to God: without this grand personality it would be impossible to describe American policy concerning Europe prior to 1914.

Roosevelt, of course, did not act alone. The president's official supporters, his secretaries of state, John Hay and Elihu Root (Secretary Robert Bacon was an appointee for a few days at the end of Roosevelt's second term), were quite different individuals, but each in his way helped ably to advance the policies of the president. Hay was given to caution and inferential statements, and when he opposed the president he did so with a deftness which Roosevelt sometimes missed and which on other occasions seemed to the president a sign of weakness, so that when Hay died in 1905, and a nation mourned, Roosevelt was annoyed at the adulation and some years later explained privately that Hay had not been a great secretary of state. As for Secretary Root, he and Roosevelt had worked well when Root was secretary of war, a holdover from the McKinley cabinet, but by the time Root came to the secretaryship of state after the death of Hay, Roosevelt had won the election of 1904 and become president in his

Theodore Roosevelt and the world.

own right, and he and Root did not always hit it off. Still, Roosevelt admired the cautiously conservative judgment of Root, for he knew that by taking Root's opinions he could seldom make mistakes. It was comforting to try out ideas on Root for size. When the secretary of state howled with pain, Roosevelt was warned. He later wrote, with affection for the man who had helped him, "He fought me every inch of the way. And, together, we got somewhere."

In addition there were the senatorial friends and the cabinet colleagues. Henry Cabot Lodge stood out among the friends in the Senate. By the time of Roosevelt's presidency, this representative of Massachusetts had become a power in the land, and he proved a power to Roosevelt. There were other friendly senators, whom Roosevelt usually could use to exert influence on that jealously emotional body. The cabinet contained fervent and effective supporters such as Philander Knox, later secretary of state and senator, who could quip affectionately with the president about the taking of Panama.

There were also supporters among the men of military affairs, like William E. Sims, whom Roosevelt saved from a near-total obscurity. Sims helped him get rid of naval dead wood. And Roosevelt and the celebrated naval publicist, author of *Influence of Sea Power upon History*, Alfred T. Mahan, were on the best of terms. Mahan acted as a presidential prophet through the influential journals of opinion in which his political articles constantly appeared.

The president also was friendly with the intellectuals, such men as Henry and Brooks Adams, President Charles W. Eliot of Harvard, and countless others. The literati, the intellectuals, were not always privy to Rooseveltian secrets, and the president used them as they hoped to use him, but there was an easy commerce between Roosevelt and these men, and they helped advance his policies for Europe and elsewhere.

Not less important were the special friends of the tennis cabinet, as Roosevelt's athletically inclined close associates were known collectively. When Cecil Spring (Springy) Rice and Hermann Speck (Specky) von Sternburg were in attendance, the president glowed with enthusiasm. An influential Britisher, Arthur Lee, had shared a tent with Roosevelt during the campaign in Cuba, and in later years Lee and Roosevelt exchanged confidences. The French ambassador, Jules Jusserand, became such a friend that on the occasion of Roosevelt's retirement from the White House in 1909, a ceremonial affair when Jusserand was to make a speech of presentation to the president, the ambassador was so overcome with emotion that he could not speak, and the presentation had to be made by someone else. Henry White, in the Roosevelt years an active member of the foreign service, often communicated directly with the president, and TR wrote White, ignoring the various gentlemen such as Ambassador Joseph H. Choate to whom White was, by the diplomatic table of organization, a subordinate. The tennis cabinet never met in full session, and the name may have had more newspaper appeal than it deserved, but the individuals to whom Roosevelt gave confidences during his presidency never forgot "the Roosevelt years" and were able, even if foreign nationals, to serve the president for the good of the United States as well as that of their own countries. Often the tennis cabinet would go into Rock Creek Park, not to play with rackets but to scramble down gorges and across streams, and up the boulders again toward daylight, puffing and panting, a line of willing and sometimes not-so-willing explorers, following the burly figure in the lead—reducing their diplomatic feelings to common thoughts and making it easier for the president to speak directly with them when the situation demanded.

2. *A Symbol for Europe, and a Meeting that Succeeded*

If there was one single symbol of America's new place in the world, or the world's new place in the calculations of America, it was possession of the Philippine Islands. It was one thing to acquire territory in the area of the Caribbean, such as the Panama Canal or Puerto

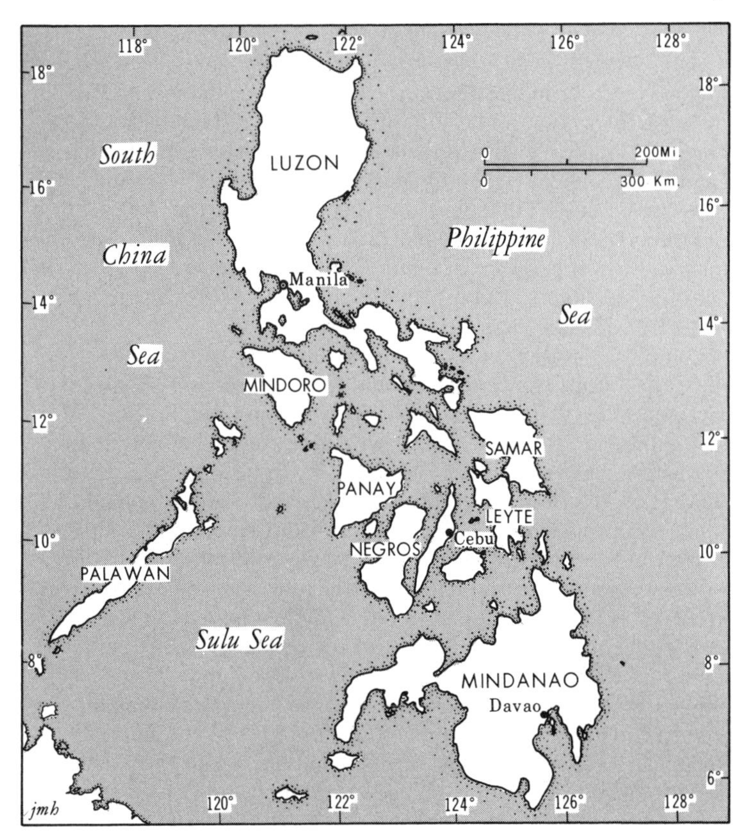

The Philippine archipelago comprises more than 7,000 islands, and totals 115,707 square miles. Eleven islands constitute 96 percent of the total land area. The second largest, Mindanao, is approximately the size of Indiana.

Rico, and many effervescent speeches were made about these acquisitions, about how they raised the United States to the situation of primary power in the Western Hemisphere, indeed the whole world. But the Caribbean was a long way from Europe and the seat of the world's important diplomacy. It was similarly almost irrelevant to the politics of Europe when the United States during the Spanish-American War had picked up the Hawaiian Islands, natural appendages to a North American power with an exposed Pacific coast. The same could be said about the acquisition, earlier, of the Samoas, not to mention Guam and Midway. The same could not be said about the Philippine Islands, which lay in Japan's sphere, not of the United States, and which could produce no logic of territorial proximity or military safety. Moreover, the Philippines were too large an island group, too populated with rebellious subjects, their acquisition too recent, for Americans to claim that they were altogether the products of chance—well, if they were the products of chance, their acquisition had careful confirmation at the long peace conference in Paris in the autumn of 1898. The Philippines therefore were a symbol of American empire, evidence that the United States was planting its flag in ways well known and understood to European powers.

Possession of the Philippines put a stamp on American policy which for a generation or two proved ineradicable, and Roosevelt—who did not mind the appearance of empire anyway—had to face up to the fact of possession, as did his countrymen. His era for the first time in American history was seriously imperial.

The president did not try to weasel out of his country's responsibilities to educate, uplift, civilize, and Christianize, as McKinley may have put the case to the Methodist clergymen in 1899. Roosevelt took up the burden of imperialism in what he described countless times as a manly way. He did this more easily, to be sure, because from the start of American intervention in the islands he had opposed Philippine independence. The local patriots had risen against the Spanish in 1896 and were ready to take over the government of the islands at the very minute that the Americans were expelling the Spaniards. Roosevelt, a lieutenant colonel in 1898, did not hesitate to defend the army's role in keeping the insurgents out of Manila, and he ardently supported the army in the years down to 1902 and the end of the Filipino War. In the campaign of 1900 when he was running for vice president, with McKinley sitting on the front porch in Canton, Ohio, Roosevelt traveled thousands of miles and dealt with every issue he could think of, and some he should not have thought of. In regard to the Filipino rebellion he described Aguinaldo's patriots as "Chinese halfbreeds" and worse. He considered it preposterous to compare Aguinaldo to George Washington. He compared the Filipino leader to Benedict Arnold. He refused to concede the legitimacy of the native independence movement. Such a view he considered akin to shirking American responsibility, handing the Philippine Islands back to barbarism or savagery.

His policies in the islands, and those of his successor Taft, were to make the islanders fit for self-government sometime in the long future. First they had to learn about good government, with the help of American assistants everywhere in the island regime. Schools likewise had to be established. Roosevelt insisted that no religious creed should appear in island education, but there should be education on the American secular model. He also moved to get the Catholic Church out of the Philippine land problem, in the case of the so-called friar lands—lands which had belonged to the friars before the revolution beginning in 1896, and which peasants had appropriated. The president settled the question by agreeing to pay the Church about 50 percent more than the lands' appraised value and to give up the demand he had made at the outset that the Vatican withdraw the friars. By 1912, 50,000 Filipinos worked small farms purchased on generous terms from the American government.

Politically and militarily the Philippine empire proved an embarrassment, as Roosevelt realized before the end of his presidency. The president told a churchman in 1907 that the best thing for the Philippines would be a succession of administrators like the islands' first civil governor, "Will" Taft, to administer them for the next century, but that changing administrations in the United States probably would prevent this, and he was not sure anyway that the American people would be willing to support the Philippine burden. It was that same year, the year the fleet started round the world, that he sent Leonard Wood, in command of the islands, coded instructions in case of attack.

In the conversation with the church leader he had commented that "from a military standpoint the Philippines form our heel of Achilles." Here was a prescient remark. The future importance of the Philippines was not altogether in evidence in 1907, and for that era their importance was as a symbol, serving to remind Americans that their nation was not unlike the imperial powers of Europe.

Being an imperial power, like the great powers of the Old World, the United States under Roosevelt's leadership had to do something for European affairs, it seemed. It could not "just stand there," speechless, motionless. It was of course to be expected that Americans seeking a safe involvement would look for something on the fringes of large events. Roosevelt therefore chose Morocco, on the geographical fringe of Europe—a territory that nonetheless, as it turned out, carried more European destinies than he had anticipated. The single major Rooseveltian intervention in Europe (apart from mediation of the peace of Portsmouth, which was more an Asian affair, though involving Russia) was over Morocco.

There were actually two Moroccan interventions, and the first was far less important than the second, though far more flamboyant. In the land where the umbrella was the mark of sovereignty, the problem for the United States was that an American citizen of Greek extraction named Ion Perdicaris had been seized by a dreadful bandit, Raisuli. Perdicaris's problem in turn was really Raisuli's problem—the Moroccan sultan, Abdul-Aziz. It was, indeed, a complicated story. The sultan had gone crazy in a minor way. Not content with innumerable bicycles, 600 cameras, 25 grand pianos, and a gold automobile (there were no roads), he wanted Western reforms. Nothing if not thoroughly Western, he also had applied to French bankers and thereby obtained a Western-style debt. All this westernization roused the tribes. He had harshly treated and aroused Raisuli some years before. What with the disaffection, the bandit chieftain decided that if he could kidnap a prominent foreigner he could extract something for himself from the ensuing trouble. Raisuli did not care about what the foreigners might threaten to do; that would be the sultan's problem. Consul Samuel Gummeré walked blindly into this trap, became duly incensed at the treatment of Perdicaris, an American citizen, and asked Secretary Hay for an ultimatum, which was readily issued because of the personal irritation and serious attitude with which TR had responded to the affair.

Raisuli and Perdicaris nonetheless had created a convenient situation. The Republican national convention had assembled in Chicago to nominate Roosevelt, and there was not much chance that they could do otherwise, because the president controlled the "steamroller," that is, the Republican delegations from the South who were all in the president's pocket, beholden for federal appointments if not for local support. Roosevelt was going to get the nomination, and probably the election. The country agreed with Viscount Bryce, who said Roosevelt was the greatest president since Washington (prompting a Roosevelt friend to remember Whistler's remark when told he was the greatest painter since Velazquez: "Why drag in Velazquez?"). The president simply needed some enthusiasm from the professional politicians in attendance. At the convention there were no bands, no parades, hundreds of empty seats. The northern Republicans were so disaffected, so listless, so unconcerned and uncaring, that they were embarrassing the party managers who had to give some impression of joy. The delegation from Roosevelt's home state, New York, was so ostentatiously cold that one reporter predicted they would all go home with pneumonia.

Mindful of the Republican convention, in such doldrums, Hay sent to Chicago a copy of the ringing cable he had addressed to the sultan of Morocco:

THIS GOVERNMENT WANTS PERDICARIS
ALIVE OR RAISULI DEAD

Simultaneously, that June 22, 1904, Hay gave out the cable to the press. He also had told Gummeré, contrary to the latter's request for an ultimatum, "Do not land marines or seize customs without Department's specific instructions." This sentence he left out of the message given to the press.

There was an uproar, Perdicaris was released, Raisuli extracted so many concessions from the sultan that the poor man must have had to sell his pianos, and Roosevelt was nominated by acclamation at Chicago; but before it was over there were seven American warships in harbor at Tangier, and the Moroccan native government was so weakened that it was hardly able to stand when, less than a year later, the German government for a very different reason produced another crisis over Morocco.

For the American government the Perdicaris affair had a quiet and embarrassing end when the State Department discovered that the man it had protected in Morocco might not have been a citizen of the United States. In 1862, during the American Civil War, Perdicaris had turned up in Greece and taken Greek citizenship, apparently as a precaution to prevent some property in the South from being confiscated by the Confederates. Hay found out about this, and so did Roosevelt. Hay clamped the lid of secrecy on the whole business, at least until after the election of November. "As to Paregoric or is it Pericarditis," the secretary of state wrote to Assistant Secretary Alvey Adee on September 3, "it is a bad business. We must keep it excessively confidential for the present." There were no leaks. Perdicaris was happy over his rescue and was not going to say anything. The truth remained unknown until 1933 when the historian Tyler Dennett published a biography of John Hay and related the affair's inner workings, and even at that interval the embarrassment of the affair was perceptible, despite a later decision that Perdicaris had after all been entitled to protection.

The second American involvement in Morocco, much less flamboyant but far more important, occurred when the German emperor William II, at the urgent request of his foreign office, stepped ashore at Tangier on March 31, 1905, rode into the city on a horse which was much too spirited for the emperor to handle easily with his withered arm, and made a speech affirming the fine qualities and independence of the sultan. The speech was a careful counter to the increasing French influence in Morocco after the Franco-British entente of 1904, an agreement which had stipulated a dominant French influence in exchange for France's recognition of British dominance in Egypt. The German government, of course, wished to nullify the Franco-British entente, to discourage cooperation between the two nations, which if exercised in colonial matters might carry over into a cooperation upon the continent of Europe against the interests of Germany.

The Germans pushed hard after the speech at Tangier, and managed so to alarm the French government that the premier, Pierre-Maurice Rouvier, dismissed Foreign Minister Delcassé, the well-known destroyer of the work of Bismarck. They told the United States, more simply, that they were seeking the open door in Morocco.

A full crisis was upon Europe, over the same insignificant locality where John Hay had produced a fuss the year before. This time Roosevelt believed that the United States had to show statesmanship, and, acting with his full powers and some that perhaps were not his, he did so. If there was a single occasion when Roosevelt did something seriously important for European peace, it was his activity in allaying the Moroccan crisis of 1905.

He talked the European powers into a conference, which was held at Algeciras in southern Spain beginning in January 1906. He sent a two-man delegation to the conference, the principal negotiator of which was his friend the experienced diplomat Henry White. During the discussions White sought to find out the precise positions of the European powers, and what lay behind those positions. The Americans gave moral support to the British and French to stand up to the Germans.

All the while, back in Washington, Roosevelt was maneuvering as rapidly as he could, which was rapid. He so maneuvered the German emperor that William's minister, Chancellor Bernhard von Buelow, made a concession in a cable to Ambassador von Sternburg which the latter interpreted as an agreement by the emperor to follow Roosevelt's lead at the conference. At a crucial point in the conference Roosevelt reminded the German government of this outstanding blank check and forced the Germans to fill it out in the way he wished. His wish turned out to be an agreement to give the French the dominance in Morocco they had been seeking to assert when the emperor, the year before, had intervened. After exerting this pressure, Roosevelt buttered up the emperor by cabling "sincerest felicitations on this epochmaking political success at Algeciras." His majesty's policy, the president said, "has been masterly from beginning to end."

Europe might have gone to war in 1905–1906, for it was not easy for the French to jettison such a foreign minister as Delcassé. The Germans on their part had laid their national prestige on the line. Roosevelt well deserved the Nobel Peace Prize, which he received for this work and the mediation at Portsmouth the preceding year.

There was some hostile talk among his countrymen about this participation in one of the major crises of European politics, but the president managed to carry through his Moroccan policy without interference by Congress or public opinion. This occurred partly because the American people did not understand how closely Europe was moving toward war and how close their president was to the fire. Roosevelt was able to point out that the United States had taken part in the Madrid Conference of 1880 which had regulated affairs in Morocco, declaring the sultan independent; the Algeciras Conference, he said, was only a successor of that meeting. Then, too, the Perdicaris affair was not long past, and it made easier the serious diplomacy toward Europe in 1905–1906.

3. *TR and Alaska*

The manner in which the United States government took part in the affairs of Europe, contrary to the supposed dictum of Mahan, was usually fairly subtle and indirect. In one respect it consisted of the personal impression made by Theodore Roosevelt, supported by his influential friends, upon the crowned heads, the elected leaders, and the peoples of Europe. In another it involved the Philippine symbol, which gave evidence that the United States was an imperial power among the other imperial powers which, with the exception of Japan, were all the nations of Europe: in this sense the United States joined a European club. Another part of America's relations with Europe during these prewar years had to do with, of all places, Alaska, where a quarrel over the boundaries of the panhandle threatened serious disagreement, if not an armed conflict, between the United States and Canada, and thereby Britain, at a time when the British were becoming extremely sensitive to their need of American support in Europe. The solution of the Alaskan boundary in 1903 was one more, perhaps the last, instance of America's advantage from Europe's distress.

The origin of the panhandle argument with Britain lay in the uncertainties of the Anglo-Russian treaty of 1825, wherein the two nations had sought to establish the boundary between Russian Alaska and British Canada. According to this treaty the line started at the southern end of the panhandle, at 54° 40′—but the next point chosen turned out, after subsequent surveys, to be nonexistent. The treaty then compounded this confusion by taking the boundary northward from crest to crest along a mythical mountain range. A third confusion appeared in the section of the treaty that stated that where a line from crest to crest would be more than ten marine leagues (a marine league equals 3.45 miles) from the ocean, the boundary should run parallel to indentations of the coastline and not more than ten leagues from it. Because the Alaskan coast was split by numerous islands, large and small, and by long narrow bays (or canals, as they are called), such a line was geometrically impossible. The only saving feature of the Anglo-Russian treaty of 1825 was its intent, which was reasonably clear: Russia was seeking, and to this the British had agreed, to retain control of the coast down to 54° 40′.

No one cared about the panhandle lands until gold was discovered in the Canadian Klondike in August 1896, whereupon it was suddenly realized that the easiest access to the gold fields was across the panhandle. The Canadians in June 1898 laid claim to a boundary which would have given them the narrow bays and hence a free passage to the Klondike fields. Their claim to one of the largest bays, the Lynn canal, threatened to bisect southeastern Alaska. On the Lynn canal were the three important settlements of Pyramid Harbor, Dyea, and Skagway, each harbor leading to a pass over the mountains to the gold fields. The Canadians offered to negotiate, provided the United States would agree in advance to give them Pyramid Harbor. The Canadian claim was a barefaced fraud, a diplomatic holdup. Secretary of State Hay wrote on June 15, 1899, to the American ambassador in London, Choate, that "It is as if a kidnapper, stealing one of your children, should say that his conduct was more than fair, it was even generous, because he left you two."

From the outset the American government refused to give in to this chicanery, and Secretary Hay in 1899 proposed a commission of six men, three Americans and three chosen by Great Britain, decision to be by majority vote—which meant that the Americans could not lose and, if one Britisher budged, would win. Nothing came of this proposition in 1899. The Canadians would not consent to it. The British were occupied by trouble with the Boers in South Africa (the Boer War began in October 1899 and lasted to June 1902). Hay had other irons in the fire, such as his announcement of the open-door policy for the Far East. In Central America he was attempting to amend the Clayton-Bulwer Treaty so as to enable the United States to begin construction of an isthmian canal. He half expected the British government to attempt to trade concessions in the isthmus for concessions in Alaska, but the government of Lord Salisbury fortunately played fair with the Americans, perhaps because of the Boer War. Salisbury apparently realized also that the Canadian claims in the panhandle were outrageous.

The issue lapsed until the year 1902 when the Canadian government through Prime Minister Sir Wilfrid Laurier intimated to the first secretary of the American embassy in London, Henry White, that the Hay formula of 1899 would be the best way out of the situation. Laurier had publicly advocated the Canadian position and could not back down before his countrymen, but he wanted to get out of his pledge and wished to do it through the Hay proposal of a six-man commission. Hay in a letter of July 14, 1902, proposed this course to his chief in the White House, Roosevelt. The commission would not be an arbitral tribunal, he assured TR. "I do not think they [the Canadians] have a leg to stand on, and I think any impartial court of jurists would so decide. At the same time I recognize the danger of submitting such a matter to an ordinary arbitration, the besetting sin of which is to split the difference. My suggestion was a submission of the question of the interpretation of the treaty of 1825 to a tribunal of six, three on a side, a majority to decide. In this case it is impossible that we should lose, and not at all impossible that a majority should give a verdict in our favor." This seemed, certainly, a safe course.

Roosevelt at this point, however, began to get difficult, and Hay's biographer, Dennett, has concluded that the president was trying to drum up a campaign issue for 1904. TR did allow Secretary Hay on January 23, 1903, to sign a treaty with the British ambassador in Washington, Sir Michael Herbert, giving the controversy to a six-man commission. But then he began to make difficulties, small and large. Five days after the treaty went to the Senate for advice and consent, the president withdrew it for a significant "correction." He had discovered that the commission of six was referred to in the body of the treaty as a "tribunal" but in the preamble was described as an

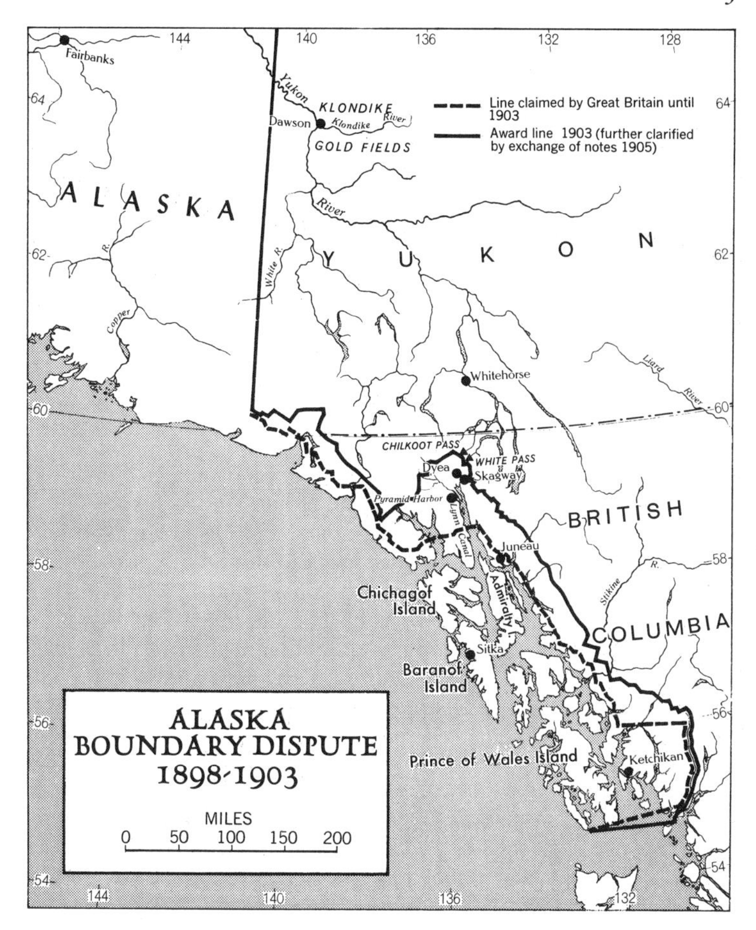

"arbitral tribunal." The adjective had to come out. Hay's assistant, Adee, reported to the secretary on January 31, 1903, that the first sheet of the treaty had to be "re-engrossed, with the necessary changes. It will be ready on Monday, when the seals can be broken, the treaty untied, the new sheet substituted, and the blame thing retied ready for re-apposition of the seals, which can be done without re-signing." The British accepted the treaty with the excised adjective.

There followed two typical Roosevelt maneuvers. First the president appointed, under the terms of the treaty of 1903, the American members of the commission. The treaty stipulated "impartial jurists of repute who shall consider judicially the question submitted to them," and TR chose ex-senator George Turner of Washington, Senator Lodge, and Secretary of War Root (Root was secretary of war, 1899–1903, and secretary of state, 1905–1909). Root was a member of the administration, presumably no impartial individual. Lodge was the president's bosom friend. Turner represented a state which was highly interested in the fate of the panhandle. The Canadian prime minister, Laurier, at this precise moment engaged in getting the treaty through the Canadian parliament, protested bitterly to Hay. The secretary of state was appalled at Lodge's appointment, though he could not intimate this to Sir Wilfrid. He wrote to his good friend Henry White how the Massachusetts senator "as if the devil were inspiring him . . . took occasion last week to make a speech in Boston, one half of it filled with abuse of the Canadians, and the other half with attacks on the State Department. He is a clever man and a man of a great deal of force in the Senate, but the infirmity of his mind and character is that he never sees but one subject at a time. . . . Of course, you know his very intimate relations with the President . . ."

Not content with this sabotage of Hay's negotiation, Roosevelt sent his views on the Alaska boundary to White and to Justice Oliver Wendell Holmes of the Supreme Court, visiting in England, and suggested that White and Holmes speak to the British prime minister, Arthur Balfour, and to Joseph Chamberlain, the colonial secretary: the president contended, via his two intermediaries, that if the commission did not decide the way it should, then he, Roosevelt, would run the boundary line and the Canadians and British could make the most of it. Hay gently protested to Roosevelt on September 25, 1903, that "Of course the matter is now *sub judice*. You can say nothing about it . . ."

Finally on October 20, 1903, the commission, meeting in London, voted in favor of the American claim. The two Canadian members championed their side to the end, but to no avail, for the British member, the lord chief justice, Lord Alverstone, voted with the United States. Hay was elated. As he informed his wife in a letter of October 24, the president "loaded me with compliments today in the Cabinet meeting. 'Nobody living could have done the work as I did,' etc. etc. 'It was the biggest success of my life.' Etc." The completeness of the victory, the secretary concluded, was "something amazing. We have got everything we claimed . . ." "I think myself," he wrote, "that Lord Alverstone is the hero of the hour. No American statesman would have dared to give a decision on his honor and conscience against the claim of his own country."

Whether Alverstone gave his decision on the basis of the evidence or because of the president's carefully communicated views is difficult to say. He doubtless learned of TR's threat to run the boundary in case the commission did not do its duty. He may have concluded that the advices of law and politics in this case nicely coincided. In a public speech after the decision Alverstone said that "If when any kind of arbitration is set up they don't want a decision based on the law and the evidence, they must not put a British judge on the commission." Perhaps this was the sole basis of the lord chief justice's stand. One should probably be content with this explanation, publicly offered, and with it draw the veil over the Alaska boundary decision of 1903.

4. *Pacts of Peace*

With the exception of Theodore Roosevelt's diplomacy during the Algeciras Conference, the acts of the government of the United States toward the governments of Europe were indirect in the years before the First World War. A careful American approach to Europe during this era was support for the creation of a network of pacts for peaceful settlement of international disputes. Americans always had been interested in international law, strengthening the laws of war and especially the rights of neutrals, and once the last great war for neutral rights, so people thought, had ended in 1814 it was easy to transfer this interest into, for example, support for treaties of arbitration. To many citizens of the United States, arbitration treaties were an American policy first explored in the mixed commissions of Jay's Treaty of 1794, and of course the policy had its most notable expression in the Geneva arbitration of 1872. Theodore Roosevelt probably saw a slightly different usefulness for arbitration treaties and general pacts of pacific intention than did many supporters of these treaties, for he envisioned them as helping the European powers through their smaller problems—it was a way in which he could contribute modestly to European peace. In this regard Roosevelt had the best of good will. He once told his friend Spring Rice that he did not wish to be an international Meddlesome Mattie, but he would try to help where he could.

At the end of the nineteenth century, in 1899, the century's last year by some definitions (there was a large argument, in which even the Pope intervened, over what year constituted the end of the century), a peace conference assembled at The Hague, sponsored by the tsar of Russia, with the avowed purpose of establishing international conventions of peace. The Russian government had taken interest in this First Hague Peace Conference because of concern for its own armaments, a desire to halt the equipping of its rivals with new and improved field artillery (the so-called French 75's). This Russian purpose, a limit to the new artillery, did not find much favor at the peace conference, but there were some other achievements. There were declarations against asphyxiating gas, expanding (dum-dum) bullets, and the throwing of projectiles from balloons. These declarations were useless, it turned out, as the powers should have devoted their attention to the machine gun and the submarine, given the importance of those weapons in the forthcoming world war. The conference did arrange for the establishment of a panel of jurists to which any quarreling nations might resort for arbiters of their disputes, the Permanent Court of Arbitration. In subsequent years this court dealt with some minor problems, and at the behest of President Roosevelt during the Venezuelan affair of 1902–1903 dealt with a major one, the question, as mentioned in Chapter 4, of what nations in the debt controversy with the Venezuelan government should have first claim on payment.

The historian Calvin D. Davis has set out carefully the preliminaries, discussions, and results of the First Hague Peace Conference, showing that the United States government sent a delegation largely because of the public sentiment for disarmament and a peace program, particularly arbitration. McKinley did not expect large results, and there were none. In view of the rivalries of the powers which were becoming so marked at this time, and the important ententes and alliances which were made or tightened in the years immediately after, it was a pity that the conference could not address itself to the major problems of Europe instead of patching a few weak places in the laws of war and setting up a panel for a world court. Davis concluded that the agreements of 1899 were "masks concealing failure." One of the American delegates, Mahan, was almost the last person in the United States who would have favored arbitration or any other serious abridgement of the war-making power of any nation.

The First Hague Conference nonetheless was followed by the Second. Roosevelt issued a call for a new conference in October 1904, but then delayed further action because of the Russo-Japanese War. When in the next year, 1905, the tsar indicated he could like to call the conference, Roosevelt easily consented, but he failed to exert the influence upon the Second Hague Peace Conference that he had exercised at Portsmouth and at Algeciras. The reason may have been that the year 1907 was less exigent personally to Roosevelt than the year in which he had issued his call, a presidential election year. More probably it was because he did not see any possibility of large results from the Second Hague Peace Conference and cautiously abstracted himself from what was likely to be an unsuccessful meeting.

After what was considered the success of the first meeting at The Hague, many people in the United States and elsewhere looked forward to the second, and Roosevelt did seek to disabuse them of their hopes. Andrew Carnegie, a self-appointed apostle of peace, was writing fervent letters to his highly placed friends, talking to the British, conferring with the Germans, bringing the British peace advocate, William T. Stead, over to converse with Roosevelt. The president stood aside. To President Eliot of Harvard, whom he suspected of being a visionary, he wrote:

In The Hague my chief trouble will come from the fantastic visionaries who are crazy to do the impossible. . . . the United States Navy is an infinitely more potent factor for peace than all the peace societies of every kind and sort. . . . At The Hague I think we can make some real progress, but only on condition of our not trying to go too far.

The preliminary negotiations for the meeting were not hopeful. Roosevelt at first believed that without great self-sacrifice the United States might favor limitation of armaments, though not reduction and certainly not disarmament. He wrote privately in 1905 that, if the American government could replace worn-out units in the navy with "thoroughly efficient ones," it might not be necessary to have any increase in naval tonnage. Mahan in December 1904 meanwhile suggested a tonnage limit for single ships, and Roosevelt favored 15,000 tons and sought to influence the great naval powers to subscribe to this limit. But both men later came to see that this single-ship tonnage limit was impractical; the British navy was just finishing the *Dreadnought*, an all-big-gun battleship which required a larger tonnage. It was at this difficult time that the German emperor said undiplomatically that Edward VII had pronounced the forthcoming conference a "humbug." Edward said virtually the same to Ambassador Whitelaw Reid one morning on the esplanade at Biarritz. Ambassador George von Lengerke Meyer, visiting England, reported similarly. The king seemed to be worrying that the change of cabinet in the British government in 1905 which had ousted the Conservatives and brought in the Liberals might have brought in some weak thinkers. He need not have feared. Foreign Secretary Sir Edward Grey had an instinctive appreciation of efforts for peace, but was a practical man and soon discovered that the forces working against the Second Hague Peace Conference were too strong. "The difficulty in regard to one nation stepping out in advance of the others is this," Grey explained to Parliament, "that while there is a chance that their courageous action may lead to reform, there is also a chance that it may lead to martyrdom." As for the German government, it openly refused to discuss disarmament at the peace conference. The German ambassador in Paris said that William was in a difficult position because of having yielded at Algeciras and could not give in on armament.

When the Second Hague Peace Conference at last assembled, there was not much in the way of results. One may agree with the judgment of "Mr. Dooley" that the "larger question" at the Second Hague Peace Conference was how future wars should be conducted in the best interests of peace. The chief American delegate at the conference, Ambassador Choate, said in one of his reports, "There is very great reluctance on the part of these fighting nations to bind themselves to anything." Roosevelt hoped to obtain a rule preserving private property at sea from capture in wartime, but the British government refused. He was willing to negotiate a general arbitration treaty, but the German government and seven other European states voted against compulsory arbitration even of legal disputes. He thought that the collection of debts à la Venezuela was one matter that nations should agree to arbitrate. The result was the Porter Resolution, a definition of when nations, after offering to arbitrate, might go to war.

A third conference, scheduled for 1915, had to be postponed, and at the end of the First World War the conference idea disappeared into the grander proposition of the League of Nations.

In addition to the Hague Peace Conferences the American government pursued several projects for groups of bilateral arbitration treaties, capped by a group of bilateral conciliation treaties sponsored by Secretary of State William Jennings Bryan just prior to the world war. These treaties are best described by the names of the secretaries of state or presidents who sponsored them: Olney, Roosevelt, Root, Taft, Bryan.

Secretary Olney in 1897 had proposed a model arbitration treaty with Great Britain to prevent such occurrences as the Venezuelan affair of 1895, and it may well be that the failure of Olney's treaty in the Senate, the failure of the very first in the series of projects for bilateral treaties for peaceful settlement of disputes, showed how futile such a course would be. It was during the defeat of the Olney treaty that the Senate asserted its right to supervise each and every arbitration arrangement concluded by the United States government even under an arbitration treaty. That is, there had to be two treaties, the one setting out an intention to arbitrate and the second defining, for a specific occasion, the terms. No administration, it seemed, could arrogate the treaty-making power of the Senate. An American arbitration treaty hence meant little or nothing, until the Senate decided what it meant in each specific case. There was no pledge to do anything. The Olney treaty failed after sixteen amendments. Its failure was a bipartisan proposition, if one may use the late Senator Arthur H. Vandenberg's unlovely adjective to apply to an era long before his own. By trying to bypass the Senate in any particular arbitration, so the disgusted Olney wrote Henry White, the treaty had "committed the unpardonable sin." It thus is possible to say that with the demise of the Olney-Pauncefote Treaty in 1897 went down all future hopes for arbitration as a practical policy advanced by the government of the United States.

Roosevelt nearly a decade later allowed negotiation of ten general arbitration treaties, signed by his first secretary of state, Hay, between November 1904 and January 1905, including treaties with the governments of France, Germany, and Great Britain. Negotiations were in progress with other countries. The treaties contained involved stipulations, but one of them set out that the parties in dispute before appealing to the Hague Court were to conclude a "special agreement" defining the issue in dispute, the scope of the arbitrator's powers, and the procedure to be followed. This proviso was the kiss of death, and by a vote of 50 to 9 the Senate amended the treaty with France so as to substitute the word "treaty" for the word "agreement." Roosevelt seems to have been only moderately annoyed, and whether his feeling was more over the Senate's pretensions than over the failure of his arbitration effort is difficult to say. He had advocated the arbitration treaties well before the presidential election of 1904, and this advocacy did not harm his campaign. Perhaps he afterward had no need for the treaties. In any event he seems to have felt that he had done his duty, and he turned his attention elsewhere until his second secretary of state, Root, championed and concluded, with Senate approval, a new set of treaties beginning in 1908.

The point noticeable about the Root treaties, which Roosevelt supported with some show of enthusiasm, was that they provided for a second treaty in each case of arbitration—the very proviso to which the president in 1904–1905 had objected; he had said openly at that time that this provision made arbitration treaties useless. Could it be that every electoral year, 1904 and 1908 at least, was a good year for arbitration treaties? Twenty-five treaties on the useless Root model of 1908 were signed and ratified, duly excepting from arbitration all questions of vital interests, independence, and national honor, or disputes involving third parties, and also containing, as mentioned, the provision for a second treaty allowing the consent of the Senate. Not a single dispute was ever arbitrated under these treaties. "I only went into them," Roosevelt explained some years afterward to his friend Spring Rice, "because the general feeling of the country demanded it."

President Taft tried to advance a new set of treaties in 1911, and began by proposing arbitration treaties with Great Britain and France. According to Taft's proposed plan there was to be arbitration of all differences "justiciable in their nature by reason of being susceptible of decision by the application of the principles of law or equity." The British and French treaties provided for a Joint High Commission of Inquiry to make advisory reports on nonjusticiable disputes and to decide whether disputes were justiciable. A special treaty in each case, setting out the powers of the arbitrators, the questions at issue, and other matters, would precede the arbitration. Each treaty was an agreement to make a second treaty. Taft pressed the issue, and the French and British signed on August 3, 1911. In the complicated terms of these treaties the Senate at once espied a flaw, the Joint High Commission of Inquiry. This harmless proviso infringed on the treaty-making power. The Senate cut the two treaties into shreds and voted overwhelmingly for the pieces, 76 to 3. A hurt President Taft with-

Three times the Democratic candidate for the presidency (1896, 1900, 1908), Bryan served as secretary of state from 1913 to 1915.

drew the treaties, or what was left of them. Soon he lost his bid for re-election. Ruefully, but with humor, Taft later described what had happened. When the treaties reached the Senate, he wrote,

> that august body truncated them and amended them and qualified them in such a way that their own father could not recognize them. . . . And since the treaties had really been framed as models, when they came back thus crippled and maimed, they were not very useful. So I put them on the shelf and let the dust accumulate on them in the hope that the Senators might change their minds, or that the people might change the Senate; instead of which they changed me.

The last set of treaties proved to be treaties of conciliation, rather than arbitration, sponsored by Secretary Bryan in the Wilson administration. Bryan long had been contemplating such instruments and, in 1912 in a letter to Taft, noted that the Peace Parliament at London had endorsed them in 1906. He diplomatically told Taft in 1912 that the latter's treaties did not offer so much for world peace as did the conciliation instruments of the sort he had in mind. The secretary of state of 1913 lost no time submitting a proposition to Wilson's cabinet. He proposed for each treaty a commission of five persons—one member from each nation; two other members, one chosen by each nation; and a fifth member chosen by the four. He proposed a time limit during which the commission would deliberate on a dispute brought before it, six months or one year, during which the disputing nations could not go to war. Thursday, April 24, 1913, at noon, the secretary presented his peace plan to some thirty-six members of the diplomatic corps in Washington.

What the hardened members of the corps thought of this proposition is difficult to say. At diplomatic receptions Bryan, a teetotaler, already had mortgaged his credit with Washington diplomats by serving grape juice, and there was talk of milk.

In the subsequent negotiations Wilson's secretary of state showed the same attractive idealism and the same bewildering simplicity of mind which had taken him so far in American politics but denied him its principal prize, the presidency. If it was true that as secretary of state Bryan often spent his time in the department talking to visiting politicos, or found plenty of time to lecture on the Chautauqua circuit for a fee, no one could accuse him of failing to pursue his peace proposal of 1913. He hounded laggard nations, pushing them along the road toward peace. When he signed one treaty, he would try to use the occasion to produce another. When his entreaties to Brazil, Argentina, and Chile led at last to an arrangement for ceremonies in Washington, he cabled his envoy in Madrid, March 14, 1914:

> I am expecting to sign treaty with Brazil, Argentina, and Chile within a few days. The three treaties will be signed on the same day. As the South American countries were formerly colonies of Spain and speak the Spanish language, it occurs to me that Spain might be pleased to arrange her treaty so as to have it signed at the same time. Please bring the matter to the attention of the Foreign Office.

No ignorance of Brazilian linguistic and political history could divert him from his course. He allowed, apparently, some of his ministers a fairly free rein for the purposes of peace. His minister in Teheran wrote on October 29, 1913, "In view of his delays in the matter of the peace proposition, I told the Foreign Minister I suspected him of being engaged in preparing a declaration of war against my country, and that I should be pleased if he would let me have either that or the other thing." There were disappointments. The chargé in Stockholm, Jefferson Caffery, later to have a long and well-known ambassadorial career, cabled on July 31, 1914, "Present minority conservative government now devoting entire energy to obtain high grade army and navy." Notwithstanding the outbreak of the world war, Bryan pursued any and all nonsignatory nations. He sent a telegram to the German ambassador at the Ritz Carlton in New York on September 29, relating that he had signed with twenty-six nations including Britain and France. "Your country and Austria have already approved of the principle. It would make our joy complete if your Government and Austria would enter into treaties . . ." As for the Belgian government, for which conciliation at the moment held few attractions, Minister Brand Whitlock wrote Bryan on November 16 that before the outbreak of war Belgium had been interested, but that after the commencement of hostilities and during its subsequent movements from place to place the government was "so overtaxed and harried" that it could not consider the matter; Whitlock had not insisted further, and would not, unless Bryan insisted.

Bryan negotiated thirty treaties for the advancement of peace, and the Senate accepted all but two, those with Panama and the Dominican Republic, seeming to believe that conciliation was unnecessary with these wards of the United States, that a one-year delay before hostilities would open a door to chaos. Six others—with Argentina, Greece, Nicaragua, Persia, El Salvador, and Switzerland—never went into effect because the other country failed to ratify. Bryan in November 1914 presented a paperweight plowshare to each of the diplomats with whom he had signed treaties. The paperweights were made of steel and nickel-plated. The steel was composed of melted swords, with the inscription on the plowshares from Isaiah: "They shall beat their swords into plowshares." The sentences on the beam of the plow set out the contributions Bryan had made to diplomatic phraseology. The war department had produced the condemned swords. The navy department rendered them into paperweights.

Like the Root arbitration treaties, these Bryan conciliation treaties were never invoked.

5. *A Gathering of Sentiment*

The first years of the twentieth century had advanced the nations of Europe inexorably toward the First World War, and when the war came it found the secretary of state of the United States negotiating a set of useless treaties, which Bryan, unperturbed, continued to do until his retirement from office in 1915. The American people seemed equally removed from the holocaust. The prewar years had passed with a rapid increase in national productivity and a continuing increase in patriotic sentiment, accompanied by—as the political crises in Europe accumulated ever more intensity—a growing belief that Americans were not like other peoples and lived in a land insulated even from the extraordinary combinations and collisions of the old continent. The one president who had sensed the movement toward disaster in Europe, Roosevelt, and had done something about it at a great international conference, had not managed, despite his extraordinary qualities of leadership, to take the American people along with him, and when he went out of office the hope of any major assistance to Europe went with him.

The affairs of Europe may not have aroused more than surface curiosity after Algeciras, and one could write that the American people were innocent, which was true, and that there would be an end to innocence, also true. The major movement of American sentiment in the years before 1914 was perhaps at the time unnoticeable and was to become apparent only in retrospect. Bradford Perkins, in a volume published a half century and more after the events it described, has pointed out that a "great rapprochement" occurred between Americans and Britishers in the two decades before 1914. This rapprochement, Perkins rightly remarks, was the signal event of the time, even if it produced few immediate results in American foreign relations. It was, of course, a change in sentiment somewhat visible in the years immediately after the Venezuelan dispute of 1895, when the British, with both the second Hay-Pauncefote Treaty and the resort to arbitration after the second Venezuelan affair of 1902–1903, showed that they were surrendering their position in the Caribbean, withdrawing in favor of the United States. The American government in turn was carefully neutral during the Boer War of 1899–1902, and Roosevelt spoke of a British Monroe Doctrine for South Africa which would warn off others, like the German emperor, as the United States had done in its own hemisphere. After 1901–1903 the ties became ever stronger between Americans and Britishers, and eventually—in 1917–1918—were to determine the outcome of World War I. But the gathering of sentiment in the United States in favor of the British people, and against their enemies, was a slow proposition and often was hidden from view. If the average American had been queried by some precursor of the Gallup pollsters, he would have denied the fact of a great rapprochement.

In this respect as in others, Theodore Roosevelt's changes of mind are interesting as reflecting changes in his countrymen, and it is helpful to set them out because Roosevelt was loquacious, eloquent, and almost instinctively right, if often prematurely so, in sensing where his countrymen should and would go in foreign affairs. Consider his attitude toward the distinguished British writer Rudyard Kipling, whose pronouncements and ideas he at first acquaintance heartily disliked. Following the practices of many other Britishers, Kipling had said unpleasant things about America, and Roosevelt bridled. TR could not abide British condescension. He hoped it was true that Kipling had been barred from the Players Club of New York. "There is no earthly reason he should not call New York a pig trough, but there is also no reason why he should be allowed to associate with the pigs." He feared that Kipling was a cad. Later he changed his mind and came to appreciate him—"a pleasant little man, bright, nervous, voluble," if "rather underbred." By 1914, Roosevelt's dislike of condescension was not enough to prevent his seeing the importance of Britain's entering the world war against German power and ruthlessness. On the day that Britain entered the war, he spoke excitedly to a small group of young men—including Felix Frankfurter, Herbert Croly, and the English reformer Charles Booth—who called upon him at Sagamore Hill. "You've got to go in! You've got to go in!" he exclaimed to Booth. For a few months thereafter he controlled his pro-British instincts, but then he turned to the grand project of Anglo-American cooperation to which he devoted himself until his death in 1919.

The whole nation changed its views in the prewar years. If in 1896 the Republicans had found it necessary to put out a precautionary pamphlet entitled *How McKinley Is Hated in England*, there was less and less of this as the years advanced. As Bradford Perkins has written of the great rapprochement, it was a combination of Anglo-Saxonism, that is, corrupted Darwinian ideology and faith in limited government; imperialism, and America with the feeling of an *arriviste*, a late arrival, happy to be a member of the British club; and finally the German shadow. A movement to celebrate the centennial of Anglo-American peace in the summer and autumn of 1914 was disrupted only by the beginning of the war. A German sympathizer in the United States pointed out that never had there been a war with Germany, and why should Americans celebrate peace with England, but this logic did not seem to matter.

An evidence of renewed American appreciation of the former mother country appeared in the ending, in June 1914, of a two-year dispute between the United States and British governments over the exemption of American coastwise shipping from Panama Canal tolls. This complex argument took its origin from the bill which President Taft signed into law in 1912, in anticipation of the opening of the canal in 1914. The British explained that the exemption was contrary to the second Hay-Pauncefote Treaty. They said that the exemption shifted to other users the share of maintenance costs escaped by coastwise shippers. It also raised a question of what ships, strictly speaking, were engaged in coastwise trade, for almost all American vessels carried mixed cargoes, part going from coast to coast, part in transit from or to foreign ports. The Americans replied that many nations subsidized their national shipping, and what was the difference between granting an exemption and returning the same amount as a subsidy? All three presidential platforms and all three candidates in the election of 1912—Taft, Roosevelt, and Wilson—favored exemption. Wilson then changed his mind and pushed for removal. To uncertain congressmen he contended that the British government at American behest had instituted a policy of cooperation in Mexico, and that removal of the exemption would be a *quid pro quo*. Both houses of Congress agreed, just before the opening of the world war, and there followed almost an outburst of pro-American sentiment in England, which kindled a complimentary and altogether timely enthusiasm in the United States.

The American president in 1914, Wilson, was probably not the most promising choice as chief executive for the dreadful problems that soon would lie before the country, submarine warfare and the trenches in France. The outbreak of war produced a notable if private outburst from former president Roosevelt, who unburdened himself to his old tentmate Lee on August 1, 1914:

> As I am writing, the whole question of peace and war trembles in the balance; and at the very moment . . . our own special prize idiot, Mr. Bryan, and his ridiculous and insincere chief, Mr. Wilson, are prattling pleasantly about the steps they are taking to procure universal peace by little arbitration treaties which promise impossibilities, and which would not be worth the paper on which they are written in any serious crisis. It is not a good thing for a country to have a professional yodeler, a human trombone like Mr. Bryan as Secretary of State, nor a college president with an astute and shifty mind, a hypocritical ability to deceive plain people . . . and no real knowledge or wisdom concerning internal and international affairs as head of the nation.

These opinions were trenchant, and not altogether inaccurate. But before long Wilson and the nation looked ahead to what they had to face.

ADDITIONAL READING

The heady, imperial qualities of the years at the turn of the century appear in many volumes, including of course the Roosevelt biographies. TR's own account is *An Autobiography* (New York, 1913), published six years before his death. See also Howard K. Beale, *Theodore Roosevelt and the Rise of America to World Power* (Baltimore, 1956), meticulous; George E. Mowry, *The Era of Theodore Roosevelt and the Birth of Modern America* (New York, 1958), in the New American Nation series; William Henry Harbaugh, *Power and Responsibility* (New York, 1961), the best scholarly account; G. Wallace Chessman, *Theodore Roosevelt and the Politics of Power* (Boston, 1969), in the Library of American Biography; and Frederick W. Marks III, *Velvet on Iron* (Lincoln, Nebr., 1980), well written. A notable double biography is by John Milton Cooper, Jr., *The Warrior and the Priest: Woodrow Wilson and Theodore Roosevelt* (Cambridge, Mass., 1983). See also Donald F. Anderson, *William Howard Taft* (Ithaca, N.Y., 1973).

General accounts are J. A. S. Grenville and G. B. Young, *Politics, Strategy and American Diplomacy* (New Haven, Conn., 1967)—although this book is a series of essays it nicely covers its period, 1873–1917—and John M. Dobson, *America's Ascent* (De Kalb, Ill., 1978).

For criticism of imperialism see titles at the end of Chapter 2.

The Philippine occupation has a retelling in John M. Gates, *Schoolbooks and Krags* (Westport, Conn., 1973); Peter W. Stanley, *A Nation in the Making* (Cambridge, Mass., 1974); Richard E. Welch, Jr., *Response to Imperialism* (Chapel Hill, N.C., 1978); and Glenn May, *Social Engineering in the Philippines* (Westport, Conn., 1980).

The Moroccan affair appears in Barbara W. Tuchman, "Perdicaris Alive or Raisuli Dead," *American Heritage*, Vol. 10 (1959):18–21, 98–101, a clever article about two scamps, Perdicaris and Raisuli, and two statesmen-scamps, John Hay and Theodore Roosevelt; and Thomas H. Etzold, "Protection or Politics," *Historian*, Vol. 36 (1974), interesting, with new information. For the Algeciras conference see Raymond A. Esthus, *Theodore Roosevelt and the International Rivalries* (Waltham, Mass., 1970).

For their subjects see Norman Penlington, *The Alaska Boundary Dispute* (Toronto, 1972), and Calvin D. Davis, *The United States and the First Hague Peace Conference* (Ithaca, N.Y., 1962) and *The United States and the Second Hague Peace Conference* (Durham, N.C., 1976). The gathering of pro-British sentiment is in Bradford Perkins, *The Great Rapprochement* (New York, 1968). See also Alan Valentine, *1913: America between Two Worlds* (New York, 1962). Failure to calculate the developments in Europe appears in Lewis Einstein, *A Diplomat Looks Back* (New Haven, Conn., 1968), edited by Lawrence E. Gelfand; and Rachel West, *The Department of State on the Eve of the First World War* (Athens, Ga., 1978).

☆ 6 ☆

The First World War

Force will not accomplish anything that is permanent, I venture to say, in the great struggle which is now going on on the other side of the sea.

—Woodrow Wilson, speech in New York, 1916

Germany has once more said that force, and force alone, shall decide whether Justice and peace shall reign in the affairs of men, whether Right as America conceives it or Dominion as she conceives it shall determine the destinies of mankind. There is, therefore, but one response possible from us: Force, Force to the utmost, Force without stint or limit, the righteous and triumphant Force which shall make Right the law of the world, and cast every selfish dominion down in the dust.

—Woodrow Wilson, speech in Baltimore, 1918

The eruption of a great European war in the first four days of August 1914 caught the government of the United States almost completely unprepared, and the result was an immediate declaration of neutrality. Signs of trouble had appeared in Europe toward the end of the nineteenth century when the leading powers began to conclude alliances with each other, presumably against their enemies. Armaments and armies increased, year by year. A series of untoward events began—trouble in Morocco in 1905–1906 and again in 1911, an Italian war on Turkey in 1911, a Balkan war the next year, another the year afterward. Then on June 28, 1914, a fanatical Bosnian revolutionary named Gavrilo Princip assassinated the heir to the Austro-Hungarian throne, Archduke Francis Ferdinand, whom Princip shot down in cold blood together with his wife in Bosnia's capital city, Sarajevo. But to all this the United States had given little attention. European problems did not seem that important, and although Americans or their ancestors had come from Europe they had almost forgotten the Continent in their desire to do well in the New World. The very existence of Sarajevo was unknown to the American minister to Belgium, Brand Whitlock, who during the crisis was at his country place outside Brussels writing a novel about rural life in Ohio. "I had never heard of Sarajevo," he later wrote. "I had not the least idea where it was in this world, if it was in this world." And so when the assassination led Vienna to declare war on Belgrade, and the Serbians appealed to their ally Russia, invoking the alliance system, soon all Europe was at war, and the American government hastily declared its neutrality.

1. *The Problem of American Neutrality*

It was Germany's submarine measures, above anything else, that brought the United States into the First World War in 1917. If the German government had used some other means of warfare against the Allies, it seems certain that the United States would not have entered the war. This is not to say that the submarine issue alone antagonized the Americans, that there were no other issues on which the American people contended with the Germans, but that the submarine issue was crucial in the American decision for war.

At the beginning of the war in 1914 the German government had blundered badly, so far as American opinion was concerned, by invading Belgium contrary to a solemn treaty of guarantee which Germany had signed. Americans were incensed by this act. Emotional and moralistic, they saw this attack by Germany on a weak neighbor, contrary to treaty, as a moral atrocity. The treaty of guarantee was admittedly old, almost a dead letter, negotiated in 1839, but it was a treaty and not a "scrap of paper" as the German chancellor, Theobald von Bethmann Hollweg, perhaps described it to the British ambassador when the latter asked for his passports. Germany violated the treaty over the protests of the Belgians, whose King Albert is credited with an epigram when asked if the German troops could march through his country: "Belgium is a nation, not a thoroughfare." The Germans had marched, Belgium had futilely declared war, and the Belgian army after a stout defense had fallen back into northern France.

A German occupation followed in Belgium, and during its four years the Germans used the harshest measures to keep the restive Belgian population in order. When the British government on May 12, 1915, published the Bryce Report giving details of German atrocities in Belgium, the American public was revolted. Here, as in the invasion of Belgium in 1914, was a second black mark against Germany. It is true that in the light of postwar investigation the veracity of some of the deeds instanced in the Bryce Report has come into question. There are no proofs of many of the wanton cruelties set down in it. But Bryce had long been a student of the United States, had made a wide reputation in America by publishing in 1888 a two-volume study entitled *The American Commonwealth*, and had been British ambassador to Washington during the Taft administration. His name, in American eyes, lent support to the official British report on German atrocities. Bryce, as we now see, should have made some effort to investigate the volume with which he associated his name, but he did not. Yet despite the falsity of many of the British charges in regard to Belgium, there was a considerable case against German occupation policy there. The Germans in their conduct toward Belgium did not behave well. They executed some 5,000 Belgian civilians, some in large groups, chosen indiscriminately as hostages for Belgian good behavior. Whenever some German soldier was shot down by Belgian patriots, the Germans retaliated by shooting hostages. If the more lurid atrocity stories of violated women and bayoneted babies contained little truth, there remained this execution of hostages which, although perhaps militarily justifiable, was humanely outrageous. To the sensitive public opinion in America, an opinion highly idealistic, German occupation policy in Belgium was unspeakably reprehensible.

But soon the submarine issue surfaced. On May 7, 1915, occurred the most shocking episode of the entire period 1914–1917, the sinking by a German submarine of the *Lusitania*, pride of the British merchant marine, largest and swiftest vessel on the transatlantic run. The Germans early in 1915 had announced their war zone around the British Isles, and this entailed sinking not merely warships and cargo ships but also liners. The Allies refused to believe that German submarines would attack the largest liners. There was a technical

The *Lusitania* leaving New York, May 1, 1915, on her last voyage.

basis for such reasoning: until the *Lusitania* went down, the Germans had not been able to sink any vessel traveling faster than fourteen knots; because the liners were swift vessels it was deemed improbable that they could be attacked. And they possessed watertight bulkheads which presumably would minimize loss of life if they were attacked. Unfortunately, and contrary to such reasoning, Captain Turner of the *Lusitania* disobeyed his instructions as his ship came within sight of the Irish coast (he slowed down his vessel and refrained from zigzagging). Thus Commander Schwieger of the *U-20* managed (the following is from his ship's log) to get a sight on "four funnels and two masts of a steamer. . . . Ship is made out to be large passenger steamer. . . . Clean bow shot at a distance of 700 meters. . . . Torpedo hits starboard side right behind the bridge. An unusually heavy explosion takes place with a very strong explosion cloud (cloud reaches far beyond front funnel). The explosion of the torpedo must have been followed by a second one (boiler or coal or powder?). . . . The ship stops immediately and heels over to starboard very quickly, immersing simultaneously at the bow . . . the name *Lusitania* becomes visible in golden letters." With this act of inhumanity—1,198 people drowned, including 128 Americans—Germany committed one of the cardinal errors of the war.

No one remembered that the German authorities, in newspaper advertisements, had warned prospective passengers that the *Lusitania* was deemed subject to attack. No matter that the German emperor on June 6, after the *Lusitania* sinking, issued secret orders to his submarine commanders not to attack liners without warning, and that after an accidental attack on the British liner *Arabic* the German ambassador in the United States, although without authorization, made the imperial orders public. The American people were horrified at the sinking of the largest Atlantic liner. "Damnable! Damnable! Absolutely hellish!" cried the evangelist Billy Sunday.

More than any other single factor, Commander Schwieger's chance torpedo shot (he had, incidentally, almost finished his cruise; it was his last torpedo) hurt the German cause in America. The American people were incensed at Germany and with almost one voice supported the Wilson administration's diplomatic protests. When Secretary Bryan refused to sign a stiff note to Berlin and resigned his office on June 7, his devotion to his conception of moral law received little public sympathy. "I must act according to my conscience," the idealist remarked sadly at a luncheon after his last cabinet meeting. "I go out into the dark. The President has the prestige and the power on his side . . ." This final sacrifice of Bryan's political career was to no avail, for anti-German feeling was far too widespread. There was never, to be sure, any serious possibility of America going to war over the *Lusitania* outrage. The country was unready for such action, but it was ready for the strongest diplomatic protests.

The German case thus suffered in the United States because of the Belgian invasion and occupation and the sinking of the *Lusitania.* These acts were monumental instances of the German policy of *Schrecklichkeit* (frightfulness). There were other irritations, such as the crude attempts to sabotage American war industry which in December 1915 resulted in expulsion from the country of the German military and naval attachés, Captains Franz von Papen and Karl Boy-Ed. The Austrian ambassador in the United States, who bore the unfortunate name of Dumba, was also expelled after the British secret service intercepted and published some compromising correspondence, showing that he had been privy to schemes for fomenting strikes in munitions factories. Then there were the continuing incidents over German submarine warfare. After the sinking of the *Lusitania* there was a lull as the Germans abandoned for the moment their unrestricted submarine tactics, but early in 1916 they again undertook to expand submarine warfare and a new crisis arose when a submarine sank the *Sussex* on March 24, 1916. President Wilson gave the German government a virtual ultimatum in the matter of unrestricted submarine warfare—that if the Germans used it again, a third time, the United States would break diplomatic relations. The German government backed down again—the Germans promised this time to exempt merchantmen as well as liners from sudden attack—and relations between Washington and Berlin became relatively placid for the rest of the year 1916, until the crisis of January 1917.

Meanwhile relations with Britain reached what was probably an all-time low during the entire war period. The British, having observed how successfully they had impressed the American people as compared with the clumsiness of the Germans, may have overplayed their hand and become too confident that no matter what they did their cause in America was safe. It was, of course, not so safe. The London government did not understand how neutral President Woodrow Wilson was trying to be. Even in 1915 the State Department had sent the British a note of such coldness that Ambassador Page characterized it as containing "nothing in its tone to show that it came from an American to an Englishman: it might have been from a Hottentot to a Fiji-islander." The British blacklist of American firms suspected of trading with the Central Powers raised particular difficulty in 1916. The British government had compiled a list of all firms, American or those of other neutral nations, suspected of trading with Germany or Germany's allies, and goods consigned to such firms were declared subject to capture and confiscation by the royal navy. Although the blacklist was generally accurate, it did mark a gross violation of neutral rights as historically interpreted by the United States. "This blacklist business is the last straw," Wilson wrote to his chief adviser on foreign affairs, Colonel Edward M. House. The British army in 1916 ruthlessly suppressed the Irish rebellion, stir-

Woodrow Wilson marching at the head of a preparedness parade in New York City, 1916.

ring up the hatred of Irish sympathizers in America. American relations with Britain in 1916 became almost as taut as those with Germany.

It was in this situation, facing a serious crisis with both the British and the Germans, that President Wilson undertook a mediation of the war, an effort to bring to an end what had become a terrible slaughter in Europe, and to end it with, as Wilson described his purposes, a peace without victory.

Unfortunately nothing resulted from this effort. In the summer of 1916 the British expected to mount a great offensive on the western front. When they were defeated on the Somme they wished to delay mediation until the military situation was more favorable. The French were fighting a gigantic battle at Verdun, and for them the time also was later, not the moment. After the French held the Germans at Verdun they were even less interested in mediation.

With the 1916 presidential elections in the United States out of the way, Wilson made a final mediation effort. He prodded the Germans into communicating their terms, but the latter were as impossible as those of the Allies. At the same time that it revealed peace terms, the German government on January 31, 1917, sent word through Ambassador Johann von Bernstorff of a new unrestricted submarine campaign.

The German admiralty had concluded that there was an excellent chance of knocking Britain out of the war by a blockade of the British Isles, the blockade including not merely munitions but everything, particularly food coming to Britain from the United States, India, and Argentina (especially the latter two countries, for harvests in the United States had been poor in 1916). The admiralty and the leaders of the German general staff knew that unrestricted submarine warfare would bring the United States into the conflict on the side of the Allies, but they were prepared to take this chance. They knew that American armaments were almost entirely naval. Great Britain controlled the seas anyway, and if the American fleet were added to the British it would make little difference in the outcome of the war. The American peacetime army was of no military importance, and the Germans calculated that before the United States could raise, equip, and train a great army, let alone transport it across the Atlantic, the war would be over. If the United States in 1917 had possessed a dozen ready army divisions the German government might well have hesitated. The United States did not have the ready army divisions, and Admiral Eduard von Capelle, Tirpitz's successor as minister of marine, declared that the military significance of American intervention would be "zero, zero, zero!" The unrestricted submarine campaign was to begin on February 1, and on February 3 Wilson severed diplomatic relations.

Between the breaking of relations and the declaration of war there was a lapse of two months during which Wilson and the country determined on a course of action. War was not inevitable even after Bernstorff received his passports, for the nation could have followed a course of armed neutrality. Wilson seems to have wavered during this crucial period, waiting until Germany had given unmistakable indication of how seriously it would take the protests of the United States.

Meantime, the course for the American government became clear. A German submarine on February 25 sank the Cunard liner *Laconia;* it was the *Lusitania* all over again. This news came to the White House almost simultaneously with the intelligence of the Zimmermann Telegram, in which the German foreign secretary, Arthur Zimmermann, sought to entice the Mexican government into war, not yet declared, with the United States, promising that Mexico might "reconquer the lost territory in New Mexico, Texas, and Arizona." This incredible missive incensed President Wilson because it had been transmitted to Mexico from Berlin via the American embassy in Berlin and the State Department in Washington. Because of British control of the cables, Wilson had allowed the Germans to use American channels; the Germans had used them to transmit a hostile message. American newspapers published the Zimmermann Telegram on March 1. On March 12 a German torpedo sank the American steamer *Algonquin;* all of the crew were saved. Then word arrived on March 18 that the Germans had sunk three American freighters; on the *Vigilancia* fifteen crew members lost their lives, six of them Americans. Two days later the cabinet unanimously advised the president to call Congress as soon as possible and ask for a declaration of war.

Wilson called Congress into special session. The Senate arranged to limit debate, but now it was asked to declare war rather than mere armed neutrality. President Wilson delivered his war message to Congress in person on April 2; the joint resolution declaring war was passed on April 6, 1917, with overwhelming majorities.

2. *Wartime Diplomacy, 1917–1918*

When the United States entered the First World War many questions at last were resolved or adjourned, and it was with considerable relief that the leaders of the American government could clear the decks, so to speak, and face the major problem that confronted them: defeating the Central Powers. Diplomacy during the war became of necessity a concern secondary to the military effort. Still, there was a place for diplomacy, and a large one, in any war such as the conflict in 1917–1918, fought by a coalition. President Wilson—as would be true of President Franklin D. Roosevelt a generation later, in 1941–1945—found himself deeply involved in what might be described as "coalition diplomacy," the holding together and in some important instances the direction of the Allied war effort. The diplomacy of interallied coordination was a major concern in 1917–1918, and the president performed it brilliantly. There were, in addition, two other diplomatic tasks which Wilson undertook. One was in regard to Austria-Hungary—bringing pressure upon the Dual Monarchy to get out of the war. The other consisted of a calculated and eventually successful effort to persuade the German people to give up fighting and make peace with the Allies.

The principal diplomatic effort of the war years came over the business of interallied coordination. In the same month that the United States entered the war, the British government sent a mission to America headed by the foreign secretary, Arthur Balfour, to discuss Allied requirements and seek to discover how the United States as a belligerent might best contribute to an Allied victory. Not to be outdone, the French simultaneously sent a mission consisting of René Viviani, a former premier, and also, to discuss military matters, Marshal Joseph Joffre. The Italians and Belgians likewise sent missions, and, as we have seen in a previous chapter, the Japanese sent Viscount Ishii to the United States to obtain some concessions for the island empire which were not connected with the Allied war effort. Little came of any of these initial missions, including the mission of Ishii, but they did serve to emphasize at the outset of American belligerency the need for Allied cooperation in the common effort against the Central Powers.

One result of Balfour's visit was the setting up of a special system of contact between the British foreign secretary, once he had returned to London, and the American government. In a private arrangement that completely bypassed the State Department, Balfour set up a special British government code by which he could communicate directly with the chief of British military intelligence in the United States, Sir William Wiseman. Wiseman maintained a suite in a New York hotel which was directly above a suite occupied by Colonel House, Wilson's confidant. House, in turn, had a direct and private wire from his suite to the White House. It was a most effective arrangement. If exasperating to Secretary of State Lansing, who thus was left completely in the dark as to many Anglo-American arrangements on the highest level, it was probably for the best in many ways, for in this manner the British government could deal intimately with the American president instead of going through the rigmarole of sending formal notes between the respective foreign offices.

This arrangement was efficacious only between the two English-speaking allies, and it was an arrangement of channels rather than a solution to the many problems of concern that confronted Britain, the United States, France, Russia, and the other powers aligned against the Central Powers. After the United States entered the war, the special Franco-British purchasing arrangements through J. P. Morgan and Company were dropped, as the Morgan Company rightly believed that it could not continue to carry on what was now a proper function of the government of the United States. This change required a new American organization, and the Morgan procedures were, unfortunately, not at once assumed by the government in Washington. There was muddle in this regard until an arrangement was made in late August 1917 for a purchasing commission in Washington. A protocol to this effect was signed by the United States, Britain, France, and Russia.

Such a purchasing commission could not coordinate the requirements of the Allies with those of the Americans, which were increasing as an American army of enormous size and power began to come into being, and so pressure appeared for more coordination, perhaps an American mission to Europe. Colonel House was mentioned as a possible head for such a mission, and without hesitation President Wilson nominated House, who with a full complement of advisers arrived in London on November 7, 1917. The House mission performed yeoman service, conferring with the British until November 21, after which it went on to Paris and joined an Interallied Conference at which eighteen nations were represented, from Belgium to Siam.

The Interallied Conference of November 1917 was one of the most fruitful diplomatic events of the war, when one considers the many decisions that resulted, directly and indirectly. The first plenary session opened with a speech of welcome by the new French premier, Georges Clemenceau, who had just formed his ministry dedicated to victory, and who had promised that he would make a brief talk. He spoke five sentences, concluding: "The order of the day is work. Let us get to work." The conference thereupon adjourned for executive sessions of committees of technical experts. From this discussion at Paris came many important decisions. One was a plan that the Americans would place in France by the end of 1918 at least thirty divisions of troops, approximately a million men, available for the campaign envisioned for early 1919. As events turned out, the Americans had their million in France by June 1918, and doubled the number by October. It was these fresh American troops which broke the back of the German army on the western front and enabled the Allies to win the war. There were other agreements at the Interallied Conference, such as the decision to send a battleship division to reinforce the British Grand Fleet. British naval authorities were extremely nervous over the accuracy of German naval gunfire as exhibited at the Battle of Jutland in 1916. Appearance of American warships in Europe, ensuring a preponderance of Allied naval power against a possible second German challenge, greatly reassured the British naval command. Another agreement at the conference in November 1917 in Paris was that the British and Americans together would close the North Sea to German submarines by the construction of a mine barrage, which incidentally marked a reversal of the American stand against the mining of the high seas. There was also agreement at the conference on blockade policy, and on methods of rationing trade with neutrals on the European continent so as to ensure that the neutrals would not transship goods to Germany or Germany's allies.

The Interallied Conference set up standing committees which met in London and Paris. There were the interallied council on war purchases and finance, the maritime transport council, the interallied naval council, the food council, the interallied petroleum conference, and the interallied munitions council. The Europeans must have been aghast at the organizational mania of the Americans, but because they needed American goods, they complied with the desires of the New World republic. As one Frenchman, André Tardieu, put it (Tardieu was France's chief of a permanent commission of coordination in the United States): "When Americans fall in love with an idea, even if their enthusiasm does not last, it is always intense. In 1917 and 1918, they had a passion for the organization of interallied war machinery, the weight of which was not always borne gladly by Europe." Eventually, he concluded, the Europeans did come to see that only through united efforts, rather than independent measures, could the war be won.

The European Allies themselves on November 7, 1917, urged on by military disaster on the Italian front, took a step in the direction of unifying their efforts. The Italian army had cracked at Caporetto on October 27, 1917, and in a short time three-quarters of a million Italian troops were killed, wounded, or made prisoner. This debacle brought the British, French, and Italians to a meeting at Rapallo early in November where they created an interallied Supreme War Council. The council was to act "as an agency for the adoption and maintenance of a general policy for the Allies in the prosecution of the war, consistent with the total resources available and the most effective distribution of those resources among the various theaters of operations." It was not a supreme command for the Allied forces—that would not come until later, in the spring of 1918, when the almost successful German general offensive in the west forced the Allies to designate Marshal Ferdinand Foch as supreme allied commander. But if it was not a supreme command, the Supreme War Council was a political organization of considerable importance. General Tasker H. Bliss, a former chief of staff of the American army, sat as one of the military advisers from the first meeting of the council. Colonel House represented the United States at the meeting in December 1917 and as Wilson's personal representative sat with the prime ministers of the other powers. After House's return to the United States, the president appointed no one in his place, although permitting the counselor of the Paris embassy, Arthur Frazier, to attend as a "listener." Wilson wished to emphasize that the United States, having not signed the formal instrument of alliance between the Allied powers and having thereby assumed only the role of "associate" in the war, was not taking part in the Allies' political discussions. This, to be sure, was a false position, and when in late 1918 the question of an armistice with Germany arose in the Supreme War Council, Colonel House entered its sessions and discussed the matter in fullest participation with representatives of the other nations.

One might conclude this discussion of the vitally important work of interallied coordination by again citing an opinion of André Tardieu. "Nations remember only the high spots of wars," he wrote in the 1920s. "What did they grasp of the tragic period of 1917–1918? The Rumanian disaster, Caporetto, the British Fourth Army, the Chemin des Dames. Were those the decisive events of the great struggle? No! The essential things were the problems of transportation, rotation of shipping and submarine sinkings, the financial problem, the problems of co-operation. Any shortcoming in the adjustment of effort, any breakdown in the machinery of supply, might have left our soldiers weaponless."

The United States, it can justly be said, was responsible for much of this work of interallied coordination.

Another of President Wilson's diplomatic tasks of the war period was his bringing pressure upon the Central Powers with the hope of persuading them to give up fighting. Like the diplomacy of coordination, this was an informal sort of negotiation. It was much different from the usual note-sending and note-receiving that marks the normal peacetime dealing of nation with nation. There were no American diplomatic representatives in Berlin or—after the American declaration of war in December 1917—in Vienna, and American moves had to be made through special emissaries and through diplomatic posts in neutral countries.

The policy of the United States was generally well adapted to the situation of 1917–1918, for it focused on Austria-Hungary. The German government had become extremely bellicose after the appointment in autumn 1916 of General Erich Ludendorff as quartermaster general of the imperial army, and there could be little hope for a peace offensive directed at Berlin. Austria-Hungary, however, had incautiously gone to war in 1914 and almost from the start was anxious to get out. The Austrian declaration of war on Serbia had set off the European alliance system, almost like a string of firecrackers, and the war had hardly begun before the old emperor Francis Joseph was wishing for peace: if Austria-Hungary could get out with a black eye and no bones broken, the emperor said, he would be happy. Upon the death of Francis Joseph in late 1916, the young emperor Charles came to the throne and was equally anxious for peace. Charles knew even better than his great uncle that the empire was torn by the dissension among its national minorities, which already had brought a high rate of desertion from the imperial army. If the monarchy did not soon have peace, it would fall apart. To this inviting situation the United States directed a considerable diplomatic effort.

President Wilson and the American government nourished the hope of getting Austria-Hungary out of the war and, at the same time, maintaining the territorial integrity of the empire—avoiding its breakup into several small national states. There were unofficial and inconclusive conversations in Switzerland between emissaries of Emperor Charles and an American resident in that neutral country, George D. Herron. There was a short exchange between Wilson and Charles, through the king of Spain. But Austria had become almost a captive state of the Hohenzollern empire. Strong bodies of German troops had deployed close to Vienna, and while the young emperor pursued his somewhat naive negotiations, the Germans by indirect pressure kept him from going too far.

Meanwhile the nationalities subject to the Habsburg throne planned to capitalize on the opportunity in a revolutionary sense, and by early summer of 1918 the situation was beyond repair. No longer satisfied with autonomy, the nationalities demanded freedom. The American government acquiesced in this change in the situation, assuming that the Austro-Hungarian empire could not survive the war. In the summer of 1918 the United States recognized the Czechoslovak National

Council in Paris and also the national aspirations of the empire's Serbs, Croats, and Slovenes. Emperor Charles in October 1918 tried vainly to federalize his empire, but the time had passed when such a move was possible. With jubilation the refugee Czechoslovak statesman, Thomas Masaryk, then in America, observed the collapse of his people's ancient Austrian enemy. This new political situation in Central Europe was, one should emphasize, created by the pressures of the war rather than any initiative on Wilson's part. The American president rather reluctantly used Central European nationalism to hasten the last stages of the war. He thereby obtained Austria-Hungary's capitulation seven days before that of Germany, in early November 1918.

Wartime diplomacy toward Germany had to move along different lines. The Second Reich, the empire of Bismarck, made by blood and iron in 1871 from the union of north and south Germany, offered no opportunity in 1917–1918—given the ardent Germanism which in the latter nineteenth century superseded German provincial feeling—to split the empire into its pre-1871 divisions. American tactics therefore were to separate the Berlin government from its people, under the somewhat meretricious but nonetheless useful argument that the government did not represent the people. With the German people, Wilson said in his war message, "we have no feeling . . . but one of sympathy and friendship." Similar statements appeared throughout his speeches in the period of American belligerency, 1917–1918.

The principal move by the American government to drive a wedge between government and people in Germany was the announcement, on January 8, 1918, of the Fourteen Points: (1) open covenants of peace, openly arrived at; (2) freedom of the seas; (3) removal, "so far as possible," of trade barriers; (4) reduction of armaments "to the lowest point consistent with domestic safety"; (5) equitable adjustment of colonial claims; (6) evacuation of Russia; (7) evacuation and restoration of Belgium; (8) assignment of Alsace-Lorraine to France; (9) readjustment of Italian frontiers "along clearly recognizable lines of nationality"; (10) "autonomous development" for the peoples of Austria-Hungary; (11) evacuation of Rumania, Serbia, and Montenegro, with access to the sea for Serbia; (12) reduction of Turkey to territory containing only peoples of Turkish descent; (13) independence of Poland, with access of Poland to the sea; (14) establishment of a league of nations. The chief motive of the Fourteen Points, one should explain, was to keep Russia in the war (the Bolsheviks had come to power on November 6–7, 1917) by a statement of more liberal war aims than Colonel House had been able to secure at the Interallied Conference at Paris in November 1917. There was also the need to reassure the Allied peoples that there was idealism in the Allied war aims. These were the immediate reasons, the impulse, behind Wilson's announcement of the Fourteen Points, but he directed his speech to the German people, hoping to persuade them to get out of the war. The Fourteen Points were a master stroke in what a later generation would describe as psychological warfare. Learning of the Fourteen Points, the German people could see that the Allies had a reasonable peace program, and they could ask themselves why they were continuing to fight in what had become a catastrophic world conflict.

Proof of the effectiveness of the Fourteen Points and other of Wilson's speeches explaining his peace program came when, prior to the armistice of November 11, 1918, the American president managed to obtain from both the Germans and Allies an express recognition—which in the case of the Allies became known as the "prearmistice agreement"—of the Fourteen Points as a basis of peace. This was one of Wilson's major triumphs as a diplomat. The prearmistice agreement became the foundation for the entire peace settlement at Paris in 1919. It was of the utmost historical importance, for without considering its pledges and exceptions no student can appreciate the Treaty of Versailles and the later German efforts to revise the treaty. The prearmistice agreement became possible when General Ludendorff, after a rupture of his lines in northern France, told the German civil government on September 29, 1918, that it must sue for peace and do so quickly. The government, which the German general staff had dominated for two years, displayed an unwonted initiative and at once asked for peace on the basis of the Fourteen Points, communicating directly with President Wilson and not the Allies. Wilson kept the negotiations in his own hands while he persuaded the Germans to democratize their government and drop the emperor. At the same time he persuaded the Allied statesmen—not without a broad hint from Colonel House, then sitting on the Supreme War Council in Paris, that the United States might make a separate peace—to accept the Fourteen Points. The British prime minister, Lloyd George, accepted the points with a reservation that there must be further discussion of Wilson's point 2, freedom of the seas. The British also desired a large financial reparation from Germany, and so they drafted a reservation on this matter—it was written mainly by Sir William Wiseman—which was accepted by the French premier, Clemenceau, and the Italian premier, Vittorio Orlando. With these reservations, communicated to and accepted by the German government, together with explanation by Wilson to the Allies (but not to the Germans) that certain of the points, such as point 10 pertaining to Austria-Hungary, had to be modified in view of recent events, the Germans on November 8 sent plenipotentiaries to Marshal Foch's railroad car, then in the forest of Compiègne in northern France, and there in the early morning of November 11, 1918, they signed the armistice.

3. *The Paris Peace Conference*

The war was over, and the making of peace could begin. American diplomacy had enunciated the Fourteen Points as a basis of peace, and in the prearmistice agreement gained Allied approval of them. The Germans had consented to them. The diplomats of the New World would now have an opportunity to see how much of the American peace program could be secured at the peace conference.

Wilson decided to go in person to Paris, and this decision at the time and later was written down as a major diplomatic error. His presence assuredly put him into the hurly-burly of what was bound to be a difficult conference. The president had much to lose in personal reputation and little to gain by going to Europe to assist in making the peace. He went; and he obtained at Paris much of his program, notably the League of Nations, which an individual with less prestige might never have secured.

But did President Wilson at Paris lose some vital issues for the United States, apart from his victory on the League of Nations? There has persisted a popular belief in his "blunders" at Paris—a belief that a gullible American president, journeying to Europe to make peace in 1919, encountered issues which he did not understand, and that cunning European diplomats at Paris persuaded Wilson to give away everything that the United States won in the world war.

The simple process by which the Paris conference accomplished its tasks, in meetings of three or four of the leading statesmen, seemed to show personal decision at the peace table. Three or four men, it was easy to believe, could make mistakes. Everyone watched with apprehension at the time, an apprehension which deepened into suspicion, as the conference followed a normal process of shrinking to a manageable size. Although it began with a large body of delegates, it was dominated at once by the Council of Ten (which was a reincarnation of the wartime Supreme War Council—foreign ministers and prime ministers of chief delegates of Japan, Italy, France, Britain, and the United States). It ended as a private meeting of the Big Four (the prime ministers of Italy, France, Britain; the president of the United States) and, frequently, the Big Three (Clemenceau, Lloyd George, and Wilson): Lloyd George, the politically agile prime minister of England, "a Welsh witch" as John Maynard Keynes described him; Clemenceau, conservative, uncharitable, realistic in the old-fashioned manner of diplomacy; Wilson, a great man in many ways, but edgy and irritable at Paris, and tired.

Even so, one must doubt that Wilson made many mistakes at Paris. Certainly on technical matters he was on almost all occasions hedged about by solid information from his advisers. There was much

A hero's welcome for Wilson in Europe.

professional advice available in Paris, and the president was seldom in the predicament of having to make a subjective decision. Wilson needed this help. His declarations during the war months had been general in nature. Despite his background as a student of history, the president was not well grounded in European history. Colonel House as early as autumn of 1917 had therefore taken steps to marshal for the peace conference a corps of American specialists, and the resulting Inquiry, a group of experts drawn mainly from university faculties, devoted itself to minute examination of the problems of Europe, especially possible boundary changes in Eastern Europe. The Inquiry was a serious group, established for a serious purpose, and its information was in the main highly accurate. At the conference the experts of the Inquiry stood available to the president and other members of the American delegation. As events turned out, the Inquiry and a somewhat similar group in the British delegation, together with experts from the other Allied nations, wrote the major portions of the Versailles Treaty with Germany and the treaties with the other Central Powers.

This is not to say that there were no large political questions at Paris subject to decision by the statesmen of the great powers, for there were such questions, running far beyond the technical into the political on a grand scale. One need only mention reparations—how much should Germany pay, and to whom? What should be done about Germany's border along the Rhine—should the border territory pass to France, or should there be provisions for demilitarization and occupation, with eventual retirement of Allied forces upon German good behavior? What should happen to the Saar, the rich coal-bearing valley—should it go to France permanently because of Germany's dynamiting of many of France's mines? There were the Polish questions, of borders and access to the sea; the difficulty of rearranging the peoples and borders of the Adriatic area, where, as in Poland, there was centuries-old confusion which had been adjourned so long as the Austro-Hungarian empire existed; the problem of the former Turkish territories in the Middle East, which had to go, apparently, to one or several of the victorious Allied powers; the need for parceling out former German colonies in the Pacific, including Germany's sphere of influence in the Shantung peninsula of China. In such political questions no experts could be of much help. Here the leading statesmen of the conference—Wilson, Lloyd George, Orlando, and Clemenceau—had to make decisions. But one should point out that even at these points, in the nontechnical areas, Wilson and the other leaders of the Allies could act only within definite limits, for each of them lacked the power of independent decision because he was curbed by the politics of democracy: Wilson was subject to advice and consent of the Senate; Lloyd George was heckled by the press in England, especially that of the sensational press magnate, Lord Northcliffe; Orlando had little power of decision because of the popular hysteria over Adriatic possessions, whipped up by patriots such

The Big Four meet in Paris: Lloyd George, Orlando, Clemenceau, and Wilson.

as Gabriele d'Annunzio; Clemenceau was the prisoner of the French passion for revenge and security.

The idea is false that Wilson had a wide area of decision at Paris and blundered badly because of his personal foibles and incapacities, thereby losing the peace. Personal decisions—blunders—could hardly characterize the peace conference of 1919. The idea of a personal conference flourished in the overimaginative brains of newspaper correspondents, and in the disappointments and disillusions of nations which after 1919 did not have what they wanted. It was easy to point to three or four elderly men sitting in a book-lined study in Paris, and to say, "*There* was the trouble," whether it was there or not.

The results of the conference gradually became evident in the months from its beginning on January 18, 1919, until signature of the treaty with Germany on June 28, 1919—the fifth anniversary of the assassination of Archduke Francis Ferdinand at Sarajevo. The majority of the 440 articles of the Treaty of Versailles were technical and noncontroversial. A few of them stood out in importance or in seeming importance. The first twenty-six comprised the Covenant of the League of Nations. The Covenant became, incidentally, the first twenty-six articles of all of the Paris peace treaties (St. Germain with Austria, Trianon with Hungary, Neuilly with Bulgaria).

In the German treaty, article 231 was the famous war-guilt clause, which blamed Germany and its allies for beginning the war in 1914. Perhaps a special error of the German treaty, fraught with future difficulty, was the postponement of setting the amount of reparations which Germany was to pay, and the fact that reparations were to include the cost of Allied pensions. The boundaries of Germany in the west underwent some changes. Alsace-Lorraine was given to France. Two small patches of land, Eupen and Malmédy, went to Belgium. The Saar Valley was placed for fifteen years under a temporary League administration, with its future status to be decided at the end of that time; the mines of the Saar went to France, and if the territory was returned to Germany by plebiscite in the year 1935 the Germans were to purchase the mines. There were to be no German fortifications west of a line fifty kilometers east of the Rhine, and certain German territory west of the Rhine was to be occupied by Allied troops for periods of five, ten, and fifteen years. In the east, Germany's province of East Prussia was separated from the remainder of German territory by a Polish corridor—a severe settlement excusable on the basis of self-determination and Poland's need for access to the sea, inexcusable to Germans, who for centuries had possessed the corridor lands. Danzig, the former German port now in the new corridor, was denominated a free city under control of the League of Nations. In Upper Silesia, in southeast Germany, there was a plebiscite to determine what lands would remain German and what would go to Poland. In the north of Germany two parts of

Schleswig were to decide their nationality, Danish or German, by plebiscite. Germany under the Treaty of Versailles lost nearly four million people in the east, a third of whom were of German nationality. Altogether it lost by the treaty over six million people, or one-tenth of its population. It lost one-eighth of its territory.

The problems of the Paris conference were extraordinarily numerous, but the treaty with Germany was not a vindictive instrument in view of the more than four years of bitter fighting which had preceded it. It compared favorably indeed to Germany's Treaty of Brest-Litovsk with Bolshevik Russia, signed on March 3, 1918, by which Russia gave up all claims not merely to Poland, Finland, and the Baltic states, but to the Ukraine and the Caucasus. If Germany had won the war in the west, it would have demanded annexation of the Briey-Longwy iron district from France, Liège from Belgium, and in addition a close economic control over Belgium. One can say therefore that Allied ambition was considerably less than Germany's during the First World War. And under the Treaty of Versailles and the other treaties with defeated nations there was always the hope of the League of Nations. President Wilson hoped that such imperfections as would appear in the peace settlement could be taken to the new international tribunal where there could be discussion, compromise, and peaceful change.

It is saddening to reflect upon the manner in which this peace settlement of 1919 was lost, of how the divisions among the Allies which became evident at the Paris Peace Conference lasted for twenty years thereafter and enabled Germany, the defeated power at Paris, to begin another world war. It was tragic that at Paris the Italian delegates had to appease their own public at home and champion more territory for Italy than would have passed to it under the terms of the generous Treaty of London of 1915 (Fiume, seized after the war by Italian patriots led by d'Annunzio, had not been offered to Italy under the Treaty of London). The Japanese used the conference to enforce their claims on Shantung, the large Chinese province containing thirty million people, and in view of the small contribution of Japan to the defeat of Germany this was an excessive demand, embarrassing to the Allies and so humiliating to China that there was bound to be future trouble. The French representatives at the Paris conference were forced by their public opinion (if they did not already think this way themselves—certainly Clemenceau did) to be bitter and grasping; this course was mistaken, although entirely understandable for a nation which had lost 1,385,000 of its finest young men, with more than three million wounded. The British under the leadership of Lloyd George were not interested in territorial acquisition, even if the colonial premiers were determined to acquire control of the former German colonies. Despite the empire's grievous loss of 947,000 men killed, British leaders desired to promote Germany's economic welfare. But

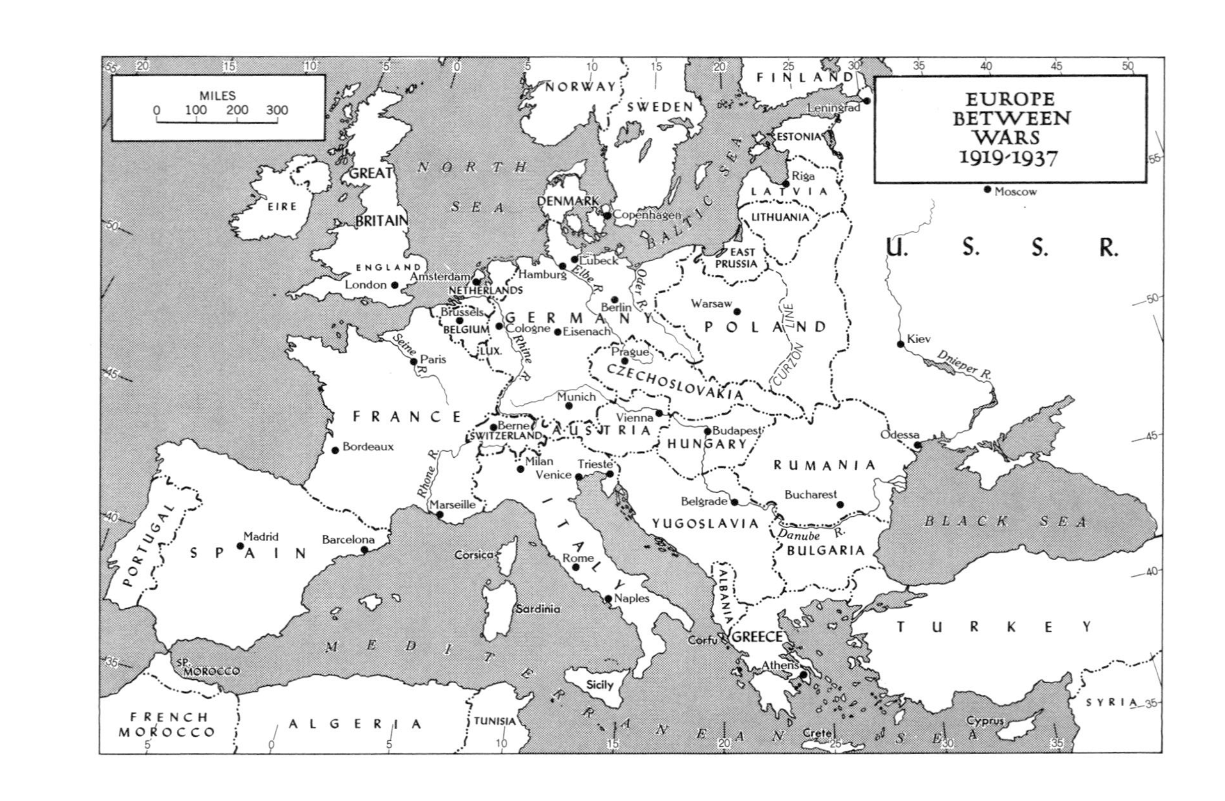
EUROPE BETWEEN WARS 1919-1937
MILES
0 100 200 300
NORWAY
SWEDEN
FINLAND
Leningrad
ESTONIA
Riga
LATVIA
LITHUANIA
EAST PRUSSIA
Moscow
U. S. S. R.
Kiev
Dnieper R.
Odessa
GREAT BRITAIN
EIRE
ENGLAND
London
NORTH SEA
DENMARK
Copenhagen
BALTIC SEA
Lubeck
Hamburg
Elbe R.
Oder R.
Berlin
Amsterdam
NETHERLANDS
Brussels
BELGIUM
LUX.
Cologne
Eisenach
GERMANY
Warsaw
POLAND
CURZON LINE
Prague
CZECHOSLOVAKIA
Rhine R.
Seine R.
Paris
FRANCE
Munich
Vienna
AUSTRIA
Budapest
HUNGARY
Berne
SWITZERLAND
Bordeaux
Rhone R.
Marseille
Milan
Venice
Trieste
RUMANIA
Bucharest
Belgrade
YUGOSLAVIA
Danube R.
BULGARIA
BLACK SEA
PORTUGAL
Madrid
SPAIN
Barcelona
Corsica
Sardinia
ITALY
Rome
Naples
ALBANIA
Corfu
GREECE
Athens
TURKEY
Sicily
Crete
Cyprus
SYRIA
SP. MOROCCO
FRENCH MOROCCO
ALGERIA
TUNISIA
MEDITERRANEAN SEA

the British prime minister was an opportunist in his approach to politics, whether national or international, and he lent uncertainty and something of cheapness to a meeting which needed dignity and a convincing atmosphere.

President Wilson, in poor health towards the close of the conference after a serious attack of influenza in April 1919, did his best to hold up American ideals to the peoples and statesmen of Europe. In this effort he was in fair measure successful, but he became so preoccupied with the task that he failed to keep in touch with the changing political situation in the United States and eventually lost at home everything that he gained abroad. He persisted in believing that domestic politics would be adjourned not merely for the period of the war, but for the period of peacemaking as well. He failed, and it was a foolish error, to appoint to the American peace delegation domestic political leaders of standing. Neither General Bliss, nor Colonel House, nor Secretary Lansing, nor the former diplomat Henry White, could keep him in touch with political developments in the United States. Wilson lost contact with American public opinion, despite a trip home in February and early March of 1919 to sign necessary legislation and plead the cause of the League of Nations to members of the United States Congress. If the Congress seemed slightly inattentive, it might have been because the Republican Party had gained control in both the House and Senate as a result of the November 1918 election. After his return to Paris the president worked incessantly, and when the moment came in June 1919 to sign the German treaty he was close to exhaustion.

Apart from the understandable errors of peacemaking forced upon the statesmen of the great powers by public opinion in their home countries, one might mention at this point a special factor, namely Russia, which, while much talked about in the springtime and summer of 1919, was left undecided at the peace conference. If the Paris conferees made a cardinal error above and beyond any other mistakes, it was their sidestepping of the Russian question. Russia, to be sure, had been much in the minds of the Allies ever since the tsarist government had disappeared with the first Russian revolution of March 12, 1917. After the first revolution, people hoped that the new government would prove more efficient than the old and that the Russian front, from being something of a holding operation, would become a serious theater of operations against the Germans. Instead the weak republic gave way in November to the Bolsheviks, whom the Allies considered a strange group of fanatics. Led by Vladimir Lenin and Leon Trotsky, they threw in the sponge and made peace with the Germans at Brest-Litovsk in March of 1918. This was a large blow to Allied fortunes, for it enabled the German army to transfer some of its troops from the Russian front to France. Luckily for the Allies, the Germans were not thorough enough in transferring troops—they could have sent across Germany many more than they did—and the western front held again in 1918 despite a great German offensive.

But at the peace conference at Brest-Litovsk the Bolsheviks led by Trotsky had talked long and loud about the rights of workers in Europe and their oppression by the capitalists, and this doctrine, though made fun of in Allied newspapers, began toward the end of the year 1918 to worry Allied leaders. When, after the German surrender, the Bolsheviks set up a Communist regime in Bavaria, and when early in 1919 the radical premier of Hungary, Michael Károlyi, surrendered his government to the Communist revolutionary Béla Kun, and when the Russians entered the Ukraine after the Germans left it—people everywhere began to wonder about this movement known as communism. There was a "red scare" in the United States, and in other countries, in 1919. The statesmen at Paris worried about the durability of any peace they might conclude, finding themselves in the position of winning a war only to make the world safe for communism, hardly an attractive prospect.

What to do about the Bolsheviks in Europe was one of the major questions at the peace conference, but unhappily the problem was never resolved. Some individuals such as Winston Churchill and Marshal Foch were all for sending troops to Russia and putting the Bolsheviks down by force. Yet such an expedition ran counter to all the feelings among Allied peoples at the time—it was impossible to stir up enthusiasm for more fighting, after November 1918, and anyway it seemed that perhaps with the passage of some months the Russian confusion would right itself. Britain and France sponsored various "white" leaders in Russia in 1919 and 1920, and the occupations of Siberia and Murmansk, originally for military purposes, tended at times to become political interventions. The Wilson administration sent 14,000 troops to Russia, which gave the appearance of supporting the purposes of Britain and France. But the attitude of President Wilson, which was to let the Russians find a new course according to their own preferences, gradually prevailed. This did not mean that Wilson was willing to recognize the Bolshevik regime, for he was not, and he so instructed his last secretary of state, Bainbridge Colby, in the summer of 1920. Colby announced the nonrecognition of Communist Russia because the regime had subverted popular government, and this policy prevailed until Franklin Roosevelt changed it in 1933. Meanwhile the opportunity for intervention in Russia, if there had ever been one, had passed away as the regime of the Bolsheviks established itself during the 1920s and 1930s beyond any chance of destroying it.

The difficulty in regard to Bolshevik Russia, the reason why the problem was not solved, was in the main, as mentioned, the war weariness of all the Allied peoples. Public opinion by 1919 had turned to concerns other than the problems arising out of the world war.

People were tired of war and wished to hear no more about it, not even about its settlement by the peace conference at Paris. By the autumn of 1919 when the Versailles Treaty was ready for approval by the nations of the world, the treaty encountered something close to indifference. "In this autumn of 1919," wrote Keynes, then in the process of composing a polemic which bitterly criticized the treaty, people were "at the dead season" of their fortunes. "The reaction from the exertions, the fears, and the sufferings of the past five years is at its height. Our power of feeling or caring beyond the immediate questions of our own material well-being is temporarily eclipsed. The greatest events outside our own direct experience and the most dreadful anticipations cannot move us. . . . We have been moved already beyond endurance, and need rest. Never in the lifetime of men now living has the universal element in the soul of man burnt so dimly."

Keynes's words were intended to describe popular feeling in England and France, but his description was true of the United States as well. In America the exertions of the war, while great, had not been beyond endurance. They had been endurable, and the nation in a war in Vietnam some fifty years later would lose nearly as many young men as in the First World War (Vietnam: 45,958 killed by the end of the war in 1973; First World War: 53,398 dead). The American exertion in 1917–1918, however, had been a great one in a spiritual sense. The American people had gone to war hoping for accomplishments not possible at the moment, such as making the world safe for democracy. To Europeans this latter phrase was a slogan but to Americans for a brief period it became a reality. When that reality faded and disappeared in the petty quarrels of the Paris Peace Conference, there came immense weariness with internationalism, and it could be said of Americans as of Europeans that "Never in the lifetime of men now living has the universal element in the soul of man burnt so dimly." Americans were ready to retreat from participation in the peace settlement, and they were ready for the general retreat into isolation which characterized the next twenty years of their diplomatic history.

4. *Defeat of the Treaty*

The withdrawal of the United States from Europe after the First World War became obvious when the Senate in 1919–1920 refused three times to consent to ratification of the Treaty of Versailles. The position on the treaty taken by the so-called irreconcilable senators, led by William E. Borah of Idaho, was of critical importance. The irreconcilables had pledged themselves to do everything in their power to achieve the treaty's rejection. Still, the most important factor militating against the continued participation of the United States in the work of world peace after 1918 was the traditionally isolationist outlook of the American people.

The role of Senator Henry Cabot Lodge in the Senate's rejection of the Versailles Treaty becomes intelligible when one realizes the forces which lay behind him and which he so well represented. To say that Lodge was the architect of America's post-Versailles isolation would be a gross misstatement. The senior senator from Massachusetts stood for traditional nineteenth-century ways of American international behavior. He represented the post-Waterloo belief that in foreign affairs America must have a free hand. Lodge loved England and visited many friends there on his summer trips abroad. He was happy to see the United States enter the war on the side of England against Germany in 1917. After the danger of German power disappeared, he wished to return the United States to the time-honored policy of the free hand. The leading element in Lodge's attitude toward the League and the Treaty of Versailles was traditionalism. The treaty's failure in the Senate was a result of this prevailing intellectual current. No single man or small group of men could change it. Political leaders, if they wished to stay snugly in office, had to act within it, and this is what Henry Cabot Lodge did.

In retrospect the motives of the several Republican factions in the Senate appear rather clearly. The irreconcilables wished for the total defeat of the treaty, including, of course, the League of Nations. Theirs was the pure, unadulterated traditionalist stand in international affairs. As for those senators who were willing to vote for the treaty with reservations of varying severity—the strong reservationists and mild reservationists—they too were traditionalists, although the wartime Wilsonian infection had influenced their judgment. They feared for what they would have loosely described as American rights and wished distinct reservations of American sovereignty. Senator Warren G. Harding, a strong reservationist, was typical of this feeling when he asserted, "I could no more support mild reservations than I could support mild Americanism." The task of Lodge as Republican manager of the Senate was clear: it was to avoid at all costs a party split. Given Lodge's traditionalist views of American policy and a personal dislike he harbored for Wilson, it should have been obvious that he would almost welcome the chance to hold his party together at the expense of the Treaty of Versailles.

By the end of the summer, the foreign relations committee under Lodge's leadership had produced thirty-eight amendments and four reservations, later boiled down into fourteen reservations. The United States, according to these reservations, in case of its withdrawal from the League reserved to itself sole judgment as to whether it had fulfilled its obligations under the Covenant. The American government could not accept a territorial mandate under the League without vote of Congress. The Council and Assembly could not consider ques-

Henry Cabot Lodge.

tions which pertained to the domestic jurisdiction of the United States. The Monroe Doctrine was "wholly outside the jurisdiction of the League of Nations" and entirely unaffected by any provision of the Treaty of Versailles. America withheld its assent to the Shantung settlement and reserved complete liberty of action. Congress might enact, if it wished, a law in regard to appointment of American representatives to the League. The reparations commission of the League would have no right to interfere with trade between the United States and Germany, without the consent of Congress. American expenses in the League would be subject to an act of appropriation by Congress. The committee asked for the right to increase armaments of the United States, under any League plan of disarmament, in case the United States were threatened with invasion or engaged in war. Nationals of covenant-breaking states, residing in the United States, might continue their normal relations. The American government must have the right to regulate private debts, property, rights, and interests of citizens of the United States. Assent was withheld to the section of the Versailles Treaty setting up an international labor organization, until Congress voted approval. The United States was to be protected against any unequal vote, in the League, of the British empire.

In particular Lodge's committee criticized article 10 of the Covenant, which the committee considered a dangerous departure from the vital principles of American foreign policy. Lodge chose to see foreshadowed in article 10 the end of a safe and wise tradition. The nation had never consented to commit itself in advance to international actions except in obvious cases such as intervention by foreign powers in the Western Hemisphere; but in article 10, according to Lodge, the nation would bind itself to decisions by an alien body sitting in Europe. Yet the perils of article 10 were largely imaginary. A close reading of the Covenant revealed the article as less than dangerous. League members undertook to "respect and preserve" (but not specifically to guarantee) "as against external aggression" (*aggression* was a difficult word to define) each other's "territorial integrity and existing political independence" (what this meant was not altogether clear). Nonetheless Lodge's committee balked at article 10. The senator's close friend, Elihu Root, pointed out that, so far as concerned the phrase "respect and preserve," he was willing to agree to "respect," but that "preserve" was tantamount to "guarantee." President Wilson, however, declared article 10 the "heart of the Covenant" and insisted that any reservation of the article was utterly unacceptable.

The tactics of the senator were to prolong the preliminaries and to delay the Senate's advice and consent to the treaty until American opinion came around to his side. Lodge in the summer of 1919 studiously procrastinated when the treaty in the course of senatorial procedure came first before the committee on foreign relations. He consumed two weeks reading the document aloud. Most of his colleagues absented themselves from the committee chamber, and on at least one occasion the committee clerk left the room, leaving Lodge reading to himself. He then arranged public hearings, an unprecedented step in consideration of a treaty, which required six additional weeks. The senator obtained for the foreign relations committee an invitation to the White House for a conference with the president, and there on August 19, 1919, Wilson answered senatorial questions for three hours.

Lodge's tactics finally drove Wilson into a rash act, a speaking tour for the treaty—and this in turn had a most unexpected result. In September of 1919, in twenty-two days, the president delivered thirty-six speeches averaging about an hour in length, traveled more than eight thousand miles, and stood up in a swaying automobile during a dozen parades. Sixty-two years old, worn by illness and the rigors of negotiation at Paris (not to speak of the requirements of twenty months of war leadership), Wilson was unable to stand the strain and collapsed at Pueblo, Colorado, on September 26, 1919. His assistants hurried him back to the White House, where he suffered a paralytic stroke.

Had Wilson died that glorious afternoon in Pueblo, while cheer after cheer swept through the huge audience, he would have met a hero's end. Ex-senator Beveridge, one of the president's critics, later remarked that if this had happened Wilson would have become a greater martyr than Lincoln. His beloved Covenant would have passed the Senate. Instead there came the collapse and the stroke, and for seven and one-half months the president lay almost helpless in the White House. The stroke thickened his speech, and withered the left side of his face and body. "My God, the President is paralyzed!" Dr. Grayson cried as he burst out of the sick man's room shortly after the attack. Mrs. Wilson later wrote that "for days life hung in the balance." For weeks and months, leaders of the administration could approach the ailing man only through his wife, who took it upon herself to decide what specific written communications she would pass in to her husband. The president did not meet the cabinet during this time, and in his sickness grew suspicious of everyone. He broke with Colonel House, and cavalierly dismissed Secretary Lansing. During his illness the Treaty of Versailles met defeat in the Senate.

On November 19, 1919, the Senate voted twice on the treaty. The first roll call was with the fourteen Lodge reservations. The vote was 39 for, 55 against (the irreconcilables voting with the Democrats). A second roll call on the treaty without reservations resulted in 38 for, 53 against. Both with and without reservations the treaty failed to obtain a simple majority. In a third and final vote on the treaty on March 19, 1920, after there had been added to the Lodge reservations a fifteenth reservation favoring the independence of Ireland, the treaty failed again—49 for, 35 against—lacking seven votes of the necessary two-thirds majority.

It was Woodrow Wilson's misfortune, unlike his counterparts in American history, Lincoln and Franklin D. Roosevelt, to live on into the final act of his era, and when he died in 1924 he had seen his handiwork discredited. One of his last moves as president was to insist that the election of 1920 be a "great and solemn referendum" on the League and the treaty. Two Ohio newspaper editors, Harding and James M. Cox, competed for the presidency in 1920, and the election was a travesty of Wilson's solemn referendum. Cox with courage came out in favor of the League, but Harding's managers played safe by taking the advice of the wily senator Boies Penrose of Pennsylvania, who told them to "Keep Warren at home. Don't let him make any speeches. If he goes out on a tour, somebody's sure to ask him questions, and Warren's just the sort of damn fool that'll try to answer them." The amiable Harding confined himself to "bloviations" (as he liked to describe his campaign oratory and statement making) from his front porch in Marion, Ohio. It was said that during the campaign he took fourteen different positions on the League. It was in one of his speeches that he accidentally made the famous declaration, "America's present need is not heroics but healing; not nostrums but normalcy; not revolution but restoration." In vain did thirty-one prominent Republicans, among them President Nicholas Murray Butler of Columbia University, Henry L. Stimson, President A. Lawrence Lowell of Harvard, and former president Taft, issue a manifesto near the end of the campaign advising that Harding favor the League of Nations. The only result of this belated effort to

Three senators refuse to give the lady a seat. Cartoon by Rollin Kirby.

remind the candidate of the large pro-League faction within the Republican Party seems to have been an inclusion of a favorable reference to the League in the first draft of Harding's inaugural address; but, so the story goes, Mrs. Harding blue-penciled the reference during one of her revisions of the text.

Such was the fate of the great crusade which had begun for America in 1917. "We have torn up Wilsonism by the roots," Lodge rejoiced after learning of Harding's unprecedented majority of seven million votes. The hopes of humanitarians that the world war would inaugurate what Lord Robert Cecil called a "great experiment" in keeping the peace, that the war to end war would not have been fought in vain, disappeared when the traditionally isolationist views of the American people reasserted themselves after the war. The League of Nations, President-elect Harding told his fellow citizens in his victory speech, was deceased. "You just didn't want a surrender of the United States of America to go under American ideals. That's why you didn't care for the League, which is now deceased." Senator Lodge announced, more bluntly, that the League was dead. The United States under the Harding administration terminated the technical state of war with Germany by resolution of Congress, July 2, 1921, and signed a Treaty of Berlin on August 25 confirming to the American government all rights stipulated in the Treaty of Versailles. Similar treaties followed with Austria (August 24) and Hungary (August 29), and a series of later pacts established diplomatic relations with Turkey and with the seven new states which had emerged from the war in Eastern Europe.

ADDITIONAL READING

For the period of neutrality the best scholarly account is Ernest R. May, *The World War and American Isolation* (Cambridge, Mass., 1959). Ross Gregory has a short, readable book, *The Origins of American Intervention in the First World War* (New York, 1971). The most spectacular event of the era is discussed by Thomas A. Bailey and Paul B. Ryan, *The Lusitania Disaster* (New York, 1975). The final decision, in early 1917, is still an intriguing subject, for which see Barbara W. Tuchman, *The Zimmermann Telegram* (New York, 1958).

For war and peace there is the present author's *Woodrow Wilson and World War I* (New York, 1985), in the New American Nation series.

The "selling" of the war appears in Stephen L. Vaughn, *Holding Fast the Inner Lines* (Chapel Hill, N.C., 1980).

As for relations with the Associates, those with Britain were the most important, for which there is Wilton B. Fowler, *British-American Relations, 1917–1918: The Role of Sir William Wiseman* (Princeton, 1969); David F. Trask, *Captains and Cabinets* (Columbia, Mo., 1973), on naval relations; and Joyce Grigsby Williams, *Colonel House and Sir Edward Grey* (Lanham, Md., 1984).

In the perspective of our own time, diplomacy involving Russia has loomed far larger than in 1917–1919, for which consult Lloyd C. Gardner, *Safe for Democracy* (New York, 1984).

Volumes on the peace conference and the Senate's defeat of the treaty could fill libraries. Two detailed books are by Arthur Walworth, *America's Moment: 1918* (New York, 1977), and *Wilson and His Peacemakers* (1986). See also Lawrence E. Gelfand, *The Inquiry* (New Haven, Conn., 1963), itself a masterful inquiry.

On the fate of the treaty in the United States there is Ralph A. Stone, *The Irreconcilables* (Lexington, Ky., 1970).

Woodrow Wilson, man and statesman, has continued to excite controversy. Wilson's career, marked by large successes and final defeat, has fascinated academic biographers, who like to recall that Wilson was the only college professor of history to become president. A definitive study of Wilson is being done by Arthur S. Link, *Wilson* (Princeton, 1947–), of which five volumes have appeared, a life and times. Arthur Walworth, *Woodrow Wilson* (3d ed., New York, 1978), is the best finished biography. For diplomacy see Link's *Woodrow Wilson* (Arlington Heights, Ill., 1979), an updating of his

Wilson the Diplomatist (Baltimore, 1957). A remarkably successful dual biography is by John Milton Cooper, Jr., *The Warrior and the Priest: Woodrow Wilson and Theodore Roosevelt* (Cambridge, Mass., 1983). Edwin A. Weinstein, *Woodrow Wilson* (Princeton, 1981), is Wilson's medical history.

For senators and other influential people there is Richard W. Leopold, *Elihu Root and the Conservative Tradition* (Boston, 1954); Robert James Maddox, *William E. Borah and American Foreign Policy* (Baton Rouge, 1969); William C. Widenor, *Henry Cabot Lodge and the Search for an American Foreign Policy* (Berkeley, 1980); and Kendrick A. Clements, *William Jennings Bryan* (Knoxville, 1984). For Wilson's successor see Robert K. Murray, *The Harding Era* (Minneapolis, 1969).

☆ 7 ☆

The Twenties

Humanity is not helpless. This is God's world! We can outlaw this war system just as we outlawed slavery and the saloon.

—Raymond Robins, article in the *Annals of the American Academy*, 1925

1. *The United States and Geneva*

Joseph C. Grew as ambassador to Japan in the 1930s became one of America's most trusted diplomats, but earlier in his life when he was not so well known and was American minister to Switzerland in the 1920s, he had to be extremely careful not to be seen near, and of course not in, the League of Nations buildings at Geneva. Once a correspondent of the Chicago *Tribune* found Grew near the entrance to that den of internationalists, and the minister spent several uncomfortable days until arrival of the Paris papers showed that the meeting had passed unnoticed.

Charles Evans Hughes, President Harding's secretary of state, for a while allowed League of Nations communications to the American government to be received at the State Department without acknowledgment.

The United States during the 1920s (and this was true also of most of the 1930s) was in the world but not of it. American foreign policy was devoted to the principle of peace, but the republic did not belong to the chief world organization dedicated to that ideal. As years passed and the heat of battle over the Covenant of the League of Nations subsided, there was an increasing interest in the nonpolitical activities of the Geneva institution. The first American flirtation with the League was over restricting the worldwide opium traffic, and a delegation from the United States, arriving in Geneva in 1924, gradually learned to take part in this cause, although not before it on one occasion temporarily walked out of a committee meeting, "acting on motives of delicacy," that is, fear lest its presence imply American recognition of the League. There followed a careful participation in such other League activities as regulation of the international traffic in arms (1925), a communications and transit conference (1927), a general economic conference (1927), abolition of import and export restrictions (1927), economic statistics (1928), counterfeiting of currency (1929), codification of international law (1930), and buoyage and lighting of coasts (1930). These activities, of course, were nonpolitical, unconnected with the large problems of international affairs.

One of the more notable American activities at Geneva was membership in the preparatory commission for the General Disarmament Conference. The preparatory commission commenced its dreary life in 1926, incident to Germany's joining the League in the same year. The duty of the commission was to draw up a draft treaty on disarmament which the nations would debate in the future conference. The commission's meetings turned into technical controversies against some types of armament and in favor of other presumably less aggressive varieties. During five years of wrangling, a subcommittee alone used 3,750,000 sheets of typescript, enough to permit the commission's Polish or Swedish delegations to walk home on a path made of committee paper. Finally in 1930 the preparatory commission produced a draft convention which upon the meeting of the General Disarmament Conference at Geneva in 1932 was promptly scrapped.

But in the annals of United States cooperation with the League, the most important issue was whether the United States should join the World Court. The League's World Court, more properly known as the Permanent Court of International Justice, has often been confused with the Permanent Court of Arbitration established in 1901 after the First Hague Peace Conference. The Hague court was not permanent but comprised only a panel of international jurors from which disputing nations might draw for arbitration of controversies. The World Court consisted of a group of judges who sat during court sessions at The Hague and passed judgment upon cases brought before them. Any state, whether a member of the League or not, could belong to the World Court by subscribing to its protocol. There was little danger to national sovereignty in joining because the jurisdiction of the court was always optional.

The idea of a worldwide international law presided over by a court has always found favor among legal-minded American diplomats, as well as among many private American citizens interested in world peace. President Harding made the first gesture toward American adherence to the World Court protocol when he commended it to the Senate in February 1923. Three years later, on January 27, 1926, the Senate approved, 76 to 17, but with five reservations of which the last was the most important: ". . . nor shall it [the Court], without the consent of the United States, entertain any request for an advisory opinion touching any dispute or question in which the United States has or claims an interest." This was a singularly foolish reservation, but it arose out of the Senate's concern about approaching the untouchable League of Nations. Why an American judge on the World Court could not have given a little advice to the League, once in a while, was difficult to understand. Of course a large political question might by some odd chance come before the court—and did, in fact, when the question of *Anschluss*, in the form of joining Austria to Germany in a customs union, was taken to the court in 1931. But if the United States had ventured an opinion in this matter, would it have made any difference in the broad course of European and world history?

The Senate in 1926 believed that for an American judge to give an advisory opinion would make a large difference. The court question continued wearily on. The elder statesman Elihu Root, who had taken part in 1920 in drawing up the World Court protocol, tried to draw up a compromise between the Senate and the forty-eight nations who were members of the court, and at the age of 84 he made a trip to Geneva in 1929 to revise the protocol. President Herbert Hoover in 1930—without much enthusiasm but, so one observer reported, to enable "old Elihu Root to die happy"—resubmitted the court proposal to the Senate with the Root compromise. There the matter languished until 1935, when Hoover was gone, Franklin Roosevelt was president, and the Senate was roused to action. But an eleventh-hour campaign of opposition led by William Randolph Hearst and the Detroit "radio priest," Father Charles E. Coughlin, deluged Washington with tens of thousands of protesting telegrams, and on January 29, 1935, the court failed to receive a two-thirds vote, 52 in favor, 36 opposed. A shift of seven votes would have saved the day.

The court issue had engendered a long debate during the fifteen years it was before the Senate, and in retrospect one must lament the energy expended on so minor a cause. Some individuals, such as Elihu Root, devoted almost all their time to the court; yet the issue was never as important as that. The American ideal of an international court could never in the 1920s and 1930s have been realized fully, given the weakness of international law. Perhaps the World Court approach to international order was logically right and thus should have had more hearing than it received. There is much to say for so rational an approach to foreign relations, and it may be a mistake to write it off completely as a waste of time. Still, in terms of the customs and habits of nations in the 1920s, the World Court was not a practical measure for bringing about world peace, and an effective court may well prove to be nothing but a noble dream in the power-dominated twentieth century. After establishment of the United Nations a second World Court appeared, this time known as the

International Court of Justice instead of the Permanent Court of International Justice. All members of the United Nations are members of the new world court, which is entitled to give advisory opinions on legal questions to the General Assembly and Security Council. Little has been heard yet from the court or of its activities.

One should not conclude this account of American cooperation with the League without mentioning the so-called war debts, a discordant factor in post-1918 United States relations with Europe. Though not directly connected with the League, the question served to raise a wall of antagonism between the United States and its debtor nations, which were virtually all League members.

During the war the Allies had stretched to the utmost their private credit in the United States; when in 1917 the limit of this was in sight, they turned to the American government, which freely lent money raised by the liberty- and victory-loan drives. Some $7,000,000,000 was advanced to the European powers in this way, and approximately $3,000,000,000 more was included in loans after the end of hostilities. After the war, the debtors halted their interest payments on these public loans pending readjustment downward of the interest rate, originally 5 percent. Congress in 1922 created the World War Foreign Debt Commission, which between 1923 and 1930 renegotiated the debts to an average interest rate of 2.135 percent and made the obligations payable over sixty-two years. The principal plus interest over that period would have totaled more than $22,000,000,000. Terms extended to the debtors varied somewhat according to ability to pay; the British government in 1923 was allowed a reduction of interest to 3.3 percent, whereas France (1926) received a new rate of 1.6 percent and Italy (1925) 0.4 percent.

It was comparatively easy to speak of debts and interest rates, and everything appeared to be settled by the mid-1920s, but the American government gradually discovered that signature of renegotiated notes by the debtor nations did not mean intention to pay. Part of the difficulty of payment consisted in problems of exchange. To obtain dollar exchange it was necessary for debtor countries to sell goods or services directly or indirectly to the United States, and the alternative was to send gold shipments. The latter interfered with the "cover" for domestic currencies. As for the former course, it was impossible to send large supplies of goods over the American tariff, raised in 1922 and again in 1930. Postwar subsidies to American steamship companies deprived the European nations of one of their traditional ways of obtaining dollars. The nations might have paid the debts somehow if they really had wished to do so. They did not, and as is frequently the case, they united against their creditor. The French set the tone of this rebellion by rechristening Uncle Sam "*l'Oncle Shylock*," and Parisian editors instructed their cartoonists to change the stars on Sam's hat to dollar signs. There followed a series of diplomatic maneuvers by the debtors. The first move, taken before American renegotiation of the debts, linked debt payment to the payment of German reparations under the Treaty of Versailles.

According to article 231 of that treaty, Germany was responsible for beginning the war, and article 232 specified that Germany would have to pay the costs arising out of war damages, including both physical damages and pensions to Allied veterans. The German government in 1919 had no choice but to accept the Allied view of reparations. But collection from Germany soon began to grow difficult, partly because of the drastic postwar currency inflation which reached its peak in 1923 when the value of the German mark sank to 1/4,000,000,000,000 of a dollar. The Germans made no effort to stop the inflation. They did not wish to pay reparations, were almost eager to appear as bankrupts. The French government, itself in financial difficulties, nonetheless hopefully maintained that *le Boche payera tout*, the Germans would pay for everything, including French obligations to the United States. The British government accepted the French idea of linking debts and reparations, and Foreign Secretary Balfour in a note of August 1, 1922, announced this formally as Britain's policy. "In no circumstances," he wrote, "do we propose to ask more from our debtors than is necessary to pay our creditors . . ." He was stating a consensus not only of London and Paris but of all America's debtors. It was to no avail that American presidents from Wilson to Hoover refused to connect debts with reparations, for the linkage had already been accomplished by the statesmen of Europe.

During the 1920s the flimsy structure of international payments to debtors and creditors preserved an appearance of stability. As holes appeared they were filled—by the Dawes Plan of 1924, which put German reparations on a plan of payment, and by the Young Plan of 1929, which reduced the original estimate of reparations, set in 1921 at about $33,000,000,000 plus interest, to $9,000,000,000 plus interest, the latter sum payable over fifty-nine years—to the year 1988—at an interest rate of 5½ percent (the total reparations bill under the Young Plan, including principal and interest, would have been about $26,000,000,000). Although the United States had no official part in these two plans, they bore the names of American financiers serving privately, Charles G. Dawes and Owen D. Young. It was curious that the number of annual installments for reparations under the Young Plan approximated the then remaining number of European debt installments to the United States as determined by the renegotiations of the Foreign Debt Commission. And there was more coincidence in the provisions for payment of debts and reparations than simply the similarity in the number of annual installments. As mentioned, the principal and interest in each case was about the same—the sum of debts plus interest owed the United States after renegotiation of the interest rate amounted to more than $22,000,000,000, whereas the sum of reparations plus interest owed by Germany to the Allies amounted to about $26,000,000,000 as fixed in the Young Plan. The annuities under the Young Plan were of two sorts, unconditional and conditional, the latter depending upon German prosperity; the unconditional annuities for the year 1931 amounted to $153,000,000, and the conditional annuities for the same year were set at $257,000,000 (total, conditional and unconditional, of $410,000,000); the conditional annuities approximated the total of war debt schedules established by the United States with its debtors in the 1920s—debt payments for 1931 totaled $241,000,000.

The whole arrangement for debts and reparations finally broke under the weight of the Great Depression in the years after 1929. The United States in June–July 1931, under the leadership of President Hoover, negotiated a moratorium on both reparations and war debts. The purpose was to save American private loans in Germany, which would have become uncollectible had reparations payments continued. The American banking structure was so weakened by the depression that for the bankers to lose their German collateral would have invited wholesale bank closures. Hoover in his moratorium was forced to acknowledge tacitly the connection between reparations and war debts, because the European nations would not consider temporarily giving up reparations unless the United States postponed debt payments. Unfortunately, despite the moratorium of mid-1931, American credits in Germany were frozen solid by the end of the summer, and American investors lost the large amounts of money which they had pumped into Germany after 1924, several billions. This money had far more than enabled Germany to make annual reparations payments (part of which, of course, went circuitously to the United States as war debt installments). It is true that had American money not gone to Germany it would have passed into the New York stock market and been lost there, but American funds in the 1920s in Germany financed the re-equipment of large segments of German heavy industry, which a decade later as armament industries were turned against their benefactors by Hitler. Much American blood and treasure had to be expended during the Second World War on the destruction of these industrial complexes. In the post-1945 period the United States has helped rebuild them once more.

When the American government by 1931 had come around to the European interpretation of debts and reparations—that they were inseparable—Germany declared itself unable to continue reparations. The European Allies, as we have seen, refused to agree to a moratorium on reparations unless the United States agreed to postpone payment of the war debts. Shortly thereafter the Allies in effect canceled reparations at Lausanne in June 1932 when they lowered the reparations bill to $750,000,000. This arrangement depended upon a renegotiation of the war debts by the United States, but the damage had been done. The Germans paid no more; neither in essence, did the Allies. When for the first time after expiration of the Hoover Moratorium the semiannual debt installments fell due on December 15, 1932, Britain paid, as did Italy, Czechoslovakia, Finland, Latvia, and Lithuania. The rest of the nations defaulted or made useless gestures such as depositing part payments in blocked accounts. Finland was the only European country after 1933 which attempted to continue paying its debt.

In anger, Congress in 1934 passed the Johnson Debt Default Act, which prohibited defaulting governments from floating loans in this country. The neutrality laws of 1935–1939—about which more later—reiterated this prohibition of government loans to debtors. The Lend-Lease Act of 1941, however, allowed the president in a latitudinarian way to "lend, lease, or otherwise dispose of" government properties, and the neutrality laws were amended in 1942 so as not to apply when the United States was at war.

In surveying the sad history of the war debts, one must conclude that when a loan is likely to be considered a gift, statesmen should accept the inevitable and make a virtue of necessity. This was the course followed in the Second World War, but during the first war there was hardly any precedent for such largesse, and time-honored custom dictated that nations should pay and not repudiate their debts. Under this prevailing practice the United States asked for payment, and no other single postwar international policy pursued by the State Department met with such cordial approbation from American taxpayers. President Coolidge allegedly remarked of the European debtors that "They hired the money, didn't they?" To his generation he seemed uncommonly sensible. His countrymen failed to comprehend the manner in which the war debts estranged them from their

Calvin Coolidge.

friends in Europe, who were already distrustful because of the American attitude toward the League of Nations. Any advantages accruing from the minor nonpolitical cooperation of the United States with the League were wiped out by the bad feeling engendered over the war debt and reparations issues. The bond of sentiment between the United States and the democratic nations of Western Europe, a bond which in 1917–1918 had been so strong, was stretched in the postwar years almost to the breaking point. With the coming of a second world war the strained friendship of Americans and Europeans would require extraordinarily careful attention.

2. *Alternatives to the League—Treaties of Peaceful Settlement*

The United States during the 1920s, outside the League of Nations, felt that it had to do something for world peace. The Department of State tried to discover alternatives to the League which would be acceptable to the American people, and from this search came two general lines of procedure in American diplomacy—treaties for avoidance of war, and treaties of disarmament. These alternatives to the League were compatible with the American tradition of isolation and neutrality in international affairs. Insofar as they were not an adequate international program in the 1920s, they indicated that the traditional principles, isolation and neutrality, were inadequate. But treaties for avoidance of war and treaties of disarmament were the American prescription for world peace in the 1920s. They were even announced as cure-alls, and in the early 1930s Secretary of State Cordell Hull supplemented them with his ideas of economic disarmament by lowering tariff barriers through reciprocal trade agreements. Such alternatives to the League of Nations, it is not unfair to add, had slight effect in promoting world peace.

What kind of treaties for the avoidance of war concerned the United States government after the refusal in 1919–1920 to adhere to the League of Nations? During the 1920s there flourished interest in a program of bilateral arbitration and conciliation treaties, and Secretary of State Frank B. Kellogg made some considerable effort to satisfy the popular demand for these pacts. He discarded in 1927 the arbitration formula used at the State Department nineteen years earlier by Elihu Root—a formula excepting from arbitration questions affecting the United States's vital interests, independence, or national honor, or disputes involving third parties—in favor of a formula reserving from arbitration only cases involving domestic questions. This was a dubious improvement, for a reservation of domestic jurisdiction was large enough to permit evading almost any arbitration.

Even so, the Kellogg arbitration treaties sounded, at least, as if they were broader than the Root treaties.

Kellogg in 1928 likewise undertook to revise and extend the United States's network of conciliation treaties as established before the First World War by Secretary William Jennings Bryan. When Bryan had concluded the treaties in 1913–1915, he had appointed the commissioners under the terms of each treaty, but with lapse of time the personnel in many cases died and nothing was done about new appointments. Kellogg filled out the commissions again.

Altogether, Kellogg and his successors concluded twenty-seven arbitration treaties on the Kellogg model. Six of the old Root treaties remained in force. Eventually, with additional negotiations by Kellogg and others, there were a total of forty-three Bryan treaties. The grand total of instruments thus reached seventy-six!

These moves had little effect upon the course of American diplomacy. No nation has ever resorted to the provisions of the Bryan conciliation treaties. Nor is there a single recorded instance of the employment in an international controversy of the Root or Kellogg arbitration treaties. Some Americans interested in the obvious merits of arbitration and conciliation have comforted themselves that the existence of the innumerable Bryan, Root, and Kellogg treaties has served somehow to allay international tensions.

Arbitration has faded away in international affairs, and little is heard about it in the latter twentieth century. It has no attraction to present-day statesmen or to popular opinion. At the turn of the century American public opinion regarded arbitration highly. Theodore Roosevelt could say of the Root treaties that he "went into them because the general feeling of the country demanded it." Perhaps people in our own time have come to realize that the nineteenth century was the most renowned legal century of modern history, a moment when it seemed as if world order might be brought into reality, when rules for peaceful intercourse among nations appeared not as dreams but possibilities. Perhaps Americans today know that after the turn of the twentieth century, with its great power conflicts, its two world wars and threat of a third, arbitration has receded into the realm of dreams, along with so many other noble projects such as binding international law and a truly powerful world court. Arbitration had passed out of the area of practicality at the turn of the century, some years before Elihu Root took it up. The idea was passé indeed by the time of the secretaryship of Frank B. Kellogg in the 1920s.

But it was not through bilateral treaties of arbitration or conciliation that the United States made its most significant effort for pacific settlement of international disputes after the First World War, for this effort came at Paris in 1928 when Secretary Kellogg, together with representatives of the great powers, signed a treaty for renunciation of all war and for settlement of all disputes by peaceful means. Nearly every nation in the world eventually signed the Kellogg-Briand Pact, except a few such holdouts as Argentina, Bolivia, El Salvador, and Uruguay, together with five uninvited little countries—Andorra, Monaco, Morocco, Liechtenstein, and San Marino.

A dull topic for discussion, the Kellogg-Briand Pact: so it might seem if superficially considered. Actually it marked some of the shrewdest diplomacy one can discover in international relations in the twentieth century. Its roots went back to the First World War and France's position as a result of that war, when after the armistice of 1918 the French had what might be described as acute feelings of insecurity. France had triumphed over Germany during the war only by alliance with Britain, Russia, and the United States, and Frenchmen not without reason were worried about the future of their country, with a small birth rate and a population of about forty million as opposed to Germany's sixty-odd million and rapidly increasing population. France after 1918 suffered from "pactomania," a desire to sign promises with anyone in or out of Europe to protect *la patrie* on some untoward day when Germany might seek revenge for the First World War. In the quest for security the French foreign minister of the later 1920s, Aristide Briand, one of the cleverest diplomats of the past half century, offered to Secretary of State Kellogg a pact between France and the United States pledging both countries never to go to war against each other.

This offer by Briand was intensely embarrassing to Secretary Kellogg, who at first sought to stall it. Briand made the proposal of an antiwar treaty in 1927 because he was attempting to drag the United States into his security system in Europe. The proposal of perpetual peace between the United States and France was in truth a negative military alliance. If America were to sign such a promise, it meant that regardless of how hard the French pushed the United States in violation of neutral rights (as the British had done in 1914–1917), in any future war when France was, say, fighting Germany, the Americans could not side in reprisal against France, for the antiwar treaty would prevent it. Kellogg, of course, wanted nothing to do with such a proposition.

The American secretary of state was furious with Briand. And not the least part of Kellogg's ill humor came because he discovered that the foreign minister had marshaled in support of this antiwar proposition the many American private organizations for world peace which had sprung up before and especially after the war. Many important private American citizens, who knew how to put pressure on the government in Washington, began to demand of Kellogg that he sign with France. Women's organizations, led by such personalities as Miss Jane Addams and Mrs. Carrie Chapman Catt, made Kellogg's life miserable with their visitations and expostulations. The secretary, who was known privately to possess a Ph.D. in profanity and invectives, swore at the "god-damned pacifists," but to no avail. He made it known through intermediaries that he wanted the peace organizations to leave him in peace. Finally he discovered a way to outwit the French foreign minister, and the resulting treaty became the Kellogg-Briand Pact, America's greatest contribution to peace in the interwar years.

There is a well-known and justly admired axiom of diplomacy to the effect that the more signatories to an agreement the less binding it becomes, and Kellogg invoked this hoary truism against his antagonist in December 1927, proposing to Briand a multinational treaty renouncing war. There was enormous glee in the State Department. Kellogg's able assistant secretary of state, William R. Castle, who had been behind the widening of the original French proposal, wrote privately in his diary that the trick had been turned, that Briand was now out on a limb, that the foreign minister was caught with cold feet which were going to be positively frozen when the State Department drove him out into the open. As for Briand, the foreign minister after Kellogg's counterproposal made one maneuver after another to drop the whole business of an antiwar pact. Every time he suggested that a committee of jurists or a conference of foreign ministers examine Kellogg's counterproposal, the secretary of state refused to be taken in, and Briand became ever more embarrassed as his American opponent invited other states to adhere to the antiwar pact. It was getting, indeed, to be a public humiliation of the foreign minister of France. It was all that Briand could do to stand up against the perverse zeal of the Americans. Himself a possessor of the Nobel Prize for peace, which he had won earlier in the 1920s for the Treaty of Locarno among France, Britain, Italy, and Germany, he could not resist indefinitely the public pressure, in Europe as well as America, that he take a position for peace.

Finally, Secretary Kellogg became enamored of the new multinational proposal, originally conceived only to counter Briand, and began to believe that such a pledge against war by the nations of the world would help prevent future wars. After he placed within the proposed antiwar treaty enough reservations of self-defense and other matters to make the pact agreeable to prospective signatories, Kellogg was able to persuade the French foreign minister to bring the powers together in Paris for a ceremony of signature, which was done by the great powers—other nations acceding thereafter—on August 27, 1928.

The treaty contained two substantive articles: first, "The High Contracting Parties solemnly declare in the names of their respective peoples that they condemn recourse to war for the solution of international controversies, and renounce it as an instrument of national policy in their relations with one another"; second, "The High Contracting Parties agree that the settlement or solution of all disputes or conflicts of whatever nature or of whatever origin they may be, which may arise among them, shall never be sought except by pacific means."

Statesmen signed the Pact of Paris, as the Kellogg-Briand Pact was alternately called, with tongue in cheek, and the only discernible influence of this grand treaty was to inaugurate a fashion whereby wars would be fought under justification of self-defense and without formal declaration of hostilities. An American senator, during the debate over ratification of the treaty, said that it was an international kiss. Senator Carter Glass of Virginia announced to his colleagues that he intended to vote for the pact, "but I am not willing that anybody in Virginia shall think that I am simple enough to suppose that it is worth a postage stamp in the direction of accomplishing permanent peace." But the pact had large popular support and in the United States was politically irresistible. Many people believed that with it they had taken a large step in the direction of peaceful settlement of international disputes. Ever since the Senate and Woodrow Wilson had defeated the Treaty of Versailles, numerous Americans had felt sorry that their country had abandoned the world after the crusade of 1917–1918. To them it seemed that the heart of the world was broken when the United States stayed out of the League. They were willing to believe that a private American measure such as the Kellogg-Briand Pact, if coupled with arbitration and conciliation treaties and cooperation with the League in humanitarian tasks and the World Court, could indirectly redress the loss to the Geneva organization of American abstention from membership. In the year 1928 there was rejoicing that the United States, once more, had puts its weight in the scales for righteousness. Few Americans understood the politique

A gathering of the signatories of the Kellogg-Briand Pact: Kellogg is in the center foreground, his arm clasped by French Premier Doumergue, looking at Briand who holds his hands behind his back.

that lay behind the Kellogg-Briand Pact. If they had they would have been sorely disappointed.

3. *Another Alternative to the League—Disarmament*

The Kellogg-Briand Pact and the bilateral arbitration and conciliation treaties were the American substitutes for the League. In addition the State Department relied on treaties of disarmament, or as the term came to mean, limitation of armament. The idea flourished after the First World War that large armaments had caused the war, and that if the nations of the world would limit their weapons, peace would follow. Disarmament gained support not merely from the American people but from their political leaders, most of whom after 1918 were sincerely anxious for the United States to set Europe an example of arms limitation. The United States's influence for disarmament lay chiefly, one should add, in naval arms, for the American postwar military establishment was weak in land armaments.

The immediate problem in naval disarmament at the end of the First World War was that, of the three major naval powers, Great Britain, the United States, and Japan, the latter two were threatening a naval race. This postwar rivalry presented serious questions for all three powers, but especially for the Japanese. Japan, despite a strengthening of its economic position during the war, could not continue a naval competition over an indefinite period of time, for by 1921 one-third of the Japanese budget was going into naval construction and maintenance. Moreover, other factors did not favor Japan. To be sure, Japan during the world war had destroyed the balance of power in the Far East, but with the armistice of 1918 the balance in Europe had also been destroyed, to the disadvantage of Japan. France and Great Britain could redistribute their sea power to distant parts of the world and were better able to defend their territories and interests in the Far East than at any time since the rise of the German navy at the turn of the century. At the end of the war, the main American battle fleet was transferred to the Pacific, the base at Pearl Harbor was developed, and there was talk of bases in the Philippines and Guam to match Britain's base at Singapore. Should Britain and the United States achieve between themselves an entente, a working relationship of their navies, there was danger of Japanese isolation. For Japan, a conference on limitation of naval arms had its attractions. It was shrewd diplomacy for Japan to begin a retreat before compulsion changed it into a rout.

For the Americans and British it was equally obvious that a naval conference might be convenient. Although there was a considerable rivalry between the high commands of the American and British navies—a feeling on each side that the other navy was too large—and although there was talk at the end of the world war of an Anglo-American naval race, still neither Congress nor Parliament would have voted appropriations for such a contest. The British government was hard pressed for money after the world war and could never have survived an expensive arms race with the United States. As for the American navy, it had emerged from the war almost as large as the British, and the high command of the American navy was all set to resume the postponed building stipulated in the naval act of 1916, but Congress by 1921 was in a balky mood and let it be known that no money for such a purpose would be forthcoming. Cooperation, not antagonism, was the obvious course for the two English-speaking nations. It was common sense that the British and American navies undertake a mutual limitation in a diplomatic conference. And by cooperating in naval policies, the two powers would be able to present a unified front to the Japanese.

In the United States, before the end of Wilson's second administration, Senator Borah was trumpeting for a conference. The Harding administration, wishing to head off the British, who were about to propose a meeting, offered on July 11, 1921, to organize a conference in Washington. The intention was to deal with both sea and land armaments, but the conference after coming together devoted itself to naval arms.

Representatives of nine invited nations met in Washington on November 11, 1921, to observe formally the third anniversary of the armistice. The following day they held their first plenary session. In addition to delegations from the United States, Britain, and Japan there were representatives of the lesser naval powers, France and Italy, and because it was impossible to deal with Japanese armaments without considering problems of the Far East, China obtained an invitation to the meeting, as did also Portugal (because of Macao), the Netherlands (the East Indies), and Belgium (interests in Chinese railways, and a concession at Tientsin). President Harding gave a stirring address, and then came the surprise of the occasion: the permanent chairman of the conference, Secretary of State Hughes, in what seemed an ordinary speech of greeting, declared suddenly that "the way to disarm is to disarm." In regard to the possibility of an armaments race Hughes said, "There is only one adequate way out and that is to end it now." He thereupon offered some devastatingly concrete suggestions.

Consternation reigned in the hall. According to the journalist Mark Sullivan, when the secretary made his enumeration of British ships to be sunk, Admiral Lord David Beatty "came forward in his chair with the manner of a bulldog, sleeping on a sunny doorstep, who has been poked in the stomach by the impudent foot of an itinerant soap-canvasser seriously lacking in any sense of the most ordinary proprieties or considerations of personal safety." All the official documents in the world, Sullivan later wrote, "can't convey as much essential fact to the distant and future reader as did the look on Admiral Beatty's face to the historian who had the advantage of being in the room when Mr. Hughes, in that sensational opening speech of his, said that he would expect the British to scrap their four great *Hoods*, and made equally irreverent mention of the *King George the Fifth*."

During the following days some American naval officers went about saying, half humorously, in a paraphrase of an old Latin *morituri salutamus*, "We who are about to be abolished salute you."

Hughes's proposals for limitation of naval armaments, considered revolutionary at the time, were in actual fact rough approximations of then existing naval strengths, although (as he made so plain in his speech) it would be necessary for the powers to scuttle some craft to achieve his proposed figures. What he had proposed amounted in tonnage to what a newspaperman happily described as a scale of 5-5-3-1.67-1.67. After adjustment to be completed in the year 1942, Britain and the United States would have parity at 5 (a battleship tonnage of 525,000, aircraft carriers 135,000), Japan a ratio of 3 (battleships 272,000; carriers 81,000), and Italy and France 1.67 (175,000; 60,000). Although for the three largest naval powers these figures were based roughly on existing naval strength, ships built and building, for France and Italy the ratio was an arbitrary figure. Neither of the latter nations had embarked upon a postwar battleship program, but it was essential to assign them a ratio because Britain was insisting upon a two-power standard against continental navies—the British fleet must equal the combined strength of the two largest continental navies—and would have refused otherwise to accept a ratio with Japan and the United States.

After the initial confusion and protests, the major conferees accepted these figures. French pique at a ratio equal only to Italy's made it impossible for Hughes to extend limitation beyond the categories of battleships and aircraft carriers (the latter were limited because the powers might otherwise have converted their excess battleships into carriers).

Limitation of armaments was the major but not the sole task of the Washington Conference, for in the work of persuading the Japanese to accept a battleship and carrier ratio inferior to Britain's and the United States's, the conference made several political arrangements in the Far East. Japan consented to refrain from further fortification and construction of naval bases in some of the island groups—the Kuriles, Bonins, Ryukyus, Pescadores, also Formosa and Amami-Oshima—and in return Britain and America agreed not to construct additional fortifications or bases in their possessions east and north of Singapore and west of Hawaii. The result was to expose Hong Kong and the Philippines in event of future war. One must add, however, that Japan's possession of the Marianas, Marshalls, and Carolines, taken from Germany during the world war, virtually precluded a successful defense of the Philippines, and Secretary Hughes at the Washington Conference was giving away only what had already been lost. Hong Kong, of course, was from the beginning indefensible. The agreement was binding until December 31, 1936, subject thereafter to termination upon two years' notice. It was believed that the Japanese, so long as they had an inferior naval ratio, could safely be allowed mastery of the far Pacific, and the peaceful behavior of Tokyo governments for the remainder of the 1920s seemed to confirm the wisdom of this decision. The Washington Conference in effect partitioned the world among the three naval powers: Japan dominated the Far Eastern seas, the United States the Western Hemisphere, and Britain from the North Sea eastward to Singapore. The naval treaty as concluded on February 6, 1922, became known as the Five-Power Treaty.

A Four-Power Treaty signed on December 13, 1921, had as its purpose the abrogation of the Anglo-Japanese Alliance of 1902, which had been periodically renewed until 1921. In the renewal of 1911 the Japanese government had suggested that the treaty be inapplicable against any nation with which either ally had a general treaty of arbitration. When the Senate loaded down with reservations the Anglo-American arbitration treaty negotiated in the administration of President Taft, the British government had a private understanding with the Japanese that under no circumstances could the alliance be invoked against the United States. After the world war, and in view of the possibility of a Japanese-American naval race, the British in 1920 announced publicly that the Anglo-Japanese Alliance would not apply in the event of hostilities, but Prime Minister Arthur Meighen of Canada became worried and at an imperial conference in the summer of 1921 demanded—against opposition of his colleagues from Australia and New Zealand, who feared an ostracized, vengeful Japan—that the mother country abrogate the Japanese Alliance. The Four-Power Treaty proved the vehicle for this task.

Ostensibly the treaty extended responsibility for keeping peace in the Far East to the United States and France, in addition to Japan and Britain, but the pact contained only (1) a pledge to respect each other's "rights in relation to their insular possessions and insular dominions in the region of the Pacific Ocean"; (2) a promise that in any controversy (excluding matters of domestic jurisdiction) between the signatories pertaining to the Pacific Ocean, not settled by diplomacy, the disputants would invite the other members to a conference; (3) an agreement for consultation in event a nonsignatory should threaten the rights of the parties; (4) specific abrogation of the Anglo-Japanese Alliance. Shortly after the Washington Conference, Elihu Root stated the effect of the pact when he declared, "I doubt if any formal treaty ever accomplished so much by doing so little."

The United States during the conference was able to obtain a Nine-Power Treaty, a pledge by all the conferees at Washington to respect the principle of the open door in the Far East and to refrain from using the unsettled situation in China to advance their special interests at the expense of nationals of other countries. The former promise, reaffirming the open door, strengthened the individual pledges given to Secretary of State Hay in 1899. The promise to refrain from exploiting the unsettled situation in China restated the second open-door note of 1900. This latter promise had been a secret protocol to the Lansing-Ishii Agreement of 1917, and its inclusion in the Nine-Power Treaty was followed a year later on April 14, 1923, by cancellation of the 1917 agreement.

There were three other Far Eastern arrangements at Washington. The attention which the Senate had given to Shantung during the debate over the Versailles Treaty indicated that this question would have to be solved before any treaty for naval limitation could be ratified, and the Japanese delegates at Washington in separate negotiation with representatives of China, with Secretary Hughes and Lord Balfour serving as impartial observers, agreed upon evacuation of troops from the Shantung peninsula and return of Chinese sovereignty and customs control, subject to retention by Japan of important economic concessions. The second arrangement by Japan at Washington had to do with the Pacific island of Yap, where cable rights were granted the United States. Third, the Japanese promised an early end to their occupancy of parts of Russian Siberia and the northern half of the island of Sakhalin. Siberia was evacuated in 1922, northern Sakhalin in 1925.

Japan thus was the principal loser at Washington. This humiliation, preceded by refusal of the Paris Peace Conference to grant the principle of racial equality, followed in 1924 by the United States's complete barring of Japanese immigration, badly hurt Japanese pride, serving to create a situation where not too many years later the Japanese would use mercilessly a deteriorating political situation in Europe to expand their power in Asia.

To the American people the Washington Conference of 1921–1922 appeared only as a triumph for peace. The Senate approved the naval treaty with a single dissenting vote—President Harding had profited from one of Wilson's most egregious errors at the Paris conference and appointed to the American delegation to the Washington Conference two senators, including Henry Cabot Lodge. There had been fear before the conference that the United States by engaging in a naval race would be acting the role of a militarist nation, not unlike imperial Germany under the kaiser and Admiral von Tirpitz. Instead the American government reaffirmed one of the doctrines of Mahan, that Anglo-American cooperation was the foundation of world order, and that policies antagonistic to Britain were the height of folly. It is noteworthy that the United States was willing to limit its naval armaments without attempting to solve the many questions of neutral rights which had so recently embroiled relations between Washington and London. The decisions of the Washington Conference much impressed the peoples of Britain and the United States, creating the somewhat questionable faith that great powers could confer successfully over their vital interests—that the conference method was one of the best ways of diplomacy. Moreover, many Americans came to believe that their country could most effectively make its contribution toward world peace by actions taken outside the League. The Republican Party announced modestly in its platform of 1924 that the Washington Treaty was "the greatest peace document ever drawn." Probably the conference was a success when one considers that battleships had a reduced part in the Second World War. A limit on their construction did not detract from the safety of the Allied nations.

The Washington Conference was not, of course, the end of naval rivalry among the great powers. A naval race developed after 1922 in the smaller categories of warships. From this cruiser race between Britain and Japan the United States abstained for several years, and early in 1927, President Coolidge called a new disarmament conference to discuss the competition. At a meeting which began in Geneva on June 20, 1927, and ended on August 4, there were representatives of Britain, the United States, and Japan. France and Italy did not attend, the French from pique because of the parity granted between them and Italy at the Washington Conference, the Italians because the French would not attend. The Geneva Conference of 1927 was a fiasco, for neither the British nor the Japanese were willing at that time to halt their cruiser race. The efforts of the Coolidge administration were embarrassing, for diplomatic rumors were set on foot in European capitals that President Coolidge had made "insufficient preparation" for the conference, which was equal to saying that Coolidge was an ignoramus in international affairs. In retaliation Congress in early 1929 passed an appropriation for fifteen heavy cruisers (10,000 tons, 8-inch guns) and an aircraft carrier.

Here was the sort of language which nations understood, and after inauguration of President Herbert Hoover there were explorations by his ambassador to London, Charles G. Dawes, and the new British prime minister, Ramsay MacDonald. Hoover invited MacDonald to visit the United States, the visit in October 1929 proved a success, and the London Naval Conference assembled on January 21, 1930.

The London Conference addressed itself to limitation of naval categories not undertaken at the Washington Conference, and the result of a three-month deliberation was a limit on cruisers, submarines, and destroyers. There were no political questions on the agenda, such as had figured so prominently at Washington. The Japanese delegation nominally accepted a ratio of 3 in the lesser naval categories as compared with 5 for Britain and the United States, but Japan achieved parity for submarines and destroyers and virtual parity, through an involved provision, in heavy cruisers—at least until December 31, 1936, by which time the entire naval question was to be re-examined. The London Treaty was a three-power engagement, although France and Italy signed the document with the other powers on April 22, 1930. The two European nations pledged themselves to negotiate their differences, but after two years they gave up in disagreement.

With the London Conference the question of disarmament virtually ceased to have meaning for European and American diplomacy. Two further conferences were held—the League-sponsored General Disarmament Conference which met on February 2, 1932, at Geneva, and a second London Naval Conference which convened in 1935—but neither achieved any results. Although the conference at Geneva opened with several weeks of enthusiastic speeches, when the fifty-nine nations set to work there was no agreement. The conference enjoyed spurts of activity when various of the great-power delegations proposed limitation schemes. President Hoover on June 22, 1932, suggested an across-the-board reduction of one-third of all arms, but this idea died when seconded by Germany, the disarmed nation. German rearmament under Hitler ended the conference, which in 1934 adjourned "temporarily," never to meet again. As for the second London Conference, commencing in December 1935, it came to grief on the demands of the Japanese delegation for complete parity with Britain and the United States, but in the background was the increasing strength of the German navy. The signatories therefore invoked the so-called "escalator clause" of the London Treaty of 1930, by which signatories were released from their commitments when a nonsignatory threatened their national safety. The grand campaign for peace through disarmament, begun in 1921 with much hope and some minor achievement, disappeared in another naval race which terminated in war in 1939–1941.

Disarmament, the principal American alternative to membership in the League of Nations, hence proved of little value. So also did the other alternatives—the Kellogg, Root, and Bryan treaties, and the Kellogg-Briand Pact. The United States did little for the broad problems of world peace by supporting the noncontroversial health and other humanitarian activities of the League.

Even so, it is doubtful if American membership in the League of Nations could have halted the drift toward a second world war. Most of the European nations were themselves unwilling to enforce peace after the armistice of 1918. France and its friends, especially Czechoslovakia under the inspiration of the Czech statesman Eduard Beneš, would have made of article 10 of the Covenant an ironclad guarantee against aggressors if they could have gained enough support for such a course, but this they were never able to do, because of the stand against enforcement of peace taken by Great Britain and the Dominions and the former neutral nations during the war—the Baltic countries and others.

As for any American initiative and success in the direction of enforcing peace (if the United States had joined the League), such would have been hardly imaginable. By the first anniversary of the armistice, the buoyant enthusiasm of the American people for making peace and justice prevail throughout the world, the enthusiasm which had carried the nation to victory in 1918, had begun to fasten itself to the almost hopeless ideas which dealt with world peace in terms of law rather than force, which offered the possibility of peace everywhere by signature rather than by continuing and ardent labor. Thereafter it was impossible to make Americans realize that a foreign policy had to be backed by military force rather than words. They wished to remain aloof from troubles outside the Western Hemisphere, and convinced themselves that they could do so by formulas.

The American people, one must conclude, had been improperly schooled for their sudden participation in the First World War. Having remained for nearly a century on the fringes of world international affairs—their last passing acquaintance being the overemphasized dangers of European intervention at the time of the Monroe Doctrine—they had forgotten the hard ways of international politics and, during the fighting of 1917–1918, had allowed their idealism such free rein that they were not mentally prepared for the rigors of peacemaking which followed. The disappointments of the Paris Peace Conference combined with the traditionally isolationist beliefs of the American people had helped the defeat of the Covenant and peace treaty in the Senate. From then on American diplomats did their best to assist the cause of peace without exciting the isolationist sentiments of their fellow citizens. It was an impossible task. The greatest nation in the world could not remain apart from the main international current of the time. Its interests were too scattered geographically and too numerous not to become entangled in those of other nations. The international education of the American people, which had virtually ceased in the 1920s, was further neglected in the dangerous years after 1933, until it began once more with startling suddenness on December 7, 1941.

ADDITIONAL READING

The best introduction to diplomacy of the 1920s is Warren I. Cohen, *Empire without Tears* (New York, 1986). See also Allan Nevins, *The United States in a Chaotic World* (New Haven, Conn., 1950), a volume in the Chronicles of America series; Selig Adler, *The Isolationist Impulse* (New York, 1957), and the same author's *The Uncertain Giant* (New York, 1965), in the American

Diplomatic History series. A recent book by Frank Costigliola, *Awkward Dominion* (Ithaca, N.Y., 1984), deals with European relations. For "atmosphere" in the United States see Frederick Lewis Allen, *Only Yesterday* (New York, 1931).

Reparations appear briefly in Herbert Feis, *The Diplomacy of the Dollar* (Baltimore, 1950). Melvin P. Leffler, *The Elusive Quest* (Chapel Hill, N.C., 1979), considers the essence of European affairs, French security. Recent studies of international economics are by Carl P. Parrini, *Heir to Empire* (Pittsburgh, 1969); Joan Hoff-Wilson, *American Business and Foreign Policy* (Lexington, Ky., 1971); and Michael J. Hogan, *Informal Entente* (Columbia, Mo., 1977).

For the peace movement see John K. Nelson, *The Peace Prophets* (Chapel Hill, N.C., 1967); Charles Chatfield, *For Peace and Justice* (Knoxville, 1971); and Charles De Benedetti, *Origins of the Modern American Peace Movement* (Millwood, N.Y., 1978). The diplomacy of the Kellogg-Briand Pact appears in Robert H. Ferrell, *Peace in Their Time* (New Haven, Conn., 1952), and J. Chalmers Vinson, *William E. Borah and the Outlawry of War* (Athens, Ga., 1957).

Disarmament as an avenue of policy has inspired a large literature. The two principal books for the present era are Thomas H. Buckley, *The United States and the Washington Conference* (Knoxville, 1970), and Raymond G. O'Connor, *Perilous Equilibrium* (Lawrence, Kan., 1962), on the London Conference. See also Thaddeus V. Tuleja, *Statesmen and Admirals* (New York, 1963); Gerald E. Wheeler, *Prelude to Pearl Harbor* (Columbia, Mo., 1963), and the same author's *Admiral William Veazie Pratt, U.S. Navy* (Washington, D.C., 1974); Stephen E. Pelz, *Race to Pearl Harbor* (Cambridge, Mass., 1974); and Roger Dingman, *Power in the Pacific* (Chicago, 1976).

☆ 8 ☆

To Pearl Harbor

"My god! This can't be true! This must mean the Philippines."
"No, sir. This is Pearl."

—Conversation between Secretary of the Navy Frank Knox and Admiral Harold R. Stark, December 7, 1941

One feels a sense of tragedy in watching a great nation enter a world war. The course of American diplomacy in the years before December 7, 1941, is a somber, melancholy spectacle. American arms had brought victory to the Allies in the First World War, but afterward the United States threw away the advantages of the victory and sought to retire into the safe and sane nineteenth century when foreign relations were one of the least concerns of the successive administrations in Washington. For a while during the post-Versailles decades, it appeared that the new American withdrawal—it was never complete isolation, for the American substitutes for the League indicated concern for world peace—would prove as successful as had the policies, or lack of them, of the nineteenth century. Especially in the golden period of the later 1920s, the tide of world prosperity supported a hope of washing away everywhere the rancors and antagonisms of the First World War. Instead, the Great Depression washed away prosperity and with it the hopes of the 1920s. By the time the United States had recovered its poise and, no longer preoccupied with domestic concerns, could look about—by the later 1930s—the peace of the world was almost irreparably lost.

1. *Trouble in Manchuria, 1929–1933*

President Herbert Hoover and Secretary of State Henry L. Stimson directed American diplomacy in the years from 1929 to 1933, the most difficult years of the Great Depression. The president and his secretary were men of ability, yet different in temperament. Hoover believed in peace and disarmament. Stimson, a Long Island squire and ex-secretary of war under President Taft, was given to quick and not always careful judgments on international affairs and overestimated the martial ardor of the American electorate. One must say immediately, however, that Stimson, like his chief, Hoover, believed in the American postwar policies of disarmament and peaceful settlement, and despite occasional snap suggestions on foreign affairs, he almost always ended with the same views as the president. Under such leadership well-meaning caution was the key to American policy, foreign and domestic.

During the Hoover administration the first entanglement of American diplomacy, the first test of the American ways to world peace, came in the Far East in 1929, when China and Russia challenged the Kellogg-Briand Pact by threatening to go to war, and then actually going to war, over the Chinese Eastern Railway in Manchuria. Here was an inkling of trouble in the future, and it occurred, oddly enough, before the world had descended into the Great Depression and before the dictatorships during the economic troubles of the 1930s took on power and strength.

The source of the Sino-Russian dispute over the Chinese Eastern deserves a short explanation. Manchuria had been an issue between Russia and Japan ever since the Sino-Japanese War of 1894–1895, when at the end of that war the triple intervention led by Russia had forced Japan to disgorge territory in southern Manchuria which it had hoped to keep. Russia thereupon sought to take Manchuria for itself. After the Russo-Japanese War of 1904–1905, Manchuria was divided into Japanese and Russian spheres of influence, roughly along the lines of the two principal Manchurian railways, the South Manchuria and the Chinese Eastern. The two lines formed a sort of "T," the traverse being the CER and the stem the SMR.

Before the appearance of Chinese nationalism in Manchuria, the Russian and Japanese spheres bothered no one in the Far East or the capitals of Western nations. The United States halfheartedly consented to the Japanese sphere in Manchuria in the Root-Takahira agreement of 1908. But after the First World War, the American government at the Washington Conference obtained with considerable diplomatic skill a Japanese evacuation of the Shantung peninsula in central China, the peninsula dominating the approaches to Tientsin and Peking which had been taken from the Germans during the world war. This gave a new turn to the history of Far Eastern imperialism. The Chinese nationalists under Sun Yat-sen and Chiang Kai-shek foolishly believed that the Western powers would look with approval and joy upon the abolition of spheres of interest and foreign possessions and extraterritoriality in all China, including Manchuria.

Pursuing this reasoning, the Chinese sought in 1929 to oust the Russians from the Chinese Eastern Railway and regain for China the Russian sphere of influence in northern Manchuria. Chinese politicians in Nanking reasoned that they should assert themselves first against the Russians, who were Communists and not respected by the powers of the West. General Chiang and his supporters also hoped to gain a victory in foreign affairs which would turn Chinese thoughts away from the difficult and still unsolved Chinese domestic problems.

The details of the Sino-Russian imbroglio over the Chinese Eastern in Manchuria during the summer and autumn of 1929 need not detain us. The Chinese acted first by expelling the Russians from management of the railway, and after violent expostulation the Soviet government beginning in August 1929 sent troops against the foolhardy Chinese and forced the Nanking regime to sue for peace. Unfortunately, after the initial seizure of the Chinese Eastern Railway by the Chinese, Secretary Stimson in Washington became excited and raised the subject of the Kellogg-Briand Pact with both China and Russia. Although the Nanking and Moscow governments promised to settle their dispute by peaceful means, the Russians in the autumn nonetheless invoked the right of self-defense and began a military campaign against the Chinese. The Kellogg-Briand Pact, which to many Americans was the very foundation of pacific international relations, looked (to use the expression of an American diplomat) like thirty cents. Stimson made still another mistake near the end of the affair, actually after the Chinese had sued for peace, when in a circular note in late November 1929 he admonished the belligerents to cease fighting. The note was communicated to the Soviet Russian government, unrecognized by the United States since the Bolshevik revolution of 1917, by the French ambassador in Moscow. The result was an insulting unofficial communication via the public press from the Russian vice commissar of foreign affairs, Maxim Litvinoff, who told Stimson to mind his own business.

Litvinoff in 1929 thus had his small moment of triumph against the well-meaning but inexperienced Stimson. The latter soon turned to other international matters than Manchuria, particularly disarmament, with which he would have to deal at the London Naval Conference of 1930 and the General Disarmament Conference in 1932. The secretary of state's first two years of office were in fact largely concerned with disarmament, being only momentarily interrupted by the diplomatic fiasco over Manchuria. Stimson, however, learned in 1929 that quick action in Far Eastern matters, even if confined to verbal admonitions, could lead to grave embarrassment. The Kellogg-Briand Pact after its initial invocation in 1929 never looked the same and proved useless when a much more important conflict broke out between the Chinese and Japanese in Manchuria, beginning with

a Sino-Japanese clash at Mukden on September 18, 1931. This conflict the Japanese liked to call the Manchurian incident; Stimson preferred, and rightly, to call it the Far Eastern crisis.

The crisis found part of its origin in the actions of the Chinese against the Russians in 1929. In their inept effort to seize Russian property in Manchuria, the Chinese managed to convince the Japanese that the South Manchuria Railway and all of Japan's other possessions in Manchuria, territorial and otherwise, which depended upon that railway, were endangered by the growing nationalism of the Chinese government. A second factor persuading Japan to move against China in Manchuria was the Great Depression, which struck with especial harshness in the Japanese islands, bringing misery to peasants and city workers. Among other difficulties for Japan, the bottom fell out of the silk market in the United States, and this catastrophe, combined with Chinese nationalist boycotts of Japanese cotton goods, meant a crisis in Japan's foreign trade, almost half of which was in cotton goods and silk with China and the United States. Manchuria, so it seemed, might provide under Japanese rule a safe area for Japan's trade, an area unaffected by foreign tariffs.

Added to these factors was increasing unrest in the Japanese army, a rebellious spirit among many of the younger officers. Until the decade of the 1920s, the Japanese officer corps was the preserve of the upper classes, who contributed the bulk of the higher-ranking officers. The army had always been a peasant army, and in the years after the First World War when democracy achieved a temporary popularity in Japan, the peasants began to rise into the officer corps, bringing into the army a new type of officer who was in reality half-educated—overly professional, ultrapatriotic, suspicious of Western ideas and intentions. These young officers, many of them old enough to know better, began in the latter 1920s to agitate and conspire against their elders, with vague ideas of overthrowing the government in Tokyo and establishing a "Showa restoration," a moral regeneration of Japan. Showa was the reign name of the Emperor Hirohito. The Meiji restoration of 1868 had rejuvenated the nation politically, they believed, by returning to the emperor the political powers usurped by the shoguns, and a Showa restoration would reform the nation's morals which had been debauched by the politicians. This was, to be sure, inexact historical reasoning, for the emperors in Japan have never enjoyed much real power, either in the early centuries before their domination by the shoguns or after the Meiji restoration. Still, the typical young officer believed in this restoration theory, and he had the courage of his ignorance. There was, one should add, a strong admixture of socialist thinking in this program of the young army officers. But after the Manchurian incident beginning on September 18, 1931, the older army officers gradually infiltrated the restoration movement of their younger confreres and in 1936 purged it of its socialist tendencies, leaving only its patriotism. This was a virulent residue. The younger officers eventually came back into control as their conservative superiors retired; the result was the attack on Pearl Harbor and a suicidal effort to achieve *Hakko Ichiu*, The Eight Corners of the Universe Under One Roof.

But to return to the incident of September 18, 1931, which inaugurated the Far Eastern crisis. That night, after alleging an explosion along the main line of the South Manchuria Railway a few miles north of Mukden and claiming that Chinese troops in the vicinity had sought to blow up the track of the South Manchuria Railway, the Japanese army in Manchuria, the so-called Kwantung Army, under leadership of its young officer elements, began occupying Manchuria. In a few days the Japanese spread out along the line of the SMR, and during the winter of 1931–1932 they audaciously took the Russian sphere of interest in Manchuria, the northern part of Manchuria

The Japanese take Manchuria, despite treaty pledges.

bordering the line of the Soviet-controlled Chinese Eastern Railway. Manchuria was set up as an "independent" puppet empire called Manchukuo with Kang Teh (the boy emperor of China deposed in 1912; also known by the names Hsuan T'ung and Henry Pu-yi) as "sovereign." In Russia the Soviet regime was so busy collectivizing the farms and forwarding the second five-year plan that it could only watch the Kwantung Army's movements in nervous fear, hoping that the Japanese would not invade Siberia (there was sentiment in Japan for such an excursion). By the spring of 1933, all Manchuria including the province of Jehol had fallen, and the government in Tokyo temporarily persuaded the army to follow a policy of relative moderation. For the next several years the Japanese government was an unsteady coalition of bureaucrats and army and navy officers. As time passed the bureaucrats of pacific inclination dropped out of the government, the navy grew more warlike as it observed the successes of totalitarianism in Europe during the years 1935–1939, and the army became supreme when in autumn of 1941 the fire-eating General Hideki (Razor Brain) Tojo, a sympathizer with the young officers, assumed the premiership.

The future did not stand revealed to American officials in Washington in September 1931, and President Hoover and Secretary Stimson spent the remainder of their time in office until March 1933, when the Manchurian affair came almost simultaneously to an end, attempting to halt Japan's aggression and if possible to persuade the Japanese to return the captured territory to China. On January 7, 1932, Secretary Stimson announced that the United States could not "admit the legality of any situation *de facto* nor does it intend to recognize any treaty or agreement . . . which may impair the treaty rights of the United States or its citizens in China, including those which relate to the sovereignty, the independence, or the territorial and administrative integrity of the Republic of China, nor to the international policy relative to China, commonly known as the open door policy; and that it does not intend to recognize any situation, treaty, or agreement which may be brought about by means contrary to the covenants and obligations of the Pact of Paris of August 27, 1928, to which Treaty both China and Japan, as well as the United States, are parties." The Stimson Doctrine had no effect on Japanese aggression, for it was later that same month that Japanese naval forces began an attack on the Chinese port of Shanghai; and Stimson on February 23, 1932, had to make a second statement of policy reinforcing his doctrine. Conceived in the form of a public letter to the chairman of the Senate foreign relations committee (Stimson felt that if he sent a note to Japan he would receive a caustic reply), the Borah Letter restated eloquently the American stand against Japanese aggression. The secretary hinted that if Japan persisted in attacking China, the United States might abrogate the Five-Power Naval Treaty of Washington. At the end of his letter to Borah, Stimson placed a noble statement of American purposes toward China which showed the essentially humanitarian instincts of American Far Eastern policy: "In the past our Government, as one of the leading powers on the Pacific Ocean, has rested its policy upon an abiding faith in the future of the people of China and upon the ultimate success in dealing with them of the principles of fair play, patience, and mutual goodwill."

Afterward Stimson regarded the Borah Letter as the most important state paper of his career, and it was an eloquent statement of Japan's wrongdoings and the American position toward them, but neither it nor the Stimson Doctrine deterred the Japanese. World public opinion, which Stimson hoped to stir, remained occupied by the increasingly acute economic problems of the Great Depression. Stimson proved himself a competent lawyer and made a most careful summation to the jury, but the jury was not listening.

This was the public mood, in the United States and elsewhere, when the League of Nations on October 1, 1932, released the Lytton Report on conditions in Manchuria. The League of Nations adopted the report with its recommendations, an autonomous Manchuria under Chinese sovereignty, on February 24, 1933, but it was too late by this time to do anything against Japan in Manchuria—and the League had never intended to, anyway. That same day, February 24, the first anniversary of publication of Stimson's letter to Senator Borah, the Japanese delegation at Geneva made a dramatic exit from the League. Japan announced permanent withdrawal from the League of Nations, taking as a souvenir the Pacific islands held under League mandate. The chief Japanese delegate at Geneva, Yosuke Matsuoka, told the League Assembly that as Christ had been crucified on the cross, so was Japan being crucified by the nations of the League. Privately Matsuoka explained that the powers had taught Japan the game of poker, but after they had acquired most of the chips they pronounced the game immoral and took up contract bridge.

This was the sad diplomatic end of the Manchurian affair. Hostilities in Manchuria petered out and were ended formally by the Tangku Truce of May 31, 1933. Japan kept its new conquest.

2. *The Diplomacy of the New Deal*

During the first and second administrations of President Franklin D. Roosevelt, the American people continued largely to live apart from the realities of international relations. The diplomacy of the United States from 1933 to 1939 relied no longer on disarmament and treaties of peaceful settlement, for by the time the Hoover administration went out of office it was fairly clear that those American alternatives to the League of Nations had proved ineffective. Even so, the only new Rooseveltian device for world peace, reciprocal trade agreements, was no more effective than the policies of FDR's Republican predecessors. Roosevelt had no opportunity, of course, to return the country to the policies of his illustrious Democratic predecessor, Woodrow Wilson. At no time after the spring of 1920, least of all in 1933 and after, had it been possible to take the United States into the League. The temper of American opinion would never have allowed it. The memory of the clever anti-League propaganda of Senator Lodge and the irreconcilables in 1919–1920 had solidified many ancient American prejudices, and an international body such as the League seemed to the average American citizen an impossible organization for his country to join. When William Randolph Hearst in February 1932 confronted the Democratic candidate for the presidency with the League issue, FDR came out flatly against membership. In the election of 1932 repeal of the eighteenth amendment was a far greater issue than any international matter.

But overreaching any issue of the 1932 campaign and dominating the policies of the first two Roosevelt administrations was the Great Depression, which had settled down over the country like an enormous blight. The depression, which lasted until 1941 and American entry into the Second World War, was the most calamitous domestic disaster in the history of the United States excluding only the Civil

War. Roosevelt came into office with a mandate to do something about the depression, and from the outset of the New Deal foreign affairs took a place subordinate to economic and social reform. No one who can remember the grim depression days will assert that Roosevelt had any choice about his program. He had to take care of the immediate problem, which was to get the economy off dead center, the condition he found it in on the morning of his inaugural when every bank in the country had closed. It does not help to say with the advantage of hindsight that for Roosevelt foreign affairs, the rapidly expanding power of totalitarian regimes throughout the world, should have been more important than domestic matters. Roosevelt had to do something about the depression.

The London Economic Conference (June 12–July 24, 1933), where the United States together with sixty-three other nations was represented, offered a typical example of the influence of the Great Depression on American foreign policy during the first two Roosevelt administrations. Here, when an international measure was suggested that might have undermined the president's domestic economic program, Roosevelt did not hesitate to withdraw all American support. Currency stabilization, the nations believed, would have a tonic effect on world trade, but such a measure President Roosevelt would not allow. When a proposal was sent to the president, he vetoed it in a sharp message to the American delegation at London on July 2, 1933. The president wished to depreciate the dollar, at least to its level in the 1920s, and depreciating it would be difficult if the dollar's value were tied to world exchange conditions and, hence, out of his control.

The administration soon showed something resembling contriteness for its behavior when in 1934 Secretary Hull announced a proposal to reduce tariff barriers all over the world. Hull's scheme was what he had hoped to offer at London the year before—tariff reciprocity.

Roosevelt, with what appears to have been mild enthusiasm, sponsored reciprocity tariff legislation in accord with the wishes of his secretary of state, and the Hull-Roosevelt Reciprocal Trade Agreements Act passed Congress and received the presidential signature on June 12, 1934. It permitted executive lowering of the tariff to an extent of 50 percent of any tariff schedule, providing that foreign nations would make similar adjustments in schedules in which the United States had an interest. Almost all concessions made would be extended automatically to other nations. The advantage of the Hull program was that tariffs could be adjusted without the express consent, on each schedule, of Congress, and hence adjustment could be made in the national interest and not that of some lobbyist.

As for the effects of the Hull-Roosevelt reciprocity program, they have been difficult to gauge. The rearmament of Europe and the coming of the Second World War and the perplexities of the postwar years obscured the results of American tariff reciprocity.

Another diplomatic act of the early New Deal period was recognition by the United States of the government of Soviet Russia. Because of the numerous outrages and horrors with which the Bolshevik Party had achieved and maintained power in Russia, and because the Communist government represented expropriation and anticapitalism and had repudiated the debts of the tsarist regime and the short-lived provisional republic of 1917, the American government had refused recognition during the 1920s. The Bolsheviks did not increase their popularity by the constant emission of crude revolutionary propaganda which kept American officials stubborn. Nonetheless many businessmen in the United States and liberal leaders who considered Communist Russia a social experiment rather than a dictatorship favored recognizing the Bolsheviks. This agitation grew in volume as the depression made businessmen sensitive to any, even remote, possibilities of foreign trade, and the result finally was diplomatic recognition.

There were some other and minor reasons for recognizing Communist Russia. For one, the increasing danger of a Japanese move against Russia in the Far East helped bring together the Soviet and American governments. Moreover, the American people had sickened of all the argument over recognition, pro and con, and remembered only that the now discredited Republican administrations of the 1920s had opposed relations with the Russians. Recognition of Soviet Russia by 1933 was a stale problem, tiresome and boring, and negotiations between Litvinoff, who had become Soviet commissar for foreign affairs, and President Roosevelt were completed with hardly a hitch. In a formal exchange of notes on the day of recognition, November 16, 1933, Litvinoff promised that his country would (1) abstain from propaganda in the United States, (2) extend religious freedom to American citizens in the Soviet Union and negotiate an agreement to guarantee fair trial to Americans accused of crime in Russia, and (3) reopen the question of outstanding claims of both governments.

A word remains about the neutrality acts of 1935, 1936, 1937, and 1939, which together with Secretary Hull's tariff-reciprocity agreements represented almost the sole discernible new moves by the United States toward the nations of Europe in the decade before the Second World War. A series of stark international events shook Europe to its foundations in the four years beginning with 1935. The first was the Italian conquest of Ethiopia, which began in 1935 and ended the next year. In 1936 came German reoccupation of the Rhineland, which made Germany militarily defensible against the French army by securing the approaches to the Rhine, and separated the French from their Czechoslovak allies. Occupation of the Rhineland broke down

France's post-1918 alliances with the nations of Eastern Europe—Czechoslovakia, Rumania, and Yugoslavia (the Little Entente). The year 1936 saw the beginning of the Spanish Civil War, a death struggle between liberals and conservatives in Spain. The liberals drew in the radicals, and the reactionaries joined the conservatives. Germany and Italy sent help to the Franco regime, Russia to the republicans. When peace came in 1939 it was a peace of exhaustion. The accession of General Francisco Franco to power in Spain, one should add, marked a sad deterioration in Western democratic fortunes, for the Spanish caudillo was a reactionary, opportunistic gentleman of the eighteenth century rather than the twentieth, who brought an intellectual, economic, and political blight to Spain during the years after the end of the civil war; during the Second World War the Allies had terribly difficult dealings with this Machiavel as he wavered between the German and Allied sides, waiting to see who would win the war. Meanwhile in March 1938, after rebuilding German military power, Hitler forced the *Anschluss* with Austria, and in September 1938 he took the Sudeten territory from Czechoslovakia after negotiations at Berchtesgaden, Godesberg, and Munich with the British prime minister Neville Chamberlain, the French premier Edouard Daladier, and the Italian dictator Mussolini. After having said in these conversations that the Sudetenland was his last demand, Hitler in March 1939 took most of the remainder of Czechoslovakia. Mussolini seized Albania in April. In midsummer the German Fuehrer precipitated the Danzig crisis with Poland, and on September 1, having waited until the crops had been harvested, he began the Second World War.

During these catastrophic four years of European history, the United States contented itself with enacting neutrality statutes. A special committee of the Senate headed by Gerald P. Nye of North Dakota had begun in 1934 to investigate profiteering in the United States during the First World War. The investigation lasted into 1936, and the Nye committee's voluminous testimony and exhibits helped condition the American people for staying neutral during Europe's new time of troubles. The Senate munitions investigating committee turned up little of a sensational nature, for it proved that many individuals had made sizable profits during the First World War, a conclusion which might have been evident without any investigation. Insofar as the committee showed that cooperation existed during the war between Wall Street banking firms (J.P. Morgan et al.), ammunition concerns (the "merchants of death"), and the Wilson administration, the American people in the mid-1930s became convinced that such cooperation was collusion, that sinister forces in 1917 had taken the nation into a war which it did not want. There would be no such nonsense again. In an act of Congress of August 31, 1935, hurried through both Houses just before the Italian attack in Ethiopia, the Roosevelt administration renounced some of the traditional rights of neutrals which had caused difficulty during the First World War, in the hope that the maritime troubles of that war which had led to American entry in 1917 would not repeat themselves in the Italian crisis. Mussolini had been making balcony speeches about Italy's destiny and gave the distinct impression that interference by anyone in the Ethiopian adventure would mean instant war. The Italian dictator believed what he said. According to the Neutrality Act of 1935, an avowedly temporary affair, the president after proclaiming the existence of a state of war had to prohibit all arms shipments to belligerents and could forbid American citizens to travel on belligerent vessels except at their own risk. Roosevelt signed the neutrality act reluctantly and remarked in irritation that it was calculated to "drag us into war instead of keeping us out." This was unlikely, but after passage of the act the president and the state department could no longer bargain with Mussolini and could make no effective protests against the Italian bully's attack on a small tribal African state, because in advance the United States had given up any possible trump cards such as sending supplies to the Ethiopians. The president managed to obtain from Congress a six-month limit on the arms embargo. He had hoped that Congress would permit him to use the embargo only against aggressor nations, but Congress refused.

In following years the United States revised and refined its neutrality laws. The act of February 29, 1936, forbade loans to belligerents. A joint resolution of Congress on January 6, 1937, embargoed shipments to the opposing forces in the Spanish Civil War (the act of 1935 had applied only to war between nations and not to civil wars). A new act of May 1, 1937, brought together the provisions of previous legislation and added some new stipulations: travel on belligerent vessels was now forbidden, rather than allowed at the risk of the traveler; the president was authorized to list commodities other than munitions which belligerents might purchase in the United States and transport abroad in their own ships (this "cash and carry" provision of the act of May 1, limited to two years, expired by the time the European war began in September 1939). The act of May 1937 did give the president some discretion, for a tricky wording permitted FDR to move only when he could "find" a war. It stipulated that "Whenever the President shall find that there exists a state of war between, or among, two or more foreign states, the President shall proclaim such fact. . . ." When in July 1937 another war broke out—this time in China between Japanese and Chinese troops near Peking, the beginning of the long conflict which closed in 1945—Roosevelt refused to invoke the neutrality legislation on the technical ground that he did not find a war. The Sino-Japanese War of 1937–1945, like the "Manchurian incident" of 1931–1933, was an undeclared war, such being the fashion of the 1930s to get around the inconvenient promises of the Kellogg-Briand Pact. On technical ground Roosevelt could claim to find no war in China, and this technicality served his purpose of making munitions available to the beleaguered Chinese.

Thus the neutrality acts by 1937 had begun to appear not always in the national interest of the United States. Their invocation in the new Far Eastern war would have assisted the aggressor, not the victim. After the Second World War broke out in Europe, Congress in November 1939 revised the neutrality laws, repealing the embargo on arms and ammunition and authorizing "cash and carry" exports of war material to belligerent powers. Because this late revision of the neutrality regulations assisted the belligerents who controlled the high seas, that is, Britain and France, opponents of changing the laws argued that Congress was committing an unneutral act, unfavorable to Germany. Actually the act of November 4, 1939, reasserted the right of the United States to sell munitions of war to any nation which had the shipping to come and get them. Neutrality according to international law had never meant that a nation had to even up its trade with opposing belligerent nations. In any event the argument over the Neutrality Act of 1939 became academic when the United States in following months unmistakably demonstrated its sympathy for the Allies with such moves as the Lend-Lease Act of 1941. By this time the neutrality acts had been proved futile. They played no part whatsoever in keeping the United States at peace.

Down to the fall of 1939, confusion and inaction characterized American policy. Many prominent Americans had only the slightest notion of the holocaust that was preparing in Europe. The dictatorships of the world had instituted a series of calamitous events: Ethiopia, the Rhineland, Spain, China, Austria, Czechoslovakia, Albania, Danzig. The British and French could take no more aggression. But to leading Americans the appalling degeneration of order in Europe seemed incomprehensible. Senator Borah in July 1939 declared that there would be no Second World War, and offered as authority his own private sources of information. When Hitler and Stalin on August 23, 1939, signed the Nazi-Soviet Pact, which gave Hitler a free hand in the West and was in a real sense the crucial diplomatic arrangement prior to outbreak of the war, the chairman of the House committee on foreign affairs, Representative Sol Bloom, called at the State Department and told a department officer that the crisis was not serious and that he had "doped out" why Hitler had come to terms with Russia: to give himself an asylum when he should ultimately be thrown out by the Germans. No other country, Bloom said, would accept him. At the height of the crisis in August 1939 there was little that American diplomats could do except await its end. The brilliant State Department career officer, Jay Pierrepont Moffat, wrote in his diary on August 26–27, 1939, "These last two days have given me the feeling of sitting in a house where somebody is dying upstairs. There is relatively little to do and yet the suspense continues unabated."

Headlines and radio flashes at the beginning of the Second World War on September 1, 1939—GERMAN PLANES ATTACK WARSAW, ENGLAND AND FRANCE MOBILIZE—found the country almost as bewildered as it had been a quarter of a century earlier, in August 1914.

3. *Lend-Lease and Its Aftermath*

When the war opened in September 1939 the Allies at once looked to American industry for assistance in building their supplies of war material. But Roosevelt had proclaimed American neutrality. Relations with the beleaguered European democracies did not change fundamentally until the spring of 1941, when Congress passed and the president signed the Lend-Lease Act.

The process of change began with the defeat and collapse of France during the German spring offensive of 1940, which prompted the president slowly into action. On September 2, 1940, in an executive agreement with the British government, Roosevelt traded fifty First World War destroyers in exchange for the right to 99-year leases on naval and air bases in Newfoundland, Bermuda, the Bahamas, Jamaica, St. Lucia, Trinidad, Antigua, and British Guiana. This he announced as "the most important action in the reinforcement of our national defense . . . since the Louisiana Purchase." It was hardly that; the bases were hardly needed, and the destroyers were old and nearly useless; but the trade did mark a show of support for Britain. Then on September 16, 1940, the Burke-Wadsworth Bill became law, providing for selective service, the first peacetime compulsory military-training program in American history.

With these measures behind him the president went before the country as a candidate for a third term in the White House, running against the liberal Republican Wendell Willkie. This campaign, one may say in retrospect, might have been used by both candidates—Willkie, like FDR, favored aid to the Allies—to educate the American people to the realities of international affairs. Unfortunately it was not. The presidential campaign of 1940 was a lost opportunity. Both candidates marred the campaign by a conscious trimming of foreign-policy issues. Willkie and FDR almost outdid each other in promising peace to the American electorate. It is true that the American people naively asked for, and were reassured by, such empty promises. It is also true that Willkie honestly, and despite the feverish injunctions of many of his political supporters, came out in favor of the Roosevelt administration's pro-Allied activities. Yet the rigors of electioneering finally drove Willkie into saying that "If you elect me president I will never send an American boy to fight in any European war." Not to be outdone, the president himself, at Boston on October 30, 1940, told American mothers, "I have said this before,

In a happy mood, President Roosevelt assures the nation that this country "is not going to war."

but I shall say it again and again and again: Your boys are not going to be sent into any foreign wars." At Buffalo on November 2 he said: "Your President says this country is not going to war." It was only a few months after the election campaign that American troops were en route to Greenland and Iceland; a little more than a year later the president had to take his promise back completely.

With the assurance of another four years of office, Roosevelt moved ahead in his plans for aid to Britain against Germany. In a fireside chat on December 29, 1940, he told the nation that it should become "the great arsenal of democracy." In his annual message to Congress on January 6, 1941, he enunciated the Four Freedoms—freedom of speech and expression, freedom of worship, freedom from want, freedom from fear. Then, having done all these things, having laid the moral and material basis of aid to Britain against the German tyranny, he turned to two new and pressing problems. British credit in the United States was running out, and the Johnson Act of 1934 prevented the floating of public loans. The requirements of British defense were so large that no private loans could possibly cover them. The president in his annual message of January 6, 1941, produced a new formula, "lend-lease." Then there was a second problem: a sudden increase in the effectiveness and rigor of German submarine warfare in the Atlantic made necessary some sort of naval protection for British ships transporting the American-made goods to England.

Lend-lease was the first major policy of assistance toward Great Britain adopted by the Roosevelt administration. It was a massive contribution to the defeat of Nazi Germany. Its inspiration lay in Britain's dire need, but more intimately it was a result of the increasing personal cordiality between the two leaders of Britain and the United States. Roosevelt had been corresponding with Winston Churchill since the beginning of the European war, and the delighted Churchill—who at the outbreak of the war was first lord of the admiralty—had replied over the mysterious signature of "Naval Person." Upon becoming prime minister in May 1940 he changed his signature to "Former Naval Person." Through the medium of this correspondence the two statesmen of the English-speaking peoples kept in contact, and the president was in a position to know quickly the difficulties of his British opposite.

It was in response to Britain's needs, so persuasively and personally represented by Churchill, that Roosevelt in January 1941 proposed to Congress the Lend-Lease Act: "H.R. 1776"—so an official of Congress had numbered the epoch-making bill when it came before the House of Representatives. According to its terms the president could "lease, lend, or otherwise dispose of," to any country whose defense was vital to the United States, arms and other equipment and supplies to an extent of an initial appropriation of $7,000,000,000. Fiscally the Lend-Lease Act made history for the size of its original appropriation, which was more than ninety times the amount of the national debt which Secretary of the Treasury Alexander Hamilton had refunded in 1790. By the end of the war the United States had appropriated for lend-lease more than $50,000,000,000, a gigantic sum which would have been incomprehensible to the nation's founding fathers. H.R. 1776 did not, to be sure, go through Congress without objection. There was a vociferous debate during the first three months of 1941 which for bitterness and passion has rarely been equaled in American history.

The reasons for the bitterness of the debate over lend-lease were not difficult to perceive. For one, it was clear that with the proposed Lend-Lease Act the Roosevelt administration was irreparably committing the United States to the Allied cause; from this act onward there could be no turning back. For another, the administration's opponents in Congress had been resisting the president's measures of help to Britain with the increasing conviction that such opposition was hopeless—and their despair translated itself easily into passionate outbursts on the floor of the Senate and House. For a third, there was much concern, part of it political but part of it utterly sincere, that the president, so recently re-elected to an unprecedented third term of office, was pushing his views too far in Congress and throughout the country, that he had an obedient congressional majority and was hoodwinking the people and moving steadily in the direction of a dictatorship. All this misgiving may seem nonsensical by hindsight, but many individuals in 1941 were agitated. Debate over lend-lease brought their feelings to the surface.

Probably the most outspoken accusation came from Senator Burton K. Wheeler, long an opponent of President Roosevelt, who in a remark which alluded to the Agricultural Adjustment Act of 1933 announced, "The lend-lease-give program is the New Deal's triple A foreign policy; it will plow under every fourth American boy." Roosevelt was outraged. He angrily denounced "those who talk about plowing under every fourth American child." He told his press conference that he regarded Senator Wheeler's remark as "the most untruthful, as the most dastardly, unpatriotic thing that has ever been said. Quote me on that. That really is the rottenest thing that has been said in public life in my generation."

Wheeler's crude metaphor was beyond question misplaced and inappropriate, and the president had reason to lose his temper. Nonetheless the administration did approach lend-lease, a momentous piece of legislation, in a not entirely candid way. Roosevelt, it has sometimes been said, was at his worst when moving indirectly, and in the case of lend-lease he came to the proposal's defense in a way which at the least might be described as inaccurate. He must have known that the measure would probably lead to war, and certainly that if it led to peace this end could come only after the United States for a long time had exposed itself to the danger of German retaliation while giving aid to the British. An administration official, Jesse Jones, said during the lend-lease debate, "We're in the war; at least we are nearly in it; we're preparing for it." This utterance FDR turned with the comment that lend-lease would be administered not as a war measure but, on the contrary, as a peace measure. Roosevelt denied that lend-lease contradicted the spirit, if not the terms, of the Neutrality Act of 1939.

"An Act to Promote the Defense of the United States" became law on March 11, 1941. As a direct result of the act, with its enormous supplying of aid to Britain against Nazi Germany, a virtual state of war broke out in the autumn of 1941 along the Atlantic seaways.

The approach of President Roosevelt to this undeclared war was, like his approach to lend-lease, indirect, and it is fair to say that the president's incapacity for direct action lent some color of untruthfulness to his words during the spring, summer, and autumn of 1941. Congress, not altogether certain of presidential intentions with lend-lease, had written into the act a statement as follows: "Nothing in this Act shall be construed to authorize or to permit the authorization of convoying by naval vessels of the United States. Nothing in this

Act shall be construed to authorize or to permit the authorization of the entry of any American vessel into a combat area in violation of section 3 of the Neutrality Act of 1939." The president denied for several months in 1941 that he had any intention of instituting convoys. Meanwhile he set on foot measures which in result if not in avowed purpose were equivalent to convoying. Soon American naval vessels were operating far out in the Atlantic "on neutrality patrol," flashing news of alien ships in uncoded messages that anyone could listen to.

The result was a series of untoward incidents. The first, probably the most important, was the attack by a German submarine on the United States destroyer *Greer*, off Iceland, on September 4. There followed a month later, on October 17, the torpedoing with severe damage of the destroyer *Kearny* by a German submarine west of Iceland, with the loss of eleven American lives. The tanker *Salinas* sank on October 30, 1941, and the destroyer *Reuben James* was torpedoed on the night of October 30, with the loss of 96 officers and men.

In the course of events in the Atlantic there remained a touch of high principle, produced by President Roosevelt and Prime Minister Churchill during their dramatic meeting in Placentia Bay off Newfoundland in mid-August 1941. It was during this meeting that they drew up the Atlantic Charter. The Charter of August 14, 1941, was not a signed document, only a press release, a statement of principles agreed to by the participants at the Placentia meeting, but its informal nature did not lessen its importance. A document analogous to the Fourteen Points, it set out what were to be American and to some extent British aims for the remainder of the war years. It later was written into the United Nations Declaration of January 1, 1942, and adopted by all the Allies against Nazi Germany. In this joint declaration Roosevelt and Churchill pledged that their countries sought no aggrandizement, territorial or other; second, "they desire to see no territorial changes that do not accord with the freely expressed wishes of the peoples concerned"; third, they announced the right of all peoples to choose their own form of government; fourth, "access, on equal terms, to the trade and to the raw materials of the world"; fifth, economic collaboration among nations; sixth, freedom from fear and want; seventh, all men had the right "to traverse the high seas and oceans without hindrance"; eighth, disarmament of aggressors and limitation of the arms of peace-loving people. The Charter admittedly was not as explicit as the Fourteen Points—it was in fact downright vague in some of its pronouncements—but it did declare in rounded terms the war aims of the American and British peoples. As the war progressed, Churchill came to see that some of the Charter's provisions were visionary, and during a dinner at Yalta in 1945 he pointedly told Roosevelt that the Charter was not "a law, but a star." The American president, however, took the Charter seriously, and Churchill and the other Allies were therefore persuaded to take it into account.

Thus the United States had come in the Atlantic, through principle and practice, to virtually a state of belligerency against Germany, although in spite of these unneutral actions there was still no declared war in the Atlantic between the two nations. For the moment it suited the German dictator's purposes that there be no declaration of war. Hitler apparently believed that with the attack upon Russia in June 1941, an attack which at its outset came within a hair's breadth of victory, he could ensure his domination of the continent of Europe—afterward, he would settle scores with both England and the United States.

4. *Pearl Harbor*

Ever since the Mukden incident of September 18, 1931, relations between Washington and Tokyo had been strained. For that matter, ever since the victory of Japan over Russia in 1904–1905 and the subsequent refusal of the Japanese to be houseboys for the open door, distrust had existed between the two Pacific nations, Japan and the United States, a distrust which on several occasions before 1931 had overcome the normal reticences of international discourse. At such moments as the segregation of Japanese school children in San Francisco schools in 1906, the Twenty-One Demands of 1915, and the exclusion of Japanese immigrants from the United States in the immigration act of 1924, Japanese anger at the American government rose to fever pitch. Long before the occupation of Manchuria, official relations between the two countries had become far from congenial.

The Manchurian affair initiated a precipitous decline in Japanese-American cordiality, and when in 1937 the Japanese army, having virtually taken over the civil government in Tokyo, went into China in a large way and began to seize China's main coastal cities and as much of the hinterland as could be easily held, relations between Japan and the United States sank lower and lower. The military operations of the so-called China incident were conducted on a ferocious scale. The Manchurian incident was marked by almost no atrocities by Japanese soldiers, but the China fighting in 1937 and thereafter was appallingly inhumane, perhaps as many as 100,000 Chinese soldiers and civilians being murdered in the sack of Nanking alone. In marked contrast to the doubted information about increasing Nazi brutalities in Europe, the American people quickly learned of this bloodletting in China, where the American missionary effort both Protestant and Catholic had for decades been large; the missionaries wrote home terrified letters about what was happening before their very eyes. President Roosevelt apparently believed at this time that public opinion was ready for some sort of positive policy. He proposed in a speech in Chicago on October 5, 1937, that there be an international quarantine of aggressors as the only means to preserve peace. He did not, it is true, pursue this policy at the Brussels Conference, held on November 3–24, 1937, by all the signatories (save Japan) of the Nine-Power Treaty. At Brussels, the United States, along with the other nations, took a weak position and the conference broke up in despair. Still, the president was beginning to think of action. When on December 12, 1937, Japanese planes sank the United States river gunboat *Panay*, with the loss of two American lives, the administration felt strong enough to demand from the Japanese government an immediate apology, reparations, and guarantee against further incidents. The Tokyo regime, hardened though it was, made no effort to defend the act of its fliers.

Relations continued to deteriorate after 1937. When the Second World War commenced in Europe in 1939, the Japanese awaited events until after the fall of France in the early summer of 1940; then the Tokyo government on September 27, 1940, signed a Tripartite Pact with Germany and Italy. High government officials in Washington at once began to worry lest the three fascist powers were now concerting their policies, and that, while Japan alone of the three aggressor nations had not yet entered the lists against the Western democracies, it would enter in due time, presumably the worst possible time for Britain and America.

What, in truth, was the purpose of the Tripartite Pact of 1940? Did it as good as tell the world that Japan intended a new move of expansion in the Far East at the expense of American interests and therefore was enlisting Germany in event of a head-on collision with the United States? If Japan expanded farther in the Far East and moved into territory other than China, it would be either (1) Siberia, or else (2) the much more attractive lands of the Dutch East Indies, French Indochina, British Malaya and Burma, perhaps Australia and New Zealand. It was axiomatic that the United States, while attempting to bolster England in the fight in Europe, could not allow Japan to knock down the British empire in Asia. An advance not into Siberia but into Southeast Asia, Australia, and New Zealand might well bring an American declaration of war. Even so, it was an error to construe the Tripartite Pact as aimed against the United States. Actually Germany in 1940 was seeking to enlist Japan in the forthcoming campaign against Soviet Russia, planned for the spring of 1941. The *Realpolitiker* in Berlin hoped that Japan would enter Siberia at the same time that the German army crossed the Russian borders in the west.

It was true, of course, that the Japanese were making up their minds to turn southward—but Allied diplomats in so reading the Tripartite Pact obtained the right conclusion from the wrong evidence.

The southward advance seemed necessary to the Japanese as the only solution of a crucial problem of military logistics. Japan's oil reserves were so small that they could not support a major and prolonged war. The Japanese depended upon imports from the United States for 80 percent of their oil. As the military planners in Tokyo saw it, they must take the oil of the Dutch East Indies. The strategists of the Japanese army and navy were resigned to the fact that the southward advance meant a war with the United States. Hence they planned to destroy at the outset the principal American military force in the Pacific, the American fleet based in Pearl Harbor in Hawaii. From such a blow, they hoped, the American navy would require months and perhaps years to recuperate. During that period, Japan could so expand through the Far East as to become impregnable to American counterattack. Then, the United States having become involved in the war in Europe, American political leaders would negotiate a peace with Tokyo and allow Japan to keep the new "co-prosperity sphere."

Such a scheme of conquest may today seem foolhardy and irresponsible in the extreme, and perhaps it was. One might ask how the Japanese military, who were not complete fools, could have sponsored it. The minds of men, one can only conclude, are always capable of self-delusion. As for the leaders of the Japanese army and navy, they were mostly men of narrow background and intensely professional experience, incapable of making the large appraisals and informed guesses which are the rudiments of statesmanship. Japan's military planning was never the careful plotting and analysis which was later attributed to it. The Japanese military leaders really did not know where they were going. Japanese aggression was a jerry-built structure which moved uncertainly forward, one event leading crazily to another. It is easy to see now that the plan of the young officer enthusiasts led by General Tojo was an immense gamble. It would have been better for Japan in 1940–1941 to have tried to get along with the United States. The Japanese military, unfortunately, were unable to see a middle way out of their predicament. They could not see that honorable peace was an acceptable alternative to capitulation or war. Typical of Japanese reasoning was the contention of an admiral at an imperial conference—that because of the vulnerability of the Japanese military machine to a cutting off of foreign oil imports, Japan was like a patient who was certain to die if you did nothing but might be saved by a dangerous operation.

The southward advance was chosen instead of Siberia. The German government learned with surprise in the early spring of 1941 that Japan was negotiating a nonaggression pact with Russia. Foreign Minister Yosuke Matsuoka signed the pact in Moscow on April 13 with Foreign Minister Vyacheslav M. Molotov. The Russians already were anticipating the German attack which came on their western border in June, and they were happy to secure their eastern flank in Manchuria against the Japanese. Japan likewise secured its northern flank, and its armies could pursue the cherished southward advance.

The first move came quickly. The Japanese announced on July 25, 1941, that together with the Vichy French government of Marshal Henri-Philippe Pétain (the Vichy government controlled that part of France unoccupied by the Germans) they were undertaking a joint protectorate of Indochina. There was no reason why Japan should protect Indochina, except that Japanese troops could thereby menace the Philippines. Access to the airport at Saigon, acquired several months before, had already brought the British bastion of Singapore within easy range of Japanese bombing planes.

Not to be outdone, President Roosevelt on July 26, 1941, issued an executive order freezing Japanese assets in the United States. This ended all trade, forcing even those Japanese ships in American ports to depart in ballast. Among other things the president's executive order cut off all exports of oil.

Back in the summer of 1940 the United States had begun to embargo some strategic materials to Japan—scrap iron, steel, and certain types of oil products—and in following months additional embargoes were placed until on January 27, 1941, Ambassador Joseph C. Grew in Tokyo warned, "There is a lot of talk around town to the effect that the Japanese, in case of a break with the United States, are planning to go all out in a surprise mass attack at Pearl Harbor." Actually this was the very time that Admiral Isoroku Yamamoto began planning the Pearl Harbor attack. When Grew's premonitions reached the United States, they were mulled over by the Office of Naval Intelligence, but ONI placed no credence in them. Between January and July 1941, much war material continued to go out from America to Japan. Only high-octane gasoline and aviation lubricating oil were openly forbidden in trade, and other types of petroleum products flowed in a stream across the Pacific to the Japanese army and navy. But on July 26 this trade came to a sudden end.

Both the United States and Japan began preparing for war. President Roosevelt in the summer of 1941 nationalized the Philippine forces and appointed the Philippine field marshal and former United States army chief of staff, Douglas MacArthur, as commanding general of army forces in the Far East. Meanwhile Japanese army planners drafted plans for major strikes against the Malay peninsula, the Philippines, and Pearl Harbor. Yet both nations needed time. The Japanese militarists needed a few months to train their carrier air groups to destroy the United States Pacific fleet, and America needed time for new naval construction and to reinforce the army in the Philippines.

There followed several months of last-minute diplomatic negotiations—which, let it be added, were sincere on both sides. On the American side President Roosevelt and Secretary of State Hull were anxious for peace if they could obtain it with honor. On the Japanese side the diplomats of the Tokyo government did not know what their military were up to. The Japanese ambassador in Washington, Admiral Kichisaburo Nomura, was an honorable man, a typical Japanese conservative, who knew that his poverty-striken country should not attempt to play the role of the frog which wanted to become a bull. Nomura with good reason was *persona grata* at the State Department. He knew nothing of the plans of the militarists in his homeland.

Nomura's superior, Premier Prince Fumimaro Konoye, was a well-meaning individual but of weak tendencies, a person known in Japan as a liberal, yet as premier in 1937 he had said that China should be "beaten to her knees." Konoye in 1941 was window dressing for the militarists, and in early September they impatiently gave him six weeks to reach a settlement with the United States. The terms: America would have to turn China over to Japan. With this impossible proposal as his only program, Konoye sought a Pacific conference with Roosevelt. But the latter, well advised by Secretary Hull, who suggested that the Japanese be invited to detail their program in advance of any meeting, refused to meet the Japanese premier. The six-week deadline came and passed. Konoye, forced to resign, gave way to a new premier, General Tojo, the Razor Brain, in whose keeping events now lay.

The crisis moved rapidly toward a showdown. Ambassador Grew in Tokyo did not know exactly what was going on in the councils of the militarists, but in a cable of November 3 he warned Secretary Hull that Japan might resort to war measures with "dramatic and dangerous suddenness." Perhaps he recalled that all of Japan's modern wars, in 1894, 1904, and 1914, had begun without formal declaration of hostilities. Nomura in Washington on November 5 received instructions that it was "absolutely necessary" to come to an agreement with the United States by November 25. A special ambassador, Saburo Kurusu, another man of good will, made a hurried flight from Japan to assist Nomura in these negotiations. On November 20, the two Japanese ambassadors made what they regarded as their "absolutely final proposal," a rather immodest request for resumption of oil exports and noninterference by the United States in Japan's China incident. Secretary Hull realized that granting these terms was impossible, given the rising American popular temper. Americans might permit trimming on European matters, but they would allow their government no compromises with the Asiatic Axis partner, Japan.

Secretary Hull escorts the Japanese ambassador, Nomura (L.), and the special ambassador, Kurusu (R.), to the White House.

The American people did not realize how close their country was to war, but it is doubtful if in 1941 they would have permitted a Munich in the Far East, even had they known the seriousness of affairs.

For a short time Washington officials did consider some sort of *modus vivendi*. Military preparations were in a perilous state—an army contingent was at sea near Guam, the marines were just pulling out of Shanghai where for years they had been protecting American commercial interests, and 21,000 troops were scheduled to sail from the United States for the Philippines on December 8. Secretary Hull prepared a three-month *modus vivendi*, which included some concessions on oil, and submitted it to representatives of China, Great Britain, Australia, and the Netherlands in Washington. The Chinese government violently opposed the idea. Winston Churchill described it as "thin diet for Chiang Kai-shek." And, in any event, a *modus vivendi* would have been unacceptable to the Japanese. Premier Tojo in Japan already had rejected any compromise along the lines of Hull's draft, and so when the State Department dropped the matter, nothing was lost.

Hull then presented the Japanese with a long document dated November 26, which among other requests asked the Japanese to get out of China. At the Tokyo war crimes trial after the end of the war, General Tojo admitted that the note of November 26 was little more than a restatement of the Nine-Power Treaty of Washington, to which Japan had been a party, but twenty years after the Washington Conference the Nine-Power Treaty was unacceptable to Japan's rulers. On December 1 a cabinet council met in the imperial presence in

Pearl Harbor.

Tokyo and ratified General Tojo's decision to make war on America, Great Britain, and the Netherlands. The Pearl Harbor striking force, which had already sailed, was notified that X-day was December 7. Nomura and Kurusu, unaware that the die had been cast, were instructed to present the Japanese reply to the November 26 proposal at 1:00 p.m. Washington time, December 7, which was twenty minutes before the striking hour at Pearl Harbor.

The intensely interesting details of the Pearl Harbor attack have been carefully described from both the Japanese and American sides in a number of books and essays easily available to serious readers. Briefly, the Japanese attack force of six carriers, escorted by two battleships and a full complement of cruisers, destroyers, and submarines, sailed undetected through high seas and fog. When the fleet changed course toward Hawaii, on the final lap of the voyage, one of the carriers hoisted to its masthead the identical flag which the revered Admiral Togo had displayed on his flagship before the battle of Tsushima Strait in 1905. It was a great moment in Japanese history when on Sunday morning, "the day that will live in infamy" (as President Roosevelt would describe it in his war message), the attacking Japanese planes roared over Pearl Harbor and found the battleship fleet exactly where it was expected, tied up to the mooring quays along the southeast shore of Ford Island.

The valor and heroism of the surprised and trapped seamen will long live in the annals of American naval warfare. More than 2,300 lives were lost that terrible Sunday morning. Eight battleships capsized or were otherwise put out of action. Fortunately for the United States, Admiral William F. Halsey was away with a carrier striking force on a special mission, and his precious ships escaped the disaster in the harbor. Fortunately too, the Japanese in their attack virtually ignored the installations and fuel tanks at Pearl Harbor, destruction of which would have presented grave logistic problems and perhaps forced a removal of the fleet's remaining ships to the American west coast. Still, the Japanese attack on Pearl Harbor, despite such miscalculations, was appallingly successful. American entry into the Second World War occurred after an unprecedented naval disaster.

ADDITIONAL READING

The Great Depression dominated diplomacy for a decade after 1929, and for general accounts see Robert H. Ferrell, *American Diplomacy in the Great Depression* (New Haven, Conn., 1957); Selig Adler, *The Uncertain Giant* (New York, 1965); Robert A. Divine, *The Reluctant Belligerent* (New York, 1965), in the America in Crisis series; John E. Wiltz, *From Isolation to War* (New York, 1968); Arnold A. Offner, *The Origins of the Second World War* (New York, 1975); and Robert Dallek, *Franklin D. Roosevelt and American Foreign Policy* (New York, 1979).

For the presidents consult Joan Hoff-Wilson, *Herbert Hoover* (Boston, 1975), the Library of American Biography series; Frank Freidel, *Franklin D. Roosevelt* (Boston, 1952–); Arthur M. Schlesinger, Jr., *The Age of Roosevelt* (Boston, 1957–); James M. Burns, *Roosevelt* (2 vols., New York, 1956–1970); William E. Leuchtenburg, *Franklin D. Roosevelt and the New Deal* (New York, 1963), in the New American Nation series; and Ted Morgan, *FDR* (New York, 1985). Also Julius W. Pratt, *Cordell Hull* (2 vols., New York, 1964), Volumes 12 and 13 in the American Secretaries of State and Their Diplomacy series.

For the Far Eastern crisis of 1931–1933 there is Armin Rappaport, *Henry L. Stimson and Japan* (Chicago, 1963); Waldo H. Heinrichs, *American Ambassador* (Boston, 1966), on Grew; and Justus D. Doenecke, *When the Wicked Rise* (Lewisburg, Penn., 1984).

For economics and diplomacy see Richard N. Kottman, *Reciprocity and the North Atlantic Triangle* (Ithaca, N.Y., 1968), and Dick Steward, *Trade and Hemisphere* (Columbus, Mo., 1975), the good neighbor policy.

On Russia see Robert K. Murray, *The Red Scare* (Minneapolis, 1955), after World War I; and Beatrice Farnsworth, *William C. Bullitt and the Soviet Union* (Bloomington, Ind., 1967).

Early diplomacy with the Hitler government appears in Arnold A. Offner, *American Appeasement* (Cambridge, Mass., 1969). For its subject see Richard P. Traina, *American Diplomacy and the Spanish Civil War* (Bloomington, Ind., 1968); also Douglas Little, *Malevolent Neutrality* (Ithaca, N.Y., 1985).

Neutrality is in William L. Langer and S. Everett Gleason, *The Challenge to Isolation: 1937–40* (New York, 1952); Robert A. Divine, *The Illusion of Neutrality* (Chicago, 1962); John E. Wiltz, *In Search of Peace* (Baton Rouge, 1963); Manfred Jonas, *Isolationism in America* (Ithaca, N.Y., 1966); Geoffrey S. Smith, *To Save a Nation* (New York, 1973), right-wing extremism with its totalitarian sympathies; Wayne C. Cole, *Charles A. Lindbergh and the Battle against American Intervention in World War II* (New York, 1974), and the same author's *Roosevelt and the Isolationists* (Lincoln, Nebr., 1983).

Gradually the United States extended help to the Allies, for which see the general account in the Langer and Gleason volume mentioned above, also their *The Undeclared War* (New York, 1953). Specific assistance is in Warren F. Kimball, *The Most Unsordid Act* (Baltimore, 1969), on lend-lease; Theodore Wilson, *The First Summit* (Boston, 1969), the Atlantic Charter conference; James R. Leutze, *Bargaining for Supremacy* (Chapel Hill, N.C., 1977), on Anglo-American naval cooperation; and Paul B. Ryan and Thomas A. Bailey, *Hitler vs. Roosevelt: Undeclared Naval War* (New York, 1979). Events in Europe are in John Lukacs, *The Last European War* (Garden City, N.Y., 1976).

American-Japanese relations are in Dorothy Borg, *The United States and the Far Eastern Crisis of 1933–1938* (Cambridge, Mass., 1964), and Jonathan G. Utley, *Going to War with Japan* (Knoxville, 1985). On Pearl Harbor see Samuel Eliot Morison, *The Rising Sun in the Pacific* (Boston, 1948), and Gordon W. Prange, *At Dawn We Slept* (New York, 1981). Research is now stressing the code problem: Roberta Wohlstetter, *Pearl Harbor* (Stanford, 1962); David Kahn, *The Codebreakers* (New York, 1968); Ronald Clark, *The Man Who Broke Purple* (Boston, 1977), on Colonel William F. Friedman. Also Ralph E. Weber, *United States Diplomatic Codes and Ciphers* (Chicago, 1978).

☆ 9 ☆

The Second World War

Russian entry will have a profound military effect in that almost certainly it will materially shorten the war and thus save American lives. . . . The concessions to Russia on Far Eastern matters which were made at Yalta are generally matters which are within the military power of Russia to obtain regardless of U.S. military action short of war.

—Henry L. Stimson to Joseph C. Grew, May 21, 1945

The two world wars of the twentieth century have been fought by coalitions, in 1914–1918 by the Triple Entente and Central Powers, and during 1939–1945 by the Axis powers and the Allies. In gathering and holding the several parts of the coalition, the diplomat was in both periods a truly important individual. In the Second World War, maintenance of the Allied coalition of the United States, Great Britain, and Russia required the exacting exercise of the art of diplomacy. There was no serious trouble in fusing the war efforts of America and Britain. After December 7, 1941, the hard-pressed British were eager to work with their new ally, the United States. Not that there never was dissension between the two English-speaking allies, for there was plenty, but in every large question no doubt ever existed that a compromise sooner or later could be made. Maintenance of the coalition with Russia was far more difficult. Sometimes relations trembled in the balance over arrangement of the smallest matter. Mutual trust was a perennial problem between the English-speaking nations and the Russians. Even in the period of extreme military hazard, the years 1941–1942, the Communist regime was sometimes difficult and uncooperative. Fortunately diplomacy managed to hold the coalition together to the end of the war.

Maintaining the coalition became the special business of conferences between the Allies. There were meetings between the British and the Americans, and between the British and the Russians. There were conferences of the Big Three: Teheran (November–December 1943); Yalta (February 1945); Potsdam (July–August 1945). These last conferences occupied an especially prominent place in operation of the Allied coalition. How much did the spectacular meetings of the Big Three accomplish? Was it not true that lower-level diplomacy, coupled with the exigencies of the war, took the coalition through to victory? Meetings of the leaders during the Second World War, it seems fair to say, if they accomplished little else, must have produced some bonhomie which helped carry forward the war effort. There doubtless were, moreover, a number of decisions of a delicate, highly political nature which were far easier to take during a face-to-face conference than through the toils of the lower-level conferences. Administratively there were problems difficult for subordinates to solve, and when issues became pointed and were of importance, a personal conference of leaders was an expeditious way of reaching decisions.

1. *The Time of Emergency*

The period of emergency in the conduct of the war was beyond doubt the years 1941–1942. In the summer of 1941, Germany had attacked Russia, and it was on December 4, 1941, that a German task force reached the gates of Moscow and momentarily breached the city's outer defenses. The exhausted German soldiers of the army group of Field Marshal von Kluge gazed off into the distance, for a day or two, and saw the towers of the Kremlin. At this moment of crisis, the Japanese government rushed precipitately into the war with a successful attack on the American fleet at Pearl Harbor.

During ensuing weeks and months, it often seemed that the Allies could not survive. To Americans, reading the wordy optimism of their newspapers, the full crisis was never quite evident, but to military planners in Washington there came during the winter and spring of 1942 a cold feeling of the imminence of defeat. The late official historian of the American army, Kent Roberts Greenfield, has written that the winter and spring of 1942 was a period of "terrific stress and anxiety." American experts gave the Russians little chance of survival. Nor did it seem that the Japanese were going to be stopped easily in the Pacific. Twenty years of Pacific diplomacy collapsed in the weeks after Pearl Harbor when the Japanese army and navy spread out to the island possessions of the United States, the Netherlands, and Great Britain, reaching southward toward an almost defenseless New Zealand and Australia.

Small wonder that when the American government arranged for a ceremony in Washington on January 1, 1942, at which representatives of the twenty-six Allied warring countries signed the United Nations Declaration, there was not much quibbling about any of the principles of the Atlantic Charter, which document had been included in toto in the declaration. The Russians adhered to the Charter with the reservation that "the practical application of these principles will necessarily adapt itself to the circumstances, needs, and historic peculiarities of particular countries." The American government did not question what measure of acceptance the Russians were offering. The military picture of the moment dominated all diplomatic considerations.

Throughout the year 1942 military necessity kept interallied dissension to a minimum, and if there was ever a time when coalition diplomacy proved relatively easy, this was it. The United States welcomed the Russians as allies, as had the British the previous summer. There was little skepticism in America's welcome to Russia. There was no undertone of opportunism such as characterized Churchill's private remark, "If Hitler invaded Hell, I would make at least a favorable reference to the Devil in the House of Commons." The hope in the United States, a hope which the circumstances of the moment would seem to have supported, was that under wartime pressure Russian patriotism had supplanted communism as the motive force of the government of the USSR. It seemed entirely possible that Russia would drop its Communist theories and return to traditional friendships in the West. The Soviets, for example, in 1943 announced dissolution of the Comintern, the international propaganda arm of the Communist Party which had caused so much strife in the 1920s and 1930s. This at the time seemed an act of signal importance—although unfortunately the Comintern would reappear in 1947 under the name of Cominform.

America's first year in the war, the time of peril, saw little Allied dissension, but it did mark some considerable American embarrassment vis-à-vis the Russians over the question of a second front in France. The Soviets wished to draw German divisions from the Russian front and pressed the issue of a second front in every possible way. It worried American planners, who knew that even if the United Nations cause could survive the trials of the first year of the coalition, at least another year would have to pass before the United States could marshal its resources and build its military power to a level where a large-scale second front in France—anything larger than a small bridgehead—was a possibility. Opinion swayed to and fro in the spring and early summer of 1942. It was embarrassing that the troops of the United States and Great Britain were not engaged in fighting the Germans at this crucial time, except for some British activity against General Erwin Rommel's mixed force of Italians and Germans in North Africa. Almost the full weight of German power was falling on Soviet Russia. American military planners wished ardently to make a move in 1942, to open a small bridgehead in France with Operation Sledgehammer and follow it the next year with the big drive, Operation Roundup. In May 1942 President Roosevelt, during a conversation with the Russian foreign minister Molotov, promised a second front within the year. Prime Minister Churchill in conferences with Roosevelt at Hyde Park and Washington (June 18–27) argued against a cross-channel attack that year, and in July the British flatly refused to support it. Roosevelt persisted in believing that an attack should be made somewhere, and out of the confusion, and the embarrassment of not providing the Russians with support, came the proposal of North Africa, Operation Torch.

The political situation in North Africa was such as to welcome an Allied invasion, so the British and Americans believed. Parts of North Africa were French protectorates, and one portion, Algeria, was an actual department of France. When the French had met defeat at the hands of the Germans in June 1940, they had reconstituted a feeble government at the southern French city of Vichy, and the Vichy regime had retained allegiance of the North African provinces of Tunis and Morocco and the department of Algeria. The Vichy government was headed by the aged Pétain, assisted by Admiral Jean François Darlan and Pierre Laval. It was in many ways a defeatist regime and seemed on occasion much too pro-German. Its political vulnerability provided the Western Allies, Britain and the United States, with an opportunity to occupy French North Africa. The Allies believed that the army and civil officers in this area would welcome British and American troops, and from North Africa the invasion of Europe might eventually be launched. In the event, this turned out to be a fond hope. The Allied landings in North Africa actually almost miscarried. In the invasion of November 1942, cooperation was obtained from the French only because Admiral Darlan happened to be in North Africa and was able to persuade the local French army commanders to welcome the Allies.

But to return to the subject of the North African invasion. This invasion, it should be remarked, was essentially a compromise move. Secretary of War Stimson argued vigorously with the president against the operation. Stimson believed that the North African invasion, decided upon in July 1942, delayed the eventual cross-channel attack for an entire year. Still, what could the Americans do in 1942 without cooperation from their British ally? The British had been fighting Hitler for three years and urged their superior wisdom in matters of strategy. Indeed, the then chief of the imperial general staff, Sir Alan Brooke, in memoirs published a dozen years after the war, argued that the Americans were strategic morons and that only through British and especially his own superior wisdom was disaster averted in 1942. Sir Alan had carefully championed Operation Torch, and told the Americans they could have Roundup in 1943, and that the North

African affair would be preliminary. The chief of staff of the American army, General George C. Marshall, and his naval opposite, Admiral Ernest J. King, predicted that North Africa's Operation Torch would kill Roundup, which it did. Sir Alan in his memoirs confessed that he intended it to do so. The North African affair was in truth a political decision, rather than a matter of strategy. Perhaps it had to be. President Roosevelt also was convinced that American troops had to become engaged somewhere, and the only feasible move—lacking support from the British for Sledgehammer—was Torch. General Marshall years after the war told the distinguished naval historian Samuel Eliot Morison that "the great lesson he learned in 1942 was this: in wartime the politicians have to do *something* important every year. They could not simply use 1942 to build up for 1943 or 1944; they could not face the obloquy of fighting another 'phony war.' The 'something' . . . was Operation Torch . . . ."

The difficulty over supporting the Russians in 1942 and the decision to go into North Africa raised in peculiarly sharp form a fundamental conflict in strategy between the British and Americans which was not adjourned for two years thereafter, namely, whether it was better to make a frontal invasion of the Continent via France, or to move northward into Europe from the Mediterranean via Italy and Yugoslavia. This issue had come to American attention for the first time during the conference between Roosevelt and Churchill at Placentia Bay in 1941, when American military planners accompanying the president were appalled at the gingerly nature of British strategy. By the year 1944, when American troops came to constitute a preponderance of the strength of the Western Allies, it was possible to insist on American strategy, and the Allies thereupon went into France. But the strategic argument of France versus the Balkans persisted throughout the war, and some postwar literary strategists have flayed the American frontal strategy in much the same manner as did Sir Alan Brooke in his memoirs. So perhaps this controversy is worth examination at this point.

The British view of proper Anglo-American strategy for the Second World War is not difficult to state. Churchill and the British government had devoutly desired the invasion of North Africa in 1942, albeit for reasoning different from that of the American president. Churchill had always in mind such military butcheries as Passchendaele and the Somme during the First World War, when hundreds of thousands of British soldiers died in a series of dreadful and futile offensives. Apropos of British reluctance to fight again on the Continent, Morison in a published lecture has recalled the simple inscription on a tablet erected by the British government in Nôtre Dame de Paris: "To the glory of God and to the memory of one million men of the British Empire who fell in the Great War, 1914–1918, and of whom the greater part rest in France." When General

Marshall, in England for staff conversations, was arguing vehemently for a cross-channel invasion of Europe, Lord Cherwell said to him, "It's no use—you are arguing against the casualties on the Somme." Churchill was not going to risk more such massacres simply because the Russians were crying for help and the Americans were eager to fight somewhere.

There were further reasons which may have prompted the British to oppose a cross-channel invasion. For one, British strategists and especially Churchill bore in mind the political purpose of the war—to defeat Hitler's Germany without bringing down the structure of Western civilization on the Continent. For this reason it appeared desirable to adopt toward Europe a strategy resembling that employed against Napoleon in the war of a century earlier, a strategy of beleaguerment, of probing at the periphery of the Continent, of feeling one's way cautiously, and perhaps moving through the Balkans and Central Europe to the Ruhr and Rhineland, North Germany and Berlin. Churchill may also have had in mind a campaign to open a route of supply to Russia through the Dardanelles and Bosporus, which if successful would have vindicated the ill-fated effort that he had sponsored during the First World War, an unsuccessful campaign that for years had clouded his political career. The British for such reasons as this elaborated their policy of cautious containment, a first step of which could be the taking of North African bases.

What can one conclude about this Anglo-American argument? Perhaps it is correct to say that Torch, the compromise of 1942, was a wise preliminary for the cross-channel invasion in 1944—that establishing a bridgehead in France in 1942 and a full-scale second front in 1943, as hoped for by General Marshall and Admiral King and President Roosevelt and Secretary Stimson and many other American leaders, would have been too dangerous, given the strength of German forces in France in those years, given Allied, especially American, inexperience in warfare, given the need for time to beat down the German submarine fleets in the Atlantic and time also to produce landing ships and tanks and the innumerable other requirements of land warfare on a vast scale. Some of the Mediterranean operations which followed the Torch landings, especially the Italian campaigning of the last year or so of the war, were strategically questionable, but the initial North African occupation did have justification pending the buildup of Allied strength to a point where the cherished cross-channel invasion was likely to succeed. It would have been a terrible blow to the Western Allies if in 1942 they had attempted Operation Sledgehammer, the proposed bridgehead operation, and been hurled off the Continent in a repetition of the British debacle at Dunkirk in 1940.

But is it not true that the cross-channel strategy which eventually prevailed in 1944 proved an unwise move from a political point of view, just as Churchill in 1942 had been sensing it would be? Did not the Allies lose Central Europe and the Balkans to the Russians because they chose the cross-channel attack in 1944, rather than an invasion up through Italy and the historic Ljubljana gap into Europe's (to use Churchill's phrase) "soft underbelly"? Actually there is little to be said for this argument, so frequently presented in the years after the Second World War. The compromise of 1942, the Torch operation, made sense at the moment, but by 1944, British strategy had become outmoded. Once the Allies had the requisite strength, there were many more advantages in an attack across France than up through Yugoslavia. It was fortunate that the Allies did not pursue the British peripheral strategy after 1943. Had they done so, it is possible that the American and British forces could have obtained control of Belgrade, Bucharest, Budapest, Prague, and Vienna, instead of those capitals passing to the Russians. But it is also possible, even probable, that an American-British advance through the Balkans and Central Europe might have bogged down in the difficult terrain of that region, with the consequence that the Russian armies, rolling across the North German plain, would have reached the Ruhr and Rhineland and passed on into the Low Countries and France—with results for the postwar political organization of the Continent which can readily be calculated. Even in its strictly political possibilities, not to speak of its military difficulty, British strategy was less effective than the opposing American strategy. It was far better to give Russia the Balkans and Central Europe rather than the Continent's vastly more valuable northern and western areas.

So Churchill's losing out on his peripheral strategy, after an initial success in 1942, was all for the best. He fought to the bitter end. At one point in 1943 he put up a terrific argument for a landing on the island of Rhodes and was still arguing after Roosevelt and Stalin at the Teheran Conference in November–December 1943 tried to dissuade him. At Algiers in January 1944, during an informal meeting with the Americans, he announced with full Churchillian rhetoric, holding onto the lapels of his coat as if making a speech in the House of Commons: "His Majesty's government cannot accept the consequences if we fail to make this operation against Rhodes!" General Marshall, present at the meeting, told the prime minister, "No American is going to land on that goddam island!"

2. *From Casablanca to Quebec*

With the year 1943, the tide of war turned in favor of the Allied coalition, and there could no longer be any serious cause for worry, after the victories of that year and the triumphs of the year that followed. The only question concerned the time necessary to defeat an enemy who was imaginative, brave, tenacious, even fanatical. By the beginning of 1943, the German and Italian troops in North Africa, numbering about 250,000, were falling into a hopeless position and would be forced to surrender on May 13, 1943. Meanwhile the beginning of a new phase of the war in Russia came with the German surrender at Stalingrad, February 2, 1943. This victory, in which twenty-two German divisions, including a galaxy of German generals, were made prisoners, was followed in the summer of 1943 by the complete failure on the Russian front of a German general offensive.

Although the crucial points in a conflict seldom become visible until after the fighting has ceased, it began to be evident in 1943 that a change for the better had come in the Pacific war as well. In the Pacific the United States first had suffered the disaster at Pearl Harbor; not too long after that had come the inevitable surrender in the Philippines, on May 6, 1942. But then in the summer of 1942 the first good news arrived from the Pacific: the Japanese were driven back from Midway on June 3–6, in a victory of naval aviation that forbade further Japanese advances. A year later, by mid-1943, United States forces in the Pacific were on the offensive everywhere.

When victory thus came into sight—and it was visible at the beginning of 1943—there appeared a need for a statement of Allied policy toward the enemy, some statement that would hold the coalition together until the end of the war. The squabbling over spoils that had broken so many coalitions must not occur. The embarrassment of not being able to provide a second front in France in either 1942 or 1943 must be relieved; there was the bare possibility that the Russians in disgust might make an arrangement with the Germans, as they had done under other circumstances in August 1939. With these purposes in mind, Roosevelt and Churchill, meeting in a conference at Casablanca, January 14–24, 1943, announced the doctrine of unconditional surrender.

At the time and later Roosevelt gave the impression that he had invented unconditional surrender, on the spur of the moment. The president, as Robert Sherwood has remarked, "often liked to picture himself as a rather frivolous fellow who did not give sufficient attention to the consequences of chance remarks," and so he made light of the calculation that went into his new doctrine, unconditional surrender. He had just managed to get two bickering French generals—Henri H. Giraud and Charles de Gaulle—to shake hands, and this, according to FDR's fanciful recollection, brought to mind a chain of ideas: "We had so much trouble getting those two French generals together that I thought to myself that this was as difficult as arranging the meeting of Grant and Lee—and then suddenly the press conference was on, and Winston and I had had no time to prepare for it, and the thought popped into my mind that they had called Grant

Roosevelt and Churchill at Casablanca.

'Old Unconditional Surrender' and the next thing I knew, I had said it."

The doctrine was premeditated, however, and was no off-the-cuff pronouncement. Roosevelt talked carefully from notes that day at Casablanca.

The new doctrine was singularly important for Allied diplomacy. Unconditional surrender, along with the policy of the Balkan versus cross-channel strategy, has stirred much debate among postwar analysts and writers. Was unconditional surrender a wise policy? Is not every surrender, by definition, a surrender on conditions? The diary of the Nazi propaganda minister, Josef Goebbels, reveals the joy with which that functionary presented to the German people the choice between fighting or groveling before the Allies. The Allied declaration of unconditional surrender appeared to him as a godsend, for it would, he thought, spark the German people to fight for an honorable peace. It proved what he had always told them, that surrender to the Allies could only be dishonorable. The military analyst of the *New York Times*, Hanson W. Baldwin, wrote that unconditional surrender was one of the blunders of American diplomacy during the war. It prolonged the war, Baldwin believed, and encouraged the Germans to fight to the last man, leaving for the Allies in 1945 a country which was the most complete shambles ever seen by conquering soldiers.

Elmer Davis, who conducted the Office of War Information and to whom in 1942–1945 fell much of the burden of explaining to the

American people the nation's wartime policy, has defended this policy of unconditional surrender. Davis argued that the policy served notice on our allies, in particular the Russians, that there would be no premature peace with Germany. Moreover, so Davis contended, "the unquestionably good effect of unconditional surrender—an effect which was its primary purpose," was upon the Germans themselves. It prevented them from telling again the story that they told after 1918, that they had not been defeated militarily in the field but had been stabbed in the back by civilian revolutionists in Berlin. To the argument that the policy of unconditional surrender left no responsible government in Germany with which the Allies could negotiate, Davis answered that there never was any chance for a government to arise with which the Allies could have negotiated. The Germans could not, certainly did not, unseat the Hitler regime. Their random wartime conspiracies against Hitler were heroic but naive affairs, easily put down by the Gestapo. Even the conspiracy to assassinate Hitler which miscarried on July 20, 1944, with such tragically terrible results for thousands of the conspirators and their relatives and friends, was an amateurish plot with little chance of success. To crush the regime required an absolute military defeat.

Certainly it was impossible to negotiate with the Hitler regime, which was the most bestial government known since the statistically clouded times of the medieval Huns and the fabled slaughters of the ancient Oriental satrapies. No negotiated peace was possible with the regime that had slaughtered literally millions of people, men and women and children, by machine guns and starvation camps and efficient gas ovens, giving to the world's languages a new word, *genocide*.

As it was inconceivable to negotiate with Hitler, it was difficult to negotiate with Stalin, to make deals with a man capable of and guilty of many murders, individual and group, such as the purge of the Kulaks, or the murder of thousands of Polish officers at Katyn Forest in 1940 and the refusal to cross the Vistula to rescue the Poles revolting within Warsaw in 1944. It was difficult for the United States and Britain to give in to the realities of the power and position of the Red Army and negotiate with Stalin.

But whatever the virtues—or defects—of unconditional surrender, it does not seem true that the doctrine, for perhaps twenty months after its enunciation in January 1943, held off the making of wartime commitments that would have prejudiced the postwar settlement. The principle of "no predetermination," a rather jawbreaking idea, was finally abandoned, and with questionable results, in a conference at Moscow on October 9–18, 1944, when Churchill and Stalin agreed to divide the Balkans into spheres of interest. According to one version—there has been no official confirmation of these figures—Russia was assigned a 75 / 25 or 80 / 20 preponderance in Bulgaria, Rumania, and Hungary, while in Yugoslavia the ratio was 50 / 50. It was agreed also that the Curzon Line, a roughly ethnographic line in Eastern Poland proposed as a boundary in 1919, would be the new postwar Polish boundary, and that Poland, having thereby lost territory to Russia in the east, would be given a western boundary along the Oder, obtaining compensation at the expense of Germany. The American government, not a party to these arrangements, let it be known that it would not be bound by them. It was American policy to refrain from division of spoils until the peace conference at the end of the war. Divisions of territory, so the United States maintained, were one of the prime methods of disrupting a coalition prior to the end of a war. The British government agreed with such reasoning in the period of emergency, the year 1942, but underwent a change of mind, if not of heart, when as victory approached it became evident that the Russians could make their own pleasure prevail in Eastern Europe, with or without agreement with the English-speaking Allies. Britain felt that an agreement might at least confirm British interests in Yugoslavia and especially in Greece (where, according to Churchill's memoirs, the ratio of Russian-British influence was to be 10 / 90, in favor of Britain). Perhaps Churchill thought it was better to anticipate the inevitable in Eastern Europe, with the hope of getting something in the process.

Having set forth the doctrine of unconditional surrender at Casablanca in January 1943, the leaders of the United States and Britain communicated it to the Russians, who for the moment accepted it. For the rest of the year the attention of the two English-speaking governments was occupied with the North African campaign, the seizure of Sicily (July 10–August 17), and the invasion of Italy (September 3). Forcing the retirement of Mussolini—who afterward escaped to North Italy and founded another Italian government under German sponsorship—the Allies began the slow movement up the boot of Italy toward Rome. They also prepared for the cross-channel invasion.

Throughout the year 1943, arguments over strategy raged between the British and American governments. The question again was whether to enter the Continent through the Balkans and Central Europe or by crossing the channel. This time the British, despite the tireless importunities of Churchill, lost to the Americans, who possessed more troops and equipment and were in a position to dictate strategy. By the end of the year there was no longer doubt as to the cross-channel operation. Planning it, however, required, in Western eyes, some coordination with the Russian front, and there followed the Teheran Conference, November 28–December 1, 1943.

Held at the capital of Iran, the conference was attended by Roosevelt, Churchill, and Stalin. It was the first three-power meeting on the highest level. The Russians promised at this conference to coor-

Stalin, Roosevelt, and Churchill at Teheran.

dinate their campaigns with the projected invasion of France. The conference also produced a plan for an international organization to keep the peace, an idea of the Americans which was accepted with some enthusiasm by the British and with less interest by the more skeptical Russians. Stalin at Teheran reiterated a promise made at the Moscow Conference of foreign ministers (October 19–30, 1943) to enter the war against Japan after hostilities ended in Europe.

Before going to Teheran, Roosevelt and Churchill had a meeting at Cairo with Generalissimo and Madame Chiang Kai-shek. The meeting was apart from the Teheran proceedings because the Russians had not yet entered the Far Eastern war and did not desire to antagonize the Japanese. At the Cairo Conference (November 22–26, 1943), the United States, Britain, and China promised to prosecute the war against Japan until the Japanese surrendered unconditionally. Japan was to be deprived of all Pacific islands acquired since 1914. Manchuria, Formosa, and other territories taken from China by Japan were to be restored to China. The three powers were "determined that in due course Korea shall become free and independent." At a second Cairo conference (December 4–6, 1943), the president and prime minister met the president of Turkey, Ismet Inönü, and received and gave pledges of support in the war against Germany—albeit without Turkish hostilities, not declared until February 23, 1945.

In concluding this account of the era when the coalition, having

Chiang Kai-shek, Roosevelt, Churchill, and Madame Chiang at Cairo, accompanied by their staffs.

passed through the emergency, stood in sight of victory, there remains the year 1944, a year of campaigning and heavy fighting. Diplomacy languished during 1944.

Churchill and Roosevelt did meet again in the late summer at Quebec (September 11–16, 1944), where the two leaders heard Secretary of the Treasury Henry Morgenthau offer a plan for postwar Germany. On September 15, 1944, the president and the prime minister initialed an abbreviated version of the Morgenthau Plan, under which Russia and other devastated countries could "remove the machinery they require" from Germany, the heavy industry of the Ruhr and Saar to be "put out of action and closed down" and these two German provinces placed under indefinite international control. The plan initialed at Quebec, phrased in Churchill's own words, included a much-quoted statement that the measures for the Ruhr and Saar "looked forward to" conversion of Germany into a country "primarily agricultural and pastoral in character." This was, beyond question, a silly proposition. Morgenthau's scheme ignored the fact that the German people could not live without the industrial complex erected in their country, the center of economic life on the Continent. Whatever the intentions of its author, the Morgenthau Plan was a starvation plan.

President Roosevelt rejected the proposal later that year, and Churchill eventually admitted that initialing it had been an error. Churchill seems to have been willing to accept the Morgenthau Plan tentatively because at the time he needed a large postwar American loan and the chief exponent of the plan was secretary of the treasury. When news of the scheme leaked out, it had an unfortunate effect in Germany, playing into the hands of Propaganda Minister Goebbels. Hitler in a New Year's message to the German people drew attention to what he described as a plot of the British, Americans, Bolsheviks, and "international Jews," which he said would result in the "complete ripping apart of the German Reich, the uprooting of 15 or 20 million Germans and transport abroad, the enslavement of the rest of our people, the ruination of our German youth, but, above all, the starvation of our masses."

In the years after the war, much was made in the United States of the fact that the Morgenthau Plan as originally drawn gave virtual control of Germany to Soviet Russia (the Russians along with other nations of the Continent were to control Germany), and that the plan had been worked out by Morgenthau's chief assistant at the treasury, Harry Dexter White, who after his death in the early postwar years was accused of Communist Party affiliations. No one, let it be added, has proved that the Morgenthau Plan was Soviet in origin. Perhaps one should simply remark, in conclusion, that the proposal and its temporary and partial adoption at Quebec in September 1944 were an unfortunate but small chapter in American diplomatic history. The scheme of the secretary of the treasury was an amateur proposal, typical of many in American diplomacy.

3. *Yalta and the End of the War in Europe*

The Yalta Conference (February 4–11, 1945) properly began the third and final period in the history of the wartime coalition, the period of disintegration, of dissolution and disillusion. By the time the conference met, the wartime coalition had outlived its military usefulness. Germany was a doomed country by 1945, with many of its cities in rubble from Allied bombing, with its eastern and western areas ravaged by the encroaching Allied armies—the Russians coming from the east, the British and Americans from the west. Americans at the beginning of 1945 were preparing to cross the Rhine. Hordes of Russian soldiers had approached to within a hundred miles of Berlin. Soviet armies had concluded a victorious peace with Finland, occupied Rumania, Bulgaria, and most of Poland, and driven deeply into Hungary, Yugoslavia, and Czechoslovakia. Understandably, when the war's end was near, there was no longer serious need for the Allied coalition, which was beginning, although ever so imperceptibly, to dissolve. A conference meeting under such circumstances was bound to encounter trouble.

The Yalta Conference was held at what had been the Crimean resort of the last tsar of Russia—the Livadia Palace built by Nicholas II in 1911 some two miles from the town of Yalta. Churchill buoyantly sent a message to Roosevelt on January 1, 1945, in advance of a preliminary Anglo-American meeting at Malta (held January 30–February 2, 1945): "No more let us falter! From Malta to Yalta! Let nobody alter!" A few days later, in a telegram of January 8, the prime minister was becoming gloomy: "This may well be a fateful Conference, coming at a moment when the Great Allies are so divided and the shadow of the war lengthens out before us. At the present time I think the end of this war may well prove to be more disappointing than was the last."Still, this was a momentary reaction, and it never infected the spirits of the Americans at Yalta. Roosevelt and his advisers concluded their labors in the Crimea in a spirit close to exultation. They felt that the postwar world was going to be safe—that the world had been saved for freedom and peace in a way which would have gladdened the heart of Woodrow Wilson. It would have been unbelievable to leaders of the American government in early 1945 had they been told that their hopes were not merely to be dashed, but that the meeting in which they had seen their vision of a new world would soon be described by critics as a conference of blunder and surrender.

What is the truth about Yalta? The Yalta Conference was the most controversial of the wartime diplomatic meetings, and in the light of later argument it deserves a close and sharp look. It dealt with essentially four issues: (1) voting arrangements in the new United Nations; (2) general policy toward the liberated governments of Eastern Europe, and specific policy toward the postwar government of Poland; (3) the immediate postwar governance of Germany; (4) Russia's joining the war against Japan.

Of these issues at Yalta, arrangements pertaining to the UN were probably of minor importance. Steps toward formation of the United Nations had already been taken before Yalta, notably at the Moscow Conference of foreign ministers in October 1943, when a joint declaration by Great Britain, the United States, the USSR, and China projected "a general international organization, based on the principle of sovereign equality of all peace-loving states, and open to membership by all such states, large and small, for the maintenance of international peace and security." It was after return from this conference that Secretary Hull declared extravagantly that, if the provisions of the Moscow Declaration were carried out, there would be no need for "spheres of influence, for alliances, for balance of power or any other of the special arrangements through which, in the unhappy past, the nations strove to safeguard their security or to promote their interests." At Yalta the date was set—Wednesday, April 25, 1945—

The Big Three and their foreign ministers at Yalta.

for opening the San Francisco Conference to work out the constitutional details of the UN. The three great powers at Yalta were in perfect agreement on their need for a right of veto in the UN. Stalin favored a veto even on discussion of matters at the UN, but Churchill and Roosevelt prevailed on him to allow the right of free speech in the new Parliament of the World. With this issue resolved, the Soviet dictator lost interest in the proposed world organization and turned to other matters.

In the meantime he had asked for and received Assembly seats for Byelorussia and the Ukraine, a concession by the Western statesmen which later brought much criticism of the Yalta Conference. The Russian argument was that the British empire was well represented in the Assembly, and that to confine a great power like Russia to one seat was unfair. The Russians at first asked for sixteen seats, one for each of the Soviet republics. The Russian ambassador to the United States, Andrei Gromyko, argued that any of the Soviet republics was more important than Guatemala or Liberia. To the query as to whether the Russian republics had been given control of their foreign relations Gromyko had answered that they soon would have such control. Finally the Russians compromised on three seats, and it was agreed that the United States also might request three seats. The American government has never asked for this bonus representation; the Russians have kept theirs. The multiple-seat concession to Russia at Yalta has provoked a good deal of criticism from American public opinion—although it is difficult to see what advantage the Russians gained by their increased Assembly representation.

In the matter of Eastern Europe the Yalta Conference has also been criticized. Here attack frequently has been directed to the Yalta Declaration on Liberated Europe, drafted by the State Department and accepted almost in toto by the conferees, which specified free elections and constitutional safeguards of freedom in the liberated nations. It was employed as a propaganda device by the Soviets, who never seriously considered putting it into effect. In retrospect the pledges of the Soviets in the declaration appear almost grotesque: "By this declaration," the United States, Britain, and Russia announced, "we reaffirm our faith in the principles of the Atlantic Charter, our pledge in the Declaration by the United Nations, and our determination to build in co-operation with other peace-loving nations world order under law, dedicated to peace, security, freedom and general well-being of all mankind." The Yalta Declaration on Liberated Europe had the immediate result of lending to the activities of the Soviet occupation authorities in Eastern Europe a certain sanctity and authority conferred by the democratic allies. Conspicuous posting of the text of the declaration throughout the liberated areas made the task of occupation easier. What followed is now well known. The Soviets pursued their own brand of democracy in the liberated countries, first by means of coalition governments. The Communist members of the coalition, supported by the red army, then infiltrated every position of responsibility in the government. Even so, the Yalta Declaration did some good, for without it the Russians might have omitted the coalition stage of their takeover of Eastern Europe in favor of a brutal takeover without attempt at legality. In this respect the Yalta Declaration may have given the East European peoples two or three years in which they had some freedom. Moreover, the declaration is the one Russian promise for this area of the Continent with which the United States and Britain have been able to reproach the Russians. It is a contractual arrangement which Russia violated.

But then one comes to the case of Poland as decided at Yalta, another matter about which the West has felt uneasy. Germany's attack on Poland had brought on the war in 1939. The British and Americans both felt during the war that an independent Polish government was essential in any acceptable postwar organization of Europe. Great Britain had guaranteed Polish national existence in 1939, and in the United States six million Americans of Polish descent laid constant and heavy political pressure upon President Roosevelt. The Western Allies at Yalta did the best they could for Poland and spent more time at the conference discussing Poland's postwar frontiers and government than any other subject. Churchill described the Polish question as "the most important question" before the conference. Still, Poland by February 1945 had been almost completely occupied by the red army, and any arrangements made at Yalta in regard to Poland had to be made out of hope rather than with certainty that they would be put into effect.

The Polish boundary question was straddled at Yalta—after much discussion—with tentative agreement on the Curzon Line as the eastern boundary but disagreement over the western boundary. Roosevelt and Churchill were not averse to a line along the Oder River, but as for continuing it southward along the Western Neisse, that was something else, and the decision was that "the final delimitation of the Western frontier of Poland should thereafter await the Peace Conference." This decision was reaffirmed at the Potsdam Conference of July–August 1945. The peace conference for Poland never met, and the Russians made their own bilateral arrangement with Poland of the Curzon Line in the east and the Oder–Western Neisse in the west.

The Western Allies reserved their consent to Poland's boundaries, but in the matter of Poland's postwar government the Americans and British at Yalta made what with hindsight appears to have been an ill-advised concession. The Russians received clearance to expand the so-called Lublin Committee, a Soviet-sponsored group of Polish-Russian Communists, by including representatives of the Polish government-in-exile then domiciled in London. The government-in-exile in London had far more right to claim the postwar government of Poland than did the cardboard Lublin Committee, propped as the latter was by the Russian army and Russian funds. The Soviets knew that their Polish organization was a fraud, and they were willing to "broaden" it and dress it in legitimacy by inclusion of members from the London Polish government. Not long afterward, all the non-Communists were squeezed out of the newly organized Warsaw government. The Western powers sensed the danger of trying to combine oil and water, Lublin and London, but they felt that they could do little more than accept Russian promises. At Yalta there was still hope that the Russians had changed their spots, that it would be possible to live amicably with the Communist regime, and in that hope and possibility the agreement on postwar Poland was consummated. In retrospect it appears that it would have been far better to have championed the London Poles, even at the risk of the government of Poland going to the Lublin Committee. It went to the committee anyway.

But perhaps this was the best that could be done. Roosevelt's adviser, Admiral William D. Leahy, said to the president at the time that the Polish agreement was so elastic that the Russians could "stretch it all the way from Yalta to Washington without ever technically breaking

it." Roosevelt agreed: "I know, Bill—I know it. But it's the best I can do for Poland at this time."

There thus was a certain inevitability at Yalta in regard to the postwar government and boundaries of Poland. The provisions at Yalta for extra Russian seats at the UN Assembly, while not inevitable, were unimportant. Division of Germany into zones of occupation was an easier part of the Yalta proceedings and was done with success because the war map of the moment, while giving Eastern Germany to Russia, gave the Western Allies the rich industrial complex of West Germany. This was no even division, but the Russians had to accept it because of the war map.

Planning for the division of Germany had preceded the Yalta Conference by a number of months, and when the Western Allies met Stalin in the Crimea, they were fairly certain of what they desired in the way of occupation zones. A European Advisory Commission met in London in 1944 and recommended that Russia receive the eastern third of Germany, and that the southeastern zone go to the United States and the northwestern zone to Britain. There was to be joint control of Berlin and an Allied Control Council for Germany. These proposals came before Churchill and Roosevelt at the Quebec Conference in September 1944, and the two statesmen agreed, Roosevelt reserving control by the United States over Bremen and Bremerhaven as enclaves within the British zone for purposes of supplying American troops in Bavaria. At Yalta this was essentially the arrangement for German occupation, with Roosevelt and Churchill persuading Stalin to allow to liberated France an occupation zone "within the British and the American zones." The Russian leader was at the outset against the idea of a French role in the occupation of Germany. Overlooking his own delinquency in the Nazi-Soviet Pact of August 1939, he said that France had "opened the gate to the enemy" in 1940 and "contributed little to this war." Churchill cagily remarked that "every nation had had their difficulties in the beginning of the war and had made mistakes." Stalin gave in, and France obtained not merely an occupation zone but a place on the Allied Control Commission.

In the matter of German reparations agreed upon at Yalta in a hedged and general way, it was decided that a reparations commission should be set up, with instructions that "the Soviet Union and the United States believed that the Reparations Commission should take as a basis of discussion the figure of reparations as twenty billion dollars and fifty percent of these should go to the Soviet Union." The British opposed naming any reparations figure and managed also to write into the instructions a statement of purpose, "to destroy the German war potential," rather than the more broadly phrased Russian statement, "for the purpose of military and economic disarmament of Germany." All in all—so a student of this complicated subject, John L. Snell, has concluded—"the reparations decisions at Yalta constituted a thinly disguised defeat for the Russians and a clear-cut rejection of the Morgenthau plan and the Quebec agreement of September, 1944."

But it was not chiefly its provisions for Germany or its stipulations for Eastern Europe or the UN that later gave the Yalta Conference notoriety. Rather it was the provisions for Russia to enter the Far Eastern war. Here one comes to the nub of the Yalta controversy. Agitation over the Far Eastern provisions of Yalta became a political matter in the United States, with the Democratic Party, in power in 1945, generally defending Yalta's Far Eastern terms, and the Republicans characterizing them as a "betrayal of a sacred trust of the American people." Entrance of Russia into the war against Japan was unnecessary—so ran the accusation—and it was not merely obtained at Yalta, it was bought, at an outrageous price.

The reason for the Yalta concessions to obtain entrance of Russia into the Far Eastern war was, simply, that President Roosevelt's military advisers told him they needed Russian help. The military situation appeared downright difficult for the United States. American military leaders estimated that the war in Europe would last until July 1, at least, and that the Pacific war would require (and this with Russian help) another year and a half, that is, until December 1946. How long the war would take without Russian help, no one knew. Japanese troop strength at the time of Yalta was impressive, in terms of men (but ignoring armaments, which it later turned out that they did not have). The Japanese had 2,000,000 to 2,500,000 troops in Japan, 1,000,000 in China, and 1,000,000 in Manchuria and Korea. The United States by the end of the war had sent only about 1,459,000 army troops and 187,500 marines into the Pacific and scattered them from Australia to Alaska. Casualties were high in operations against the Japanese. Shortly after the Yalta Conference came the costly attack on Iwo Jima, an island two and one-half miles wide by four and two-thirds miles long, on which the marine corps lost 4,189 dead and 15,308 wounded. Okinawa, invested soon afterward, cost 11,260 dead and 33,769 wounded. At Okinawa the Japanese sank 36 ships and damaged 368 others. It is understandable that Roosevelt and his advisers at Yalta wanted Russian entrance into the Far Eastern war. American military leaders estimated that an invasion of Japan would cost at least half a million American casualties, even if Japanese forces in China, Manchuria, and Korea stayed on the mainland. Douglas MacArthur, who later described as "fantastic" the Yalta concessions for Russian entrance into the Pacific war, told a Washington staff officer in early 1945 that Russian support was essential for the invasion of Japan. According to a memorandum of a conversation of February 25, 1945, sent by Brigadier General George A. Lincoln to General Marshall, "General MacArthur spoke of the strength of the opposition to be expected in invading the Japanese home islands. He declared that planning should start at once, that heavy firepower would be needed to cover the beachheads, and that as many Japanese divisions as possible should first be pinned down on the mainland, principally by Soviet forces." When Russia on August 8, 1945, invaded Manchuria, MacArthur declared flatly, "I am delighted at the Russian declaration of war against Japan. This will make possible a great pincers movement that cannot fail to end in the destruction of the enemy." Such was the feeling of Roosevelt's advisers at the time of

Yalta, and it explains a number of the Yalta concessions to Russia.

As everyone now knows, the military estimate of Japan's strength was inaccurate. Actually Japan was on its last legs at the time of Yalta. In the summer of 1944 the marines had captured Saipan, and this defeat spelled the beginning of the end of Japan's will to fight. The cabinet of General Tojo resigned on July 18, 1944, in shame and disgrace, and from that moment onward it was a matter not of *if* but of *when* Japan would surrender. Russian assistance was not needed when, by the early summer of 1945 (after the Yalta Conference, and before the Russians entered the Far Eastern war), United States submarines sank ferry boats passing between the islands of Japan, and when the American fleet engaged with impunity in offshore bombardments. The taking of bases other than Saipan—Iwo Jima, Okinawa—secured air strips within easy bombing range of every part of Japan. The huge B-29 bombers in their fire raids wreaked havoc upon the island empire. Even before the dropping of the atomic bombs at Hiroshima and Nagasaki the dreadful daily bombing raids had proved roughly comparable in deadliness to the atomic explosions. At Hiroshima between 91,233 and 423,263 people died as a result of the atomic bombing (the figures are highly uncertain). In the conventional raids on Japan the total of deaths ran to several hundreds of thousands. It was an apocalyptic end for the Japanese. No intervention by Russia was necessary to bring down the Japanese empire.

At Yalta the Russians agreed to join the war against Japan in "two or three months" after defeat of Germany. In return for this dubious service (which at the time seemed necessary), the Russians received the territory and privileges in China and the Pacific region that they had enjoyed prior to the Russo-Japanese War of 1904–1905: Southern Sakhalin and the Kurile Islands, railroad concessions throughout Manchuria (disguised as a joint Sino-Russian venture in railroading), and Port Arthur and Dairen (the latter was internationalized, meaning that it was free for Russian use).

It was embarrassing, but necessary, to obtain Chiang Kai-shek's acquiescence to these territorial infringements on Chinese sovereignty, and this necessity has since agitated some of the critics of Yalta. Even so, anyone conversant with the wartime military situation in China must grant that Chiang had done virtually nothing to expel the Japanese from his country. In 1945 he was still in his miserable and remote capital at Chungking. His troops had no control of any sort in Manchuria, not to speak of the seacoast, which had passed to the Japanese in 1937–1938. For Chiang to give Russia rights in territory which he did not possess was no concession. True, the Western Allies at the Cairo Conference in 1943 had promised complete restoration of Chinese sovereignty. Yet there had been no real Chinese control over Manchuria since the end of the nineteenth century when Russia received the first large concessions, and a restoration of Chinese sovereignty did not preclude restoration of Russian privileges. It is technically possible for a nation to exercise sovereignty at the time that its territory is encumbered by servitudes. Extraterritoriality had been a commonplace in the Orient in the nineteenth century, and the United States had not relinquished its extraterritorial privileges in China until 1943. Admittedly this is a bit of a technical argument in favor of the Yalta agreement on Russian privileges in China. There is something to be said for the broad, more equitable interpretation of international arrangements. The difficulty in 1945 was the seeming necessity of getting Russia into the Far Eastern war. This meant obtaining an ally for Chiang Kai-shek, which the latter statesman, in view of his own minuscule contribution to the war, should have welcomed. Chiang signed a treaty with the Russians in August 1945. The unfortunate aspect of the matter was that he was not consulted in the Yalta arrangement—but again, had he been consulted there almost certainly would have been a leak to the Japanese of the imminence of Russian intervention. As Roosevelt said at Yalta to Stalin and Churchill, anything told to the Chinese "was known to the whole world in twenty-four hours."'

Yalta was beyond dispute the climax of coalition diplomacy. It was the moment when the issues of the war, in all their complexity, came to focus. Most of these issues were not decided at Yalta, for they already had been decided in one way or another. Stalin had twice promised, informally at the Moscow foreign ministers' meeting of October 1943, formally at Teheran, to enter the war against Japan. Arrangements for the postwar Polish government, over which so much bitterness later would appear, had been anticipated during the October 1944 meeting in Moscow of Stalin and Churchill. Eventual settlement of the problem of Eastern Europe, despite the promises at Yalta, was also set forth at the Moscow Conference of 1944. Other illustrations could be cited to show how the Yalta Conference in most cases focused issues rather than "settled" them.

The conference was memorable, too, because it was the second and last meeting of the wartime Big Three. In the United States the death of Roosevelt on April 12, 1945, after a massive cerebral hemorrhage, brought to the presidency FDR's vice-president, Harry S. Truman. The third and last wartime conference would take place at Potsdam, near Berlin, in the summer of 1945. This meeting (for which see Chapter 10) saw the departure of Churchill from the prime ministership, replaced by Clement R. Attlee, head of the Labor Party, which had won the recent elections.

The appearance of Truman in the White House did not have much effect upon the course of the war, although it was the new president who announced the surrender of Germany on May 8, 1945. The collapse of German forces on both the Russian and Western fronts was almost at hand when Roosevelt died. Hitler, in his bunker head-

Inauguration of Harry S. Truman as president of the United States, April 12, 1945.

quarters in Berlin, celebrated the death of his great opponent, but at the end of April he too died, a suicide. His successor, Grand Admiral Karl Doenitz, soon afterward asked for an armistice, which was signed on May 7 in the headquarters of General Eisenhower at Rheims. Hostilities ceased the next day.

4. *Hiroshima and Nagasaki*

Harry S. Truman was president of the United States not only at the time of the German surrender in May 1945, but also when the Japanese surrendered on August 14, 1945 (their formal surrender came aboard the battleship *Missouri* on September 2). In the ending of the war against Germany, the forces of the Hitler regime simply collapsed. In the instance of Japan's surrender, however, a decision was taken that still must haunt the government and people of the United States—the decision to use nuclear weapons against two Japanese cities, Hiroshima and Nagasaki.

In extenuation, though perhaps not in absolution, it must be said that Truman's decision to drop nuclear bombs on the Japanese was in a very real sense a "nondecision." A long series of forces and factors that reached back to the beginning of the Pacific war on December 7, 1941, had been moving Washington officials toward use of what proved to be the world's most effective weapon of mass destruction.

Among the reasons that persuaded the Truman administration to use nuclear weapons, first and foremost was the manner in which the Japanese government conducted the Pacific war, without regard to international law. The "sneak" attack at Pearl Harbor was unforgettable, resulting in the deaths of 2,300 Americans, mostly sailors aboard the trapped ships of the Pacific fleet. Aboard the battleship *Arizona*, which blew up, more than a thousand men were cut down in a single, searing flash. In subsequent years the war in the Pacific was fought, on the Japanese side, without reference to the Geneva Convention. Word of the Bataan "death march," in which thousands of prisoners died, including hundreds of Americans, easily got back to the United States, and people were horror-struck. Individual acts of enemy ferocity against Allied, including American, prisoners were sometimes photographed and, whether circulated that way or by word of mouth, were hardly in need of exaggeration.

Second among the factors that led to the use of nuclear weapons upon Japan was the simple fact that the bomb project in the United States was highly secret, and hence there was little possibility of a serious, public debate. As matters turned out, the Truman administration engaged in no real discussion of alternatives to the bomb. The president did not ponder the morality of dropping the bomb. Early in the war, when he was a senator, he had learned of some sort of scientific project; a Senate committee that he headed had uncovered unprecedented expenditures by the War Department. Secretary of War Stimson was forced to call upon Senator Truman and ask him, in the name of national security, to stop this particular investigation. In August 1944, when Truman was the vice-presidential nominee on the ticket with President Roosevelt, the president during a luncheon meeting at the White House told him about the bomb project. He learned no more, and did not think about the bomb. After he became president Truman found he needed advice quickly, for scientists predicted a finished bomb by the summer of 1945. The new president arranged for a high-level committee of cabinet and other officials to consider use of the bomb. But the committee members could not examine the issue philosophically: they were almost all officials of a government conducting a war in Europe and Asia that was at its very height.

In the spring of 1945 a scientist at the Chicago Metallurgical Laboratory, Eugene Rabinowitch, began to mull over the prospect of so awesome a weapon of mass destruction. As he walked among the skyscrapers of Chicago he easily envisioned the destruction that could be wrought by this novelty of physics. Sensing the similar unease of his fellow scientists in the laboratory, he organized a petition, which took the name of the Nobel laureate James Franck, and the Franck Report was presented to the president's advisory committee in Washington. Not knowing quite what to make of it, the committee members referred it to a panel of eminent scientists that included the head of the bomb design laboratory at Los Alamos, J. Robert Oppenheimer. The panel rejected the petition as being without merit. Oppenheimer later admitted that no one had briefed them on the military situation in the Far East, where Japanese forces were facing defeat.

He confessed that "We didn't know beans about the military situation."

Third in the calculus of using the atomic bomb was the huge cost of the bomb project. Government support for nuclear weapons had begun modestly after the distinguished émigré physicist Albert Einstein wrote President Roosevelt about the theoretical practicability of an atomic bomb. In September 1939 the president created an ad hoc committee which awarded $6,000 to the physicist Enrico Fermi to purchase graphite for construction of an atomic pile at Columbia University. Gradually government support increased, and an all-out Anglo-American effort to make a bomb was announced in Washington on Saturday, December 6, 1941, at a secret meeting chaired by the president of Harvard, the chemist James B. Conant. Thereafter the Manhattan District Project, as it was known, moved forward, but with difficulty, because the technology was formidable. The first necessity was to obtain sufficient quantities of fissionable material, or "bomb stuff." Three German scientists had managed the fission of a uranium atom at Berlin's Kaiser Wilhelm Institute in 1938. Two years later the American physicist Ernest O. Lawrence, inventor of the cyclotron, achieved fission of the artificial element plutonium, derived from uranium. Scientists of the Manhattan District Project, a galaxy of Nobel laureates domestic and émigré, British as well as American, decided to work with both uranium and plutonium to achieve bomb stuff, and this meant construction of two huge separation plants in areas of the United States close to hydroelectric power: at Oak Ridge, Tennessee, and at Hanford, Washington.

Months passed before the two separation plants yielded sufficient bomb stuff, and indeed so much time proved necessary that no bombs were ready until the summer of 1945, after the end of the European war. Even then, the Oak Ridge plant secured only enough fissionable uranium (U-235) for a single bomb. The plutonium plant at Hanford did better, and produced enough for two additional bombs.

The cost of the separation plants, the laboratory in Chicago, and the bomb design laboratory at Los Alamos was enormous, $2 billion. It was the largest government project in the history of the country up to that time. Its very cost militated in favor of using any resultant bomb. Scientists and military leaders were eager to try out any weapon created at such expense. The project's cost also put pressure on the president of the United States. The president's chief of staff, Admiral Leahy, and Roosevelt's before him, said later that "I know F.D.R. would have used it [the bomb] in a minute to prove that he had not wasted $2 billion."

Another factor in favor of using nuclear weapons, once developed, was the faulty intelligence of the American armed forces regarding the condition of Japan's army, navy, and air force. Penetration of the Japanese home islands by Allied agents had proved nearly impossible. Photographic intelligence was reasonably good, but whether because of insufficient photoreconnaissance, or inability to read or assess the results, the joint chiefs of staff in Washington came to believe that Japanese military capacity was far higher than it was. By the summer of 1945 these estimates were coming down, but still were high.

Added to pessimistic intelligence estimates was the fatigue of the men in the European divisions that had fought the Nazi armies to a standstill during a hard winter, and now looked with intense reluctance upon their transfer from Europe to Asia. These men had seen plenty of death and devastation, and the possibility of more devastation in Japan was morally no different than the horror they already knew. They did not know about the nuclear bomb project. Leaders of the American government understood, however, that the European troops would support any decision to use the bomb.

It is easy to forget the attitude of American troops at the time, and this applied to troops in the Far East as well as in Europe. In retrospect it seems callous. The writer Paul Fussell, himself a young infantryman in Europe in 1945, stirred a fury of accusation with his commentary in the *New Republic* in 1981: "The dramatic postwar Japanese success at hustling and merchandising and tourism has (happily, in many ways) effaced for most people important elements of the assault context in which Hiroshima should be viewed."

The decision to use the nuclear bomb was eased as well by the frightful precedents of bombing civilian populations with conventional weapons earlier in the war. The escalation of violence in less than two decades of modern warfare had been dramatic, from the Japanese bombing of Chapei, the Chinese sector of Shanghai, in 1932 to population bombings by the Italians in Ethiopia in 1935–1936 and by Germans in Spain during the Spanish Civil War. The Germans bombed Poland in 1939 and destroyed Rotterdam in 1940, then turned their weaponry on the British, who retaliated for the blitz of London, Coventry, and other cities by raiding civilian targets in Germany. After America entered the war it sent to England the Eighth Air Force, which bombed by day while the Royal Air Force raided by night. Dresden, a treasure house of German art and architecture, was largely destroyed by bombs on February 13, 1945; the number of dead may have reached 135,000. Meanwhile, in the Far East, American B-29s reduced killing to a science. Five weeks before Truman took office, they dropped 2,000 tons of napalm on Tokyo, whipping up a firestorm of hurricane force. Flight crews could smell burning flesh below as they incinerated sixteen square miles of Tokyo, leaving an estimated 125,000 dead. After similar attacks on Nagoya, Osaka, and Kobe, the bombers went back over Tokyo and in the resulting holocaust killed another 80,000.

As the nuclear project came close to success, the scientists were quite uncertain of the TNT equivalent of the bombs they were making. They believed nuclear weapons would provide an explosive force equal to between 500 and 1,500 tons of TNT. They did not discover the true force of the bomb until the explosion of a plutonium test device in the desert near Los Alamos on July 16, 1945. The device vaporized the steel tower from which it was suspended, exploding with the force of 20,000 tons of TNT. The uranium bomb that was dropped on Hiroshima exploded with a force, it was ultimately determined, equal to 13,000 tons of TNT.

When the plutonium test device exploded in the Los Alamos desert on July 16, the leading officials of the United States government were already at the Potsdam Conference, preparing for the first formal conference session the next day. This meeting of Britain, the United States, and the Soviet Union ran from July 17 through August 2, 1945. Truman kept a makeshift diary at Potsdam, only recently discovered. According to this Potsdam diary the president was horrified by the prospect of nuclear weapons. On July 25, 1945, he wrote his own vision of the apocalypse: "We have discovered the most terrible bomb in the history of the world. It may be the fire destruction prophesied in the Euphrates Valley Era, after Noah and his fabulous Ark." The entry continued, "This weapon is to be used against Japan between now and August 10th. . . . It seems to be the most terrible thing ever discovered. . . ." The diary makes clear that Truman intended the bomb to be used against "military objectives . . . and not women and children," and that he would issue a warning asking the Japanese to "surrender and save lives." Unfortunately the result was the ambiguous statement known as the Potsdam Declaration, an announcement by Britain and the United States (Russia had not yet entered the Far Eastern war) that the Japanese should give up the fighting in the Far East. "We call upon the government of Japan," Truman and Churchill announced on July 26, "to proclaim now the unconditional surrender of all Japanese armed forces, and to provide proper and adequate assurances of their good faith in such action. The alternative for Japan is prompt and utter destruction." Had the Japanese known that the words of the declaration were barbed by the test explosion, they might have heeded the warning from Potsdam, but they did not know of the successes of Allied science.

The result of this tragic concatenation of experience and expense and surmise and ignorance and inadvertence was the deaths of tens of thousands, perhaps hundreds of thousands, of human beings. The first atomic bomb was dropped on Hiroshima on August 6, 1945. Three days later a second hit Nagasaki. In retrospect the dropping of nuclear bombs on Hiroshima and Nagasaki was an enormous error. Humanly it was appalling. Militarily it was unnecessary. Japan would have surrendered in a few weeks without the bombs. The U.S. army, navy, and air force already had brought sufficient force to bear with their conventional weapons. On August 10, when news of the bombs reached Tokyo, the Japanese requested an armistice. They had been shocked not only by the devastating bombings but also by Russia's entry into the Far Eastern war on August 8.

In Washington, August 14, 1945, Truman announces the cessation of hostilities against Japan.

After the war a contention arose that the United States had used the atomic bombs not so much to end the war as to impress the Soviet Union—that they were a demonstration of America's new weapon, its "ace in the hole" for postwar diplomatic relations with the Soviets. This plausible theory has never enjoyed the slightest proof, although it has had much currency. During the last months of the war, relations between the Anglo-Americans and the Soviet Union had been deteriorating. President Roosevelt himself had become disenchanted with the Russians, and there is evidence that shortly before he died he was preparing for much firmer diplomacy with them. A cable exchange with Stalin over the secret American negotiations in Switzerland for surrender of German forces in Italy had infuriated Roosevelt, and, according to a visitor to the White House shortly before the president left for Warm Springs, he had banged his hands on the arms of his wheelchair and said he would not abide such behavior, such distrust. Truman had become angry with the Soviets over their decision not to send a high-level representative to the opening of the United Nations Conference in San Francisco in late April 1945. After Stalin relented and sent Foreign Minister Molotov the president had "talked turkey" to Molotov in Washington and told him that relations between the West and the Soviet Union were not a one-way street. "I have never been talked to like that in my life," Molotov said. "Carry out your agreements," snapped the president, "and you won't get talked to like that."

If circumstances called for a strong reminder of American power, the nuclear bombs could have provided it. But in actuality the decision to use them surely had no connection with Russian intransigence. Ambassador Averell Harriman lived for many years after 1945, to a great old age, dying in 1986, and to his dying day was capable of becoming infuriated at the very thought that the Truman administration would have dropped the bombs to impress the Russians. And nowhere in the voluminous and frank Truman records is there any testimony that the bombs were used to startle the Soviets.

ADDITIONAL READING

The Second World War, like the war of 1914–1918, produced a spate of books, and a good starting place is Gaddis Smith, *American Diplomacy during the Second World War* (2d ed., New York, 1985), a volume in the America in Crisis series. Samuel Eliot Morison, *Strategy and Compromise* (Boston, 1958), considers strategic issues. See also Raymond G. O'Connor, *Diplomacy for Victory* (New York, 1971).

Any account of diplomacy toward Germany must begin with the most inhuman event of the war, or of any war within memory—the Holocaust. See David S. Wyman, *Abandonment of the Jews* (New York, 1984), which maintains that the Western governments did not do all they could to save Europe's Jews. Allen W. Dulles, *Germany's Underground* (New York, 1947), describes the tragic uprising on July 20, 1944, by the German opposition to Hitler. The same author's *The Secret Surrender* (New York, 1966) sets out the end of the war in Italy. Dulles was the representative in Switzerland of the American wartime intelligence organization, the Office of Strategic Services.

Julian G. Hurstfield considers *America and the French Nation* (Chapel Hill, N.C., 1985). Wartime relations with Russia are in Vojtech Mastny, *Russia's Road to the Cold War* (New York, 1979).

The question of Yalta—whether Yalta was a sell-out—agitated Americans for years, and a congressional request to the State Department resulted in publication of the conference papers in 1955 in a special volume in the series Foreign Relations of the United States. General MacArthur's allegations on the subject of Yalta led to another documentary publication by the Department of Defense, *The Entry of the Soviet Union into the War against Japan* (Washington, D.C., 1955), showing that MacArthur approved of the Yalta arrangements for Soviet assistance against Japan. Scholarly analysis is in Diane Shaver Clemens, *Yalta* (New York, 1970); Athan G. Theoharis, *The Yalta Myths* (Columbia, Mo., 1970); Floyd H. Rodine, *Yalta* (Lawrence, Kan., 1974); and Russell D. Buhite, *Decisions at Yalta* (Wilmington, Del., 1986).

For the Pacific war the best general account is Ronald H. Spector, *Eagle against the Sun* (New York, 1985). On the decision to drop the nuclear bombs see R. J. C. Butow, *Japan's Decision to Surrender* (Stanford, 1954), and Martin J. Sherwin, *A World Destroyed* (New York, 1975). Gar Alperovitz, *Atomic Diplomacy* (New York, 1965), contends that the American government used the bomb to impress Soviet Russia. See the discussion of "revisionist" books on the origins of the cold war at the end of the next chapter.

Books on wartime relations with China appear at the end of Chapter 11.

For titles about Roosevelt, see books at the end of Chapter 8. An excellent short account is by Robert A. Divine, *Roosevelt and World War II* (Baltimore, 1969). The last three volumes of Churchill's memoirs take the war from 1942 to 1945. See also Warren F. Kimball, ed., *Churchill and Roosevelt: The Complete Correspondence* (3 vols., Princeton, 1984). Also Forrest C. Pogue, *George C. Marshall* (4 vols., New York, 1963–1987); Charles E. Bohlen, *Witness to History* (New York, 1973); and W. Averell Harriman and Elie Abel, *Special Envoy to Churchill and Stalin* (New York, 1975).

☆ 10 ☆

Europe, 1945–1950

I remember, when I was Secretary of State, I was being pressed constantly, particularly when in Moscow, by radio message after radio message to give the Russians hell. . . . When I got back I was getting the same appeal in relation to the Far East and China. At that time, my facilities for giving them hell—and I am a soldier and know something about the ability to give hell—was 1⅓ divisions over the entire United States. This is quite a proposition when you deal with somebody with over 260 and you have 1⅓. We had nothing in Alaska. We did not have enough to defend the air strip at Fairbanks. . . .

—George C. Marshall, address to an audience at the Pentagon, 1950

After every one of the major wars in American history—the Revolutionary War, the Civil War, the First and Second World Wars—there has been a time of relaxation, when people felt a sort of letdown after wartime trials and enjoyed peace with unaccustomed vigor and abandon. The greater the war the greater the letdown, and the first few months after 1945 were a relaxed, loose, and frivolous time; the nation enjoyed itself as never before in its history. The end of gas rationing came in 1945, and soon afterward the end of other rationing; "the boys" came home; the cars moved out on the roads; the night clubs expanded their seating capacities. The United States in 1945 and 1946 in no sense experienced what occurred in postwar Britain—continued rationing, and a general tightening of belts. Neither did it experience the troubles of continental nations—dropping production, rising unemployment, and lack of food and fuel by large segments of the population. Americans enjoyed themselves in a burst of postwar spending and self-indulgence, which when compared to the austerity of other nations, victor and defeated alike, seems in retrospect almost callous.

This wonderful feeling of relaxation after the war accounts for some of the indecisiveness of American diplomacy in the first year or two after V-E and V-J days. The purposes of American diplomacy understandably took second place in the general hubbub. After all, who wanted to think about diplomacy when the nation had just won the largest war in human history? Peace was to be enjoyed; meanwhile, let the diplomats play their private games—so many Americans thought.

There were other, if less important, factors influencing American diplomacy after 1945. For one, the leadership of the republic's diplomacy was not all that it might have been. When Vice President Harry S. Truman on April 12, 1945, was elevated to the presidency by the death of President Roosevelt, he had little knowledge of foreign affairs. He had been vice president for a few weeks and had had almost no briefing on the conduct of American foreign relations. Nor could he receive quick assistance from James F. ("Jimmy") Byrnes, his inexperienced appointee as secretary of state (Byrnes replaced Edward R. Stettinius, Jr., in July 1945; Stettinius had replaced Hull in December 1944). Jimmy Byrnes was an able politician who during the war had made himself almost indispensable to President Roosevelt as a troubleshooter, ferreting out problems and their solutions with admirable efficiency, but when translated into the State Department he discovered himself in a milieu different from American domestic politics.

The nation's diplomacy, thus in trouble, was further crippled by the precipitous demobilization of the American armed forces. During the war the enormous military power of the United States had given a strength to the country's diplomacy that it had not possessed since the time of the First World War, when for a fleeting moment the nation had had another large army. If only some of American wartime military power could have been retained, if the draft could have continued to feed into the army, navy, and air force just a part of its wartime levies of young men, the series of defeats that befell American diplomacy in the postwar years might not have occurred. Hindsight makes this easy to see. At the time no one worried. There was a compelling pressure for demobilization, and the Washington government had little choice except to let the complicated war machine of May 1945 disintegrate within half a dozen months under a ruinous point system that released first the armed forces' most experienced members.

But the overwhelming desire for letdown, for return to normal ways of behavior and thought, was the chief cause of our woes after the Second World War. Desire for relaxation carried everything before it. Few individuals looked for trouble in foreign affairs, and almost everyone chose to enjoy the postwar domestic prosperity to the limit. The United Nations, President Roosevelt had believed, would care for future international rivalries. There would be few problems from

Soviet Russia. The Russians, almost all Americans thought in 1945, would be peaceful and easy to get along with. General Dwight D. Eisenhower concluded after a trip to Moscow that "nothing guides Russian policy so much as a desire for friendship with the United States," and this was the prevailing view. When in 1946 and 1947 Soviet intentions became all too clear, written in actions and verbiage that everyone could understand, it was nearly too late to do anything. Americans found that they were without the means to make their will prevail, short of a preventive atomic war, which was humanely unthinkable. There was no conventional military machine to back the nation's diplomacy, and two or three years were necessary to rebuild the military forces. Besides, the country was repelled by the idea of turning again to military pressure in foreign relations. It sought for a while with considerable success to institute a program of economic aid to Europe and the Middle East and Asia. Part of that program, the Marshall Plan, resuscitated the faltering economies and wrought startling improvements in the material well-being of the Continent. Even so, the threatened subversion of pro-Western regimes in Greece and Turkey, the need to buttress them militarily, as was recognized in the Truman Doctrine of 1947, and the continuing use of strong-arm methods by the Russians in such cases as the Berlin blockade of 1948–1949 all gave indication of trouble ahead. Something more than economic measures was necessary. The nation in 1950 woke with a start when the invasion of South Korea demonstrated the importance of a military as well as economic policy. For five years the United States had sought, with increasing distraction, to pursue its own national prosperity, and in 1950, on June 25 to be exact, the postwar letdown came to an end.

1. *The United Nations*

In the months after victory, probably nothing characterized the times more hopefully for Americans than did the creation in 1945 of the United Nations. The UN would provide, its American supporters believed, a solvent for national rivalries. It would be the Parliament of the World of which poets long had sung. An American president in 1919 had revealed a vision of world government which failed to obtain popular support. Woodrow Wilson, his supporters were saying while the Second World War was still being fought, had been "ahead of his time." By 1945, time had caught up with the prophecy, and many Americans were approaching the new world organization with a childlike faith that within a few years was humbling to recall. The UN was to be the government of the brave new world; the mistakes of 1919 would not be repeated. Because of the United Nations, so carefully established before the war had ended,

Stettinius signs the UN Charter for the United States as Truman looks on.

there would be no muddle and descent into international anarchy such as had marked the two decades after the armistice of 1918.

The intention of the United States to establish and participate in a new world organization had become obvious well before the end of the Second World War. In the year 1943 both houses of Congress passed resolutions—the Fulbright Resolution in the House (September 21, 1943), the Connally Resolution in the Senate (November 5, 1943)—stipulating, as Representative J. William Fulbright put it, "creation of appropriate international machinery with power adequate to establish and to maintain a just and lasting peace, among the nations of the world." The Senate, with due attention to its traditions, added in the Connally Resolution that the "general international organization" should be "based on the principle of the sovereign equality of all peace-loving states." A year later, in 1944, the United States invited Britain, Russia, and China to meet in Washington to plan for the new organization, a meeting held from August 21 to October 7, at a mansion known as Dumbarton Oaks—the meeting thereby becoming known as the Dumbarton Oaks Conference. Its draft proposals became the basis of the UN Charter when the latter was drawn up at the San Francisco Conference of the following year.

Delegates of fifty nations attended the grand conference at San Francisco which opened on April 25, 1945. President Truman gave the speech of welcome. The resultant UN Charter was signed on June 26 and established a General Assembly of all member nations to meet periodically, each nation with a single vote, together with a Security Council of eleven members in continuous session. There were to be such other organs as an Economic and Social Council, an International Court of Justice (sitting at The Hague, replacing the old and similarly titled League organization, the Court of International Justice), a Trusteeship Council, and a Secretariat. The Senate of the United States advised and consented to the UN Charter on July 28, 1945, by a vote of 89 to 2. Other nations quickly added their assents, and the Charter went into effect on October 24, 1945. The first meeting of the General Assembly was held in London on January 10, 1946; the Security Council convened the same month. The headquarters of the new organization was not to be in the location of the discredited League—Geneva, Switzerland—but in the metropolis of the Western Hemisphere, New York City, in a new skyscraper along the Manhattan range. This splendid slim tower of steel and glass, sumptuously appointed, has since been visited by (to use the skeptical description of Reinhold Niebuhr) multitudes of Americans prompted by piety or school principals or women's clubs. These Americans seemed to regard the UN as a kind of supergovernment that could guarantee peace if only devotion to it were absolute. Viewing the UN's headquarters in their own country, Americans apparently believed that this time the world organization, the UN, would work.

Had they examined the UN Charter with greater care they might have found in it reason for skepticism, or at least for reservation, because in some ways the new organization was a less imposing institution than the old League of Nations. The preamble to the Charter was impressive enough, though rather bittersweet when read in the light of the world's history after 1945. "We the peoples of the United Nations," it began in a vein reminiscent of the constitution of the United States,

> determined to save succeeding generations from the scourge of war, which twice in our life-time has brought untold sorrow to mankind, and to reaffirm faith in fundamental human rights, in the dignity and worth of the human person, in the equal rights of men and women and nations large and small, and to establish conditions under which justice and respect for the obligations arising from treaties and other sources of international law can be maintained, and to promote social progress and better standards of life in larger freedom, and for these ends to practice tolerance and live together in peace with one another as good neighbors, and to unite our strength to maintain international peace and security, and to ensure, by the acceptance of principles and the institution of methods, that armed force shall not be used, save in the common interest, and to employ international machinery for the promotion of the economic and social advancement of all peoples, have resolved to combine our efforts to accomplish these aims.

Such was the auspicious beginning. But further in the Charter there were some qualifications in its detailed constitutional arrangements. The very length of the Charter—the Covenant of the League of Nations had 26 articles; the UN Charter required 111—gave it an air of uncertainty, recalling the manner in which state constitutions in the United States frequently have been drawn to great length so that the governments inaugurated under them would not merely be precisely informed of their duties but limited in their powers. Perhaps, however, the length of the Charter was a scheme to hide the inevitable reservations of national sovereignty—the "loopholes," as the two express reservations of the Covenant of the League had been known. There were two similar loopholes in the Charter, just as all-encompassing as those in the Covenant. Part 7 of the UN Charter's article 2 reserved to member nations "matters which are essentially within the domestic jurisdiction of any state." Article 51 thoughtfully set forth, "Nothing in the present Charter shall impair the inherent right of individual or collective self-defense . . ." Taken together, the provisions for domestic jurisdiction and self-defense would allow any scheming nation to wiggle out of its UN commitments, if it so desired. An additional loophole was the veto power over any UN actions held by the five permanent members of the Security Council, the United States, Great Britain, the USSR, France, and China. Every possible contingency thus was fenced in, in advance.

If one analyzed the Charter carefully, it could be seen that it bound its membership to little more than good behavior. It certainly was no stronger than the League of Nations. And it was positively weaker when one considered that the Charter showed a startling lack of the procedures and regulations for members in event of international trouble that had marked the Covenant of the League of Nations. The Covenant specified procedures in case of war or threat of war. The Charter did little except declare "breaches of the peace" (the word "war" does not appear in the articles of the Charter, except twice in the phrase "Second World War") as the proper business of the membership, without stating what should thereafter be done. A skeptic or a cynic might have asked what was gained by the 111 new articles, other than the admission to membership of Soviet Russia. The Russians, having been expelled from the League in 1939 during the war with Finland, would have nothing to do with the old world organization and insisted upon a completely new one. Now there was the new one, weaker organizationally than the old.

Quite apart from its constitutional inadequacies, the UN developed a special functional weakness in the years after 1945, a weakness which deserves some mention. This was the unanticipated rise of the General Assembly to a position of importance within the UN organization, accompanied by the decline in prestige of the Security

Council. The increased role of the Assembly was not, as said, anticipated by the UN's founders. The San Francisco Conference had established the Security Council in a belief that in this select body of eleven members, dominated by five great powers possessing permanent seats and the right to veto any action deemed detrimental to their interests, the work of watching over the world could easily be accomplished. In the springtime of 1945, there was little anticipation, at least on the American side, that American-Russian relations would soon deteriorate to a point where the Council could hardly function at all. The Americans in drawing up their list of powers for permanent membership in the Council also did not anticipate how drained of energy the British were in 1945, how Great Britain's stature in a year or two or three would decline to that of a virtually second-class power. France also had appeared to the United States as a far more important nation than postwar events proved. Likewise it was at the outset a mistake to have included China among the permanent members of the Council, for neither was Nationalist China a great power in 1945, nor could it fairly represent the Chinese people after 1949, when the Kuomintang was driven from the mainland to Formosa. The Security Council, as constituted in 1945, was crippled from the start. This most important policy-determining arm of the UN did not in any major respect represent the true distribution of strength, military and diplomatic, throughout the world.

The idea behind the organization of the Security Council as a body dominated by the great powers was essentially a good one, for this meant, if the idea worked as planned, that nations holding dominant power in the UN were also the nations truly responsible for maintenance of peace throughout the world. The UN structure, as conceived in this way, contained the prime requisite for any well-planned political organization—a linking of power and responsibility. But the idea went awry in the unforeseen diminution of power of Britain, France, and Nationalist China, and the new antagonism between the United States and the Soviet Union. This development soon led to confusion within the UN; then the United States confounded the confusion by adopting a policy of taking major political questions to the General Assembly, many of them with profound implications for the controversy between the two superpower groups. The Assembly, the planners of the UN had assumed, was to be a talking place, a kind of town meeting with extremely limited powers, a forum where the smaller nations of the world could have representation without power. After the North Korean invasion of South Korea in June 1950 the United States decided that it would be good to have "decisions," resolutions of support, from the General Assembly, and inaugurated this procedure with the "uniting for peace" resolution of November 3, 1950.

By soliciting support from the Assembly, the United States placed itself in a delicate position. It would not always be convenient for the American government to solicit Assembly support. But the Assembly, having been solicited by the United States, began to take its support seriously, as something to be given or withheld as the case might require. The Assembly was a large and unwieldy organization, including the numerous new nations of Southeast Asia and the Middle East and—in the 1960s—Africa. Hence, whenever the Assembly gave or withheld support in the form of a resolution, many nations voted—nations other than the United States, Great Britain, Western Europe, and the British Commonwealth—and it was difficult to be sure of the votes. If the United States was not constantly on guard, the Asian-Arab bloc could team up with the Latin American nations and secure an Assembly majority. The African bloc became so strong by the latter 1960s—by 1968 it contained forty nations—that it could join with Latin America and almost obtain a majority. Assembly majorities frequently did not have the faintest correspondence to world power. But for better or worse, a modicum of power passed to the Assembly, after the abdication of the Security Council, and how the United States would handle this new development was a matter for time to tell. Some thoughtful people, observing the irresponsibility of the Assembly and the difficulty of reaching decisions in the Security Council, were beginning to believe that the UN was finished so far as constructive work was concerned. It was, they believed, a place of passion, of unreason, frequently of utter confusion, with little regard for the problems of the great powers of the world.

An especially confused polarization developed in the UN, often discussed as a division between "East" and "West." These two terms have probably become inextricably imbedded in the language, but they need comment, even if in a digression. They are inaccurate if only in that the "West" division includes such eastern nations as the Philippines and Japan, and would also like fervently to enroll India and many other Asiatic countries. It is unfortunate that the language of discussion in Western countries thus tends to concede all Eastern countries to communism.

In the first years after the war the confusions of the UN's organization, structural and functional, were only in part apparent. The UN in its first days was a forum of deadlock, with the *nyet* of Russian representatives echoing through the meetings of the Security Council, with the two superpowers at odds over all kinds of international proposals. It was, perhaps, unfortunate that the new world organization should have been asked to help solve at this time one of the most difficult problems ever presented to any government, national and international—the problems of limitation and reduction of atomic arms.

It was on January 24, 1946, two weeks after its opening meeting, that the UN Assembly created a commission to study the control of atomic energy. The American elder statesman, Bernard M. Baruch, on June 14, 1946, proposed an international atomic development authority to which the United States would turn over its atomic bomb secrets, provided that there was an international control and inspection of bomb production not subject to big-power veto, and that further manufacture of bombs would cease and existing stocks be destroyed. "We are here," Baruch told the UN's Atomic Energy Commission, "to make a choice between the quick and the dead. That is our business. Behind the black portent of the new atomic age lies a hope which, seized upon with faith, can work our salvation. If we fail, then we have damned every man to be the slave of Fear. Let us not deceive ourselves: We must elect World Peace or World Destruction." The Soviet Union, unfortunately, was not willing to accept the Baruch proposals, balking in particular at the American elder statesman's demand for international control and inspection. The Russian representative in the Security Council, Andrei A. Gromyko, in a speech on March 5, 1947, remarked, "Logic tells us that any thought may be reduced to an absurdity. This applies even to good thoughts and ideas. The transformation of atomic-energy control into an unlimited control would mean to reduce to an absurdity the very idea of control of atomic energy in order to prevent its use for military purposes. Unlimited control would mean an unlimited interference of the control and controlling organ—or organs—in the economic life of the countries on whose territories this control would be carried out, and interference in their internal affairs. . . . the authors of the so-called Baruch plan completely ignore national interests of other countries and proceed from . . . the interests actually of one country; that is, the United States of America."

The issue of atomic limitation and control by the UN thereupon deadlocked. Testimony to this saddening fact was the McMahon Act of 1946, reorganizing the American domestic atomic program under a new civilian five-man Atomic Energy Commission. There were two atomic tests at Bikini in July 1946. The UN had proved incapable of halting the atomic armaments race.

2. *The Nadir of American Diplomacy*

In the early postwar period of 1945–1946, faith in the UN was coupled, as we have seen, with a dominant American mood of letdown, relaxation—which insofar as it expressed itself in policy was marked by a desire to "get out of" Europe and "get out of" Asia. Troops and military forces in those distant places should come home. The world should return to its prewar habits, nations "standing on their own feet" without American aid and sustenance. The nations should "get off the U.S. taxpayer's back." If this were done, so Americans thought, everything would be just fine. In the merry chase at home, the effort to get caught up in cars and refrigerators and deep-freezers and all the other items that had gone out of production during the war, there was enough to do without thinking of foreign countries.

Despite the popular mood, diplomacy could not come to a stop. International relations continued, whether most Americans saw any value in them or not. In the initial postwar period, accommodation with Russia was the purpose and goal of American diplomats. This turned out to be largely a negative rather than positive effort, to preserve a wartime alliance that the Russians found no longer useful. The wartime alliance had begun to break, even before the end of the war in Europe, and the stresses and strains had been visible at the Yalta Conference, but for some time thereafter the West sought futilely to arrange some kind of friendly settlement with the East. Everyone in 1945 hoped for one world, a family of nations. The UN "*has* to work," people said. One world or none. The atomic bomb would unify or destroy the world. Such ideas as coexistence, containment, and cold war, utterly foreign to American wartime hopes, were not talked of by the people and statesmen of the United States until 1947 and thereafter.

In one particular, the trying before international military tribunals of the leaders of Germany and Japan, the Soviets and Americans cooperated without difficulty. The trials of the major German war criminals, held at Nuremberg, led to the hanging of ten defendants (Reichsmarschall Hermann Goering committed suicide on the eve of the executions). The Japanese trials, held in Tokyo, brought death by hanging to seven defendants, including former Premier Tojo. At the time and later there was a good deal of contention that the sentences of the tribunals were illegal, according to international law—that the arguments of the prosecution had rested on such fragile supports as natural law and the Kellogg-Briand Pact (neither of the authors of the treaty of 1928 ever had envisioned that it would apply to individuals as well as nations). The problem was the overwhelming guilt of at least some of the defendants, the involvement in plainly criminal acts by others. It was in some sense the plight of all individuals in dictatorships. To survive was to collaborate, although most of these individuals had collaborated with unusual zeal. In retrospect perhaps the defendants should have gone free, as an international mark of charity if not justice.

This, then, was a successful cooperation, by some evaluations. It was hardly enough to affect the general course of U.S.-Russian relations. There had been rumblings of trouble between the U.S. and USSR as early as the spring of 1945, but they were unknown to the American public. President Roosevelt a short time before his death had admitted to Senator Arthur Vandenberg, "Just between us, Arthur, I am coming to know the Russians better . . ." President Truman had discovered shortly after entering the White House that American dealings with Russia had been a one-way street and on May 12, four days after V-E Day, Prime Minister Churchill sent a memorable telegram to President Truman: "What is to happen about Russia?" he asked. "What will be the position in a year or two, when the British and American Armies have melted and the French has not yet been formed on any major scale, when we may have a handful of divisions, mostly French, and when Russia may choose to keep two or three hundred on active service? An iron curtain is drawn down upon their front. We do not know what is going on behind. There seems little doubt that the whole of the regions east of the line Lübeck-Trieste-Corfu will soon be completely in their hands. To this must be added the further enormous area conquered by the American armies between Eisenach and the Elbe, which will, I suppose, in a few weeks be occupied, when the Americans retreat, by the Russian power. . . . Thus a broad band of many hundreds of miles of Russian-occupied territory will isolate us from Poland. . . . Surely it is vital now to come to an understanding with Russia, or see where we are with her, before we weaken our armies mortally . . ."

This magnificent advice went unheeded. It came too soon to be followed. The American government prepared hopefully for the Potsdam Conference, held on July 17–August 2, 1945. As a signal of good will toward Russia, President Truman ordered American troops to begin withdrawal from the advanced positions they held in central Germany. In the final rush of the war, the Western Allied troops had penetrated beyond their Yalta-allotted zones of occupation on a front 400 miles in length and at one point 120 miles in depth. Despite Churchill's plea, the United States gave up this territory, beginning the withdrawal on June 21. Americans hoped that at Potsdam no force or threats of force would be necessary, that the good work begun so auspiciously at Yalta, the work of establishing the hopes of peoples everywhere for a lasting peace, would be carried forward decisively to a settlement of European problems and, perhaps, a preliminary settlement of Far Eastern affairs.

The diplomacy of accommodation with the Russians was pursued at the Potsdam Conference amid the gardens and brownstone splendor of the Cecilienhof, once the country estate of the last Crown Prince William of Hohenzollern. Surrounded by history, the conference had every inspiration for success, but what had gone before—the eagerness to please the Soviets, the withdrawal by the Western Allies into their zones of occupation, the disavowal of Churchill's leadership by the British people, the uncertainties of American lead-

The triumvirs at Potsdam. The surrender of Germany seemed to require yet another conference of the victorious powers. On July 17 Churchill, Truman, and Stalin met in Potsdam. Before the conference had finished its work, Churchill was replaced by Attlee.

ership—these were the decisive factors at Potsdam, together, of course, with Russia's vast army in possession of all Eastern Europe: Poland, Czechoslovakia, Hungary, Rumania, Bulgaria. Yugoslavia and Albania were under control of local Communists. The decisions of Potsdam, like those of the preceding wartime conferences, were foreordained. The Russians admitted that they had made a private deal with the Polish Provisional Government of National Unity (dominated by the Lublin Committee) whereby Poland received a slice of Germany, the line of the Oder and Western Neisse Rivers, in compensation for Poland's loss to Russia of the territory east of the Curzon Line. The Western Allies at Potsdam could do nothing about this accomplished fact, the new Polish border drawn within Russia's zone of East Germany, except to vow in the conference's protocol that "the final delimitation of the western frontier of Poland should await the peace settlement."

After the Potsdam Conference came the interminable meetings in Europe and America of the Council of Foreign Ministers, in which nothing seemed to be accomplished. There were four meetings of the foreign ministers during the first year of peace, and the meetings went on and on. The ministers talked and argued but could come to no agreement. The apogee of disagreement was reached at the Moscow meeting in the spring of 1947, when there were forty-four sessions devoted to economic and political problems in Germany and Austria.

The regular meetings of the Council of Foreign Ministers, as had been the case with the Potsdam Conference, were disappointing in their results. Nor was the Paris Peace Conference of 1946, a series of special meetings of the foreign ministers of Great Britain, France, the Soviet Union, and the United States, held between the dates of April 25 and October 15, a triumph for American diplomacy. It gave a short-lived independence to Hungary, Rumania, and Bulgaria, which the Russians soon snatched away. It provided for Finnish independence, which Finland somehow maintained, perhaps because as an independent country Finland was able to pay more reparations to Russia than would have been the case if the Finns had not received their independence. As for the conference's deliberations on Italy, that nation was a province of the Western Allies, Britain and the United States, and they could have controlled Italian destinies with or without a Paris Peace Conference. The Paris meetings ratified the Western decision to give Italy independence. The conference had the effect, although the democratic allies at the outset had fervently hoped that this would not be, of confirming the military settlement made in Europe at the end of the war in 1945. Indeed the combined results of the Paris Peace Conference, the various regular meetings of the foreign ministers during 1945–1946, and the Potsdam Conference might have been predicted by any neophyte: where the red armies stood, there the Russians organized and manipulated governments to their own taste; wherever the West had stationed its forces, it retained local political control.

Despite what in retrospect appears to have been an obvious situation, the loss of Eastern Europe to the Communists was at the time an unnerving experience for the Western powers. At the end of the war there had been high hope that the Russians in their preserve of Eastern Europe—Hungary, Rumania, and Bulgaria, together with the already nominally free Yugoslavia, Albania, Poland, and Czechoslovakia—would maintain political freedom in the occupied nations, in accord with the Yalta Declaration on Liberated Europe. There would be, so Americans hoped, free elections in Eastern Europe, after which the reconstituted governments would continue to allow political freedom. It was one of the most disillusioning experiences of the postwar era to see the Russians ignore the Yalta Declaration and subvert the East European governments to communism. At the Potsdam Conference in 1945, Stalin had made the Soviet position clear when he said, "any freely elected government would be anti-Soviet and that we cannot permit." Western statesmen did not think the Soviet dictator would follow such a course of open domination as he did in Eastern Europe.

Observing this process of communization, American diplomatic representatives in Eastern Europe, in Budapest and Bucharest and Sofia and Belgrade and Warsaw and Prague, protested without end, but to no avail. The diplomacy of the United States in 1945 and 1946 reached a nadir. Never in the twentieth century had American prestige in Europe fallen so low. And this within two years of the tremendous victory of 1945.

Some commentators at the time and later would believe that Soviet actions in 1945–1946 were shrewdly calculated and that the undoubtedly low estate of American diplomacy by the end of the year in 1946 was a masterly piece of work achieved by the genius of the Soviet dictator. Here, it might have seemed, was diplomacy worthy of Bismarck, Talleyrand, or Vergennes. Stalin had accomplished everything he wished, and without war.

One must take exception to this view that Russian postwar actions were, as examples of the diplomatic art, masterpieces of calculation and achievement. Soviet diplomacy was beyond doubt shrewd, but it was a cheap kind of shrewdness, a petty, narrow shrewdness that gained short-term advantages while losing long-term advantages of far greater value.

First of all, one must say that many of the Soviet actions in the early postwar years were unnecessarily irritating to the West. The Russians could have accomplished the subversion of the East European governments with much greater finesse. Indeed, subversion of those governments, from the Russian point of view, should not have been necessary. An independent government can be subservient without enslavement, and subservience might have sufficed for Russia's purpose of economic exploitation. Few military advantages were to be gained from control of the satellites. The USSR at the outset was of course highly desirous of dominating Eastern Europe militarily, for in the past this area of the Continent had been the invasion route into Russia. With this purpose, closing the route of attack, Americans at the time and later surely have been sympathetic. But at the beginning of the postwar era the USSR might as well have withdrawn its troops back to the homeland; the sheer weight of the Soviet army, within easy distance of Eastern Europe, would have dominated the area. Nor was there advantage in raising satellite armies; so carefully trained, they have proved politically unreliable. Moreover, a few years after the end of the Second World War military tactics began to change, what with acquisition by the Soviet Union of atomic weapons. The development of missile technology in the 1950s and 1960s underlined the fact that satellite territory was of little or no military value.

There were other Soviet blunders in the years immediately following the war. At Yalta and Potsdam, the Russians had agreed to a demarcation of occupation zones in Germany that gave the West the most valuable part of the country, the industrial portion that later became the heart of the West German state. The setting up of the German Democratic Republic made this a permanent division of territory. Moreover, when in Great Britain the Churchill government lost the election in 1945 and gave way to the Labor Party, an avowedly socialist party, there was opportunity for the Soviets to flatter this new Labor government, and perhaps try to separate it from its ally, the United States. Instead the Russians rebuffed the British Laborites. They chose to treat the British Labor Party with the same contempt that they had shown the Churchill regime. There was similarly shabby treatment of the French government. Already, during the war, the Russians had refused to consider the French a great power, and it was with difficulty that Britain and the United States persuaded Stalin to permit the French to supervise a zone in Germany and a section of the Anglo-American area in Berlin. In such manner the new Fourth Republic of France found itself insulted by the Eastern colossus at a time when honeyed treatment might have drawn France into the Communist camp. In somewhat similar fashion the Russians frightened the smaller nations of Western Europe into association with the Western Allies. By these tactics—shrewd in the short term, erroneous over the long run—the USSR by its own ineptitude unified the West instead of dividing it, creating by its actions that which it most feared. Soviet tactics by 1947 produced the Western policy of containment. The following year the Soviets, by forcibly taking over Czechoslovakia in the so-called Czech coup, made possible the passage of the Marshall Plan through Congress.

A famous article, "The Sources of Soviet Conduct," appeared in the American journal *Foreign Affairs* in 1947. Written by a "Mr. X," later identified as George F. Kennan of the State Department, the article made a classic plea for a new Western policy toward Russia. Kennan, incidentally, when chargé d'affaires in Moscow the previous year, had sent a long cable to the department in which he had sketched many of the points of his *Foreign Affairs* article. Russian wartime and postwar expansion, he now argued publicly, was only another example of the migrations westward of barbaric peoples from the recesses of the Asiatic heartland, a migration similar to that of the Mongol conqueror of the thirteenth century, Genghis Khan. The best diplomacy for the United States, the persuasive Kennan said, was containment, a policy less than war itself, but a policy of opposing force with force, of drawing a line, a defense perimeter (as the military men liked to describe it), and warning the Russians "Thus far shall you go, and no farther." It was clear, Kennan wrote, "that the main element of any United States policy toward the Soviet Union must be that of a long-term, patient but firm and vigilant containment of Russian expansive tendencies . . . such a policy has nothing to do with outward histrionics: with threats or blustering or superfluous gestures of outward 'toughness' . . . demands on Russian policy should be put forward in such a manner as to leave the way open for a compliance not too detrimental to Russian prestige." Kennan's article ended with an apostrophe to manifest destiny: ". . . the thoughtful observer of Russian-American relations will find no cause for complaint in the Kremlin's challenge to American society. He will rather experience a certain gratitude to a Providence which, by providing the American people with this implacable challenge, has made their entire security as a nation dependent on their pulling themselves together and accepting the responsibilities of moral and political leadership that history plainly intended them to bear."

Shades of 1898. And in the enormously troubled era of fifty years later.

3. *The Truman Doctrine*

It was in the early spring of 1947, with Western Europe in economic peril, with the nations of Eastern Europe falling like ninepins under complete Communist control, that the United States turned to a policy of containment. And at the outset of discussing the Truman Doctrine—which of course was only the first of a series of American moves against what seemed to be the USSR's expansionist policies—one must confront the question of whether the Soviet Union, so badly hurt by the Second World War, was really expansionist, or simply was giving the appearance of expansion. After all, the Soviets if perhaps crudely and erroneously (from the point of view of military necessity) were only taking control of the countries on their borders; in view of the vast depredations suffered by the Russian people during the war, was this simply a prudent policy? In long retrospect it now is fairly clear that the Soviet Union in 1945 was in a condition close to exhaustion. Would it not have been better American policy to have gone slowly against the precautionary territorial arrangements of its great wartime ally, and to continue to offer the hand of friendship, in hope that time and example would persuade the Soviets that the outer world under control of capitalist governments was not in essence hostile to the Communist experiment? Then there might have been no cold war, and all of the extraordinary confrontations, including the Cuban missile crisis of 1962, which came out of it, not to mention the extraordinary cost of the cold war to both the United States and the USSR.

There are many issues, and one must admit many uncertainties, in examining the origins of the cold war, and historians will debate this grand issue for years to come. Suffice to say that the pronouncements and actions of the Soviet Union in 1945, 1946, 1947, and later years so aroused the leadership of the American government that on

The triumvirs. An informal pose.

its part there was never any sense that the Soviet Union was acting out of weakness. The frequently hostile statements of the Russian leaders gave the distinct impression that the USSR was proceeding according to Marxist logic and looking even toward some sort of Armageddon in which capitalism and socialism would fight to the death. This view probably was propaganda; it is difficult now to believe that the Soviet leaders believed it. But they said it. And their actions, which usually were moves of power, supported their words. American leaders beheld words and acts and drew the obvious conclusion. And there is no reason to be sure that if American leaders had pursued another policy, of friendly accommodation, the Soviet leadership would have responded in a friendly way. Stalin may not have been the man of steel, the literal meaning of the revolutionary sobriquet that he had taken in place of his family name, Djugashvili, and perhaps Molotov likewise was not the hammer, as his acquired name indicated (his real name was Scriabin; he was related to the nineteenth-century composer). But Soviet leaders had become accustomed to taking advantage of the weakness of enemies, and even of friends, and American friendship might well not have worked. Moreover, as one theory of Kremlinology has it, Stalin almost needed a foreign enemy in order to tighten his control upon the Russian people. The USSR at the end of the war was in a very difficult condition: its western lands were devastated, industrial capacity down perhaps to half of prewar; the Red Army had seen Europe (and Europe had seen the Red Army) and become infected with Western ideas, especially Western standards of living; many Soviet citizens who had lived under German occupation, in particular the Ukrainians, had proved disloyal. For all these reasons—lack of resources, tens of millions of suspect citizens—if hostility with the United States had not existed it perhaps would have had to be invented.

So Soviet-American wartime friendship turned into hostility and cold war. The first serious postwar confrontation between the United States and the USSR was over Iran in early 1946, when the Russians gave indication of attempting either to make permanent their wartime occupation of the Iranian province of Azerbaijan or else install a satellite government there and divide the country in the manner of Germany, Austria, and Korea. In an agreement signed during the war they had promised to get out of Iran. The date of departure came and went without their exit. President Truman was receiving hundreds of cables and messages from his envoys abroad that the Russians would not leave without heavy American pressure, and so he passed the issue to the United Nations and meanwhile made plain that the United States would support the government in Teheran. After weeks of intransigence the Russians slowly retired.

Troubles meanwhile were looming elsewhere, in Turkey and Greece. The Turkish problem was less visible, as it did not involve Soviet occupation or (as in Greece) a civil war, but it seemed equally exigent. The Turks had managed to sit out most of the war without joining either side, until in the last weeks of the conflict they went over to the Allies. It was obvious that they wished nothing so much as to be let alone. Almost immediately with the end of hostilities the Soviets began to bring heavy pressure on Ankara, demanding control of the Straits and return of territory along the Anatolian border lost at the end of the First World War. The Turkish economy was largely agricultural, and the Turks were not up to supporting a large army against Soviet troops massed on their borders. In the first months of peace the Americans tried to bolster them with words and minor aid, but the situation clearly required more than that.

The Greek problem—the third of these difficulties on the periphery of Europe (it almost seemed as if the Soviet Union was encouraging trouble in places which, considered by themselves, were not vital to American security, but provided test cases for further moves)—had developed out of a civil war that had broken out toward the end of the Second World War, after British troops had entered Greece and re-established the Greek monarchy. Greek Communists were fighting Greek monarchists. There were excesses on both sides. The British troops in Greece in 1945 and 1946 were barely able to maintain order in the vicinity of Athens and Piraeus. The government in London was in financial trouble and foresaw the need to do something about the drain of resources to such apparent sinkholes as Greece.

As events turned out, it was the Greek issue that moved the United States government into the statement of purpose which, when made by the president on March 12, 1947, became known as the Truman Doctrine. Early that year the government of Great Britain had found itself unable to guarantee further support to the government of Greece. The British on February 21 communicated this intelligence privately to Washington, with the advice that if after April 1 the United States could not pay the bill, economically and militarily, then Greece would have to shift for itself, presumably falling to communism. It was a difficult situation. President Truman took the only acceptable course in the face of this threatened disaster and prevented it by a program of economic and military aid to Greece and Turkey and other nations willing to resist aggression, a program that in its sweeping general justification of aid took the appellation of the Truman Doctrine.

Senator Arthur Vandenberg, the Republican Party's leading expert on foreign affairs, urged that Truman make his proposal of aid in a speech before Congress, and in accord with this advice the president went before a joint session on March 12 and asked for $400,000,000 for military and economic aid to the Greek and Turkish governments. In a message notable for its frank and forthright approach, he estimated that the United States had contributed $341,000,000,000 toward winning the Second World War. He pointed out that the assistance he was recommending to Greece and Turkey amounted to little more than 1/10 percent of the wartime investment. "I believe," the president said, "that it must be the policy of the United States to support free peoples who are resisting attempted subjugation by armed minorities or by outside pressures." Great responsibilities, the president remarked, had been placed upon the United States by the swift movement of events, and he was confident that Congress would face these responsibilities squarely.

Congress proved decisively in favor, and the aid bill passed by a vote in the Senate of 67-23 (April 23) and in the House of 287-107 (May 9). This first appropriation under the Truman Doctrine, signed by the president on May 15, was a relatively small program, in view of the outlays that followed under the Marshall Plan and the North Atlantic Treaty Organization, but it was a beginning, and as such marked an upward turn in American diplomatic fortunes. If Greece and Turkey had succumbed to the increasing pressure—Greece was almost surrounded by Albania, Yugoslavia, and Bulgaria, all Communist states; Turkey had its long border with the USSR—Western Europe might have followed in the wake of such a disaster. The two eastern Mediterranean nations had never before been associated with the American national interest, and it was a novel procedure for President Truman to convince the national legislature and the American people that two such foreign localities had now, perforce, come within the American defense perimeter.

Opposition to the Truman Doctrine nonetheless was voluble and sharp. One of the arguments against the program was that the Greek government was undemocratic, corrupt, and reactionary, that Turkey was not a democracy and had been neutral during most of the war. Why (so ran the argument) attempt to defend the free world by aiding such questionable governments? Or, why not let Greece and Turkey pass into the Communist orbit, since those two nations merely would be exchanging one form of undemocratic government for another? The Truman administration could only argue that in matters of foreign policy it was not always possible to choose between white and black. Then too, the government of Greece might evolve toward more democratic ways if it could be economically buttressed. The government of Turkey was already moving from its era of tutelage under Mustafa Kemal toward an era of fuller democratic government. Future governments in Ankara and Athens might turn out to be different from the governments of the moment.

Some opponents of the Truman Doctrine in Congress and in the public press during the spring of 1947 raised the argument that the doctrine bypassed the United Nations. The UN, they claimed, was the place to develop plans for economic assistance on such scales as were required in Greece and Turkey. This argument appeared frequently in the speeches and pronouncements of members of Congress and others whose friendship for the UN had never been warm, and whose sudden stand in favor of handing over the fate of Greece and Turkey to the UN sounded suspiciously like buck-passing.

During the debate over the Truman Doctrine, Representative Walter H. Judd, a former medical missionary to China, drew a comparison between American aid to Greece and Turkey and American aid to China which was momentarily embarrassing to the Washington administration. Judd wanted to know why the United States in 1947 was urging the Communists in one country—China—to cooperate with China's accredited regime, and opposing Communists in other countries with arms and economic aid. Here was a sincere argument, using an analogy not easy to refute. Undersecretary of State Dean Acheson hedged in his answer to Judd, saying that the situation was different. China was a place unlike Turkey and Greece. The point, of course, was that despite the global implications of the Truman Doctrine it was difficult to aid such a large country as China. Later, in the 1960s and early 1970s, it turned out that it was too late to assist even such a small Asian country as South Vietnam. The Truman Doctrine in its practical effect was limited to Western and Mediterranean Europe.

It was a noble gesture, the Truman Doctrine, but it had applied only to Greece and Turkey. In the spring of 1947 Americans began to realize that all Europe was sick, and that something had to be done quickly, some measure of relief to Europe undertaken on a grand scale, or else the local Communist parties would take over. Hanson W. Baldwin in the *New York Times* of March 2, 1947, reviewed the "plague and pestilence, suffering and disaster, famine and hardship, the complete economic and political dislocation of the world." He remarked that the United States was "the key to the destiny of tomorrow; we alone may be able to avert the decline of Western civilization, and a reversion to nihilism and the Dark Ages." The economic situation in all Europe in the spring of 1947 was desperate. With support from the temporary relief organization, the United Nations Relief and Rehabilitation Administration (UNRRA), due to end (UNRRA was launched late in 1943 and came to an end on March 31, 1947), Poland, Hungary, Greece, Italy, Austria, and Yugoslavia found themselves in a bad way. It was at this time that Winston Churchill described Europe as "a rubble heap, a charnel house, a breeding ground of pestilence and hate." Everywhere in Europe people lacked sufficient food, clothing, and shelter. Drought had killed most of the 1946 wheat crop, and the severe winter of 1946–1947 cut the prospects for the crop of 1947. In France, between three and four million acres of wheat planted in the autumn were destroyed in January and February 1947. In England at this time, a coal shortage became so serious that London found its electric power shut off for hours every day. What would the United States do about a Europe on the verge of economic breakdown? Would it pursue a do-nothing policy?

Having already taken a step in the direction of economic aid to Greece and Turkey, the Truman administration found the way clear to a more general and ambitious program of aid to all Western Europe. President Truman on January 21, 1947, had replaced Secretary of State Byrnes with General George C. Marshall. The new secretary in a commencement address at Harvard in June 1947 announced the program that was to bear his name, the Marshall Plan.

4. *The Marshall Plan*

In conceiving the Marshall Plan, the American secretary of state brought together various ideas and opinions of his subordinates in the State Department, linked them to the eagerness of President Truman to arrest the progress of world communism, and contributed his own decisive and open approach. The resultant plan as the secretary elaborated it tentatively before the Harvard assemblage on June 5, 1947, was preeminently the result of staff work in the Department of State. It was the kind of work that the department had not done for a long time, since fifteen years before when Henry L. Stimson was secretary of state. When Marshall had taken over the State Department he had told his undersecretary, Acheson, to straighten out the lines of command, and to set the unwieldy organization on the kind of footing that would enable it to function and would prevent the suffocation of every idea that sought to make its way from desk officers through the hierarchy to the office of the secretary. When the Truman Doctrine injected a new note of decision into American diplomacy, the already reorganized department sprang to life and produced a ferment of ideas that set the secretary to thinking about a general plan of European economic assistance. The original impetus for the Marshall Plan came from a series of extraordinary memoranda by Marshall's able undersecretary of state for economic affairs, the Texas cotton merchant William L. Clayton. If anyone truly was the "father" of the Marshall Plan, it was "Will" Clayton, who reported in detail to Marshall not merely about Europe's economic problems but about the need for a massive injection of American public funds. About this time, George F. Kennan, as head of the department's new policy-planning staff, produced an able memorandum sometimes cited as the beginning of the Marshall Plan, but one must say that Clayton's memoranda were the force behind the new policy. Charles ("Chip") Bohlen, a department career officer who later became ambassador to Russia and to France, then proceeded to draft Marshall's Harvard speech.

The secretary of state himself produced two ideas which went into his speech and were of high importance in the resulting proposal. In his speech Marshall called upon the European governments to help themselves by drafting a program of mutual economic aid, to which the United States would make a substantial contribution. He told the European nations that instead of bringing their various shopping lists to the United States, as had been the case with lend-lease and

George C. Marshall, at Harvard University where he received an honorary degree and delivered his famous "Marshall Plan" address.

UNRRA, the nations should get together and decide among themselves the best allocation of resources. Only after such decision would the United States contribute. "It is already evident," he said, "that before the United States Government can proceed much further . . . there must be some agreement among the countries of Europe as to the requirements of the situation and the part those countries themselves will take. . . . The initiative, I think, must come from Europe. . . . The Program should be a joint one, agreed to by a number, if not all, of the European nations."

Second, there was no stipulation in Marshall's original proposal that it should include only the nations of Western Europe. The Marshall Plan encompassed Russia and satellites in Eastern Europe, and the Soviets could participate if they wished. Both Kennan and Bohlen advised the secretary that the Russians would not come in, but the secretary took some chance in opening the plan to them.

In this provision for an all-European program there might have been the death of the Marshall Plan, even before it passed beyond the stage of proposal. If the Russians had participated in the plan, they could have wrecked it, either through their devious activities or else by their mere entrance. For it was almost inconceivable that Congress would have voted the appropriations necessary to put the Marshall Plan in business if the Russians had chosen to join in Secretary Marshall's proposed program. Fortunately the Russians did not join.

They certainly had their opportunity, as Foreign Secretary Ernest Bevin arranged for a planning meeting in Paris of the European foreign ministers—Britain, France, and Russia. The Paris meeting of foreign ministers opened on June 27, with Molotov present. Bevin dominated the proceedings. After two or three days of desultory conversation, he took a proposal by the French foreign minister Georges Bidault, reduced it to a single page by taking out the extra words, and sent this page to Bidault and Molotov on the morning of July 1. Bevin was urging that the three foreign ministers draw up a proposition for the American government. Molotov had been saying that each nation should send its own shopping list. Bevin coolly told Molotov that the Russians wanted a blank check from the Americans, and what would happen if he, Bevin, went to Moscow and asked for a blank check from the Russians? The meeting of July 1 adjourned on this note. The final meeting, next day, brought a clean break. Bevin presided. Molotov repeated his arguments and finished by saying that any joint Anglo-French action without Russian consent might have very grave consequences. Bidault said the French would go with the British. Bevin said that he, like Bidault, proposed to carry on. The following day, July 3, the British and French governments invited all European states to meet in Paris and draw up a proposal for the American government.

Molotov departed the Paris meeting without a sign that his government would cooperate. The Russians foolishly turned against the Marshall Plan and announced their own bogus program of economic aid to Eastern Europe, known as the Molotov Plan.

Before the Russian policy of obstruction became clear, there was an attempt by two of the satellites, Poland and Czechoslovakia, to accede to the Marshall Plan. Both nations expressed willingness to attend the general planning session scheduled to open in Paris. The party line immediately went out from Moscow, and the Polish foreign minister had the unenviable task of explaining to the American ambassador why his country was turning down participation in the Marshall Plan. When he made his explanations, the foreign minister refused to look the ambassador in the face, and his discomfiture was perfectly clear. In the case of the Czechoslovaks the embarrassment was far worse, as they had shown more interest than the Poles. A delegation from Prague was summoned to Moscow, and Stalin thereupon conversed with Prime Minister Klement Gottwald. The Czechoslovak leader met Stalin alone and came back to his hotel visibly shaken, saying he had never seen the Russian dictator so angry. After a second conference of the Czechoslovaks and Russians, a general meeting in which the Russians more politely set out their objections to the Marshall Plan, the Prague government took back its words and sent back the Paris invitation.

The way was open for action by the American Congress, and action was forthcoming. Debate on Marshall's proposal of June 1947 had begun during the autumn and early winter, and in January 1948 the time of decision arrived. By this date it was apparent that Congress would not balk. Senator Robert A. Taft believed that there was not much good that could come out of helping foreigners, for it would only spread bankruptcy from Europe to America, but he said he would vote for the European Cooperation Act. Anguished individuals such as Henry A. Wallace, the former secretary of agriculture and of commerce who was moving toward open political opposition to the president, denounced the proposed aid program as a wanton attack on the Soviet Union, a "Martial Plan." But Wallace had little support in Congress. The Marshall Plan passed easily and was signed by President Truman on April 3. The initial appropriation, aid for the fifteen months from April 3, 1948, through fiscal 1949 (ending June 30, 1949), amounted to $5,850,100,000. China received Marshall Plan aid, through fiscal 1949, of $275,000,000, and an additional $125,000,000 for military aid. This gesture—and it could be nothing more, for China was fast going down the drain, the country passing to the Communists—was to quiet the "China first" members of Congress.

Sixteen European nations, together with the zones of West Germany and the Free State of Trieste, gathered in Paris in March 1948 and formed the Organization for European Economic Cooperation, or OEEC, an international coordinating body that would represent all European partners in the plan. To these states the United States, via the Marshall Plan, gave through the Economic Cooperation Administration, or ECA (and its successor at the end of 1951, the Mutual Security Administration), between April 3, 1948, and June 30, 1952, the sum of $13,348,800,000. Three nations took over half this amount. The United Kingdom obtained $3,189,800,000, France $2,713,600,000, West Germany $1,390,600,000. Italy (including Trieste) received $1,508,800,000, the Netherlands $982,100,000. Iceland took the smallest amount, $29,300,000. Such was the Marshall Plan in operation.

It was a noble effort by the United States, and in its effect upon the European economy it showed itself vastly worthwhile, for European production in 1950 was 45 percent higher than in 1947, 25 percent higher than in 1938, the last prewar year; in 1952 production was 200 percent over 1938. By the end of the Marshall Plan in 1952, there was an economic base in Europe, a solid foundation on which the United States could build an alliance against the USSR. An effective military alliance would have been impossible in 1947.

All this for the reasonable expenditure of $13,348,800,000, a negligible sum compared to the near $1,000,000,000,000 income of the

American economy during that same period. The Marshall Plan expenditures were only a fraction of America's liquor bill over the same period. Unconvincing were the claims of some political leaders in 1947 and thereafter that European aid was bankrupting the nation, that the billions sent to Europe would force the United States treasury into fiscal chaos, ending the American way of life. The country in 1947–1952 enjoyed an unprecedented prosperity and hardly felt the expenditures of the Marshall Plan.

When the plan ended in 1952 after the beginning of the Korean War, with production in Europe still rising in a manner most encouraging to the people and government of the United States, there were perhaps two problems that Marshall aid had undertaken to solve without complete success. If the plan had hoped to make Europe more efficient in production and marketing techniques, and if it had sought to capture the sympathy of European workers so as to wean them away from communism, it had been something of a failure, for those two goals were not altogether achieved. Europe by 1952 was still inefficient economically. Much of its trade was throttled by cartels, if not by trade barriers at national borders. As for the workers of Europe, in Italy and France (although not in England, Scandinavia, Germany, Austria, Luxembourg, the Netherlands, and Belgium) they had failed in the early years of the Marshall Plan to receive much benefit from the new production that the plan achieved. The poor in Italy and France had not become poorer, but the rich grew richer. Italian and French workers were dissatisfied with their lot and not unwilling to express their feelings by voting Communist in national elections. Even so, despite such difficulties, the Marshall Plan provided a healthy economic base in Europe from which reforms, economic and democratic, might be made in the future. This was no ordinary accomplishment.

The Korean War eventually brought an end to the Marshall Plan, an end to exclusively economic aid to the countries of Western Europe. There had been a stipulation that not a cent of Marshall Plan aid should go into military supplies. Early in 1951 the United States informed Europeans that further American assistance would have to be allotted for defense purposes. (This, incidentally, was not as large a blow as it appeared, for Europe and chiefly Germany benefited hugely from the "Korean boom" in the world market.) By 1952 the United States was giving 80 percent of its aid to Europe in military weapons and the other 20 in defense support. By 1952 the plan, the Economic Cooperation Administration or ECA, merged with its competitor, the Military Defense Aid Program or MDAP, in the Mutual Security Administration, MSA (in 1953 rechristened the Foreign Operations Administration or FOA; in 1955 rechristened the International Cooperation Administration or ICA; in 1961 rechristened the Agency for International Development or AID).

5. *The Berlin Blockade*

A crisis of more than momentary importance in the first half-decade after the war was the Berlin blockade of 1948–1949, which for a time appeared to be a prelude to a third world war. Prior to the Korean War, no crisis looked so dangerous as this Russian attempt in 1948 to seal off Berlin from Western access by rail or road and to force the Western Allies thereby into a change of their German policy.

The blockade took its origin in the deplorable condition of the German economy. The West Germans lived on a "cigarette economy," in which the American cigarette had replaced the inflated Reichsmark as a standard of value. Food rations in the Allied zones were set at 1,500 calories daily, well below the normal requirement. Steel production in Germany in the year 1946 was down to 2.6 million tons. There was little incentive to work, Communist Party memberships began to increase, and the American army was spending $1,000,000,000 a year in relief funds to feed the hungry Germans.

The American military governor, General Lucius D. Clay, naturally sought to change the situation. He persuaded the British to fuse their zone in Western Germany with the American zone, and the result was "Bizonia," which with addition of the French zone became "Trizonia." In June 1948 the Allies instituted a drastic currency reform in Western Germany, repudiating 90 percent of the Reichsmarks then circulating and substituting a new and soundly controlled money. Almost at once the sparks of economic life began to flare up throughout the cities and countryside of Allied-occupied Germany. There commenced such a renaissance of economic life as has hardly been seen during the course of modern history. Meanwhile, in the spring of 1948, a conference of the Western powers in London invited the Germans to elect delegates to a constitutional convention which would create a new government for West Germany.

The economic revival, and the prospect of political revival, thereupon inspired the Russians to a land blockade of the Western sectors of Berlin, beginning April 1, which became total on June 24, 1948.

That there could have been such a thing as a Russian blockade of Berlin and an Allied airlift would have seemed incredible to Americans in 1945. The United States had been uninterested in Berlin in 1945. In the closing days of the war, General Eisenhower's victorious Western armies had moved far into Germany. Troops were not far from Berlin, but they were not in force. The Russians had hundreds of thousands of troops massed close to the city and wanted to take it anyway. Since it was plain that the taking of the city would be costly in lives, Eisenhower advised against the Western Allies' taking Berlin with or ahead of the Russians. As he informed Washington, "May I point out that Berlin is no longer a particularly important objective."

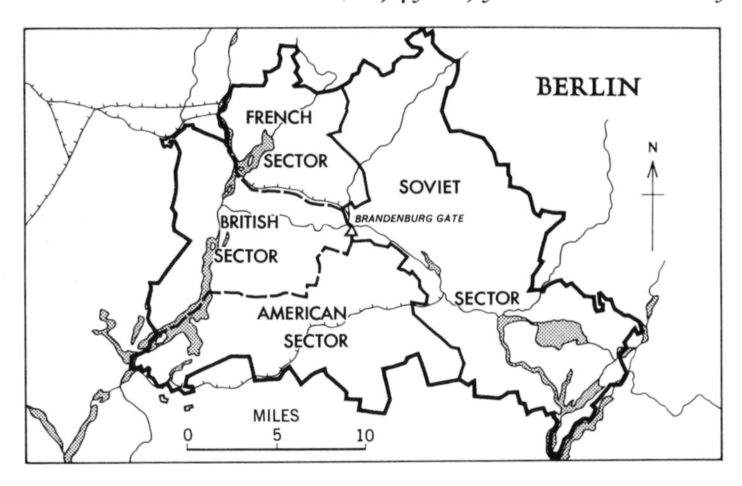

The chiefs of staff in Washington agreed, and President Truman concurred, and Berlin was conquered by the Russians, who allowed the Allies to occupy specified sectors within the city. Access to those sectors was through Russian-held territory. But few individuals worried in 1945 over the security of the Western Allies' position in Berlin, over the fact that the Soviets could blockade at will the Western sectors of the city.

The only thing that saved West Berlin in 1948–1949 was the Allied right to air corridors to the city across the Soviet zone of East Germany. Fortunately, on November 30, 1945, the Allied Control Council in Berlin had approved a paper providing three corridors of communication between Berlin and West Germany, and flights through these three corridors could proceed without notice. The powers, including Russia, established a four-power Berlin Air Safety Center in February 1946. This center continued to operate through the Berlin blockade of 1948–1949, with Russian members coming daily to their offices as if everything were normal.

The only alternative means of supplying West Berlin with food and fuel was to push through armed road convoys, or an armored train.

An airlift seemed at the outset impossible in 1948, but the Allies were determined to stay in Berlin. The odds appeared impossible but General Clay had informed the Pentagon on April 10, 1948:

> When Berlin falls, Western Germany will be next. If we mean . . . to hold Europe against communism, we must not budge. . . . If we withdraw, our position in Europe is threatened. If America does not understand this now, does not know the issue is cast, then it never will and communism will run rampant. I believe the future of democracy requires us to stay.

The Berlin airlift.

The challenge, therefore, was taken up. The Allied air forces by dint of quick work and improvisation brought together enough planes from all over the world to accomplish what by any standard was a gigantic task. General Clay had estimated that by the winter of 1948–1949 it would be necessary for the Allies to bring in 4,500 tons of food and fuel a day. By October 1948 the average daily airlift haul was approaching 5,000 tons. One day in April 1949, 1,398 Allied planes landed a record 12,941 tons. The planes came in every 61.8 seconds. Altogether, from June 24, 1948, until May 12, 1949, Allied planes ferried 1,592,787 tons, over half a ton apiece, for each of the 2,250,000 Berliners in the Western sectors.

In the course of the blockade there was a bit of humor in Berlin. The American commandant, Brigadier General Frank L. Howley, in his *Berlin Command* (1950), has recounted the Russians' difficulty in constructing a war memorial at Pankow during the blockade. The Soviets had contracted to a West German builder for a large statue of Lenin, and the German thoughtfully sent over all the material except Lenin's head, which he kept as security until he should receive payment for his work in the more valuable West marks. The Russians wanted to pay in East marks and appealed to Howley.

"But we must have the head!" wailed General Kotikov. "How can we unveil the monument next week without it?"

"Too bad," was Howley's reply.

The Russians paid in West marks.

Once during the blockade Howley was compelled to invite Kotikov to a lunch conference. Chicken was served, and the Russian commandant complained that it was tough.

"It ought to be," Howley pointed out, "it had to fly all the way from Frankfurt."

At the outset of the blockade the Americans caught the Soviet commander for Germany, Marshal Sokolovsky, in a speed trap on an autobahn, and the marshal—whose bodyguard had jumped out to face the Americans with guns—cooled his heels for an hour, with an American gun in the pit of his stomach, until an officer came along and identified him. And there were two other episodes involving Sokolovsky. One related to his house, where Howley discovered the heating arrangements were via a gas main which ran through the American sector. Howley turned off the gas. Sokolovsky had to move. The marshal's assistants then foolishly put his furniture in a van and tried to truck it surreptitiously through the American sector, and Howley captured the furniture.

But to return to the more highly diplomatic, and serious, aspects of the Berlin blockade. Not merely, of course, did the Western powers supply the people of their sectors in Berlin. The airlift produced in Berlin and throughout Europe a tremendous wave of pro-Allied enthusiasm. Sight of the hundreds of giant transports circling down over Tempelhof airdrome was an indication of Western power that thrilled Berliners, and the morale of the inhabitants of that embattled city rose to such heights that the Russians in disgust called off their blockade on May 12, 1949. The way was clear for a West German government. The way was clear in all Europe for the Marshall Plan. And with the Marshall Plan, Americans hoped, would come sufficient economic power that the Europeans in a not too distant future might be able to participate in defense of their countries against a possible Russian invasion.

In this chapter nothing has been said about the origin and development of the North Atlantic Treaty Organization, which occurred in 1949 and subsequent years. NATO was a logical accompaniment of the Marshall Plan: the plan prepared the economic base from which a European military plan could be constructed. NATO, however, remained subordinate to the Marshall Plan until 1950 and the Korean War, and so it is perhaps better to put off discussion of it until a subsequent chapter dealing with Europe from 1950 onward.

As for President Truman's program of Point 4, the fourth of a series of suggestions that the president elaborated in his inaugural address of January 1949, this in a sense was a world counterpart to the Marshall Plan. It promised technical assistance—American agricultural, mechanical, medical, and administrative knowledge—to the so-called emerging countries (incidentally, those countries heartily disliked the word "underdeveloped" with its unintended meaning of American superiority, and even the word "developing," which carried the same meaning). Unfortunately the program was always more promise than fulfillment. It was announced without much forethought, having been proposed to one of the president's speechwriters by a subordinate official at a crucial moment. The Department of State was not much in favor of it. Quite a lot of time passed before appropriations were arranged; then only $26,900,000 was made available, and funding thereafter was never large; Congress provided $147,900,000 in 1952 and $155,600,000 in 1953, after which the Technical Cooperation Administration, which managed Point 4, lost its identity and specific appropriations. Despite vast wealth the United States could not underwrite the economies of all the poorer nations of the world. Only here and there could efforts at amelioration be made, at places where either a small amount of money could do a large amount of good, or where "pilot projects," demonstrations of the effectiveness of aid, could hope to bring in further assistance from other quarters. And it was difficult to obtain public support in the United States for Point 4; Americans in the war and postwar years already had paid out a great deal for foreign assistance and were disinclined to finance economic development indefinitely for no more precise purpose than developing emerging countries. Many were ready to hear ridicule; the head of the International Cooperation Administration (predecessor of the present-day Agency for International Development), in charge of Point 4 work, was accused of various absurdities and delinquencies: providing striped pants for Greek undertakers and bathtubs for Egyptian camel drivers; supplying wild grass seed for sowing along Lebanese highways; flying Arabs to Mecca; building roads for the royal Cadillacs in Saudi Arabia; and—that ancient political accusation!—iceboxes for Eskimos. (There was "absolutely no trace of iceboxes for Eskimos," the harassed administrator protested, "nor are we in the business of furnishing aid to the Eskimos.").

The first five years of peace in Europe after the Second World War, one might conclude, marked a period of numerous trials and troubles. The course of power and politics on the Continent had proved far different from what Americans had expected in the rosy haze of V-E Day 1945. Europeans and Americans by 1950 had nonetheless come together against what they considered the menace of Russian communism. Matters were not yet out of danger, but the worst, so Americans hoped, was over.

ADDITIONAL READING

Books on the postwar era and afterward include John Lukacs, *A New History of the Cold War* (3d ed., Garden City, N.Y., 1966); Daniel Yergin, *Shattered Peace* (Boston, 1977); Terry H. Anderson, *The United States, Great Britain, and the Cold War* (Columbia, Mo., 1981); Robert M. Hathaway, *Ambiguous*

Partnership (New York, 1981); John L. Gaddis, *Strategies of Containment* (New York, 1982); John W. Spanier, *American Foreign Policy since World War II* (10th ed., New York, 1985).

German problems are in Eugene Davidson, *The Death and Life of Germany* (New York, 1959); Stephen E. Ambrose, *Eisenhower and Berlin, 1945* (New York, 1960); and John Gimbel, *The American Occupation of Germany* (Stanford, 1968).

For Eastern Europe see Lynn Etheridge Davis, *The Cold War Begins* (Princeton, 1975); Bruce R. Kuniholm, *The Origins of the Cold War in the Near East* (Princeton, 1980); and John Gimbel, *The Origins of the Marshall Plan* (Stanford, 1976).

Accounts by or about individuals close to decision include Harry S. Truman, *Memoirs* (2 vols., Garden City, N.Y., 1955–1956); Richard L. Walker and George Curry, *Edward R. Stettinius, Jr. and James F. Byrnes* (New York, 1965), Volume 14 in the American Secretaries series; Robert H. Ferrell, *George C. Marshall* (New York, 1966), Volume 15; Dean Acheson, *Present at the Creation* (New York, 1969), a masterly autobiography; Gaddis Smith, *Dean Acheson* (New York, 1972), Volume 16 in the American Secretaries series; David S. McLellan, *Dean Acheson* (New York, 1976); Richard L. Walton, *Henry Wallace, Harry Truman, and the Cold War* (New York, 1976); and Robert L. Messer, *The End of an Alliance* (Chapel Hill, N.C., 1982). An interesting effort at joint biography is Walter Isaacson and Evan Thomas, *The Wise Men* (New York, 1986): Acheson, Harriman, Kennan, John J. McCloy, Robert Lovett, Charles Bohlen.

One turns, last, to the debate among historians some years ago concerning the origins of the cold war. In 1959 a volume appeared by William A. Williams, *The Tragedy of American Diplomacy* (2d ed., Cleveland, 1962), that advanced a theory about the open-door policy of 1899–1900. That policy, Williams wrote, in fact had started after the end of the frontier in 1890 and applied to all the world—Americans were forcing their goods upon everyone. Williams himself gave the thesis a historical underpinning: *The Roots of the Modern American Empire* (New York, 1969). The result was a series of books, mostly about the cold war, with the Williams interpretation, notably Joyce and Gabriel Kolko, *The Limits of Power* (New York, 1972); Walter La Feber's widely read survey in the America in Crisis series, *America, Russia, and the Cold War* (5th ed., New York, 1985); and Thomas G. Paterson, *On Every Front* (New York, 1979). Gradually so-called traditionalist scholars began to argue: Arthur M. Schlesinger, Jr., "Origins of the Cold War," *Foreign Affairs*, Vol. 46 (1967–1968): 22–52; John Lewis Gaddis, *The United States and the Origins of the Cold War* (New York, 1972); Lisle A. Rose, *After Yalta* (New York, 1972). Robert James Maddox, *The New Left and the Origins of the Cold War* (Princeton, 1973), then focused the wrath of cold war revisionists by concentrating on their footnotes, discovering awkward uses of ellipsis points and in one case plagiarism. Ernest R. May, *The "Lessons" of History* (New York, 1973), announced a plague on the houses of both the revisionists and their critics, saying they were all extremists. William H. Becker, *The Dynamics of Business-Government Relations* (Chicago, 1982), sought to remove the historical underpinning of the Williams thesis. But in the last few years the controversy has died down and virtually ended, with the participants perhaps exhausted.

☆ 11 ☆

China, Japan, and the Korean War

Now, the tradition of which he wrote—that of meeting force with maximum counter-force—is in itself not one that exists outside military textbooks. To be sure, it is a good rule for the employment of troops, but it has no bearing on the relations between governments or between peoples. The American people have accomplished much and attained greatness not by the use of force but by industry, ingenuity, and generosity. Of course the third paragraph of MacArthur's letter [to Representative Joseph W. Martin] was the real "clincher." I do not know through what channels of information the general learned that the Communists had chosen to concentrate their efforts on Asia—and more specifically on his command. Perhaps he did not know just how much effort and how much sacrifice had been required to stem the Communist tide in Iran—in Greece—at Berlin. . . . But then MacArthur added a belittling comment about our diplomatic efforts and reached his climax with the pronouncement that "there is no substitute for victory." . . . there is a right kind and a wrong kind of victory, just as there are wars for the right thing and wars that are wrong from every standpoint. . . . The kind of victory MacArthur had in mind—victory by the bombing of Chinese cities, victory by expanding the conflict to all of China—would have been the wrong kind of victory.

—Harry S. Truman, *Memoirs: Years of Trial and Hope* (1956)

Americans in the years since the end of the Second World War have heard more about Far Eastern affairs than ever before in their history. In magazines and newspapers, from public rostrums and private platforms, information and misinformation about the Far East has poured forth in flood proportions, and there is no indication that the flood is in any way receding. The years since 1945 have been an era of intense interest in the Orient. John Hay could announce a policy of the open door at the beginning of the twentieth century and hear polite applause from certain interested segments of the American people, but even a minor pronouncement on Far Eastern policy from Dean Acheson or John Foster Dulles, not to mention George P. Shultz, at once touched off long, sharp, and acrid debate.

One easily understandable reason for public interest in the Far East has been the vast extent of American involvement in the area during and after the war of 1941–1945. After fighting and winning the war against Japan, the United States was forced to occupy the Japanese Islands, half of Korea, parts of the Chinese mainland, and island groups off the Asian coast: Ryukyus, Bonins, Volcanoes, Marshalls, Carolines, Marianas.

There also has been in recent years a new intellectual attraction of Americans toward the Far East, which has accompanied the diplomatic-military events and further increased American interest in the Orient. During the Hay era at the turn of the century, people in the United States considered the East a strange place, quaint and backward. There was from earliest times little inclination to welcome Orientals into the Western Hemisphere; it was all right to take Western civilization to them, but it was not right if Chinese, Japanese, Indians, or Southeast Asians wished to leave their own area of the world. In the years after 1945 American views changed drastically.

As for the idea long held by American businessmen that the East contained unlimited markets for the products of the nation's industry, that notion had died; it had little to do with American concern over the Far East after 1945. After the Second World War, one heard little about four hundred million customers or the other old-time cries for commercial expansion.

1. *The Communization of China*

Why did China go Communist in the first four years of the postwar era? How could China, after a century of friendship for the United States, since the Cushing Treaty of 1844, turn on its good friend and benefactor at a moment when Americans faced in Soviet Russia the most implacable and dangerous foe they had ever had? This, in truth, is not an easy question to answer. The victory of the Chinese Communists was no simple proposition, and to understand what happened to China in the years after the war one must look back to the events of Chinese history in the 1920s and 1930s and early 1940s.

China, as mentioned in previous chapters, had undergone a time of troubles near the beginning of the twentieth century because of the breakdown of the Manchu dynasty's control over large areas of the Chinese subcontinent. The Manchus had been governing China ever since the mid-seventeenth century, and their power, as had held true of the dynasties before, was in a decline following an initial era of some vigor. In the mid-nineteenth century serious trouble had come with the Taiping rebellion and the Nien Fei uprisings, and by the turn of the century there was no question but that a new regime was due. The Western powers and Japan sought momentarily to partition the empire themselves, but because of the imminence of war in Europe—not, incidentally, because of the American open-door policy—the powers abandoned this effort, and matters rocked along uncomfortably until, almost without effort, the Chinese themselves overthrew the Manchu dynasty in 1911.

The next years were a swirling period when government after government assumed power in a nominal way in Peking, and when in the provinces there was competition for place and power by a large number of local warlords. As events gradually revealed the course of the future, a revolutionary movement in the south of China proved the most important intellectual and military movement in China for the 1920s and 1930s and the first years of the 1940s, for it was from Canton that the Kuomintang or Nationalist Party took its origin and in time moved northward to assume the rule of China in the name of the Chinese people.

The years between 1927 and 1937, from the Kuomintang taking of Nanking to the Japanese attack on China, in which Japan occupied Nanking and began forcing the Nationalist regime into the Chinese hinterland, were the era when General Chiang Kai-shek tried as best he could to secure his control over China, to present a united front toward the foreign powers. There was talk early in this era of relinquishment of extraterritoriality by the Westerners and Japan. Then the Chinese went too far—first with the Russians in the Chinese Eastern Railway affair of 1929, next when they began to tinker with Japanese prerogatives in the South Manchuria Railway, precipitating in 1931 the Manchurian incident by which Japan seized, within two years, all of Manchuria. Pressure thereafter mounted against the Nationalist regime, and Chiang's government tottered on several occasions. In 1937 the Japanese, observing the preoccupation of the Western nations with the series of untoward events in Africa and Europe, decided that the time had come, as Premier Konoye put it, to beat the Chinese to their knees. The Japanese attack on China's coastal cities in 1937 began a new and miserable era for the Nationalist regime.

It was the Sino-Japanese War of 1937 and thereafter which at last brought in the Americans and involved them in the politics of China. The war began with a series of horrible massacres of Chinese civilians and soldiers by the Japanese troops, at Nanking and other places, and the character of the war, thus established in ferocity, never changed during the years that followed. The Japanese were angered that the regime of Chiang Kai-shek retreated to Chungking and there received American support. Their anger and frustration resulted finally in an alliance with Germany and the attack on Pearl Harbor. But American aid to the Chinese only increased after this catastrophic event, and by the years 1943 and 1944 the American government was virtually propping up the Nationalist regime in Chungking—the regime might well have fallen otherwise—by shipping over the hump of the Himalayas supplies and instructors for the Chinese army, and by maintaining in Chinese territory Major General Claire L. Chennault's Fourteenth Air Force. General Joseph W. Stilwell established himself in Chungking not merely as American commander of the China-Burma-India theater, the CBI, but also as military adviser and chief of staff to Chiang Kai-shek. Stilwell thereupon sought to galvanize the Chinese armies to resistance against the Japanese.

Part of Stilwell's endeavors consisted of trying to obtain the military cooperation, perhaps with American supplies, of the Chinese Communist armies; and this effort by the American high command during the Second World War raises the question of the strength of Chinese communism by this time. The Communists in China by the war years were a strong group but not the dominant group, and as late as 1945 (when Stalin on August 14 made a treaty with the Nationalist regime, apparently in the belief that the Nationalists would remain the dominant group in China), it did not seem possible that mainland China within a short period could pass under Communist control. Communism in China had been a faltering affair, and whatever strength the Communists possessed by 1945 had come only after years of labor and some serious setbacks. Russian Communists had attempted in the early 1920s to spread the revolution to China, but they had sought to do it by revolutionizing the views of city workers, an effort that failed miserably. According to the accepted party line, communism was to make its first conquests intellectually in the cities of China, the workingmen were then to be made Communists, and their efforts, according to Russian theory imported into China, would promote and eventually realize the revolution. The city Communists in the mid-1920s attached themselves to the Nationalist movement of Dr. Sun Yat-sen and his successor Chiang Kai-shek, and perhaps their leaders hoped that with time they could control that movement. But Chiang surprised them and put them out in 1927 at Hankow. Communism in China languished after its defeat by the Nationalists, and until a deviationist named Mao Tse-tung undertook to revolutionize the peasantry rather than the city workers, achieving the revolution by a means other than that prescribed by the doctrinaires of Moscow, there was no success at all. When attacked by the Nationalists, the country Communists resisted heroically, and in 1934 they set out on the Long March from Kiangsi province to remote Shensi in China's northwest, where they sought to establish themselves for a revolution which they foresaw distant in the unknown future. The coming of the war between the Japanese and the Nationalists in 1937 was a heaven-sent boon to the Chinese Communists, who because of united front tactics were enabled for a while to present themselves as patriots against the Japanese and in the meantime were relieved of Nationalist military pressure. Gradually they improved their position in their capital city of Yenan and established areas of control behind Japanese lines throughout China, but their power by the end of the Second World War was by no means dominant.

During the war, naturally, they feared entering any coalition with Chiang Kai-shek, remembering the draconian measures he had taken against them nearly twenty years before in 1927 at Hankow and the many years required before communism had again gained strength in China. When Stilwell tried to get the Communists and Nationalists together, he doubtless misguessed the situation.

Stilwell's main effort in China was to reorganize and invigorate the troops of Chiang Kai-shek. Here, surely, was a heroic proposition. General Chennault believed that airpower alone would save China and had many private channels through which he sent these views to Washington; and there were many well-wishers of China in the United States who thought that whatever General Chiang desired should be given to him and not with advice as to how to use it. But the largest difficulty that developed was the dislike of Stilwell for Chiang and vice versa. Stilwell came to dislike Chiang intensely. The American commander referred to the generalissimo of China as "Peanut" and "a crazy little bastard." At one point in their relations, when Stilwell had presented to Chiang what appeared to be virtually an ultimatum from President Roosevelt that he reform his armies, Stilwell repaired to his quarters and wrote out a bit of doggerel, the "Peanut Poem," which must go down as a wartime classic:

> I've waited long for vengeance—
> At last I've had my chance.
> I've looked the Peanut in the eye
> And kicked him in the pants. . . .
>
> For all my weary battles
> For all my hours of woe,
> At last I've had my innings
> And laid the Peanut low. . . .

This was very probably read by General Chiang, whose agents constantly were about Stilwell's quarters in Chungking and made every effort to read his correspondence and dispatches.

But very probably Stilwell did not care, for he had observed the miserable morale of Chinese troops in the field, the corruption that ran rampant through the entire Nationalist government and down through the Nationalist army command to the junior officers, and he saw that if the endless manpower of China were ever to be marshaled effectively in a military way there would have to be the most serious sort of reform of the Chinese armies and probably the Chinese government.

Stilwell had the faithful backing of his military superiors in Washington, General Marshall and Secretary of War Stimson. Even so, the dissatisfaction of various of General Chiang Kai-shek's supporters resulted in President Roosevelt's ordering Stilwell relieved in 1944.

Stilwell's successor, Lieutenant General Albert C. Wedemeyer, did not take a strong stand against the military and other delinquencies of the Nationalist government. The efforts of the American government became more diplomatic than military thereafter.

Wedemeyer was assisted by Major General Patrick J. Hurley, who in November 1944 was appointed American ambassador to Chungking and sought to help Nationalist China through the war. Hurley (who had been born in Choctaw Indian country) liked to demonstrate a blood-curdling Comanche yell. He chose to loose this salutation to the Chinese Communists at Yenan—Mao Tse-tung, Chu Teh, Chou En-lai, and others—when he first met them on an official ambassadorial visit at the airport of their city. He admittedly did not like the Chinese Communist leaders. He referred to them as Mouse Dung and Joe N. Lie. He nonetheless did his best in China. His was not an easy mission, and he found himself crossed by his nominal subordinates in the foreign service accredited as observers at Yenan and elsewhere, such highly talented and trained foreign service officers as John Stewart Service and John Paton Davies, who naturally thought he did not know much about China. At any rate Hurley's disgust

Mao Tse-tung confers with Patrick J. Hurley. (Between them is Army observer Col. I. V. Yeaton.)

mounted to a point where, after recall to the United States in the autumn of 1945, he resigned in a huff in November of that year. He charged publicly that his work had been sabotaged, and he engaged thereafter in a crusade against disloyal Americans that eventually found much sympathy among his fellow countrymen.

In the years that followed, down through 1949, the Communists achieved control of China. Ambassador Hurley was replaced by a long-time Presbyterian missionary in China, the distinguished president of Yenching University in Peking, Dr. John Leighton Stuart, who remained ambassador to China until his resignation in 1952. Ambassador Stuart presided at the American embassy in Nanking during the downfall of the Nationalist regime, and his detailed and touching memoir, *Fifty Years in China*, is one of the best accounts available on why China went Communist.

The ambassador watched a succession of American special missions to China and saw them fail, one after the other. The Chinese problem was too much for them. The essential difficulty, as he wrote in his memoirs, was "a gigantic struggle between two political ideologies with the overtones of democratic idealism perverted by bureaucratic incompetence on the one side, succumbing to a dynamic socialized reform vitiated by Communist dogma, intolerance and ruthlessness on the other. And the great mass of suffering inarticulate victims cared for neither but were powerless to do anything about it."

The first and major diplomatic attempt by the United States to assist Nationalist China in the postwar years was the mission of General Marshall, who went out to the Far East as special ambassador in December 1945, following Ambassador Hurley's resignation, to attempt to bring together the Communists and Nationalists. The hopes of the Marshall mission were bright at first; Ambassador Stuart later believed that the two sides came close to agreement. General Marshall later said, apropos his efforts to form a coalition government, that the Communists favored the idea because they "felt the Kuomintang was just an icing on the top and all its foundations of public support had become almost nonexistent or at least hostile, so if they could ever get the thing in the political arena they would win . . . it would not have been hard but a rather easy thing for the Communists to dominate the government."

After the smoke began to clear in China, following the Japanese surrender, the weakness of the Nationalist regime became apparent. When both sides violated the Marshall truce, and when the Nationalists in 1947 began a full-scale military campaign against the Communists in Manchuria, the fate of the Chiang Kai-shek government was sealed.

If one were to assess the relative contribution to the fall of Nationalist China on the mainland, the chief portion would lie with the Chiang regime, the second with the Communists, the third with the Russians who supported the Chinese Communists at least spiritually (there is little or no proof of any Russian material support to the Chinese revolution), and the least portion with the United States.

The Chiang regime was nearly hopeless. Government affairs by early 1949 were in utter confusion. Until the last, incompetence was the order of the day. The Nationalists sought to stop the wild inflation of their final months by instituting on August 19, 1948, a new currency, the gold yuan, equal to four United States dollars, which was handled not by their own treasury officials but by a private and respected group of Shanghai citizens who were to publish statements each month of the issues and backing of the currency. Despite brutal measures taken by Chiang Kai-shek's eldest son, Chiang Ching-kuo, against speculators in Shanghai, by the end of September 1948 the gold yuan had lost 98 percent of its value.

All the money that the United States had put into China between 1937, the beginning of the Sino-Japanese War, and the departure of the Nationalists from the mainland in 1949 had gone down the drain, so far as concerned shoring up the Nationalist regime. Grants and credits in the twelve-year period 1937–1949 had come to the large total of $3,523,000,000. About 40 percent had been authorized before V-J Day and the remainder thereafter. This did not include so-called sales, virtually gifts, to the Chinese government of American military- and civilian-type surplus property made since V-J Day, material with a procurement cost of over $1,078,000,000. Nor did such totals include large quantities of ammunition left by American forces in China and transferred by the United States to the Chinese government at the end of the war, or the cost of special missions to China, or relief contributions through such agencies as the World Health Organization. It is a strange commentary on United States policy toward China that in the postwar years 1945–1949 the American government contributed about $2,000,000,000 in grants and credits to the Chinese, while at the same time the Russians before their retirement from Manchuria took $2,000,000,000 worth of machine tools and other booty, stripping many factories bare, hauling off to Siberia everything that was portable; it is also strange that the net result of this subtraction and addition by the two powers was the almost universal impression among the Chinese people that the Russians were their benefactors and the Americans their oppressors.

On October 1, 1949, the Central People's Government of the People's Republic of China was formally inaugurated at Peking and began to seek recognition from foreign governments. The Soviet Union recognized it the next day, October 2. The Nationalist government, now resident in Taipei, the capital of Formosa (which the Nationalists renamed Taiwan), severed relations with the USSR on October 3, and the following day the United States announced that it would continue to recognize the Chiang Kai-shek government.

2. *The Occupation and Democratization of Japan*

Of the many unexpected events and strange occurrences in the Far East after the Second World War, none was more spectacular than the occupation of Japan by the United States armed forces and the democratization of that country under the rule of General Douglas MacArthur. At the end of the war, MacArthur set himself up in Tokyo and began to order the course of Japanese affairs. The American general became a latter-day shogun, something of an emperor, a dictator. Who in 1941 could have foretold such a turn of affairs?

MacArthur proved a happy choice for the job in Japan. His critics would always describe him as a little larger than life, as an ambitious man who had done everything in his career with a success more complete than he deserved, but no matter how one felt about the general there could be no doubt that in his first years in Tokyo he lent a prestige and authority to the occupation that no other American could have given it. When MacArthur's limousine drove up to his office, a respectful crowd of Americans and Japanese was always on hand. When the general left Tokyo on his homeward trip in 1951, recalled in the atmosphere of censure by President Truman, Japanese lined the route to the airport. MacArthur in Japan became a strange kind of democratic autocrat who ordered the new Japanese constitution to be composed by his underlings, apparently writing in a few phrases himself, and then presented the constitution to the Japanese people with such commanding presence that they ratified it and were thankful. When he finished his work at Tokyo, the Japanese were largely governing themselves, the economy of the nation was booming, the Japanese government was on the high road to independence and foreign recognition.

The occupation made many changes in Japanese life. American occupation authorities promoted a revived labor movement, land reform, freedom of the press, women's suffrage, educational reform, and efforts to give the average Japanese some protection against what had been an oppressive and brutal police. These measures acquainted all classes of Japanese society with ideas of freedom and liberty. When the Japanese received their national independence in the Japanese Peace Treaty Conference held at San Francisco on September 4–8, 1951, and when the occupation came to an end with ratification of the peace treaty early the next year, it proved impossible to turn the clock back completely, impossible to repudiate all the occupation reforms.

Admittedly, some American measures during the occupation were not altogether successful. The Americans sought to "humanize" the emperor, and in a New Year's rescript of January 1, 1946, Emperor Hirohito repudiated (as he described it) "the false conception that the Emperor is divine." How much change this announcement could make in Japanese attitudes was difficult to say. Likewise, American efforts failed to break up the concentration of business enterprise in Japan. Ever since the industrialization of Japan in the later nineteenth century, business enterprise had concentrated in the hands of a small group of wealthy families, the *zaibatsu* such as the Mitsui and Mitsubishi, and it was the hope of American occupation authorities that decartelization might create economic democracy. Despite an active program of decartelization, it proved an extraordinarily difficult task to change the pattern of an economy. To play safe, to avoid risking a collapse of the Japanese economy through perhaps economically dangerous methods of cartel control, it was finally decided to keep the cartels, to follow a policy of "putting the cartel before the hearse."

But by and large the occupation proved highly satisfactory, in that many of the reforms continued after the peace treaty. The postwar Japanese government has been much more responsive to demands of its citizenry than any previous government of the islands. Doubtless there are possibilities for revival of the ways of the past, but they are hardly important enough to remark. Consider militarism, so omnipresent in prewar Japan. In postwar Japan militarism has almost disappeared. Too many Japanese were killed in the war: the battle losses among soldiers, sailors, and airmen, the casualties from the American air force's fire bombings in Tokyo and elsewhere, and the holocausts at Hiroshima and Nagasaki were terribly costly. The tragedy of the Second World War was by 1945 so omnipresent in Japan that militarism could no longer have had its old attraction. The so-called MacArthur constitution contained a clause renouncing war that was reminiscent of the Kellogg-Briand Pact of 1928 and sounded for this reason altogether American in expression, but the Japanese apparently accepted this remarkable clause in good faith, glad to be excused from further fighting. According to the constitution the Japanese people "forever" renounced "war as a sovereign right of the nation and the threat or use of force as a means of settling international disputes." To carry out that hope, the constitution continued, "land, sea, and air forces, as well as other war potential, will never be maintained." When these provisions of American military government first appeared they evoked little or no criticism. Later, during and after the Korean War when it seemed necessary that Japan establish defense forces of strength and size, the general public antipathy in Japan toward military men and measures had hardly lessened. It prevails to the present day.

One of the most interesting aspects of post-occupation Japan has been the extraordinary economic success. In the years after 1952 the Japanese economy passed the "take-off" stage that the American economy had entered many years before, and moved with unanticipated rapidity into an era of so-called consumer culture that has made Japan a showcase throughout Asia and perhaps even for nations of the West (by the end of the 1960s the Japanese had surpassed West Germany in production, their economy was the third largest in the world, after those of the United States and the Soviet Union). Year after year, the Japanese economy expanded. The visible symbols were there for everyone to read: the well-kept houses with television aerials, and inside the very latest household appliances; highways filled with automobiles and trucks; trains that moved like clockwork along the welded rails; ultramodern airports. In automobile production the Japanese threatened to overtake the Americans. Toyota became one of the three largest car makers in the world. Japan's exports of cars to the United States exploded from fewer than 2,000 in 1960 to nearly 2 million by 1980. Hondas were now made in Ohio, Nissan erected a plant in Tennessee, General Motors and Toyota assembled cars in California. Japanese engineers meanwhile had taken on and seemingly defeated American engineers in designing semiconductor products; Japan claimed to have most of the world market for the advanced 64K RAM microchip.

The reason for the astonishing dynamism of Japan's economy was difficult to discover, although there were several theories. Economists did not quite know what to make of it. The observer was reminded of the old remark that according to all the laws of aerodynamics the bumblebee cannot fly. Perhaps the American occupation had freed Japan from the remnants of feudalism, making possible an outburst of individual initiative. Or there was an unexpected potential in the economic circumstances of Southeast Asia after the Second World War that burst its bonds—but, then, Japan was competing all over the world, and such a theory did not explain too much. Some Western businessmen were complaining about the sluggishness, the uncooperativeness of their work forces, and noticed that in Japan a kind of client relationship had developed between workers and employers; they spoke wistfully of the Japanese work ethic as opposed to the goof-offs in their own factories. The truth was that no one knew why Japan had made such a huge economic advance.

Politically the new Japan behaved in a cautious manner, seeking to avoid offense not merely to the erstwhile victor, the United States, but to all other governments that had suffered because of Japan's deplorable choice of allies during the Second World War. The Japanese government easily could have "gone atomic," had it wished. Scientific know-how and the means to create weapons were there. Propriety would have demanded a revision of the peace treaty. As mentioned, the Japanese people showed no inclination to take on the accouterments of major military power.

Internationally the Japanese were pursuing an astute policy. It seemed to show that restraint, modesty, and decorum could bring as many tangible results as the old advices about power advanced by Prince Bismarck in the latter nineteenth century. For the other nations of the world were careful in their behavior toward the Japanese, allowing Tokyo the best of both worlds—all the respect and care due an atomic power, without the expense and danger. The United States in 1960 renegotiated the treaty of alliance signed nine years earlier at the time of the peace treaty; the earlier alliance had contained signs of the virtually vassal relationship of the Japan of that time, and those signs were absent from the instrument of 1960.

One may fairly conclude that the new Japan has thus far proved worthy of American confidence. Under MacArthur the Japanese nation was not remade in six years. "The Japanese people since the war," MacArthur told Congress in 1951, "have undergone the greatest reformation recorded in modern history." There could be some doubt about this. Still, the new Japan is a nation far different from the one that upset the peace of Asia in the years before and immediately after Pearl Harbor.

3. *The Korean War*

American occupation of Korea, unlike that of Japan, encountered grave troubles of an unexpected sort which led not to peace but to further war. The difficulties in Korea were caused in general by the post-1945 antagonism between the United States and the Soviet Union. In particular they stemmed from the division of Korea in 1945 into two zones of occupation, Soviet and American, separated by the thirty-eighth parallel.

After this division of Korea in 1945, the events that led to the Korean War are not difficult to trace. In September 1947, when East-West tensions were in evidence, the United States informed the USSR that it was referring the question of Korean reunion and independence to the United Nations. In January of the next year, the Russians announced that the UN commission scheduled to visit Korea would not be permitted to enter North Korea. Elections were held in South Korea in May 1948. The government of the American-sponsored leader in South Korea, Syngman Rhee, in December 1948 signed an agreement with the United States for economic and military assistance. A People's Republic meanwhile had been set up in North Korea in September.

At this juncture there occurred a certain confusion, or apparent confusion, on the part of American government and military leaders. The American secretary of state during the second part of the Truman administration, from 1949 to 1953, was Dean Acheson, who as undersecretary from 1945 to 1947 had taken a large part in the drawing up of the containment policy for Europe—the Truman Doctrine and the Marshall Plan. Acheson was not greatly interested in the Far East, but he knew enough about its confusions and complications to realize that the best policy probably was to avoid interference. His friend and mentor, General Marshall, who in 1947–1949 preceded him as secretary, had found out during a mission to China that there was little to do there until the dust settled. Beyond keeping control of the bases in Japan, Okinawa, and the Philippines, neither Marshall nor Acheson elaborated a Far Eastern policy. It is clear that in 1949–1950, Acheson was attempting to stay away from involvement.

On June 25, 1950, the North Koreans attacked the South. Was this a simple effort to embarrass the United States in an area of the world where it was unprepared? Militarily the commitment of American troops to the Korean Peninsula was undesirable. But for a diplomatic reason—the need to block, if only momentarily, what was seen as Soviet adventurism in the Far East—this had to be done.

The decision of June 1950 to commit American troops in Korea amounted to a complete turnabout. In terms of America's commitments in Europe, and of the danger of the war's spreading in the Far East from one tactically disadvantageous place to another, the decision was embarrassingly difficult. Without blinking, believing that the Soviet Union had challenged the United States through its proxy, the government of North Korea, Acheson and Truman went ahead. Truman on June 27 instructed the Seventh Fleet to patrol Formosa Strait (and thus defend Taiwan against a Communist attack from the mainland) and authorized use of the navy and air force in Korea. On June 30 he gave MacArthur permission to use army combat and service troops in Japan "to insure the retention of a port and air base in the general area of Pusan." He and Acheson knew that at the outset they had very little military force to work with, only the weak occupation garrison, but they were determined to resist.

Incidentally, there is considerable reason to believe, though there have been no confirming revelations from the Russian side, that the Soviet Union's leadership, especially the redoubtable Stalin, was astonished at the American *volte face* over Korea—that this American move was entirely unexpected, and that it rattled the Kremlin's calculations for months thereafter and indeed created an aspect of high uncertainty about American moves which made the Soviets very careful with their great antagonist during the next few years.

Because of Soviet unpreparedness for American opposition it was possible for the United States to obtain the sanction of the United Nations for its military action in Korea, and this eventually had some

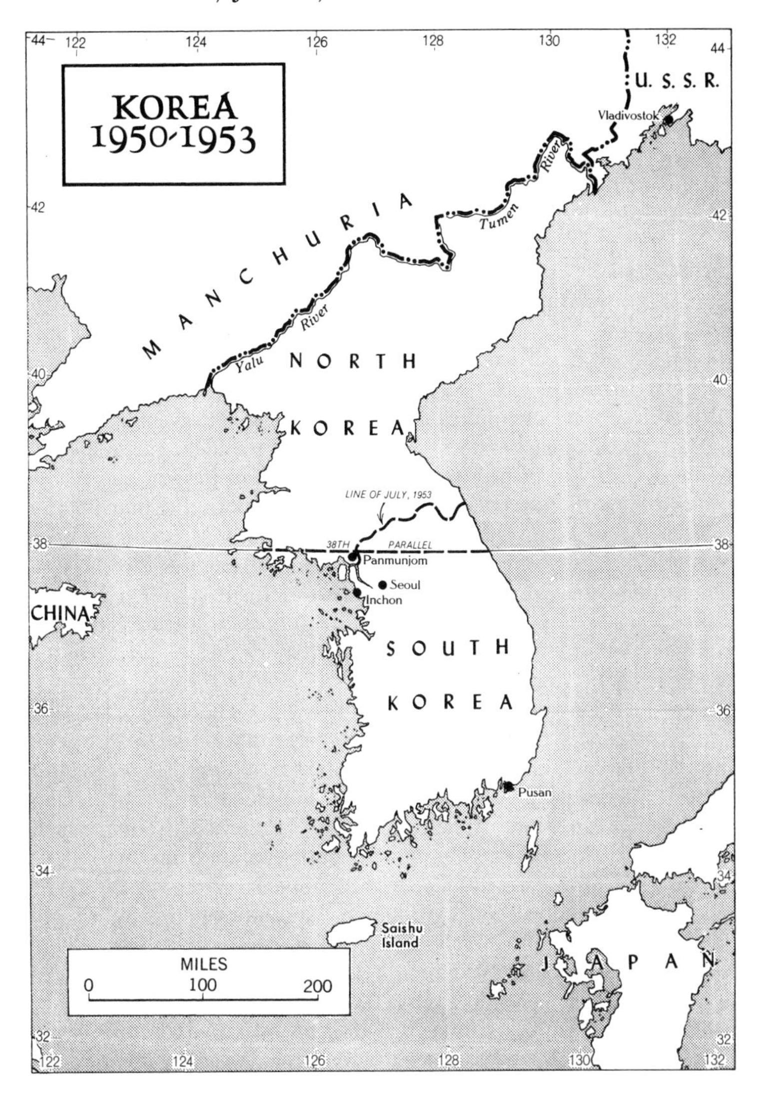

military—though far more diplomatic—advantage. The USSR had been boycotting meetings of the UN Security Council since January 1950 when its delegate, Jacob Malik, had walked out in protest against continued Western recognition of the diplomatic envoys of Nationalist China. Malik was unable to obtain instructions to reenter the Security Council until August 1, 1950, by which time the United States had received UN support for the Korean War. On June 27 the Council, its Russian colleague absent, called upon UN members to "furnish such assistance to the Republic of Korea as may be necessary to repel the armed attack and to restore international peace and security in the area." It was the same day that Truman ordered air and naval forces into Korea, three days before he authorized ground troops. The UN voted a unified UN command in Korea under a commander to be designated by the United States, and General MacArthur was so designated on July 8, 1950.

In view of its diplomatic and military consequences, perhaps the most debatable episode in the conduct of the war was the UN invasion of North Korea undertaken in October 1950. Invasion of a Russian satellite was unique in American post-1945 strategy and diplomacy. It never has been attempted since. And here again, it is necessary to suspect, Secretary Acheson made a miscalculation. He had received warnings of the possibility of Chinese intervention, should UN troops advance beyond the thirty-eighth parallel. The mainland Chinese government had just established itself in Peking, and Acheson evidently did not believe it was capable of mounting much if any military opposition. Without much investigation he seems to have concluded that the Chinese probably were just talking. He chose to ignore them. Having already had to reverse his general Far Eastern policy (or lack of policy) by intervening militarily in Korea, he now compounded that error by permitting the war to widen with the entrance of the Communist Chinese.

The invasion of North Korea, following General MacArthur's brilliantly conceived Inchon landings in September, brought Chinese intervention on a massive scale. The intervention produced a second American retreat down the peninsula below Seoul, this time during the cold Korean winter. One large group of American troops, which MacArthur had placed under a command separate from the bulk of his forces, had to evacuate men and equipment by sea. It was a harrowing retreat, in the course of which the commander of the Eighth Army, General Walton Walker, was killed in a road accident. There was serious worry in Washington whether the American troops could hold on in Korea or would have to be evacuated to Japan. MacArthur spoke dejectedly of evacuation. British Prime Minister Clement Attlee came to Washington in a panicky state of mind. At this point Secretary Acheson and President Truman showed real resolution, as did the new secretary of defense, General Marshall, and the chairman of the joint chiefs of staff, General Omar Bradley. A new commander hurried out to Korea, General Matthew B. Ridgway, and by quick action managed to stabilize the lines. It had been a very close call.

After recouping their strength, the Americans began another push upward, a sort of slow-but-sure "meat grinder" advance known in army parlance as Operation Killer, followed by a tactic picturesquely named Operation Ripper. Encountering this new American power, the Communists through the Russian delegate on the Security Coun-

Truman and MacArthur at a meeting on Wake Island, October 1950. The general assured the president that the Chinese would not intervene in force.

cil, Malik, raised the subject of a truce. After a frustrating two years of talk between American and North Korean representatives meeting most of the time in an improvised "truce tent" at Panmunjom, the truce went into effect on July 27, 1953.

Meanwhile had come a great debate in the United States over the conduct of American diplomacy in the Far East—one of the most vociferous arguments in many years.

The great debate mainly was over Korea, but it also concerned President Truman's abrupt dismissal of MacArthur in 1951. President Truman removed the general from command because he had flagrantly disobeyed a presidential order against pronouncements on foreign policy by government officials without prior clearance from the state department. MacArthur had disagreed with some of the strategic and diplomatic views of the Truman administration, and with little regard for the consequences and perhaps as a direct challenge to the president, the general had talked openly to reporters and sent communications to friends at home, one of them a letter to the Republican leader of the House of Representatives, Joseph W. Martin, which was an open invitation to President Truman to dismiss him or acquiesce in the general's judgment. With the unanimous support of the joint chiefs of staff in Washington, Truman dismissed MacArthur from all Far Eastern commands.

The American people, irritated over Korea and China, used the occasion of MacArthur's relief to give the discharged general a welcome the like of which had not been seen since the Lindbergh enthusiasm of 1927 and Admiral Dewey's reception in 1899.

MacArthur came home in triumph. San Francisco, New York, and innumerable other localities went wild for the general. After MacArthur Day in New York City, the department of sanitation reported that the MacArthur litter weighed 16,600,000 pounds; the previous record had been 3,600,000. It was the general's first visit to his country since a short trip from the Philippines in 1937, and the homecoming may have been warmer for this reason, perhaps also because he and the nation were to each other such unknown quantities. But whatever the ingredients of his welcome, it could have been construed only as a demonstration against the Truman administration. The president did not greet the general on the steps of the White House, but MacArthur achieved the next best recognition in being invited to address a joint session of Congress, with his speech broadcast over the national radio and television networks.

The MacArthur hysteria provided an occasion, however, for a careful public statement by the Truman administration of the basic principles and purposes of American diplomacy during the Korean War, and this statement deserves some attention. When the general's greeting had run its course, two senatorial committees in May and June of 1951 held "an inquiry into the military situation in the Far East and the facts surrounding the relief of General of the Army Douglas MacArthur from his assignments in that area."

The MacArthur hearing, for those American citizens who followed its stenographic reports closely, was extremely enlightening. After the Chinese had intervened in North Korea in late November 1950, MacArthur had spoken out in favor of attacks on the Chinese mainland. The general had been giving the impression that the slow pace of the war, the moving up and down the Korean peninsula, had derived entirely from strategic blunders by politicians and political generals in Washington. Such allegations were major political attacks in the pre-presidential campaign atmosphere of the capital in 1951–1952, and the Truman administration's answer to its deposed proconsul may have taken some inspiration in the political need for a defense. Certainly much of the great debate of 1951–1952, defense and offense, carried implications for the presidential campaign. Even so, the administration's response had a ring of sincerity. General Bradley put the administration's reasoning succinctly. "Taking on Red China," Bradley said at the hearings, would have led only "to a

MacArthur addressing a joint session of Congress, wherein he made his famous statement, "Old soldiers never die, they just fade away."

larger deadlock at greater expense." "So long," he said, "as we regarded the Soviet Union as the main antagonist and Western Europe as the main prize," the strategy advanced by MacArthur "would involve us in the wrong war at the wrong place at the wrong time and with the wrong enemy."

Nothing could have been clearer than Bradley's statement of the American position. It was a position that derived not from blunders by politicians and political generals, but from careful consideration of all the factors in the United States's politico-military policy. MacArthur had failed to understand the many responsibilities of his government and had advocated a policy in the Far East that was exclusively military in nature. He had been so ill-advised as to push his views in the public press and in letters to congressmen, rather than keep his opinions in proper military channels. After the controversy over his dismissal had cooled, the Bradley-Truman view of strategy and diplomacy seemed sensible.

There remained the presidential campaign, toward which much of the great debate over foreign policy, as mentioned, had been directed.

The Korean War became perhaps the prime issue of the campaign, although it was accompanied on the Republican Party's side by two others, corruption in the government and communism in the government. The GOP's formula for victory was K^1C^2 (Korea, corruption, communism). The Republican platform argued that Allied morale in Asia was crumbling because Russia's "Asia first" policy contrasted so markedly with the American policy of "Asia last." The Republican nominee for president, General Eisenhower, eventually was moved to declare that if elected he would "go to Korea" and straighten things out. For this reason among others, Eisenhower was elected. Soon after his inauguration, and perhaps because of his trip to Korea, the Korean War came to an end with the armistice of July 1953. The great debate ended with it.

The Truman administration's views on Korean strategy had prevailed. Eisenhower in his short period of office during the war did not change the Korean strategy of limited war—of war for a limited purpose, the containment of Soviet-inspired aggression in Korea—and achievement of this purpose, one can fairly say, marked the basic achievement of the Korean War. This was a large success of American policy, this turning into victory of what on all sides in June 1950 and again in November–December of that year had looked like imminent defeat.

Other events of diplomatic importance followed from the Korean conflict. The war encouraged the United States to a far larger rearmament than it had begun in 1948 and 1949. The United States roused its allies in Europe and made a heroic effort to put teeth into NATO, engineering the appointment of General Eisenhower as supreme commander of NATO forces.

Likewise there were some marked economic effects of the Korean War. It seems fairly certain that although the Korean War did not pull the Untied States out of an economic recession—the downward economic trend that had begun in 1949 had reversed itself well prior to the North Korean invasion—it did give an impetus to the American economy that sent it spinning ahead to what over the next years proved ever higher levels of production, wages, and employment. Two months after the Korean War began, employment crossed the 62,000,000 mark, two million beyond the fondest dreams of New Dealers at V-J Day. And there was even a sort of mental fillip that came with the Korean War. Many of the post-1945 worries about an economic depression, memories of the Great Depression that had only been temporarily stilled by the prosperous years of the Second World War, were laid to rest during the Korean boom. With release from this fear, the economy moved ahead with unheard-of confidence.

The facts set out above do not make a triumph of the tragedy of Korea. No one in the United States is soon going to forget the casualties during that conflict: 33,629 young men killed in action. And the cost of the war was many billions of dollars.

In long retrospect it sometimes is tempting to think that a more forceful strategy toward the Chinese intervention in the Korean War might have given a better object lesson to the aggressive leaders of Communist Asia, and perhaps prevented the Vietnam War. Individuals who wish to ruminate on this possibility should also consider the kind of strategy that General MacArthur would have liked to serve up in Asia during the war of his time. Shortly after his retirement he talked confidentially to two newspaper correspondents, and their accounts of his conversation were published within days of his death in 1964. He said that victory had been in the palm of his hand but because of the supine behavior of officials in Washington (President Truman was so mistaken that "the little bastard honestly believes he is a patriot") together with those in London it had been turned into a stalemate that eventually would produce a calamitous defeat for America and the Western world. The general had wanted to drop between thirty and fifty atomic bombs in North Korea and take out the enemy's air force, both installations and men. Then he would arrange a pincers in the upper part of the peninsula, with help from a half million troops furnished by Chiang Kai-shek and "sweetened" by two marine divisions. Four-fifths of these troops would land on the west coast and the remainder on the east. They would throw a cordon across the peninsula, cutting enemy communications, and within ten days the starving hostile forces would have had to sue for peace. To keep out reinforcements MacArthur would have sown—by plane, truck, wagon, and cart—a five-mile belt of cobalt across the border between Korea and China. Cobalt has an active life of at least sixty years, and hence would deny access to any army on foot for that length of time. As for possible Russian intervention:

> It makes me laugh . . . that Russia would commit its armies to a war in China's behalf at the end of an endless one-track railroad to a peninsular battleground that led only to the sea. Russia could not have engaged us. She would not have fought for China. She is already unhappy and uncertain over the colossus she has encouraged. . . . It was in our power to destroy the Red Chinese army and Chinese military power. And probably for all time. My plan was a cinch.

Years later a strange postscript to the Korean War occurred, the *Pueblo* case of 1968. It raised once again the debates of 1950–1953, in particular the issue of whether a limited war was a sufficient solution to aggression in the Far East. The lessons of the Korean War were brought to bear upon the capture of this United States navy ship by the naval forces of the North Korean government, for the government of the United States chose not to make a retaliatory attack on North Korean military installations or cities, took the long, tedious route into negotiation, and actually issued an abject apology for violation of North Korean rights. Then upon release of the *Pueblo*'s crew it made the remarkable assertion that the statement of apology had been offered under duress. After release of the *Pueblo*'s crew, the case almost immediately focused upon the conduct of the captain, Lloyd Bucher, who had surrendered the ship and crew without a fight, and the conduct of all crew members who, while in jail in North Korea, violated the military services' injunction that after capture every member of the armed forces is restricted by the pledge, "I am bound to give only name, rank, service number and date of birth." There followed a long, inconclusive trial of the captain, and the American public was treated to an extraordinary recital of North Korean brutality and American suffering. The real issue, however, was not the fate of the crew but the course of American policy, the fact that the government of the United States, despite the passage of years, was not willing to give up the lesson of the war of 1950–1953, namely, that a limited war had to be kept limited. Even when the North Koreans on April 14, 1969, shot down an American reconnaissance plane in international waters off the North Korean coast, a lumbering, propeller-driven Super Constellation carrying 31 Americans, all of whom were killed, the government of the United States did no more than protest through diplomatic channels.

In the early 1970s the relations of the Untied States and the government of South Korea entered a new period of possible strain. During the preceding quarter-century relations generally had been satisfactory and after departure of the aging Syngman Rhee in 1960 to Hawaii, where he died a few years later, had become fairly close. Then President Park Chung Hee in October 1972 turned South Korea into a dictatorship. He rearranged the constitution and began to run the country himself.

What to do about President Park's regime? In a matter of months there was trouble. Koreans resident in the United States were being sought out and warned not to talk against the policies of Park. And in August 1973 agents of the South Korean Central Intelligence Agency apparently abducted from a Tokyo hotel Park's vociferous critic, Kim Dae Jung, who in the 1971 presidential election had amassed 46 percent of the vote. The agents spirited him out of Japan, back to Korea. There was an uproar, with sharp protests by the Japanese and American governments, and Kim turned up safely, released in the vicinity of his house in Seoul. He had been beaten and trussed up but otherwise was in fairly good shape. Having protested Park's dictatorship from what he thought was the safety of a foreign country, he had discovered that it was not so safe. The presumption was that without the immediate diplomatic protests from Tokyo and Washington he would have been killed by his abductors (Kim said that he was to have been dumped into the sea, so that no trace of him would ever be found). This presumably with the knowledge and approval of the president of the Republic of Korea.

In 1979 a palace revolution in Seoul displaced President Park, by the simple expedient of his murder by the chief of Korean intelligence, and a new Korean president took office, General Chun Doo Hwan. He proved no more of a friend of human rights than his predecessor, and yet like President Park his hold upon his office seemed vise-like.

The one encouraging aspect of American-Korean relations was that beginning in the 1960s the economy of Korea began to bound upward, and "bound" was the word, for it rose more rapidly than did that of Japan after the Second World War. South Korea rapidly became an industrial country, and in shipbuilding, steel, automobiles, and textiles commenced exporting to neighboring countries. Its technicians and workers went to countries of the Middle East to aid the vast construction projects there. In the late 1970s, Korean industry began to challenge that of Japan, for the cost of Korean labor was a fraction of that of Japanese. By the mid-1980s, Korean automobiles were entering the American market.

Politically South Korea nonetheless is drifting on a dangerous course. In case of serious political trouble in South Korea, perhaps a revolution, it is possible that the northerners might try another invasion. Forty thousand United States troops have remained in South Korea, and the United States is bound to come to the defense of the government there by the terms of the alliance of 1953, signed shortly after the armistice ending the war.

ADDITIONAL READING

Excellent introductions to their subjects are John K. Fairbank, *The United States and China* (4th ed., enlarged, Cambridge, Mass., 1983); Edwin O. Reischauer, *The United States and Japan* (3d ed., Cambridge, Mass., 1965); and Burton I. Kaufman, *The Korean War* (Philadelphia, 1986).

For China see Kenneth Shewmaker, *Americans and Chinese Communists* (Ithaca, N.Y., 1971); Barbara W. Tuchman, *Stilwell and the American Experience in China* (New York, 1971); E. J. Kahn, Jr., *The China Hands* (New York, 1972); Russell D. Buhite, *Patrick J. Hurley and American Foreign Policy* (Ithaca, N.Y., 1973); Ross Y. Koen, *The China Lobby in American Politics* (New York, 1974); Lisle A. Rose, *Roots of Tragedy* (Westport, Conn., 1976); Michael Schaller, *The U.S. Crusade in China* (New York, 1978); Gary May, *China Scapegoat* (Washington, D.C., 1979), on John Carter Vincent; Dorothy Borg and Waldo H. Heinrichs, eds., *Uncertain Years* (New York, 1980); Nancy B. Tucker, *Patterns in the Dust* (New York, 1983); and William W. Stueck, *The Wedemeyer Mission* (Athens, Ga., 1984). Participant accounts are by John Leighton Stuart, *Fifty Years in China* (New York, 1954); John F. Melby, *The Mandate of Heaven* (Toronto, 1968); John Paton Davies, *Dragon by the Tail* (New York, 1972); O.

Edmund Clubb, *The Witness and I* (New York, 1974); John S. Service, *Lost Chance in China* (New York, 1974).

Many books deal with Japan. Scholarly studies include Toshio Nishi, *Unconditional Democracy* (Stanford, 1982); William S. Borden, *The Pacific Alliance* (Madison, Wis., 1984); and Michael Schaller, *The American Occupation of Japan* (New York, 1985). The Tokyo war crimes trial is in Richard H. Minear, *Victors' Justice* (Princeton, 1971), and Philip R. Piccigallo, *The Japanese on Trial* (Austin, 1979). Participant accounts are Harry E. Wildes, *Typhoon in Tokyo* (New York, 1954); William J. Sebald and Russell Brines, *With MacArthur in Japan* (New York, 1965); John M. Allison, *Ambassador from the Prairie, or, Allison Wonderland* (Boston, 1973); and John K. Emmerson, *The Japanese Thread* (New York, 1978). For the American shogun consult Courtney Whitney, *MacArthur* (New York, 1956), a fulsome biography, which stands correction in D. Clayton James, *The Years of MacArthur* (3 vols., Boston, 1970–1985).

For the war of 1950–1953 see John W. Spanier, *The Truman-MacArthur Controversy and the Korean War* (Cambridge, Mass., 1959); Robert R. Simmons, *The Strained Alliance* (New York, 1975); Francis W. Heller, ed., *The Korean War* (Lawrence, Kan., 1977); Bruce Cumings, *The Origins of the Korean War* (Princeton, 1981); Charles M. Dobbs, *The Unwanted Symbol* (Kent, Ohio, 1981); William W. Stueck, Jr., *The Road to Confrontation* (Chapel Hill, N.C., 1981); and Rosemary Foot, *The Wrong War* (Ithaca, N.Y., 1985).

☆ 12 ☆

Eisenhower Diplomacy

Nationalism is on the march and world communism is taking advantage of that spirit of nationalism to cause dissension in the free world.

—Eisenhower diary, January 6, 1953

In the first dozen or so years after the end of the Second World War, the forward movement of Russian communism, politically and militarily, seemed distressingly predictable in its large outlines. The initial Soviet move appeared to be toward the nations of Western Europe, where the troubles of the war had brought military, social, and economic ills and where, according to Communist dogma, the contradictions of the capitalist system were about to deliver these nations into the hands of the revolutionary workers of the world. Such a possibility was blocked largely by American policy—the Truman Doctrine, the Marshall Plan, and the North Atlantic Treaty Organization (NATO).

At this point the North Koreans started a war in the Far East which if successful might have spread communism throughout Asia and made Russian satellites of the weak governments in that part of the world. Again the United States responded, this time with military force, and the UN-U.S. action in Korea of 1950–1953 brought proof that the United States would allow no easy rearrangements of territory in Asia by the USSR.

During all the movements of what one might consider to have been Russian policy, doubtlessly urged on by chance, opportunity, and inertia, the continent of Europe remained the most important part of the world, and both the Russians and the Americans understood this continuing fact of international relations. If the Soviet Union moved its pawns around the corners of the board, the important pieces were in Europe.

1. *The Strengthening of NATO*

The North Atlantic Treaty was signed in Washington on April 4, 1949, by representatives of the United States and eleven European powers. NATO's original members were, in addition to the United States, the nations of Benelux (Belgium, the Netherlands, and Luxembourg), France, Britain, Canada, Italy, Portugal, Denmark, Norway, and Iceland. Greece and Turkey joined NATO in February 1952, and West Germany joined in 1955, making a total of fifteen countries. Spain joined in 1981. By article 5 of the treaty the signatories agreed that an attack upon one would be an attack upon all, to be followed by individual or collective resistance under the stipulations of the UN Charter's article 51, the "collective self-defense" article. For the United States, membership in NATO was an epoch-making proposition, for not since the Treaty of Mortefontaine of the year 1800, when the United States disengaged itself from its French alliance, had the American government been bound in peacetime by a treaty of alliance. Signature of the North Atlantic Treaty in 1949 indicated clearly that the era of isolation had ended.

Three Russian moves of strength—the Communist coup in Czechoslovakia in February 1948, the Berlin blockade of 1948–1949, and the Korean War of 1950–1953—had led first to the creation and thereafter to the buildup of NATO. The Communist seizure of power in Czechoslovakia aroused the West and led to talk of military action to counter such Russian moves. During the turmoil in Prague, the Czech foreign minister Jan Masaryk, son of the founder of the republic and well known in the West, died in an apparent suicide under circumstances suggesting that the Communists pushed him out of a window. Soon afterward came the Berlin blockade, which made the West wonder how far the Russians were willing to go in violating the war's territorial settlement—to move the iron curtain westward to the Atlantic Ocean? NATO was organized while the blockade was in progress.

If there were any uncertainties as to Russian intentions, these were resolved by the outbreak of the Korean War in 1950. Thereafter the Allies set out in earnest to construct a strong military force in Western Europe, for it seemed that only by opposing force with force could the position of the West against Russia be made tenable. General Eisenhower, the American military commander of the Second World War, went to Europe in 1951 to establish the Supreme Headquarters, Allied Powers in Europe, known as SHAPE, and his command received the available standing forces in Western Europe which at the time consisted of 15 army divisions together with a handful of planes.

Eisenhower's presence in Europe galvanized the NATO powers,

and large plans were drawn for a NATO force that on the ground would be almost able to defend Western Europe against the red army divisions in East Germany and the satellite nations. At the NATO Council meeting in Lisbon in February 1952, a plan was developed to raise in Western Europe (not counting Italian, Greek, and Turkish troops) a force of 50 divisions, ready and reserve, and 4,000 aircraft by the end of that year. At the defined time, the plan was largely met: 25 divisions were to be ready for combat, and all were on hand by December 1952; 25 more divisions in reserve were to be available in thirty days, and all but three or so were ready. The aircraft goal fell short by between 200 and 300 planes.

This achievement came at a time when the Korean War was drawing to an end, and in the year 1953 the European powers, surveying the better prospects for peace in the Far East, began to reconsider their NATO goals. The goal for 1953 in Western Europe had been 75 divisions (ready and reserve) and 6,500 aircraft; this figure was revised downward to 56 divisions and 5,500 aircraft. For the following year, 1954, the provisional goal had been 100 divisions; this goal was reset at 60, with 30 ready divisions.

The goal of NATO in Western Europe in the latter 1950s and the 1960s was approximately achieved—by 1974, NATO's strength stood at 29½ divisions. Of this force the United States contributed 300,000 men, including 4⅓ divisions in West Germany, 70,000 air force men all across Europe, and 40,000 navy and marines including the Sixth Fleet in the Mediterranean. The Soviet Union kept a somewhat larger force in the East European countries—about 330,000 men in 31 divisions. In numbers, firepower, and tactical air support the Warsaw Pact was usually considered superior to NATO, but the United States joint chiefs of staff considered that a tenuous military balance had been struck on the critical front in Central Europe.

In connection with the buildup of NATO—whatever the insufficiency of the resultant forces—the new state of West Germany was able to increase its bargaining power with the Western Allies by obtaining a grant of full sovereignty on May 5, 1955, exchanging as a *quid pro quo* a contribution of German troops to NATO. The West German government found itself in the enviable position where both the *quid* and the *quo* were to its advantage, although the Western powers, especially the United States, felt rewarded by the German troop contribution. Ten years after the defeat of 1945, a German government received full sovereignty in Europe, a remarkable event which few individuals would have predicted. In view of the French preoccupation in the mid-1950s with the rebellion in Algeria, a relatively small German rearmament was enough to create on the Continent a German army larger than the French.

The issue of Germany's troop contribution to NATO was complicated and is worth some comment, although with the passage of time it has begun to take on the appearance of a detail within the larger scene of diplomacy in Europe and the world. At the beginning of the Korean War, the United States was anxious to include a German contingent within NATO and without much finesse impressed this sentiment upon its NATO Allies. The French were disturbed by this notion of German rearmament within so short a time after the recent troubles and not unnaturally became cautious. In October 1950 the French premier of the moment, René Pleven, pulled a special rabbit out of his hat, the Pleven Plan, which by 1952 was called the European Defense Community (EDC). This scheme was readily understandable as a linked expression of French dislike of German rearmament and concession to the need for German troops in NATO. EDC was a compromise by which German contingents would be included within NATO but in a military organization no larger than the divisional level: the divisions of members of EDC would be mixed at the corps and army level. This was the chief point of EDC, and there were subsidiary provisions for a joint military budget of the multinational European defense force, the budget to be raised by assessing each member country a share based on its national income.

EDC commended itself to American diplomats in 1952 because of their desire for haste in bringing together a European force to oppose Soviet forces. The Americans thrust it upon Pleven's successors until the French, who had repudiated Pleven, scuttled EDC by a rousing vote in the National Assembly in August 1954. This despite Secretary of State Dulles's pronouncement of December 1953 that if EDC did not pass the Assembly, the United States might have to make an agonized reappraisal of its European commitments.

The Germans soon afterward were admitted to NATO by another stratagem, more involved if less soothing to French fears of a new German army. The solution was to refurbish a treaty concluded between Britain, France, and Benelux in 1948: the Brussels Pact alliance, known also as Western Union. In its revised form, christened Western European Union or WEU, its original signatories offered membership to West Germany and Italy, which the two former enemy nations accepted. WEU was not an organic union like EDC, but an alliance, and it allowed Germany to keep more control over its armed forces than would have been the case under EDC. After joining WEU, West Germany was invited to become a member of NATO, and all armed forces of WEU were to be subject to the NATO supreme commander, who now was referred to as the Supreme Allied Commander, Europe, or SACEUR. The French assembly approved WEU on December 30, 1954.

In any discussion of West Germany's entry into NATO, one should point out that this move had an economic as well as military basis which was well understood by the European powers, especially Great Britain. The trouble was that the West Germans, with their defense problems taken care of by their erstwhile enemies, had been able prior to 1955 to have a special advantage in competition for foreign markets—they had no production facilities tied up in military work and could produce goods for export at an advantage over their Western European competitors. The British in particular felt the competition of West Germany during the Korean War boom and after, and when 9 percent of Britain's total national product and 15 percent of its metal and two-thirds of its scientific brain power was being consumed in the armament race, this business of German competition was no laughing matter.

Even after the Germans were persuaded to take up the burden of their own defense, Britons were inclined to point out how the Germans were still the leading war profiteers of Europe. The American army in the latter 1950s was spending so many dollars annually in West Germany that this expenditure helped the West Germans keep ahead nicely in dollar exchange. One British statesman was moved to say plaintively to an American colleague that it might be advisable for Scotland to threaten an attack on England so the English could have a rich American army stationed in their midst.

In addition to the issue of a German contingent within NATO, another aspect of the alliance—concerning a choice of weapons—is worth some attention. The organization's weakness in firepower led the United States in 1953, even before securing the inclusion of West German forces, to introduce "tactical" atomic weapons into the armament of the American divisions in NATO. This was a questionable decision. Perhaps it was necessary because of NATO's weakness, but it was a move that raised at least as many questions as it answered. United States military forces in Europe thereupon received delivery of a number of atomic cannon—"Atomic Annie," as the new gun was affectionately named. Shortly thereafter, the American army in West Germany announced acquisition of field artillery battalions equipped with Nike and Honest John missiles. It became known that atomic bombs were stockpiled in Germany. In public speeches the leaders of the American armed forces announced that their cannon and missiles would see use in any future war with Russian forces in Europe. The impression they gave was that atomic cannon and missiles were just a little more powerful than ordinary artillery and represented only one more and rather minor miracle of American science. Magazines in the United States published army press releases with pictures extolling the virtues of the huge new cannon, and the cannon looked like a cannon, which was reassuring.

What most people failed to understand were the consequences if armies in the field used such small atomic weapons for tactical purposes. An atomic explosion was an atomic explosion whether propelled out of cannon or by missiles or dropped from planes, and equipment of American armies in Europe with these small atomic weapons meant conversion of the armed forces to atomic strategy. And in any future war, tactical use of atomic cannon and missiles would be a signal, so many informed commentators in the United States and Europe believed, for all-out use of atomic weapons. The tactical use of atomic weapons was impossible. Who could tell when tactical employment shaded into strategic employment? No military writer or practitioner has ever been able to draw a clear line between tactics and strategy. Choice of atomic weapons for America's NATO forces was a fateful and perhaps fatal step. At the time of their introduction Viscount Sir Bernard Montgomery put the case frankly: "The reason for this action is that we cannot match the strength that could be brought against us unless we use nuclear weapons." He said that with this decision "we have reached the point of no return as regards the use of atomic and thermonuclear weapons in a hot war." Bluntly, the use of tactical weapons in the field meant hydrogen bombs on the homeland.

And yet error once committed, like policy undertaken, could go on and on without reexamination. Thirty years after the introduction of tactical atomic weapons into NATO's arsenal the whole issue still seemed in a state of confusion. Shortly after the first weapons appeared in Germany the young Henry A. Kissinger, fated for high office beginning in 1969, had published a much remarked upon book in which he championed the new weapons. A few years later, recognizing his mistake, he backed away from this position. One might have thought that when he entered the Nixon administration he would have taken along with him his new position, but apparently he took the old one, or else was unable to make his changed views prevail, or preferred—a likely hypothesis—to let sleeping dogs lie. For whatever reason the U.S. Army in the early 1970s continued to maintain a veritable arsenal of tactical nuclear weapons in Western Europe, primarily in West Germany. There were some 7,000 in position or stored. Many of them had warheads with an explosive power of several hundred kilotons, much more powerful than the 13-kiloton bomb that destroyed Hiroshima.

Early in 1973 the army sought to negotiate with the Atomic Energy Commission to receive new-model, lower-yield tactical weapons. Congressional testimony by NATO's supreme commander, General Andrew J. Goodpaster, released in 1974, stressed the need for weapons of perhaps a kiloton or less, to be used mainly against troops. Small-yield weapons could be exploded at a lower altitude, and that would increase the pulse of radiation striking the ground. The AEC's weapons laboratories were working on design changes that might enhance the radiation effects by as much as a third. These were the so-called "neutron bombs," essentially anti-personnel weapons that would preserve built-up areas (cities) and presumably wreak vengeance on Soviet tank crews as well as, generally, advancing Warsaw

Pact troops. The small warheads also could be used against hardened targets, counting on blast effects, with suppression or reduction of radiation effects. But this kind of talk was not reassuring. Americans, reading of Goodpaster's proposed new tactics, could still imagine how an unfortunate misunderstanding might arise on the battlefield and a nuclear escalation occur, as Viscount Montgomery had predicted. As for Europeans, they still could think of what a tactical atomic weapon, large or small, might do to some portion of the Continent's crowded living space. The West German government began to have second thoughts about the use of tactical weapons in its territory. The Bonn regime refused to allow the digging of "pre-chambered holes" into which the U.S. army, in time of trouble, would drop atomic demolition mines. The army planned to set off these mines at "choke points" along likely invasion routes that would be used by the Soviet army, such as mountain passes. The West German government appeared to be afraid of fallout. Together with other, unnamed members of NATO it seemed to be bothered about the use of any tactical atomic weapons—not merely demolition mines but missiles or bombs. Whether these concerned NATO countries would be able to change U.S. military planning remained highly uncertain.

The positioning of atomic weapons in Europe could cause problems that were almost unpredictable. Consider the problems raised by the Cyprus revolution during the summer of 1974. Who in NATO had planned for them? The revolution was of course another turn in the perennial Cyprus question. It led to Turkish intervention in Cyprus and to a revolution in Greece. The American government foolishly entered the melee with diplomatic advice and gained the ill will of everyone. The new Greek government already was down on the United States because Americans had been conspicuously friendly to the old regime in Athens; the Sixth Fleet had moved its base from Italy to Greece. One of the first acts of the new regime on taking office was to announce that it was leaving NATO. It then hedged the announcement, and Americans were unsure what was going to happen, a partial withdrawal such as the French had made some years before or a complete withdrawal. Meanwhile something had to be done about the Greek air force planes standing out on runways with atomic bombs under their wings. The Defense Department said that American technicians had taken the bombs off the wings and stored them in special places under American supervision. It said the bombs were safe because of a complex system of two-key locks, and one key was always in American possession. But how could one be sure? And how did the department propose to cart the bombs out of Greece? Suppose a Cypriot got the idea of acquiring a bomb or two? The Cypriots were angry enough; during the revolution one of them had fired into the American embassy and killed the ambassador. Or suppose a Greek national, angered over Turkish use of NATO equipment for the intervention in Cyprus, decided to borrow a NATO bomb?

In the 1980s the issue of tactical weapons continued to roil the diplomatic waters. The Reagan administration insisted upon placing in Europe Pershing II ballistic missiles and Tomahawk cruise missiles, and managed to get its way. The British and German governments went along despite furious Russian objection. Other NATO governments were not so friendly to such hardware, and it was not clear that they would support it on their territory. All in all, one wondered again if such tactical dispositions—so one might describe them—were wise.

2. *Theory and Practice in a Revolutionary Era*

The diplomacy of the United States entered upon a new and virtually revolutionary era beginning about the year 1953, when Dwight D. Eisenhower became president and chose John Foster Dulles as his secretary of state. It was revolutionary in the sense that never before had an American secretary found it necessary to negotiate under threat of nuclear annihilation. The initial periods of the atomic era, the years from 1945 to 1949 when the United States possessed a monopoly of nuclear weapons, and then the period from 1949 to 1953 when the United States held a clear superiority, were much easier times for the conduct of foreign relations than were the years which followed. As seen in previous chapters, James F. Byrnes, George C. Marshall, and Dean Acheson all had to wrestle with extremely difficult questions and crises and met with success and with failure. But the fact of monopoly, and after that, until 1953, of superiority, gave a security, however tenuous, to the conduct of American policy. Then, because the Russians by about 1953 had obtained enough atomic bombs to devastate most of the continental United States, even if they did not possess a nuclear arsenal as large as American bomb stocks, the diplomatic revolution began to affect almost every large action of American statesmen. Commencing with the secretaryship of John Foster Dulles, appointed by President Eisenhower in 1953, diplomacy became truly difficult.

In its opening years the Eisenhower-Dulles team hopefully announced several new policies, or new courses announced as new policies. There was talk of liberation of the captive nations of Eastern Europe, of an agonizing reappraisal of America's relations with its allies, of a new look in American military defenses based on a decision to meet Russian aggressive military moves with "massive retaliation." Each of these policies was born under the exigencies of the diplomatic revolution and took its course under the compulsions which attached to that revolution in 1953 and thereafter, the virtual equality of Russian and American atomic power.

Consider the policy of liberation, so boldly announced during the presidential campaign of 1952. By that year containment had begun to wear a little thin, just from being around for five years. The time had come for a new proposition. Logically, liberation also made sense. There was a logical problem with the slogan of 1947, containment, in that it was negative: everyone knows that positive teaching is far more valuable than negative; no one wishes to be negative, at least not for five years. Containment also did not appeal to many American citizens whose ancestors had come from behind the iron curtain and who habitually voted Democratic. For the Republican Party, liberation was politically irresistible. And it had great philosophic possibilities. As the historian Louis L. Gerson has shown, John Foster Dulles prior to appointment as secretary of state had been philosophizing about how dynamic forces always prevail over static, active over passive; that nonmaterial forces have a more powerful effect than material; that moral or natural law, not made by man, determines right or wrong, and that in the long run only those nations conforming to this law escape disaster; vigor, confidence, sense of destiny, belief in mission, all had led to the growth of the American republic; there needed to be a second American revolution; by conduct and example the United States could project its political, social, and economic ideas which were, he said, "more explosive than dynamite"; America was once the conscience of mankind, and it was foolish to let Marx replace the American thinkers of the eighteenth century; ideas were weapons. Dulles wanted "genuine independence in the nations of Europe and Asia now dominated by Moscow." The United States, he said, should not be a party to any "deal" confirming Soviet rule over the satellites. Dulles wrote the foreign relations planks of the Republican Party platform for 1952 and remarked brightly in one of them:

> We shall again make liberty into a beacon light of hope that will penetrate the dark places. It will mark the end of the negative, futile and immoral policy of "containment" which abandons countless human beings to a despotism and godless terrorism, which in turn enables the rulers to forge the captives into a weapon of our destruction. . . . The policies we espouse will revive the contagious, liberating influences which are inherent in freedom. They will inevitably set up strains and stresses within the captive world which will make the rulers impotent to continue in their monstrous ways and mark the beginning of the end.

But when all this platform promising had led the Republicans into power, what happened? The only discernible results of the epoch-making policy of liberation were the establishment of an annual celebration in the United States known as Captive Nations Day, and the sending of balloons over Eastern Europe bearing cheery messages of good will from the United States to the peoples of the satellite nations. The American government did absolutely nothing when the workers of East Berlin and other East German cities revolted in June 1953, nor during the Hungarian and Polish revolts of 1956. At these critical moments the Eisenhower-Dulles policy of liberation became indistinguishable from the Truman-Acheson policy of containment. The United States could not risk driving the USSR into atomic war to liberate the captive peoples of the satellite nations between Western Europe and Russia. It is worthy of note that the Western spokesmen of the captive peoples, leaders of the East European emigration to the West after 1945, did not favor forcible liberation, and for the same reason that deterred the American government—the terrible nuclear vengeance that Russia might wreak on all Europe in the event of an attempted Western military liberation of Eastern Europe.

The second item on the list of Eisenhower-Dulles diplomatic pronouncements, the projected agonizing reappraisal of 1953, was the attempt to scare France, militarily embarrassed in Algeria, into cooperating with NATO when the United States was doing its best to incorporate West Germany in the military alliance against Russia. One well can understand why Dulles had lost patience with the shuffling of French politics in 1953, which was much worse than during most of the political eras of the French republics. He felt that only a blunt announcement would move the wayward French. On a visit to France that year, he twice announced the possibility of an agonizing reappraisal, once at the NATO Council meeting and then at a press conference in Paris. The language of the mid-twentieth century, he perhaps believed, had to be dramatic to cut through the world's great daily outpouring of oratory and words in general.

It was unfortunate that he resorted to this kind of statement that the United States might pull out of Europe if the European Defense Community failed, because by such talk he said the very thing that the Russians might well have wanted. His talk of agonizing reappraisal was a double failure, short range and long. The immediate result of the pressure was to touch the *amour-propre* of the French Assembly, which voted down the proposed European Defense Community that would have brought German divisions into NATO. In this immediate sense the threat of a new American policy failed. The more long-range effect of it was that Dulles was reinforcing false and even dangerous worries and concerns in the minds of the sensitive Western European allies. For the United States, the less such reinforcement the better. The Western European nations were exposed to Russian nuclear vengeance; if the United States pulled out of Europe they would come immediately under Russian dominance. The threat of an American departure in 1953, combined with the actions of the United States three years later during the Suez crisis in which the Americans sided with Russia against Britain and France, gave a chancy aspect to American policy of the 1950s, tending in subtle ways to erase the affirmations of the late 1940s. Europeans always have been slightly cynical about American policy. They distrust big policy shifts and have a tendency to underrate the major moves of American opinion by taking seriously the constant minor statement-making in the press and in Congress. They have had trouble believing in what Americans, at least, knew was a major shift of policy in 1947–1949. They think that sooner or later we will crawl back into our holes, go back to the wisdom of 1796 and the Farewell Address. Dulles's statement of a possible reappraisal of American policy was a dangerous remark during a time when the Western Europeans could not maintain an independent policy and the United States itself was under more pressure than ever before.

The new look, another Eisenhower-Dulles principle, better known as a military policy of massive retaliation, was an attempted return to an atomic strategy rather than continuance of the combined atomic-conventional strategy which the United States had adopted after the opening of the Korean War in 1950. This sort of reshaping of the American military establishment was in the cards at this time, as the testing of hydrogen devices and bombs by both the Americans and Russians was tending to stress atomic warfare. The Russians were making great claims of their new atomic prowess, and it probably was necessary for the American government to announce its own atomic ability if only for diplomatic reasons, both with the publics of the United States, Britain, and France and with the many flighty publics of the neutral nations. It was hard to say the right thing here, but something needed to be said in 1952–1953–1954, what with the changing atomic picture. Then there was the problem of changing the American army, which just had finished fighting the Korean War on the old-time, Second World War basis. It was clear that the army had to be reorganized, but few people knew how. There was need to cut military expenditures from the level of the Korean War's last year, $53,000,000,000—but how far? The $14,000,000,000 budget of pre-Korea years? The new Republican administration needed to demonstrate ability with money, after the profligacy of the Democrats, and so the Eisenhower administration looked to the sinkhole of most of the budget, the military expenditures. There was a melange of reasons behind the proposed new policy of massive retaliation, including the fact that Eisenhower early in 1953 had threatened the Chinese in Korea with nuclear war if they did not stop fighting. The war somehow had stopped. Early in 1954 trouble was looming in Indochina, perhaps another Chinese intervention. Secretary Dulles said on September 2, 1953, "The Chinese Communist regime should

John Foster Dulles, the exponent of massive retaliation and brinkmanship, assures Uncle Sam, "Don't be afraid—I can always pull you back."

realize that such a second aggression could not occur without grave consequences which might not be confined to Indochina." Dulles in January 1954, in a famous address to members and guests of the Council on Foreign Relations in New York, announced a basic government decision "to depend primarily on a great capacity to retaliate by means and at places of our own choosing." With this, he later said, "you do not need to have local defense all round the 20,000-mile perimeter of the orbit of the Soviet World." In March 1954, Vice President Richard M. Nixon announced a corollary, the "nibble-to-death doctrine": "We have adopted a new principle. Rather than let the Communists nibble us to death all over the world in little wars, we will rely in future on massive mobile retaliatory powers." This strategy was defined visibly about this time when there were hair-raising revelations of a thermonuclear device exploded by the United States at Eniwetok in November 1952. A three-megaton (equivalent to 3,000,000 tons of TNT) hydrogen force had ripped a mile-wide crater in the ocean's floor and devastated an area of six miles in diameter. On March 1, 1954, the United States exploded a large H-bomb at Bikini, with a force of fifteen megatons. A radioactive cloud swirled far out from the explosion area, much farther than anticipated, down on the Japanese tuna trawler *Lucky Dragon*, which was seventy miles away, bringing sickness to the crew and eventual death by a collateral cause to one crew member.

In 1954–1955, and again in 1958, massive retaliation was spoken of, in connection with a dispute over the so-called offshore islands, close to mainland China, dozens of miles from Taiwan. The Nationalist Chinese possessed the islands, and the mainland Chinese desired them. The United States signed an alliance with Nationalist China on December 2, 1954, in which both countries guaranteed each other's security and promised that either country before taking action toward mainland China would concert its measures. Early in 1955 the Nationalists evacuated the Tachen island group and resolved to hold two other groups, the Matsus and Quemoys, which commanded the approaches to important harbors in the Fukien province of mainland China and were possible staging points for a Nationalist invasion. The affair of 1954–1955 quieted down. But in 1958 the mainland Chinese began shelling the Quemoys. Within the Eisen-

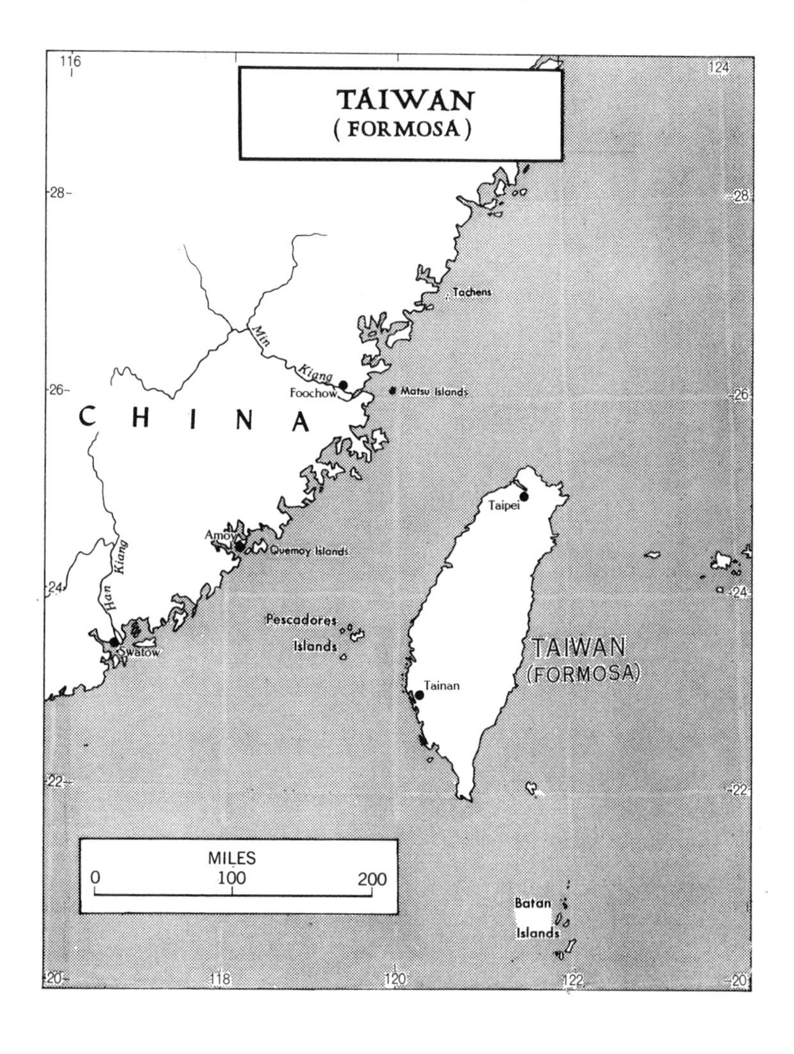

hower cabinet talk arose of nuclear weapons. Their use would have been possible constitutionally, for three years earlier Congress had given Eisenhower a blanket resolution that he could defend the island groups any way he saw fit. Fortunately the bombardments stopped, and the offshore-islands question lingered in uncertainty, with no massive retaliation. Even at the time, certainly in retrospect, nuclear weapons did not seem the proper way to defend two groups of islands that, prior to the 1950s, Americans had not known existed.

The new look, massive retaliation, had its own contemporary inspirations, but as a theory of foreign relations it did not fit well into the military requirements of the nuclear age, and it came to grief. "More bang for the buck" sounded good, the slogan was compelling, until the administration realized that reductions in conventional military power would have an automatic effect on the conduct of American diplomacy. "Diplomacy without armaments," Frederick the Great once said, "is like music without instruments." If this aphorism has needed qualification in the latter twentieth century, it still carries truth. A wide range of armaments was necessary in the day of limited war (for limited war was the only feasible kind of armed conflict after invention of the new weapons; total war had become almost too repulsive for practical consideration). The years 1953–1954 were no time to rely primarily on atomic weapons when the type of war to be anticipated was limited war, totally unsuited to atomic strategy.

Still another principle of diplomacy advanced to the publics of Europe and America in the middle 1950s deserves some mention here, because while this proposition did not become part of American foreign policy (for reasons which, one must assume, showed a more mature thinking by policy makers than earlier in the decade), it had much attraction and for a while dominated public forums on foreign policy.

The proposed policy was called "disengagement," and any student who undertakes to plumb its rise and fall in the American and European discussion of the 1950s can measure accurately the nuclear and other problems of world politics at that time and, indeed, down to the present time. At the outset, disengagement seemed so attractive. It took its origin out of the attempts by the Soviet Union early in the decade to prevent West Germany from joining NATO, in the course of which the Soviets proposed the unification of Germany as a neutralized state. There could be no German alliances within German unity so conceived. This initial blandishment held attraction, although any careful observer would have noted the cantonments of Russian troops in the nearby Eastern European nations, notably Poland, and hence the exposed nature of any Germany so unified. The West German government of Chancellor Konrad Adenauer was hardly taken in by such a proposition, and the idea quietly lapsed. Gradually, though, the original Soviet suggestion was transmuted into a proposal, or set of proposals, never clearly elaborated, for a nuclear-free zone in Eastern Europe which might include only Germany, or some of the Eastern European countries, or all of them. In the minds of its proponents such a zone might be all of Europe. It might include the British Isles. In the latter case the Russians would be back within their borders and the Americans within theirs. The only difficulty was that the Russians would be much closer than the Americans.

The temporarily retired American diplomat-turned-historian George F. Kennan (Dulles had retired him in 1953 by refusing to give him an ambassadorial or other high appointment) took up disengagement and advocated it in a series of broadcasts over the British Broadcasting Corporation in 1957, the Reith lectures, which were published next year under the title of *Russia, the Atom and the West*. Kennan went so far as to advocate American disengagement from some of the emerging nations of the world, telling those nations (in event that they were seeking to blackmail the United States for more aid) that they could give themselves to the Russians if they wished.

The doctrine of disengagement, so enchantingly portrayed, evoked a furious response in the journal *Foreign Affairs* by former secretary of state Acheson, who said that the only disengagement possible in this world was disengagement from life, which was death. He remarked that the passage of time, twenty years from 1918, had brought the errors of 1938, and after another twenty years the errors, distressingly similar, of 1958. Disengagement, it was now called. It was the same futile and lethal attempt to crawl back into the cocoon of history. Such doctrine would undo all the work of 1947–1949 which had produced a livable, prosperous situation in Western Europe.

Kennan like any good debater resorted to metaphor in meeting the arguments of his former chief. He said the very purpose of containment was creation of a position of strength from which to negotiate, not construction of a blockhouse. Containment presumed eventual compromise, not the crushing of Soviet power. Hence the link between containment and disengagement. He believed that if the Russians moved five hundred miles to the east, behind their own borders, only the most dire of circumstances, general war, would bring them back. They had to watch for the requirements of public opinion in their own and in the free areas. Through their propaganda, he said, the Russians had mortgaged themselves to such notions as peace and noninterference. He referred to an "overmilitarization of thought" about the cold war.

Disengagement gradually disappeared as a talked-about theory, and little was heard from it after the year 1959. The reason, so it now seems, was not so much the arguments of its proponents or adversaries but the enormously difficult business of taking a new diplomatic step in so complicated an era. The sides of policy, the unforeseen results, complexities, counterforces, were almost too many. One preferred to stay where he was, to live with what he knew. The British military analyst and historian Michael Howard summed up the problem well when he wrote that "The frying-pan is hot, but where will we land if we jump out of it?"

3. *The Middle East*

Problems in the Middle East bedeviled the middle years of Eisenhower's presidency. They took their origin not from the difficulties of NATO, or from diplomacy in a time of Russian nuclear power, but from three sources that were local and easy to see. This, to be sure, did not prevent the Russians from taking advantage, to the intense irritation of the American president and his assistants.

The sources of Middle Eastern problems were nationalism, oil, and the independence of the state of Israel. Nationalism was a psychic phenomenon, impossible to predict or channel, and a great fact of modern history after the American and French revolutions. The discovery of enormous pools of oil in the Middle East led to exploitation beginning in the present century and notably after the Second World War. Invariably, the least populous of Middle Eastern nations possessed the most oil. Discovery of these riches of the earth usually inspired heightened nationalism. And last in the forces that have churned the Middle East in our time was the independence of Israel, the appearance of a Western state in the midst of weak Arab neighbors, a state supported by the people and government of the United States.

The independence of Israel was a result of several forces and factors, in which the United States took almost no part. One was of course the Holocaust itself, the event that precipitated the founding of Israel. In this once administrative district of the Turkish empire, which had passed to Great Britain as a League of Nations mandate after the First World War, a civil war had broken out between Arabs and Jews that 60,000 British troops could not put down. In 1947 the British, afflicted by a floundering domestic economy, abandoned India, Greece, and Turkey, and with good reason passed the problem of Palestine to the United Nations.

The issue at the UN soon became clear. After the UN sent an investigating committee to Palestine, a resolution was introduced into the Assembly which, while calling for a customs union and for individual transit across all boundary lines and for a separate regime for Jerusalem and for protection of holy places, looked to the independence of a Jewish state and an Arab state. The Jewish Agency, an international Zionist organization, quickly came to see that the question would be which community in Palestine would be able to dominate the area militarily once the British withdrew. If any single act

created the state of Israel, it was the UN decision of November 29, 1947. Immediately afterward the British announced that they were relinquishing the mandate, their forces leaving Palestine, on May 15, 1948. No such thing as a UN force existed which could occupy Palestine in place of the British and enforce the UN decision. The American government by itself certainly was not able to send troops to Palestine to enforce the UN decision. A debate within the cabinet, set forth clearly in Secretary of Defense James V. Forrestal's memoirs, shows that the American army of the time could not have sent more than a division to Palestine without a partial mobilization, which was impossible in an election year, 1948, and impossible anyway, given the temper of public opinion so soon after the end of the Second World War. The U.S. army estimate of troops necessary to enforce the UN decision was a minimum of 80,000 and a maximum of 160,000.

It was said then and later that President Truman did everything possible to assist in the creation of Israel—so that he could obtain the electoral votes of New York State in the very close presidential election of 1948. There is no truth in this allegation. Truman personally favored a Jewish state in Palestine, but he did little to make it possible. In any event the state went to his Republican opponent, New York governor Thomas E. Dewey, and Truman won the election anyway.

On May 15, 1948, after the event, the Truman administration did recognize the new Israeli state with a slight haste. Midnight, May 15, Palestine time, was 6:00 P.M., May 14, Washington time. Eleven minutes later, when the new regime had not even had time to cable its existence, basing his action only on a request from Eliahu Epstein of the Jewish Agency in Washington, Truman extended presidential *de facto* recognition—a recognition in eleven minutes, compared with the three days necessary to recognize Panama in 1903, the eleven months necessary after San Jacinto to recognize Texas in 1836–1837.

The appearance of the state of Israel in 1948, when the British abandoned the Palestine mandate, did not represent any large calculation by Western statesmen and for a while everything looked all right, but the eventual result was the Suez crisis of 1956. Few Americans or citizens of Britain and France had time to give much thought to the Middle East in that hectic year 1948, the year of the Marshall Plan's first operations, of the Berlin blockade, and of Communist successes in China. That area of the world rattled along, so to speak, and the nations of the Middle East went their new ways with apparent stability and little attention. In the year 1950, Britain, France, and the United States concluded a Tripartite Declaration under which they promised, among other things, to prevent any border changes by the Arab states or Israel: "The three Governments, should they find that any of these States was preparing to violate frontiers or armistice lines, would, consistent with their obligations as members of the United Nations, immediately take action, both within and outside the United Nations, to prevent such violation." Although this part of the declaration proved later to be a dead letter, another part provided for a virtual arms embargo, a careful measuring of requests for arms by the Arab nations or Israel, so that there would be no arms competition by these small nations. In such fashion everything continued in fairly good order until February 1955, when Israeli troops, in retaliation for border incidents by the Egyptians, made a large raid against Egyptian army forces in the so-called Gaza Strip area adjoining Israel. Thereupon, the Egyptian government, under its new nationalist leader Gamal Abdel Nasser, announced negotiation in September 1955 of an arms deal with Czechoslovakia. This was the thin entering wedge for serious trouble.

The Egyptian arms deal with Czechoslovakia alarmed the Israelis and led them to what they knew would be an easy military operation against the Egyptians. The Israelis numbered something over a million and a half souls and they saw around them forty million Arabs. Anti-Israel propaganda came night and day from the Cairo radio which blanketed the Middle East. Many of the Israelis who had known Hit-

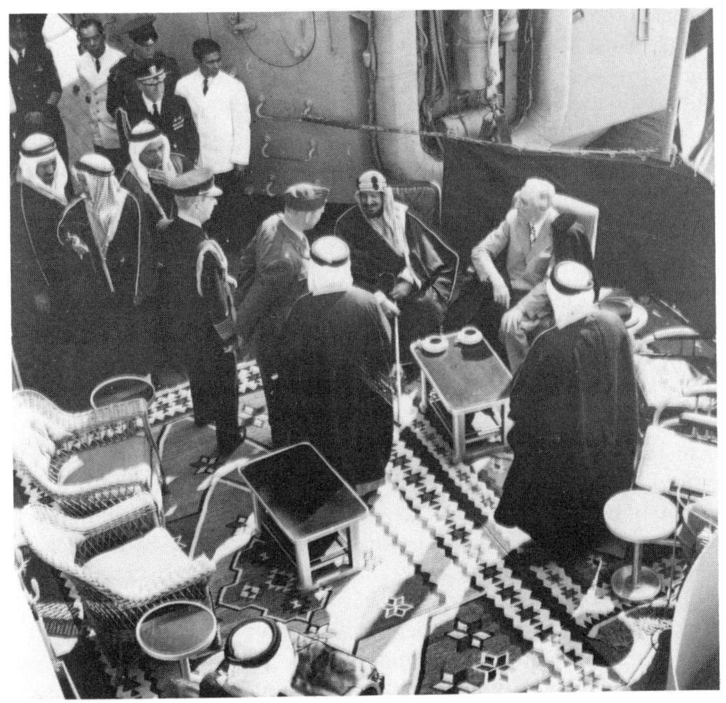

Three years before the independence of Israel, President Roosevelt met King Ibn Saud of Saudi Arabia aboard the U.S.S. *Quincy* anchored in the Great Bitter Lake in Egypt. At this meeting after the Yalta Conference the president sought to obtain Saud's support for a home in Palestine for the Jews of Europe. Saud said that the Arabs had not oppressed the Jews, and that the latter should receive land in Germany.

ler were not unwilling to believe that President Nasser of Egypt was another Hitler. The government of Israel in 1948, when it was just a few weeks old, had decisively defeated the combined armies of the Arab states in war. The Israelis were eager to do it again.

In July 1956 President Nasser complicated his position (as well as everyone else's position) by nationalizing the Suez Canal, an act which won him the enmity of the British government. He had been negotiating with the Western powers to obtain funds to raise the level of the Nile by a higher dam at Aswan in upper Egypt, which would generate electricity to promote Egypt's industrialization, in addition to increasing the area of cultivable land. The failure of this effort was his avowed reason for nationalizing the canal. He announced that he would use the income from the canal to build the dam. For the British, who had been treated to many humiliations since the end of the Second World War, to be thus humiliated by the Egyptians seemed at the moment unbearable. President Nasser engaged the intense dislike of Prime Minister Anthony Eden, who had made a reputation in the 1930s for being willing to stand against Hitler and had broken from the Neville Chamberlain government over this issue.

Meanwhile the French, who like the British owned a large amount of stock in the Suez Canal, had become more particularly angered at Egypt because of the Egyptians' support for the rebels in Algeria.

The makings of trouble were at hand. In the summer of 1956 the French commenced an intrigue with the Israelis, who wanted to have a whack at Nasser. The British joined the intriguers. The agreement was that Israel would attack Egypt, and Anglo-French forces then would take over the canal area, with the British air force meanwhile neutralizing the Egyptian air force. The Anglo-French would enter the canal zone under the guise of an intervention to keep the Israelis and Egyptians apart.

In the subsequent military operations, between October 29 and November 2, 1956, the forces of Israel brilliantly finished off all Egyptian troops in the Sinai Peninsula and could have cut straight to Cairo and taken all Egypt if they had not been stopped by their prior arrangement with Britain and France. The two Western powers gave both the Israelis and Egyptians an ultimatum on October 30 that they refrain from military operations within ten miles of the canal. This phrasing of the ultimatum allowed the Israelis to occupy a hundred miles of Egyptian territory. When the Egyptians ignored the ultimatum, the British and French brought their forces into the canal area, shelled and occupied Port Said. The Egyptians blocked the canal with wrecks. There followed a diplomatic, military, and economic impasse at Suez until the United Nations at the request of Canada created a UN Emergency Force, UNEF, which beginning in mid-November arrived in the Middle East and by Christmas 1956 had replaced the British and French, with the Israelis retreating to their home base.

In the course and sequels of this complex crisis the United States joined with Russia in opposing Britain and France; the Russians threatened to shoot missiles into the Western capitals and to send "volunteers"—that is, troops—to the Middle East; the United States said that volunteers meant war; the Egyptians in effect held the blocked canal as a hostage; there was sabotage of the Iraq oil pipeline through Syria; the British pound sterling came within an ace of devaluation; two British ministers resigned; there was indication that India and Pakistan might withdraw from the Commonwealth and join forces with a new international African-Arab-Asian bloc; the United States and especially Secretary of State Dulles received an exceedingly bad press in Britain and France; the Israelis were angry because they did not receive a chance to destroy Nasser; Nasser rose in stature to be the most powerful and attractive of all the Arab leaders; Prime Minister Eden lost the Nobel Peace Prize for which before the Suez operation he had been a candidate, went to Jamaica for three weeks to recuperate from what could not have been a more maladroit piece of diplomacy, and not long afterward relinquished the seals of his office to Harold Macmillan.

The lesson of Suez was plain for everyone to read: use of armed force by the Western powers could no longer secure their interests in the Middle East. As Guy Wint and Peter Calvocoressi wrote in an excellent little book, *Middle East Crisis:* "The fundamental British error has been to persist too long in a policy that has been overtaken by events. . . . The alternative to staying is going away. In 1947 the British left India lock, stock, and barrel. . . . Withdrawal may be repugnant and is certainly risky, but once the facts dictate it, it needs to be made sharply. Failure to realize this in the Middle East led to . . . an achievement for which it would be hard to find a parallel in the history of British diplomacy."

An especial sadness of the British fiasco over nationalization of the Suez Canal was that the whole operation on the Anglo-French side—the intervention in Egypt after the Israelis had attacked—was shadowed in collusion. This was not an appropriate aura for twentieth-century British diplomacy, even if it had enveloped French diplomacy on innumerable occasions. What about the British idea of the behavior of a gentleman, the notion of fair play? Not without reason had Sir Harold Nicolson in his well-known manual on diplomacy set out as a prime attribute of the good diplomat the telling of the truth. Suez inspired many official half-truths. And two notable falsehoods had been uttered in the British government's holy of holies, the House of Commons. Randolph Churchill pointed out in *The Rise and Fall of Sir Anthony Eden*, published soon after the debacle, that only a fool would believe that the British government had not conspired with the French and Israelis to arrange for the Israeli attack followed by the Franco-British intervention. He recalled the famous remark of the Duke of Wellington on another occasion, "If you can believe that, you can believe anything." Not, however, until a decade later, when the number two man in the British foreign office at the time of Suez, Anthony Nutting, published a little volume entitled *No End of a Lesson*, did the full truth come out. Nutting related the inner workings of British diplomacy prior to Suez. He told how the French and British and Israelis had conspired against the Egyptians. When he had protested to Foreign Secretary Selwyn Lloyd, the latter said, employing a facetious joke, "There's only one worse thing than having a yes-man on one's team, and that's having a no-man like you." When Nutting suggested to Eden a consultation with the foreign office's legal adviser, Sir Gerald Fitzmaurice, he met the flattest of negatives: "Fitz is the last person I want consulted. The lawyers are always against our doing anything. For God's sake, keep them out of it. This is a political affair." The Eden government then used Israel as a stalking horse against Egypt. The British, of course, had to come in after Israel attacked, because the Israelis had insisted upon neutralization of the Russian-equipped Egyptian air force, and only the British had enough planes in the area to do this job. After the debacle, Lloyd lied in parliament, although one could interpret his words as technically correct: "It is quite wrong to state that Israel was incited to this action by Her Majesty's Government. There was no prior agreement between us about it." Eden did worse, by saying simply that "there was not foreknowledge that Israel would attack Egypt." In British politics it is unforgivable to deceive the Commons, whatever deception a leader or member must employ outside. When in 1963 the secretary of state for war, Sir John Profumo, falsely told the House that he had no connection with a London prostitute, he was disgraced and forced to resign.

Because of what was known and suspected of the Suez affair, British and French prestige vanished from the Middle East. Arab resentment was for a moment deflected from the United States because of the undeniably firm American stand against the Suez venture of its allies. But the Americans were susceptible to the same illusions, if not the same methods, as the British and French, and two years later, in a not exactly analogous situation, they also made a show of armed force in the Middle East and focused upon themselves the hostility of the Arab world.

The Lebanon crisis of 1958 was an aftermath of the Suez fiasco. In a footloose effort to buy its way out of its Middle Eastern troubles the Eisenhower administration announced a $200,000,000 crash program of economic assistance to the area, "aid against overt armed aggression from any nation controlled by international communism." The so-called Eisenhower Doctrine led to instant trouble, for the sole Middle Eastern leader who asked for money (the others doubtless would have liked money, but were afraid to risk their popularity by asking) was President Camille Chamoun of Lebanon, who desired an unconstitutional second term. There had been a civil war in Lebanon, a confused struggle of political factions, embittered by a Christian-Arab antagonism, the pro-Nasser and anti-Nasser feeling of the Lebanese, and a general division of the tiny country between its westernized city dwellers in Beirut and the inhabitants of the small towns and the hill areas. Then a revolt opened in nearby Iraq, against the government of a pro-Western premier, which promptly led to the murder of the premier and of the king of Iraq. When Nasser began to stir in response to this revolt, Lebanon's President Chamoun felt threatened and called on President Eisenhower for American marines, which Eisenhower sent. A division of marines and army troops landed under protection of the U.S. Sixth Fleet. It was reported that the fleet was carrying nuclear weapons.

Within weeks everything died down, a shuffle occurred within the Lebanese government, and all was back almost to normal. But in the small Lebanese crisis of 1958 lay the seeds of much larger conflict in the Middle East, and another Lebanese crisis a quarter-century later that was far more bloody.

4. *End of an Era: The U-2*

The trouble in the Middle East that had been stirred up by Soviet policy in 1956 was highly convenient because it covered a deep Russian embarrassment over rebellions in two of the satellites, Poland and Hungary. The Soviet leader of the latter 1950s and early 1960s, Nikita Khrushchev, had informed the Twentieth Party Congress early in 1956 of Stalin's many errors, transgressions, and outright anti-state actions, leading to terrible slaughters of his enemies, all because of "the cult of personality." Destalinization, as it became known, encouraged the Communist leaders in Poland and Hungary to oppose the Russians. The opposition managed to survive in Poland by cleverly giving the appearance of subservience to the Soviets, but in Hungary, where the government sought to become neutral, the Russian army moved into action, shelling and occupying Budapest and executing the dissidents. All this occurred at the time of the Suez crisis, which constituted a helpful distraction while the Russians put their East European house in order.

After the Polish and Hungarian rebellions the Soviets became tentative and almost oblique in asserting their power, as befitted a nation that was no longer ruled by "the cult of personality." For a while in the latter 1950s it seemed as if the post-Stalin Russian leaders were willing largely to let the successes of Soviet space science speak for their nation's power. The first sputnik went up in 1957, and the world, not merely Europe, looked agog as the scientific marvel glided silently around the globe. Other sputniks quickly followed, and eventually manned flights. All the while the American government appeared far behind in what became known as the space race. The result was predictable for European politics. Many Europeans began to ask how the American government could continue to shield them against Russian aggression, considering the scientific superiority of the institutes in Moscow and Leningrad.

For some years after 1957 the American government was embarrassed before its own public and those of other nations, friends and foes, because its small-thrust missiles could not easily lift satellites. There were several well-publicized failures, inducing clowns in the Moscow circus to enter the ring bearing balloons, to announce to their audiences that the balloons were American sputniks, and then to stick pins in the balloons. The first American satellites were small, and for manned flights the United States had to miniaturize its space capsules, keeping the weight down by painful compromises and extremely costly lightweight metals.

The truth of the space race was that from the outset the Russians acted from weakness, not strength. The race for space that began in 1957 between Russia and the United States was never understood by the American public, not to mention the publics of Western and Eastern Europe and of the many other nations of the world. For years, in relating its spectacular feats in space, the Soviet government was able to bank on popular ignorance. People understood the meaning of a race, and this ordinary understanding ignored what space feats were important, and what were not, within the real power balance between the United States and Russia. Back in 1954 the United States government had exploded its first hydrogen bomb at Bikini (at Eniwetok in 1952 it had fired a device, not a bomb), and this huge bomb was not merely a triumph of explosive power—the Russians required seven years to fire a bigger one—but a triumph of American scientific ingenuity. American scientists had taken the sixty-odd-ton device in 1952—it was so heavy, J. Robert Oppenheimer said, that it would have to be hauled to its target in an oxcart—and reduced it to a small size in the bomb of 1954. Because of this reduction, American intercontinental ballistic missiles no longer needed the tremendous thrust for which the country's experts were designing them. The government immediately abandoned its plans, already well toward completion, to build a huge missile to carry hydrogen warheads into the Soviet Union. It turned to much smaller missiles, with smaller thrust, which easily could lift the miniaturized H-bomb of 1954. The result became embarrassingly obvious in 1957 when the Russians, who apparently had been unable to miniaturize their H-bombs and hence had developed huge-thrust missiles, threw their sputnik into the air. The principal requisite to put a satellite in orbit was thrust, not a large amount of scientific know-how.

Of course, a decision was made to build missiles with huge thrust, not merely enough to send aloft earth satellites with larger scientific payloads, or more space observers, but to hurl unmanned and manned capsules into flights to the moon and to Mars. The National Aeronautics and Space Agency (NASA) became a very big operation, and at its peak in 1966 was employing 35,000 people at fifteen scattered centers, plus some 400,000 scientists, engineers, and workers among its thousands of contractors. Between 1958 and 1974, NASA spent about $50,000,000,000 to get America ahead in the space race.

Then, at last, in 1969 an American astronaut got to the moon. No Russian cosmonaut was in sight.

Long before that time the Soviet Union had focused its attention on other concerns, and similarly sought through them to confuse people over the true state of the U.S.—USSR power balance. The so-called

U-2 affair was one of these issues and for a while it took the headlines. It came at a most unpropitious moment, just before a scheduled "summit meeting" of the leaders of the United States, Britain, France, and Russia in Paris.

What happened in May 1960 is common knowledge and needs no long recital. Ever since the beginning of the cold war, the United States had been spying on the Soviet Union with fast-flying reconnaissance planes, which often flew along the coast of Soviet territory carrying cameras that could photograph far inland. Once in a while the Soviets would violate international waters and shoot down one of these planes to discourage the operation. There were fourteen known incidents prior to the U-2 affair. The Soviets, on their side, had been overflying Alaska and Canada. In 1957 there were reports that the United States air force was flying a remarkably efficient jet reconnaissance plane, and these planes by 1960 had been making "milk runs" over the Soviet Union for four years. The Soviets knew the United States was violating their airspace but could not shoot down the American planes and did not like to admit inability to defend their territory. Then on May 1, 1960, one of the new spy planes used by the Central Intelligence Agency, the Utility-2, as it was known, piloted by Francis Gary Powers, was disabled by a rocket while flying over the Soviet Union and crashed near Sverdlovsk, the Soviet Pittsburgh. Through a series of stupidities understandable in all large organizations (government, businesses) the United States government tried to cover up what had happened, and Premier Khrushchev was able to trap the Americans in a whole series of lies. President Eisenhower at last admitted personal responsibility for the U-2 flights.

The American handling of the U-2 affair came to a small crisis during the Paris summit meeting, which Khrushchev "wrecked" by allowing it to convene just long enough to accuse the president of the United States of hypocrisy and then go back to Moscow in a huff, although not before making other angry pronouncements while on French soil and holding a press conference at which he harangued a roomful of reporters while his defense minister, Marshal Rodion Y. Malinovsky, sat glowering at his side.

The basic achievement of the U-2 flights was almost completely lost from view during the hullaballoo over the downing of Powers's plane and the failure of the summit. By 1960 when the president ordered the flights to cease, the American government had closed an important intelligence gap. At the end of the Second World War the United States had come into possession of German air force maps of most of European Russia, detailed maps that gave a great deal of information. For several years after the war these were supplemented by interrogation of returned German prisoners who had been doing forced labor in Russia. Then in the early 1950s the sources of information about the Soviet Union were drying up. President Eisen-

Francis Gary Powers at the opening of his trial on espionage charges in Moscow. At left is defense counsel Mikhail Griniev.

hower in 1955 at a Geneva summit conference had proposed "open skies," but the Soviets did not like that interesting idea. So the U-2 flights were begun. The U-2 planes' high-resolution, long-range aerial cameras could photograph ground features in fantastic detail. They produced a close analysis of the Russian territory overflown, giving American military planners a most helpful understanding of the USSR's industrial and military capacity.

It is perhaps worth remarking that shortly after the end of the overflights the United States, starting in November 1960, began to employ reconnaissance satellites to spy on the USSR. The program had commenced in the mid-1950s; it was no small program, and by the early 1970s had cost about twelve billion dollars. One of the first results of this new kind of photography proved even more important than the information provided by the U-2 flights. In the course of the American presidential election of 1960 the initial Soviet technological lead in long-range missiles during the latter 1950s had given rise to much uninformed talk about a missile gap in Russia's favor. The satellite photos indicated that Russian intercontinental ballistic missile (ICBM) strength had been vastly overrated as compared to that of the United States, that instead of a force of 400 ICBMs, which would have enabled the Russians to make a devastating surprise attack on the United States, the Soviets had all of 14! The missile gap was in favor of the United States. During the ensuing meeting between Khrushchev and President John F. Kennedy in Vienna in June 1961, and a subsequent crisis over Berlin, it was possible for the American government to take a much harder line with the Russian government because of this knowledge derived from satellite reconnaissance.

Satellites now constitute the principal means by which each of the superpowers keeps tabs over the other. They are far less risky than manned overflights. And American scientists have ingeniously developed them. A powerful new camera provides resolutions (that is, detection of objects) of slightly better than one foot, which is close to the theoretical limit. Satellites have been equipped with special sensors to penetrate camouflage on military installations. This is done with "multispectral sensors," a group of cameras which simultaneously photograph the same area, each through a different color filter. It no longer avails for a foe to paint canvas as if it were grass; painted canvas will reflect sunlight with greater or lesser greens, reds, yellows, and blues than does real grass, and the multispectral sensors will catch what the eye cannot. As for underground silos, an infrared scanner can detect the presence of warm objects against a cool background, or vice versa—such as an underground silo, heated to keep its ICBM warm during the long Russian winter.

Curiously, neither of the superpowers has ever confessed publicly that it is employing reconnaissance satellites, although by mutual agreement they both report the times and orbits of all satellite launches and it is easy for specialists to figure out which launches are for reconnaissance. A recognition of this not-very-secret activity was written into the treaty on antiballistic missiles and the executive agreement for a five-year freeze on intercontinental ballistic missiles and submarine-based missiles concluded by President Nixon in Moscow in 1972 (for which see Chapter 15). Both of these instruments delicately mention "national technical means of verification," by which each power meant reconnaissance satellites. Without satellite reconnaissance, which would give proof of violations on the ground or underground (although not undersea), the two powers could not have concluded the Moscow agreements.

Some evidence appeared beginning in 1968 that the Soviets were testing a satellite-destroyer designed to blow up a reconnaissance satellite. It was difficult to be certain. Soviet specialists at the Strategic Arms Limitation Talks (SALT) (Chapter 15) denied any knowledge of such a weapon. To employ it in warfare would, of course, be contrary to the multilateral treaty prohibiting the use of outer space for military purposes which the UN opened for signature in December 1966, and the United States and USSR signed shortly thereafter, and also contrary to the Moscow agreements which relate that each party "undertakes not to interfere with the national technical means of verification of the other party." In the 1980s the United States appeared to be well ahead of the USSR in the technology of satellite destruction, perhaps because of its "star wars" strategy (Chapter 16), although neither country has chosen to denounce the outer space treaty.

ADDITIONAL READING

For the founding of NATO see Lawrence S. Kaplan, *A Community of Interests* (Washington, D.C., 1980) and *The United States and NATO* (Lexington, Ky., 1984). On nuclear problems in the 1950s see Michael Howard, *Disengagement in Europe* (Baltimore, 1958); Herbert York, *Race to Oblivion* (New York, 1970), and the same author's *The Advisors* (San Francisco, 1976), the decision to go ahead with the H-bomb.

Russian-American relations are in George F. Kennan, *Memoirs: 1950–1963* (Boston, 1972), by the ambassador of 1952; Charles E. Bohlen, *Witness to History* (New York, 1973), ambassador in the early Eisenhower years; Michel Tatu, *Power in the Kremlin* (New York, 1970), by the Moscow correspondent of *Le Monde*; and Adam B. Ulam, *The Rivals* (New York, 1971).

The literature about Israel is large. For introductions see Nadav Safran, *The United States and Israel* (Cambridge, Mass., 1963), and Seth P. Tillman, *The United States in the Middle East* (Bloomington, Ind., 1982). See also Kenneth Ray Bain, *The March to Zion* (College Station, Tex., 1979); Evan B. Wilson, *Decision on Palestine* (Stanford, 1979); Peter Grose, *Israel in the Mind of America* (New York, 1983); Miriam Joyce Haron, *Palestine and the Anglo-American Connection* (New York, 1986); and Cheryl A. Rubenberg, *Israel and the American National Interest* (Urbana, Ill., 1986). Frank J. Adler, *Roots in a Moving Stream* (Kansas City, 1972), is a history of the Kansas City synagogue of which the late Edward Jacobson, President Truman's haberdashery partner in 1919–1922, was a member, and offers new material on Truman and Israel. The well-known crusader against Israel, Alfred M. Lilienthal, has published four hostile books: *What Price Israel* (Chicago, 1953); *There Goes the Middle East* (3d ed., New York, 1960); *The Other Side of the Coin* (New York, 1965); and *The Zionist Connection II* (New Brunswick, N.J., 1978).

The Suez crisis is covered in the books mentioned in the text, together with the Eisenhower and Dulles titles below.

The U-2 affair appears in Francis Gary Powers, *Operation Overflight* (New York, 1970), and Michael R. Beschloss, *Mayday* (New York, 1986).

Memoirs and biographies include Dwight D. Eisenhower, *Mandate for Change* (New York, 1963) and *Waging Peace* (New York, 1964); Herbert S. Parmet, *Eisenhower and the American Crusades* (New York, 1972); Charles C. Alexander, *Holding the Line* (Bloomington, Ind., 1975); Robert A. Divine, *Eisenhower and the Cold War* (New York, 1981); Robert H. Ferrell, ed., *The Eisenhower Diaries* (New York, 1981); and Stephen E. Ambrose, *Eisenhower* (2 vols., New York, 1984). Also Louis L. Gerson, *John Foster Dulles* (New York, 1967), Volume 17 in the American Secretaries series; and Townsend Hoopes, *The Devil and John Foster Dulles* (Boston, 1973). G. Bernard Noble, *Christian A. Herter* (New York, 1970), Volume 18 of the American Secretaries series, presents the regime of Dulles's successor at the department, 1959–1961.

☆ 13 ☆

Crises in Latin America

No state has the right to intervene in the internal or external affairs of another.
—Article 8 of the Convention on the Rights and Duties of States, adopted by the Seventh International Conference of American States at Montevideo, 1933

President Franklin D. Roosevelt in the early 1930s presided over a marked change in the diplomacy of the United States toward Latin America—the adoption of a policy of the good neighbor, and the abandonment of the role of colossus of the north. This "good neighbor policy" has characterized American relations with the many independent republics of the Western Hemisphere down to the present day. At the outset the good neighbor policy contained a certain ambivalence, for to the government in Washington the phrase meant that it would behave with more care and punctilio, whereas to Latin American governments it meant that the United States was subscribing openly, making a public testimony, in favor of nonintervention in their internal or external affairs. The Roosevelt administration was not keen on a pledge of total abstention and never really committed itself to keeping its hands off Latin America. Nonetheless, as time passed it became apparent that the United States no longer was going to play the part of instructor and chastiser of the hemisphere. Despite three interventions in the 1950s and 1960s, of which one was fully the most important world crisis of the entire era after the Second World War, the government in Washington accepted the view of its Latin American friends as to the true, inner meaning of good neighborliness.

The phrase "good neighbor," incidentally, was not original with Roosevelt when in his inaugural address of March 4, 1933, he declared, "In the field of world policy, I would dedicate this nation to the policy of the good neighbor . . ." It was a phrase which in Latin American relations went back at least to the early nineteenth century, and was assuredly one of the most familiar clichés in the language of international intercourse. Roosevelt, indeed, used it in regard to the entire world in his address of 1933. President Herbert Hoover, his predecessor, in 1928–1929 used the phrase on several occasions during a pre-inaugural tour of Latin America. But it was in Roosevelt's time that American policy obviously changed to that of the good neighbor, and the phrase has become associated, perhaps unjustly, with his name.

1. *Pan-Americanism*

The relations of the United States with Latin America in an organized, international sense, a sense of Pan-Americanism, which led naturally to the policy of the good neighbor, began as early as 1826 when the liberator Simon Bolívar called the Congress of Panama as a convention of the states newly independent of Spain. The United States sent two representatives, who failed to arrive in time for the meeting. Decades later, in 1881, Secretary of State Blaine undertook to revive Pan-Americanism. He primarily wished to halt the War of the Pacific then raging between Chile, Peru, and Bolivia. And there were other troubles. Argentina was in danger of entering this conflict. Mexico and Guatemala were at odds. Costa Rica and Colombia were engaged in a boundary dispute. Largely to preserve peace in the hemisphere, Blaine invited the nations to a conference at Washington scheduled for November 1882. With the death of President Garfield, he left office, and his successor as secretary of state, Frederick T. Frelinghuysen, canceled the invitations. Cleveland's secretary of state, Bayard, renewed them for a conference in 1888. In the following year, under Benjamin Harrison, Blaine again became secretary of state and had the pleasure of presiding over the first Pan-American Conference, which met from October 1889 until April 1890. Seventeen Latin American states attended, all except the Dominican Republic. Although the goal of the United States, formation of a customs union, was defeated, and although no machinery was set up for arbitration of disputes—another of Blaine's purposes—the International Bureau of American Republics was established. Later it became known as the Union of American Republics (with its secretariat, the Pan-American Union), and since 1948 as the Organization of American States (so phrased that it might include Canada; the Pan-American Union is now known as the Secretariat).

There followed three Pan-American Conferences in the early twentieth century—Mexico City in 1901–1902, Rio de Janeiro in 1906, and Buenos Aires in 1910—but little came from them. The fifth Pan-

American Conference met at Santíago de Chile in 1923, again with few notable results. The sixth conference, at Havana in 1928, was notable not for the results of the meeting but because of the way in which the affair turned into a virtual rebellion of the Latin American nations against the power and influence of the United States. It was at this meeting that the envoy of El Salvador introduced a resolution against intervention, "that no state has a right to intervene in the internal affairs of another," a proposal directed, of course, against the interventions by the United States. President Coolidge's special representative at the meeting in Havana, Charles Evans Hughes—Coolidge himself had opened the conference by a visit and speech in the Cuban capital—finally could contain himself no longer and stood up in the assemblage to speak impromptu about what he denominated the "interposition" of the United States in the affairs of its neighbors. Hughes's speech, the last defense by American representatives of the policy of intervention, was terse and to the point. The distinguished former secretary of state asked the representative of El Salvador what the United States was to do "when government breaks down and American citizens are in danger of their lives? Are we to stand by and see them butchered in the jungle . . .?" After this reply the Salvadorean withdrew his motion and the conference turned to other matters, less politically sensitive.

Hughes had made the final defense of the old policy, and even in the year he made it the United States recognized that the old method of intervention was neither effective nor necessary. Both the appearance of Coolidge at Havana and the appointment of Hughes to head the American delegation showed a new policy toward the Latins. The president's old college friend, Dwight Morrow, had gone to Mexico the year before, in 1927, and Morrow's appointment too showed the fear of the Coolidge administration that something needed to be done with Latin American relations. President-elect Hoover undertook his tour of Latin America in November 1928, and although some individuals claimed that he did this to get away from office seekers in the United States, one must guess that there were less strenuous ways of escaping them than making twenty-five speeches and traveling for ten weeks in ten Latin countries. His tour, like the moves of Coolidge that same year, showed a change of policy.

Hoover in 1930 established through Secretary Stimson the new recognition policy. He tried also, without too much success, to settle a boundary controversy in the Chaco between Paraguay and Bolivia and the Leticia affair between Peru and Colombia (Peru had taken Leticia from Colombia). He also permitted publication of a long memorandum drawn up in 1928 by Undersecretary of State J. Reuben Clark, which after an exhaustive exegesis of 236 pages showed that the Roosevelt Corollary of 1904 had no reason to be attached to the Monroe Doctrine. In a seventeen-page covering letter to Secretary of State Kellogg, Clark explained, in authentic Department of State passive-voice style, that "it is not believed that this corollary is justified by the terms of the Monroe Doctrine, however much it may be justified by the application of the doctrine of self-preservation." Clark thus did not deny that the United States possessed the right in Latin American affairs of "interposition of a temporary character" (so Hughes liked to describe American intervention policy), but he denied that the Monroe Doctrine justified intervention. This notable memorandum received reinforcement by statements from Stimson and Undersecretary of State William R. Castle. Stimson declared that the Monroe Doctrine was "a declaration of the United States versus Europe—not of the United States versus Latin America." Castle explained that the Monroe Doctrine "confers no superior position on the United States." The era of tutelage and instruction by force was plainly over.

The good neighbor policy was really a nonintervention policy, and this policy, announced by both Hoover and Franklin D. Roosevelt, was made formal in resolutions of the many Pan-American Conferences that have met since 1933.

The conferences of 1933 and 1936 were probably crucial in obtaining from the United States specific expressions of intention not to interfere any more in Latin America. At Montevideo in 1933 the Latins, having seen the signs of change of policy, rose to the occasion with speech after speech. The distinguished historian of Cuba, Dr. Herminio Portell-Vilá, told the conferees: "Delegates, perhaps no other country has as important and special reason as Cuba for presenting a point of view on the very important problem of intervention or nonintervention. . . . Intervention is not only the 'curse of America,' but as a Cuban internationalist has said, it is the 'curse of curses' of any country, the cause of all evils of the Cuban Republic. Cuba was born with the congenital vice of intervention. . . . I wish to say . . . that the Platt Amendment and the Permanent Treaty have the evil of compulsion, for the people of Cuba did not accept either one freely, due to the fact that the country was full of North American bayonets."

The foreign minister of Argentina, Dr. Carlos Saavedra Lamas, said that any intervention, regardless of the reasons, was bad (Lamas in the mid-1930s received the Nobel Peace Prize for a grand project for peace which many of the Latin nations signed and which virtually duplicated several treaties already concluded for Latin America and the Kellogg-Briand Pact for world peace sponsored in 1928 by the United States).

The Haitian delegate (the Americans were still unwelcome guests in his country) said that American marines and the American government had brought to his nation "indescribable anguish."

To such arguments, based not entirely on history, the United States representatives at Montevideo made no effort to reply, but instead accepted, to the surprise of the other delegates, the crucial part of the Convention on the Rights and Duties of States: "No state has the right to intervene in the internal or external affairs of another." The chief of the American delegation, Secretary of State Hull, added a reservation mentioning "the law of nations as generally recognized and accepted," a broad enough hole to crawl through if the occasion demanded. International law, the secretary knew, was sufficiently obscure about intervention so that to invoke it was to invoke uncertainty.

The Montevideo pledge, Hull nonetheless announced, marked "the beginning of a new era." To effect its resolution for a new course, the United States evacuated Nicaragua in 1933, and the marines left Haiti in 1934. The Platt Amendment for Cuba was abrogated by a treaty between the United States and Cuba in 1934, and a similar treaty abandoned the American protectorate of the Dominican Republic in 1940.

At the special Buenos Aires Conference of 1936 called by the United States, the American government made a strenuous effort to better its friendships in Latin America. President Roosevelt journeyed to the Argentine capital on a cruiser to open the conference in person, and the United States agreed to an undertaking of nonintervention more inclusive than that of Montevideo: "The High . . . Parties declare inadmissible the intervention of any one of them, directly or indirectly, and for whatever reason, in the internal or external affairs of any of the Parties." The text did not define intervention, thus leaving a useful loophole for the United States. Seeking to close this gap, the Latin states invited the Roosevelt administration to sign at Buenos Aires a Declaration of Principles of Inter-American Solidarity and Cooperation, in which the signatories "proclaim their absolute juridical sovereignty, their unqualified respect for their respective sovereignties and the existence of a common democracy throughout America." But this was put in the form of a declaration, rather than a convention which after ratifications by the several states would have been binding. Undersecretary of State Sumner Welles, referring to the nonbinding declaration, said diplomatically that it was a Magna Carta of American freedom and collective security.

The last two words of Welles's pronouncement, which appeared in international verbiage about this time, indicated that the purposes of the United States in the Western Hemisphere were changing. The good neighbor policy had begun at the end of the 1920s as a reaction to the policy of intervention, a policy which was no longer necessary to protect the canal—matters in Europe seemed peaceful enough in 1928—and which had raised much ill will in Latin America. Intervention policy needed to be replaced by a policy more in line with Latin American nationalism and *amour propre*. By the year 1936, Nazi

Germany was moving actively in Europe to effect revision of the Treaty of Versailles, with the plan that soon emerged of tearing up the treaty and creating a new order in Europe and perhaps the world. Because of this new exigency, the United States at the Buenos Aires Conference began to speak in terms of collective security, which thereafter became the theme of Pan-American meetings. When war came in Europe, the Declaration of Panama of 1939, a result of a meeting of foreign ministers of the American republics, established a security zone around the Americas south of Canada, which by 1941 was patrolled in vital areas by warships of the United States. The Declaration of Havana in 1940, made by another meeting of the foreign ministers, transformed into a Pan-American task what had long been a part of United States foreign policy, the No-Transfer Principle, that territory held in the Western Hemisphere by a non-American power could not be transferred to another non-American power. The declaration of 1940 was designed to prevent Dutch and French territories in the New World from passing under German control after the fall of those nations in the Nazi spring offensive of 1940.

In the war of 1941–1945 against Germany and Japan, the United States found that the Latin American republics all came to its support in one form or another. Eventually all of them declared war, and two of the republics, Brazil and Mexico, sent military contingents abroad—Brazil sent a division to Italy and Mexico an air squadron to the Far East. The Cuban navy cooperated against German submarines in the Gulf of Mexico. The American government obtained military bases on the soil of Brazil, Cuba, Ecuador, and Panama. In exchange for this assistance the United States gave all the republics except Argentina and Panama (Argentina did not declare war until March 24, 1945) $491,456,432.64 in lend-lease supplies.

Argentina proved difficult until almost the end of the war—a "bad neighbor," Secretary Hull called that country in his memoirs—and the United States used practically every means except severe economic sanctions and war to bring the Argentines into line. Most of the other Latin American nations gave lip service to the efforts by the United States to coerce Argentina. They were afraid of Argentina and also did not wish a principle of coercion introduced into their relations when with so much trouble they had just rid themselves, they hoped, of American intervention.

The Argentines, declaring war on Germany in March 1945, were able to take part at the United Nations conference in San Francisco when it met in April 1945. But after the war as during the war, the Argentines refused their cooperation to the United States, and in the immediate postwar era the fascist government of President Juan D. Perón in Argentina probably caused more concern in the United States than did any other development in Latin America. In its policy toward Argentina during Perón's rise and rule, the United States government seems to have been thoroughly unsuccessful. In 1943–1945 it exerted heavy pressure to prevent Perón's rise to power, and in 1946 at the time of Perón's candidacy for president of Argentina the Department of State published a Blue Book virtually denouncing as a Hitler satellite the government of a country with which the United States maintained diplomatic relations. Perón enlisted the indignation of his countrymen at this interference and was handily elected president. Later the United States made an uneasy peace with his regime in return for measures taken in Argentina against former Nazis and Communists. By 1955 the United States was beginning to give the dictator financial support. Thereupon his countrymen rose up and threw him out. After a long exile in Spain, in the course of which his countrymen cherished the memory of his accomplishments (he had almost ruined Argentina's economy and bankrupted its government), he returned home in triumph in 1973 and again was elected president. He died in 1974, was succeeded in office by his wife who had been vice-president, and power slipped rapidly from her hands. The Perón era thus ended.

American diplomacy toward most of the Latin republics other than Argentina was not nearly so eventful after 1945 as in the years before the war. President Harry S. Truman in April 1945, upon assuming the presidency, said that he would continue the good neighbor policy. But there were no large gestures of the sort made by his predecessor at Montevideo and at Buenos Aires. Since the end of the Second World War the problems of the United States in Latin America usually—with three notable exceptions set forth in the following pages—have seemed small compared with those in other areas of the world. For this reason, perhaps, and because in essentials the good neighbor policy had been accomplished by 1945, there was a lapse of diplomacy in the region.

The only international act in Latin American relations after the war which has had any considerable importance is the Inter-American Treaty of Reciprocal Assistance (the "Rio Pact") of September 2, 1947, concluded at the special conference held expressly for the purpose in Rio de Janeiro that year. This treaty, under article 51 of the UN Charter, which allows regional agreements for collective security, set forth that in case of a dangerous "fact or situation" short of armed attack, the parties would hold a special consultation and decide what to do. And under the new treaty there was not merely a right but an obligation of every American state to help meet an armed attack upon another American state or its territory until the UN Security Council should take effective measures to repel the aggression. The nature of the action to be taken by the American states was to be determined by a two-thirds vote in a meeting of foreign ministers of the Western Hemisphere, parties to the dispute not voting. No state could be required to use armed force without its consent—

hence the United States by vote of the foreign ministers might have to cut diplomatic relations with another state, or cut trade, but it did not have to use (without its consent) armed force. The treaty went into effect after ratification by two-thirds of the signatories in December 1948 (it became effective, of course, only among the signatories who had ratified). In due time twenty-two republics adhered. This was the principal formal diplomatic act of the postwar era.

2. *Guatemala*

It might appear curious that in the 1950s, when the Rio Pact presumably was working, the United States government intervened in Guatemala, and that in the next decade it intervened in Cuba and the Dominican Republic. Shades of Theodore Roosevelt! Was the era of the 1950s and 1960s, then, a throwback to the older ways of behavior? Actually the three interventions of recent times, such apparent contradictions of Pan-Americanism, of the policy of the good neighbor, all had their separate rationales and, considered individually, made sense. They were not deviations from the policy of inter-American cooperation to which the United States had turned after the First World War. Each of these interventions concerned international communism, and for reasons peculiar to the inter-American movement and the countries which were parts of it, the United States believed that it had to act unilaterally, one might say under the Monroe Doctrine, to protect its vital interests. The members of the Organization of American States did not greatly question these interventionist moves by the United States, which seems to say that they covertly approved of them.

The first of the interventions, in Guatemala, involved mainly the rise to power of a talented local troublemaker, Jacobo Arbenz Guzmán, who wished to succeed President Juan José Arévalo. Arévalo had been in office since the late 1940s and constitutionally could not succeed himself. Arbenz's supporters in 1949 arranged the assassination of their leader's principal rival for the presidency, the chief of the armed forces, Francisco Javier Arana. Arbenz in January 1953 was inaugurated president of the republic. Thereupon difficulties arose. The country seemed to be turning toward communism. The Communists in Guatemala came out in the open and were extremely active. Trouble broke out in Honduras, where Arbenz seemed to be causing strikes by labor organizations. A Swedish freighter, the *Alfhem*, sailing from Stettin, brought into Puerto Barrios a cargo of 15,424 cases of Czechoslovak-made military equipment, totaling 2,000 tons of arms, which were unloaded in the presence of the minister of defense.

At Caracas in March 1954, at the Tenth Inter-American Conference, Secretary Dulles had an experience which showed which way the wind was blowing and what the United States might do about it. Dulles was seeking to obtain a resolution against Communist subversion and came to see that such a resolution would prove attractive to the Latin American nations because it would provide a basis for intervention by the United States in the affairs of the state threatened by communism but, at the same time, would allow the other states of the hemisphere to stand aside and preserve the purity of the nonintervention doctrine while the United States did the dirty work. It was awkward for the Latin states themselves to intervene, even for a good reason like getting rid of communism. Communism was entering Latin America under the guise of democratic nationalism, and the Communists would be the first to raise the banner of nonintervention. The nations were willing for Dulles to take the lead, and the vote on his resolution proved extremely interesting: 17–1; two states abstained—Argentina and Mexico; Costa Rica was absent; the objector was Guatemala.

The Guatemalan crisis came to white heat early in June 1954 when Arbenz proclaimed a dictatorship, in the course of which there was cold-blooded killing of opponents. In mid-June a force of a few hundred revolutionists led by Colonel Carlos Enrique Castillo Armas invaded from Honduras and within two weeks gained control of the country. Arbenz went to Czechoslovakia. Guatemala returned temporarily to peaceful ways, but Castillo was assassinated some months later.

Who in the United States government took the leading role in this first postwar intervention? This point is of interest, because it was commonly said at the time that the Central Intelligence Agency had masterminded the Guatemalan revolution. Was the CIA pursuing a private foreign policy? Did it have the active support of President Eisenhower? It is surprising to relate that the leading part in the government's decision in favor of Castillo was not taken by CIA Director Allen W. Dulles, supposedly Castillo's *éminence grise*, but by the chief executive of the United States. According to the first volume of Eisenhower's memoirs, published in 1963, in the midst of the crisis the assistant secretary of state for inter-American affairs, Henry F. Holland, armed with three large law books, one day joined a small group in the presidential office. The rebels in Guatemala had lost two of their three old bombing planes, and the question was whether the United States government should replace them. Holland was against any American action.

"What do you think Castillo's chances would be without the aircraft?" Eisenhower asked Allen Dulles.

The answer was unequivocal: "About zero."

"Suppose we supply the aircraft. What would the chances be then?"

Again the CIA chief did not hesitate: "About 20 percent."

Eisenhower considered the matter carefully, knowing about the blame that always descended upon the United States in any cases or supposed cases of intervention in the affairs of Latin America. But he "knew from experience the important psychological impact of even a small amount of air support. In any event, our proper course of action—indeed my duty—was clear to me. We would replace the airplanes."

It was a small affair, and no blame appears to have come to rest upon Eisenhower's action, which after all he did not reveal until nine years later. By that time it did not seem like an intervention at all.

3. *Cuba—the Real Crisis*

Tad Szulc and Karl E. Meyer, reporters respectively for the *New York Times* and *Washington Post*, have written that there is "a curious contrast in American relations with Cuba, Puerto Rico and the Philippines—the three territories whose destiny was determined by the Spanish-American War." In the Philippines and Puerto Rico, which became American colonies, the United States established a series of reforms which if not altogether successful seem to have been modestly so. At any rate, in both of these places a large pro-American sentiment appeared which has flourished down to the present day. In Cuba the Americans arranged for independence in 1902. American lighthanded supervision in Cuba appears to have produced a veritable hive of anti-Americanism.

In seeking to understand how Cuban-American relations reached their tangled state of the early 1960s, one also should remember that Cuba boasted a fairly large society and culture at the time of the Spanish-American War, whereas Puerto Rico and the Philippines were more backward. Could it be that Cuban sensibilities were therefore more easily offended?

The turns and twists of international affairs are difficult to analyze, and it may be that, as in so many cases, the plunging of Cuban-American affairs into the abyss of 1961–1962 and the enmity which continued in subsequent years had no roots in logic, and that it was the chance appearance of a "maximum leader," Fidel Castro, who has raised anti-Americanism into an article of faith for his fellow Cubans. When Castro departs from his authority, as sometime he must, perhaps a resurgence of friendly feeling for the United States will follow his exit, although by that time the Cuban educational system may have twisted the minds of a generation of his countrymen.

Castro, one must say, did not come to power because of anti-Americanism, but because of the revulsive dictatorships of his two principal predecessors, Gerardo Machado and Fulgencio Batista, whose names together were synonymous with Cuban politics for thirty and more years, from the mid-1920s through the 1950s. Machado entered the presidency in 1925. His dictatorship became oppressive when the worldwide Great Depression descended upon Cuba after 1930. At last he promised genuinely free elections for the year 1934; but in August 1933 a violent general strike paralyzed the island and Machado was forced to retire. The maker of governments for most of the years thereafter, until the appearance of Castro, was Colonel Batista, whose rule, like that of Machado, became ever more oppressive until he too was forced from office.

In discussing Castro's rise to power and the American intervention which followed, it is of some interest to point out that years before, in 1933, just after Machado had gone, a considerable discussion occurred within the American government as to whether the United States should intervene against the successor regime. Had the United States intervened and remained, Castro today might be an American citizen. There was fear in 1933 that Cuba was turning unduly radical, perhaps Communist. Ambassador Sumner Welles in Havana asked for the marines. Ambassador Josephus Daniels in Mexico—secretary of the navy during President Wilson's intervention there a generation earlier—argued vociferously with his former assistant secretary who had become president, Franklin D. Roosevelt, that the United States should not intervene in Cuba. In the summer of 1933 Daniels wrote the president a pointed letter:

> You know that the things we were forced to do in Haiti was [sic] a bitter pill to me, for I have always hated any foreign policy that even hinted of imperialistic control. Frank Lane knew my feeling, and during the Haitian direction, with mock seriousness, he would rise at the Cabinet meeting and say to our colleagues "Hail the King of Haiti." The danger of that pivotal country, so near our shores, falling into the control of some European nation, added to the business of assassinating presidents, made it imperative for us to take the course followed. . . . I never did wholly approve of that Constitution of Haiti you had a hand in framing or the elections we held by which our handpicked President of Haiti was put in office. I expect, in the light of experience, we both regret the necessity of denying even a semblance of "self-determination" in our control of Haiti, when we had to go in and end revolutions or see some European government do so. Your "Good Neighbor" policy will not, I hope, be subjected to any such emergency as we were up against.

Roosevelt saw the light. He deprecated any talk of armed intervention in Cuba. He told reporters on September 6, 1933, that the United States was not sending any massive naval forces to Cuba, but only "three, four, five little fellows." He told them to "Lay off on this intervention stuff. As you know, that is absolutely the last thing we have in mind. We don't want to do it." At his press conference two days later, he reminded them that the American naval forces in Cuban waters were "little bits of things." Early in 1934, after Batista had replaced an objectionable president with a more acceptable leader, the American government recognized the new Cuban regime.

Batista's rule in Cuba lasted from 1934 to 1944 and from 1952 to 1959, and during this long era the American government tried to allay tensions between the two countries. It gave up the Platt Amendment in 1934. That same year it concluded a reciprocity treaty under which Cuban sugar obtained a price in the United States of approximately two cents above the price in the world market. Some people believed that this bounty only kept Cuban sugar noncompetitive with domestic cane and beet sugar. True enough, but the American government had singled out Cuban sugar for this advantage in the domestic market and could just as well have placed a tariff on all foreign sugar. The critics also said that the bounty helped American sugar companies in Cuba. Likewise true. It also helped make Cuban sugar workers the highest paid in the world, except for those in the United States and its possessions. Labor costs in Cuba were so high that the island's sugar had to sell at cost on the world market.

As Batista's mandate began to run out in the 1950s, the American government made some efforts to persuade him to step down. These efforts tended to be countered by the friendliness of Ambassador Earl E. T. Smith. There did not seem to be great danger whether Batista stayed or left. The State Department assumed that the American-equipped Cuban army would prevent too far a swing to the left. Secretary of State Dulles paid little attention to Latin America. President Eisenhower likewise was concerned with European and Asian problems, unlike his brother Milton, the president of Johns Hopkins University, who undertook several Latin American missions and later wrote a book entitled *The Wine is Bitter* (1963).

Then Batista, together with his entourage, departed by plane on January 1, 1959, for the Dominican Republic, and Cuba suddenly belonged to a young man who for two years had been carrying on an insurrection from the Sierra Maestra Mountains. Castro and a few followers had holed up there, issued pronouncements, given interviews to American correspondents. The Cuban government collapsed into the hands of this then thirty-two-year-old bearded revolutionary, over six feet tall, dressed in fatigues, riding in a jeep, and carrying a submachine gun.

The first months of Castro's rule probably were confusing to him, but they were more confusing to the government of the United States. The Eisenhower administration recognized the Castro regime six days after the fall of Batista, and American firms in Cuba hastened to pay their taxes in advance to show their approval. In February 1959, Castro became premier, preferring not to take the title of president. Already, however, the executions had begun, circus-like affairs, for the trials were held in stadiums and other public places. Cuba had no tradition of executions, and the constitution of 1940 which Castro said he would restore had prohibited the death penalty. Americans, and many Cubans, were horror-struck. President Eisenhower was understandably angry when, in that spring of 1959, the American Society of Newspaper Editors invited Castro to the American capital to give a speech. Eisenhower would have liked to have denied him a visa. He did not invite him to the White House. Castro nonetheless went to the capital of the erstwhile colossus of the north, now the good neighbor, and made the speech. It was a neighborly address, in which he denied any Communist influence in his government.

It was after his American trip that relations rapidly deteriorated. Shortly after his return to Cuba the revolution began to pick up speed and become not merely a Cuban affair but one for all of Latin America, even the world. In 1959, the Castro-styled Year of the Revolution, Cuban propaganda began to spread leaflets in Spanish and English in the American South and in New York's Harlem urging Puerto Ricans and American blacks to rise against oppression. The Cubans made contact with the native Americans too, and in July 1959 the premier received Mad Bear, an Iroquois nationalist, as a guest in Havana. The next year, 1960, was the Year of the Agrarian Reform, and before that year ended Castro had seized the approximately one billion dollars of American-owned property in Cuba. The United States was organizing an invasion. That autumn he came again to the United States, this time to New York to attend the Assembly of the United Nations in company with many other foreign leaders, including Nikita Khrushchev, the prime minister of India, Jawaharlal Nehru, and the president of Yugoslavia, Marshal Tito. When he spoke at the UN, Castro took four and one-half hours to present his case. His most memorable remark was that the two American presidential contenders of that year, John F. Kennedy and Richard M. Nixon, lacked "political brains," for which comment he was reprimanded by the chair. At this UN Assembly session he met Khrushchev and physically embraced him. Khrushchev feigned delight at the encounter, and probably was delighted, although the Russian leader afterward privately told the Indian prime minister that Castro was a "romantic."

Early in 1960 the Central Intelligence Agency surreptitiously began to move against Castro, and one thing led to another and eventually to the ill-fated invasion effort of April 17, 1961. As planning matured, the CIA (known jocularly to the cooperating Cuban exiles as the Cuban Invasion Authority) mounted its forces in Guatemala, the locale of its successful effort against communism a few years before. The plans for invasion were approved by the U.S. joint chiefs of staff. Their execution then was delayed until after the inauguration of the Kennedy administration. The new president approved the invasion project because it seemed so far along and because it had such august

The CIA fails in Cuba.

backing, not merely by Director Dulles but by the joint chiefs. He did put a condition on the invasion, that the United States forces must not be directly involved—that it, there would be no air cover. When the 1,500 Cuban exiles went ashore into the marshy Bay of Pigs, this condition proved sufficient to ensure their defeat. One should point out, though, that Castro could have pitted 250,000 militia against the invaders, a force which, whether or not the invaders had airpower, would have overwhelmed them. One result of this fiasco was that President Kennedy never afterward placed full faith in the advice of the joint chiefs and he thereafter maintained a command post in the White House from which to watch over the projects of the sprawling United States government.

A fiasco is itself bad enough for a large and prestigious government, but it is forgivable. This fiasco, however, led directly into the most frightening international crisis since the end of the Second World War—the Cuban missile crisis of October 1962.

The essential point of contention in the missile crisis was that, as President Kennedy subsequently said, the Soviet leaders were trying to change materially the balance of power and were seeking to do it on territory in the Western Hemisphere. The Hungarian ambassador in Washington at the time, who later defected and published his memoirs, would recall a confidential explanation by the Soviet minister of trade and Politburo member, Anastas Mikoyan, to the effect that the purpose of the missiles was to achieve a definite shift in the power relationship between the socialist and capitalist worlds. The Soviet Union's difficulty vis-à-vis the United States in 1962, which impelled them into this Cuban adventure, was the same trouble that had plagued the USSR ever since the Russians had exploded their first atomic weapon in 1949, namely, that the Americans had been staying far ahead in the atomic weapons race. The Soviets seemed much stronger than they were. They held a local superiority in Europe and had threatened the French and British with missiles during the Suez crisis of 1956—safe in the knowledge that the United States did not approve of the diplomacy of its NATO allies. In the next year, 1957, the Soviets had been able—as mentioned in Chapter 12—to put up their first sputnik, evidence of their superiority in the space race. To undiscerning peoples of the world it seemed as if the Russians, given their actions in 1956–1957, were ahead in the atomic race. Such was hardly the true state of affairs. By the end of the Eisenhower administration, the Americans held a commanding lead not merely in nuclear weapons but in ability to take those weapons into Russian territory. In brief, the Soviet Union knew that the missile gap—so ignorantly talked about by Kennedy supporters in the 1960 presidential race in the United States—was not in its favor. The new administration soon recognized its power and openly asserted it. The Soviets were embarrassed and were looking for a "quick fix" for their position, a short-term arrangement of missiles on Cuban soil until they could install intercontinental ballistic missiles in great numbers on their own soil, and until they could construct missile-launching nuclear submarines.

Premier Castro's quarrel with the United States became Soviet Russia's grand opportunity. Castro's apparent fear of the United States might make the emplacement of Russian missiles seem a sensible reaction to American power, justifying to the world's innocents what was a sheer power play by the Soviet Union. For it is evident now that the kinds of missiles almost emplaced in Cuba by Premier Khrushchev would have far exceeded in quantity and quality the requirements of Castro—if such there were—for protection against the United States. After all, Castro only needed one nuclear-armed missile with a range sufficient to get to Miami. He did not need the capacity to blanket the United States as far as the Mississippi River. And who knows what kind of weaponry the Soviets would have brought into Cuba if President Kennedy had failed to react against the weapons the Russians did cart in? By the time the president acted against the Russians (with Castro, of course, by that time unwittingly in the middle) there were at least 42 Il-28 light bombers and an equal number of strategic missiles in Cuba. Technicians were readying nine missile sites. Six of them had four launchers each for so-called medium-range ballistic missiles (range: 1,100 miles), and three of them were fixed sites for intermediate-range missiles (range: 2,200 miles). The three fixed sites each had four launching positions.

The Kennedy administration through U-2 reconnaissance discovered precisely what the Soviets were up to, and after an extraordinary series of conferences and consultations at the White House, State

Department, and Pentagon, the president decided upon a careful course. Already Congress on October 3 by joint resolution had authorized Kennedy to take measures "to prevent in Cuba the creation or use of an externally supported military capability endangering the security of the United States." The president recently had read Barbara Tuchman's *The Guns of August*, an account of how the major powers of Europe had been drawn into the First World War largely out of miscalculation. He vowed to his intimates that if some future historian were to consider his acts in the missile crisis it would be understood that "we made every effort to find peace and every effort to give our adversary room to move"; he was not going to have anyone write, at a later date, a book entitled "The Missiles of October" and say that the United States had failed to do all it could to preserve peace. The president already had given the Russians a warning, to no avail. On September 4 he had said that he would not permit installation in Cuba of surface-to-surface missiles. The Soviet news agency Tass had disclaimed such an intention, and Ambassador Anatoly Dobrynin in private had denied flatly that the Russian government contemplated such a course. The Soviets, however, had refused to take Kennedy seriously for a number of reasons: the maladroit invasion of the year before, Khrushchev's dim view of Kennedy's nerve during a meeting in Vienna in the summer of 1961 when the president had confessed to the Russian leader that the Cuban invasion had been a mistake, and the U-2 affair of 1960, which inspired many Americans to feelings of remorse. Khrushchev had ignored Kennedy's first warning and displayed every evidence of belligerency. The president therefore gave the Russians a public warning which no one, in or out of government, in the United States or the Soviet Union, could mistake. There would be no miscalculation by the Russian government in 1962.

On October 22, Kennedy in a television "spectacular"—of a sort which no one on this earth wishes to see again—announced his policy about the missiles in a manner that not merely Khrushchev but anyone listening and watching could understand. ". . . it shall be the policy of this nation," he said, "to regard any nuclear missile launched from Cuba against any nation in the Western Hemisphere as an attack by the Soviet Union on the United States requiring a full retaliatory response upon the Soviet Union."

The unnerving, frightening aspect of this public message was not its content but the fact that it was public. It was a facedown. It was eyeball-to-eyeball, to use a current graphic expression. Kennedy raised up the national interest of the United States in a public showdown with the Russians. There always is danger that the extreme publicity in such a move will produce equal intransigence on the other side. In October 1962 there then could have been no recourse except Armageddon.

The president, one should add, believed that he had no choice, and that if he did not act he would be impeached. "It looks really mean, doesn't it?," he said to his brother Robert. "But then, really there was no other choice. If they get this mean on this one in our part of the world, what will they do on the next?"

Two days after the address of October 22, the government of the United States, with unanimous support of the Organization of American States, inaugurated a blockade of Cuban waters, and the grand question became whether the Soviet ships then approaching, laden with military hardware, would try to run the blockade. On that Wednesday morning, October 24, an intelligence report stated that two Russian vessels, the *Gagarin* and the *Komiles*, accompanied by a Soviet submarine, were nearing the 500-mile blockade barrier. They were within an hour of interception. The aircraft carrier *Essex* was to signal the submarine by sonar and ask it to surface and identify itself, and if the Russian craft refused then the Americans would drop depth charges with small explosives until the sub surfaced. Robert Kennedy in his book *Thirteen Days* remembered his brother sitting in a White House conference room during this dreadful moment of waiting:

> His hand went up to his face and covered his mouth. He opened and closed his fist. His face seemed drawn, his eyes pained, almost gray. We stared at each other across the table. For a few fleeting seconds, it was almost as though no one else was there and he was no longer the President. Inexplicably, I thought of when he was ill and almost died; when he lost his child; when we learned that our oldest brother had been killed; of personal times of strain and hurt. The voices droned on . . .

Tension in the room that dread morning was broken when a messenger brought a note to Director John A. McCone of the CIA disclosing that some Soviet ships approaching the quarantine line had stopped

The Executive Committee meets in the White House during the Cuban missile crisis. The president is bending over the table at the right, next to Secretary of State Rusk. Robert Kennedy is standing to the far left.

dead in the water, a sign that Moscow was not going to offer an immediate confrontation.

The crisis wore on for several days as messages went back and forth between Kennedy and Khrushchev. Russian technicians in Cuba were hurriedly uncrating and assembling the Il-28 bombers, and working frantically to ready the missile sites. On Friday night, October 26, Khrushchev sent an emotional message which showed how far the relations between Russia and the United States had deteriorated:

> If you have not lost your self-control, and sensibly conceive what this might lead to, then, Mr. President, we and you ought not now to pull on the ends of the rope in which you have tied the knot of war, because the more the two of us pull, the tighter that knot will be tied. And a moment may come when that knot will be tied so tight that even he who tied it will not have the strength to untie it, and then it will be necessary to cut that knot, and what that would mean is not for me to explain to you, because you yourself understand perfectly of what terrible forces our countries dispose. Consequently, if there is no intention to tighten that knot, and thereby to doom the world to the catastrophe of thermonuclear war, then let us not only relax the forces pulling on the ends of the rope, let us take measures to untie that knot. We are ready for this.

But the end of the crisis was no easy matter, even after the Soviet premier had sent his message of Friday, October 26. The next day, Saturday, the president received another message, not so emotional, indeed rather stiff in tone, presumably composed in the Soviet foreign office. By this time the president's advisers had analyzed and reanalyzed the Soviet position so much that they were becoming confused. Any course of action seemed fraught with danger. No action at all was impossible; time was running out, what with the Soviet technicians in Cuba hurrying their work. The president's brother, Robert, and the president's counsel, Theodore C. Sorensen, suggested a solution. They recalled that an important official of the Soviet embassy in Washington had approached a reporter for the American Broadcasting Company, John Scali, and proposed that the Soviet Union would remove the missiles in Cuba, under United Nations supervision and inspection, if the United States would lift the blockade and give a pledge not to invade Cuba. The Soviet official had asked Scali to transmit this proposition to the American government, which Scali had done. Robert Kennedy and Sorensen contended that the president should "accept" this proposal, even though it was unofficial and Khrushchev could have disavowed it. In forty-five minutes that Saturday afternoon the two men wrote a draft of a note. The president worked on it, had it typed, and signed it.

At last, on Sunday, October 28, Khrushchev backed down and agreed to take the missiles out of Cuba. He had received far more of a confrontation than he had anticipated. Shortly after the premier's decision the Soviets dismantled their bases and hoisted their missiles into the holds of waiting ships. The American navy convoyed the Soviet vessels out of Cuban waters and watched them slowly sail off into the Atlantic, back to their distant bases in the USSR.

For students who wished to learn lessons from the Cuban missile crisis, insofar as one could learn from an affair in which the full truth may never be known, a notable fact was that many well-meaning Americans had not understood that the Soviet Union had made a large aggressive move in the cold war. To a remarkable extent the Soviets were able to hoodwink people. There was a considerable feeling that Castro needed protection against the United States, however wrong Castro was. Some individuals also believed that, after all, the United States maintained missiles abroad, and why should not the Soviet Union have its overseas missile bases? Letters appeared in newspapers asking for a mutual missile withdrawal, that the Soviet Union should take its weapons out of Cuba in exchange for removal of the squadron of fifteen American Jupiter missiles then on Turkish soil.

The Jupiter issue was a fairly complicated proposition, and public opinion easily could have misunderstood it—and of course did so, to the benefit of the Soviet Union. In retrospect it is disquieting to see how the Soviet Union was able to exploit public ignorance during a tremendous international crisis. At one point during the 1962 crisis, Khrushchev requested an exchange of the American Jupiters in Turkey for his own country's missiles then in Cuba. The Russian leader knew what he was doing. He was putting an outrageously plausible face upon what had been a great act of aggression. The Americans who argued for an exchange had no idea that the 1,100-mile Jupiter system was equal only in part to the Russian delivery system being established in Cuba. The United States had no missiles in Turkey or anywhere else equivalent to the intermediate-range, 2,200-mile missiles Khrushchev had shipped into Castro's island. Moreover, because of the near-certain American ability to strike the Soviet Union with atomic weapons carried from within the continental United States, or by submarines, and the USSR's then very weak delivery capability beyond intermediate ranges, the emplacement of Soviet missiles in Cuba was a far more important military advantage than was a comparable American base in Turkey.

Also, if the Russians had wished only to force the United States into withdrawing the missiles from Turkey, there were easier ways to do that than to emplace missiles in Cuba. In previous months President Kennedy had been anxious to get the Jupiters out of Turkey, for the stationing of Polaris submarines in the Mediterranean had made the liquid-fueled, "soft"-sited Jupiters virtually useless. Secretary of State Dean Rusk had approached the Turkish government in the spring of 1962, but the Turks had balked about removal of the missiles. The president had instructed the State Department to go ahead anyway, negotiating withdrawal of the missiles whether the Turks liked it or not. The State Department made another approach. The Turks balked again. Nothing more happened, though Kennedy assumed that everything was being arranged. During the Cuban missile crisis the president then discovered to his consternation that his own government, through the State Department's inefficiency, had given the Russians a plausible justification for the Cuban affair, permitting them to argue that they were only doing in Cuba what the United States had done in Turkey. The State Department's failure also had given the Russians an opportunity, if the United States had attacked Cuba, to attack Turkey and thereby challenge the whole structure of NATO (would the predominantly European NATO allies respond to an attack on the Turks?). And would the United States, with or without NATO support, thereupon fire the Jupiters at the Soviet Union? It was a complex situation. But public opinion, not being privy to the United States government's conversations with the Turks, not understanding how obsolete were the Jupiters, or what the United States would do with the Jupiters if the Russians attacked Turkey, tended to fall in with the barefaced Russian suggestion of a trade. Curiously, the United States did make a deal with the Soviet Union over the Jupiters—but it necessarily was a secret deal. Robert Kennedy dealt with Dobrynin, with the understanding of top secrecy; if word got out, Kennedy said he would deny the agreement and the deal would be off. The Jupiters were out of Turkey, as agreed, in five months.

Another instructive—and also, one should add, more reassuring—facet of the crisis was the fact that Berlin had not become involved. President Kennedy was on the lookout for trouble, remarking: "We must expect that they will close down Berlin—make the final preparations for that." But when the crisis came over Cuba, Berlin did not enter the conversations. Berlin would have complicated an already too-complex equation. It might have made the Cuban crisis too dangerous. Russian action in Berlin could have triggered the American missile forces. Soviet Foreign Minister Gromyko said to the Supreme Soviet in December 1962 that the Cuban crisis "made many people think how the whole matter might have developed if yet another crisis in Central Europe had been added to the critical events around Cuba."

After the Cuban crisis, American prestige, so hurt by the invasion effort of 1961, was not merely restored but mightily increased. President Kennedy did not threaten a rain of American atomic weapons on the Soviet Union to raise American prestige, but his successful resolution of the crisis served such a purpose.

Parenthetically one should note that Kennedy gave orders to all of his officials never to claim a victory over the Soviet Union. "He respected Khrushchev for properly determining what was in his own country's interest and what was in the interest of mankind," the president's brother recalled. "If it was a triumph, it was a triumph for the next generation and not for any particular government or people."

It is also of interest that some years later, after Kennedy's assassination, and after Khrushchev's fall from power, the ex-premier in moody retirement was interviewed by an enterprising American reporter and said that, of all the Americans he had known, the one he respected most was John F. Kennedy.

In the shaking out of positions and reputations that occurred after the crisis of October 1962, no one emerged with a more pathetic appearance than the premier of Cuba. Castro with his jeep and submachine gun had become almost irrelevant to the great scene he had helped create. He did not seem to know what had happened, once the diplomacy left his feeble grasp. When everything was over, he did not even have a pledge from President Kennedy not to invade Cuba. Kennedy had made such a pledge contingent upon on-site verification of the removal of Soviet weapons—which the United States never obtained. The Russians claimed that the president had made an out-and-out pledge. Castro complained to the United Nations that "officials of the U.S. Government declare that they do not consider themselves bound by any promise."

4. *The Dominican Republic*

After the missile crisis had blown over, the Dominican crisis blew up—but it was almost a relief compared to the problems and prospects which had opened over Cuba. From beginning to end the intervention of the United States in the Dominican Republic, which arose after the assassination of President Trujillo, was a small affair, compared to what had preceded it.

The Trujillo dictatorship had lasted from 1930 until the shooting of the Dominican president in 1961 and beyond question had constituted one of the worst dictatorships ever to have flourished in Latin America. If there was any single explanation for the untoward political events which followed after Trujillo's death, it was the excesses of his regime, which so poisoned all of Dominican life—society, economics, politics—that it may well be that the rest of the twentieth century will not see peace and quiet, not to mention true democracy, in the Dominican Republic. The dictator's follies have now become public knowledge in the United States. During his regime the mastheads of newspapers and the country's license plates celebrated his virtues with such legends as "Twenty-fifth Year of the Era of Trujillo." He changed the name of the capital city from Santo Domingo to Ciudad Trujillo. Signs everywhere read "*Dios y Trujillo*," and it apparently is true that the dictator wished to change the signs to read "*Trujillo y Dios*." The dictator was not always president; he sometimes inaugurated other individuals and for a short time appointed himself ambassador to the United Nations and ascended into New York. He was, however, the country's only five-star general, the *Generalísimo*. (After his death he was called the *Difuntísimo*, the Most Defunct.) He was careful to provide for his relatives, of whom there were many, including six brothers and four sisters. His son, Ramfis, became a colonel at the age of three and a general at the age of nine. As a juvenile-adult Ramfis spent some time at one of the U.S. Army's war colleges but left under a cloud. He was accustomed to living luxuriously aboard his father's yacht off California waters, where he entertained assorted movie stars. No one will ever know how much money the Trujillo family accumulated, or what happened to it. Much of the Dominican Republic belonged personally to the Trujillos, and those holdings at least were confiscated after the dictator was assassinated. Estimates of funds sent abroad to numbered accounts in Swiss banks range wildly up toward a billion dollars. A former American ambassador, John Bartlow Martin, has related that one conservative estimate published in Europe in 1962 put the total Swiss account at $800,000,000. Martin himself estimated the total at only between $150,000,000 and $200,000,000.

The frightful cost of the dictatorship was due not so much to the amounts of money sent abroad or the inanities of the dictator and his family, but to what all this meant for the everyday life of Trujillo's countrymen. For them the cost of his rule was enormous. The assassinations, the tortures, the degradations were beyond calculation, and some of them beyond description—they rivaled the worst of the Nazi atrocities. It is difficult to realize that one man could do all these things to the poverty-stricken people of the Dominican Republic, many of whom Ambassador Martin in the early 1960s found living almost outside of the money economy, people in the *barrios* with virtually nothing, no past and no future. And Trujillo's rule affected not merely his countrymen. In the first days of October 1937, Dominican troops killed an estimated 12,000 Haitians inside the Dominican Republic (no one knows the total, which may have been as high as 30,000) in a mad orgy, the purpose of which is difficult to imagine.

Contrary to common interpretation, Trujillo did not have much support from the United States government, although he managed to get along. He had obtained his start in politics by entering the marine-trained constabulary during the occupation. Years later he arranged an end to the customs supervision, and he traded heavily on this treaty of 1940 with the United States. The good neighbor policy became odious to his countrymen, and after Trujillo's fall the statue of Cordell Hull was one of the first to be pulled down. Nonetheless the American government was wary of the dictator and from the beginning of foreign aid in 1946 down to the time of Trujillo's death gave the republic only some $5,000,000, no large amount considering that in 1962–1963 alone the Americans gave or lent some $70,000,000.

The dictator's excesses at last became too much. In a 1956 plot, the full details of which are still unknown and perhaps always will be, he had arranged the disappearance from the Columbia University campus of Jesús María Galíndez, an exiled critic who had written a doctoral dissertation hostile to the regime. Ambassador Martin believed Galíndez's body, never discovered, was thrown to the sharks, together with that of Gerald Murphy, the pilot who reportedly ferried the kidnapped professor to the Dominican Republic. There was an uproar in the United States over this affair, and Trujillo retained an eminent New York law firm to make an impartial investigation, which it did and gave the regime a fairly good bill of health. In the year 1960, though, Trujillo went too far when he arranged for an automobile containing explosives to be parked along the route of a parade in Caracas, Venezuela, so that the president of that republic, Rómulo Betancourt, would be blown up. Something went wrong; the person sitting next to Betancourt was killed, and only the president's hands were burned. Betancourt was furious and took his case to the Organization of American States. In an unprecedented move the OAS imposed diplomatic and economic sanctions on the Dominican Republic. The dictator's position began to weaken, and at that point his enemies gunned him down.

The assassins failed to organize immediately after the dictator's death, and Ramfis presided over a bloodbath. Slowly the republic got back on its feet, expelled the Trujillo family, and in 1962 elected a president, Juan Bosch, who had been an exile for twenty-five years.

Ambassador Martin, a free-lance writer from Indiana who for a while was a Kennedy speechwriter, has published a brilliant, huge volume of 743 pages, *Overtaken by Events* (1966), setting out an almost day-by-day account of Dominican politics from the time he came as ambassador in 1962 until after he returned in 1965 during the wild military melee of that year. Martin has written of how he sometimes felt that the Dominicans received the governments they deserved. He liked the citizens of the island republic, yet was repelled, he said, by their impracticality, their laziness, their extremism—traits which together meant they could not seize the opportunity that presented itself with the death of Trujillo. Bosch was almost an incarnation of the good and bad qualities of his countrymen and during his seven months in office managed to do little. As Martin relates, he did avoid political persecutions or killings, and for that short time the Dominican Republic knew freedom. Martin did his best to support Bosch, even though the president was his own worst enemy and had a genius for alienating people whom he needed. It was slow, uphill work, even for an able ambassador such as Martin, surely one of the best representatives the United States government has sent abroad in many a day. President Kennedy backed him up, and sometimes kidded him, as when after one White House conference Martin was walking out of the presidential office. The president followed and said loudly for his outer-office assistants to hear: "There he goes—the Earl E. T. Smith of this Administration." Martin, startled, could only reply, "What a thing to say."

Like Mazzini, the nineteenth-century revolutionary, Bosch inflamed a generation he could not lead, and in 1963 he was ousted in a military coup led by a military man by the name of Elias Wessin y Wessin, a deeply religious, fanatical anti-Communist, born of middle-class Lebanese parents, a man completely honest, politically naive, seeing no difference between the non-Communist revolutionary left and communism, seeing only black and white.

Then two years later, in 1965, a coup occurred against the military regime. This latter revolt soon turned into a serious business, as arms were distributed to the citizens, who took up the weapons for an enormous variety of purposes. Extremism was loosed. The heritage of Trujillo had triumphed. "Men and women like this," Martin afterward wrote, "have nowhere to go except to the Communists." The rebel leader, Colonel Francisco Caamaño Deñó, seemed to have some of the makings of a Dominican Castro.

President Lyndon B. Johnson brought in the marines, a total of 22,000 troops and 8,000 sailors manning some 40 ships. The marines set up a neutral zone between the fighting Dominicans. The Organization of American States voted 14 to 5 to send an inter-American force to the Dominican Republic, commanded by a Brazilian general. United States forces eventually were withdrawn. The new president of the troubled republic became Joaquin Balaguer, a former appointee of Trujillo who presumably had turned over a new leaf. It was an unsatisfactory solution, achieved with far more expense than the American government had put out in the Dominican Republic for economic and other aid. The cost of American military intervention in the Dominican Republic in 1965 was $150,000,000.

ADDITIONAL READING

Pan-Americanism appears in Gordon Connell-Smith, *The Inter-American System* (New York, 1966). See also Alexander De Conde, *Herbert Hoover's*

Latin American Policy (Stanford, 1951); Bryce Wood, *The Making of the Good Neighbor Policy* (New York, 1961), *The United States and Latin American Wars: 1932–1942* (New York, 1966), and *The Dismantling of the Good Neighbor Policy* (Austin, 1985); Irwin F. Gellman, *Good Neighbor Diplomacy* (Baltimore, 1979); and Richard E. Welch, Jr., *Response to Revolution* (Chapel Hill, N.C. 1985). Special studies are Frank D. McCann, Jr., *The Brazilian-American Alliance* (Princeton, 1973); Michael J. Francis, *The Limits of Hegemony* (Notre Dame, Ind., 1977), Argentina and Chile during World War II; and Randall B. Woods, *The Roosevelt Foreign-Policy Establishment and the "Good Neighbor"* (Lawrence, Kan., 1979), Argentina in World War II.

For Guatemala see Blanche W. Cook, *The Declassified Eisenhower* (Garden City, N.Y., 1981), and Richard H. Immerman, *The CIA in Guatemala* (Austin, 1982). For Cuba: Lester D. Langley, *The Cuban Policy of the United States* (New York, 1968); Irwin F. Gellman, *Roosevelt and Batista* (Albuquerque, 1973).

The missile crisis is in Arthur M. Schlesinger, Jr., *A Thousand Days* (New York, 1965); Theodore C. Sorensen, *Kennedy* (New York, 1965); Elie Abel, *The Missile Crisis* (Philadelphia, 1966); Roger Hilsman, *To Move a Nation* (New York, 1967); Graham T. Allison, *Essence of Decision* (Boston, 1971); Howard Trivers, *Three Crises in American Foreign Affairs and a Continuing Revolution* (Carbondale, Ill., 1972); Janos Radvanyi, *Hungary and the Superpowers* (Stanford, 1972), from the vantage point of a satellite embassy in Washington; Herbert Dinerstein, *The Making of a Missile Crisis* (Baltimore, 1976); and Warren I. Cohen, *Dean Rusk* (Totowa, N.J., 1980), Volume 19 in the American Secretaries series.

For the Dominican crisis see John Bartlow Martin, *Overtaken by Events* (New York, 1966); Theodore Draper, *The Dominican Revolt* (New York, 1968); and especially Abraham F. Lowenthal, *The Dominican Intervention* (Cambridge, Mass., 1972).

☆ 14 ☆

The Vietnam War

The United States is in clear danger of being left naked and alone in a hostile world. . . . American foreign policy has never in its history suffered such a stunning reversal. . . . What is American policy in Indochina? All of us have listened to the dismal series of reversals and confusions and alarms and excursions which have emerged from Washington over the past few weeks. . . . We have been caught bluffing by our enemies. Our friends and allies are frightened and wondering, as we do, where we are headed. . . . This picture of our country needlessly weakened in the world today is so painful that we should turn our eyes from abroad and look homeward.

—Senator Lyndon B. Johnson, 1954

To an American of the 1960s and the initial years of the next decade, until the collapse of Saigon in 1975, Vietnam was a name to conjure with. The foreign policy of the United States has had many worries and concerns since the end of the Second World War, but in no case was there so much confusion and travail as over the fate of this little country which, in 1945, and indeed for several years thereafter, most Americans had hardly heard of and could not have placed upon their maps of the world within hundreds or thousands of miles of its true location. The war in Vietnam led to the garrisoning of 540,000 American troops, with perhaps 300,000 more men backing up the supply lines from the United States. The annual rate of sacrifice went as high as 10,000 American lives. Loss of life in Vietnam outran the death toll in the Korean War (33,629); between December 22, 1961, when the first American soldier was killed in Vietnam, and the withdrawal of American forces in 1973, 46,397 American lives were lost in Vietnam.

There were other costs of the war. When President Johnson took office following the assassination of President Kennedy, he announced with assurance that there would be victory in the war on poverty, and that other domestic conflicts would be solved. The Vietnam War delayed these developments, for the war cost as much as $30,000,000,000 a year. American participation in the war sparked explosive protests, especially after 1965, that too frequently became violent. The nation's political and social fiber was sorely tested. Worst of all was the effect of Vietnam upon the Nixon administration, which took office in 1969. A series of events connected to protests over the war led high officials, including the president, to violate the law in a growing scandal that became known as Watergate. The popular uproar over the Vietnam War so worried the Nixon administration that it was willing to take illegal measures against dissidents, including the Democratic party, which seemed to them to be encouraging dissidents.

1. *The Heritage*

American involvement in Vietnam came after the 1954 collapse of the French position in Indochina. The government of France had entered Indochina (Vietnam, Laos, and Cambodia) a century before, at a time when all the great nations were practicing imperialism. French settlers moved to Indochina, not so much to settle on land as to settle on the natives who worked the land. By the time of the world war of 1914–1918 the French had done handsomely for themselves and their descendants. Their only failure was in political knowledge, a sense of how far they might go in personal ways without encountering political forces that would end their personal prosperity. They failed altogether to sense the incipient nationalism of the Vietnamese.

This mistake of the French in failing to see the growing nationalism in Vietnam was not apparent even at the end of the world war in 1918, when Ho Chi Minh, not long before a pastry cook for the renowned chef in London, Escoffier, went to the Paris Peace Conference and sought to argue his nation's cause in the anterooms and coffeehouses of the French capital. Ho's was an impossible mission. Like so many other persons whom the American journalist Philip Bonsal, an aide to Colonel House, described as "suitors and suppliants," Ho went back to his native land with a feeling that there was not much of a future for his country.

Ho spent the interwar years in intrigue, with some attention to the writings of Russian Communists, and did not become an important personage until the time of the Second World War, when he headed Vietnamese resistance to the Japanese. During the war's latter stages a few American agents were dropped behind the lines, and gave Ho such encouragement as they could. Then the war was over, and Ho found himself a national hero.

When the Japanese surrendered, a vacuum of power opened in

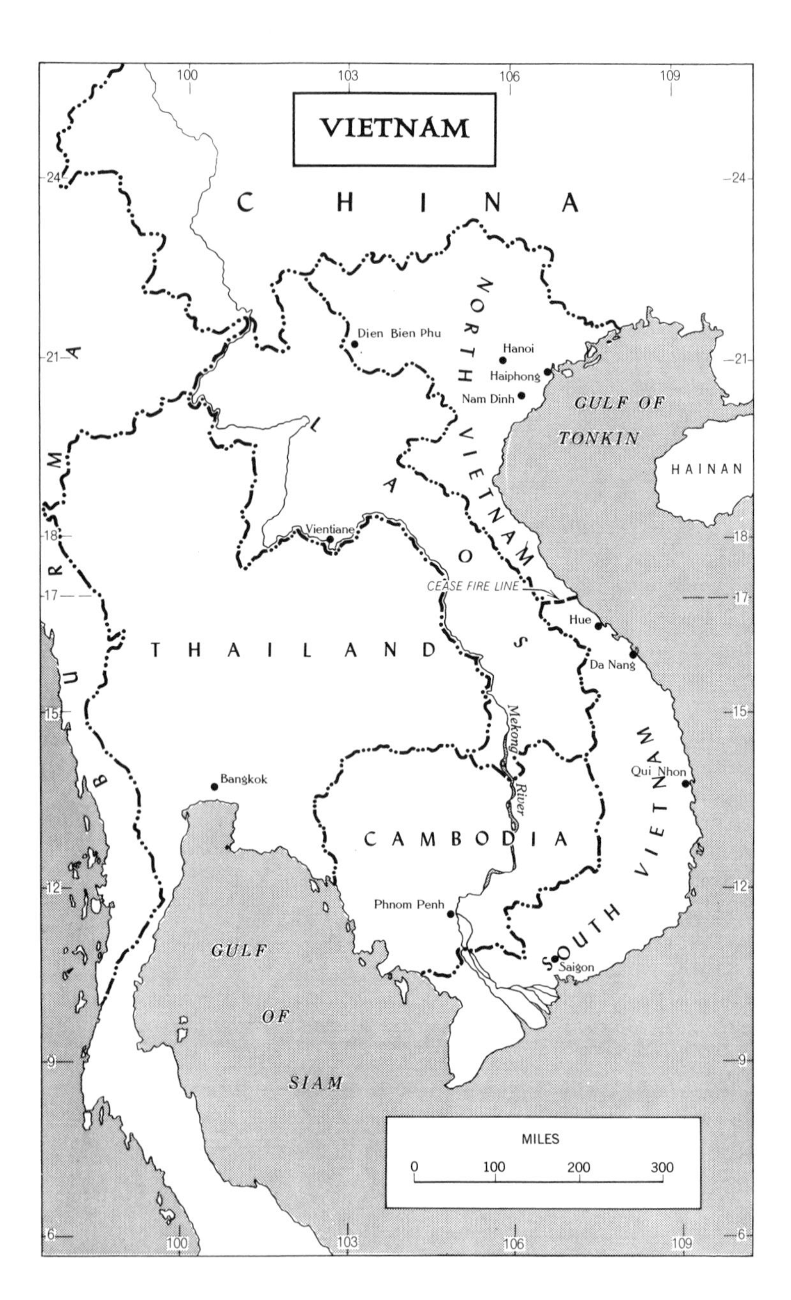
VIETNAM
CHINA
BURMA
LAOS
NORTH VIETNAM
THAILAND
CAMBODIA
SOUTH VIETNAM
GULF OF TONKIN
HAINAN
GULF OF SIAM
Dien Bien Phu
Hanoi
Haiphong
Nam Dinh
Vientiane
CEASE FIRE LINE
Hue
Da Nang
Mekong River
Qui Nhon
Bangkok
Phnom Penh
Saigon
MILES
0 100 200 300
100 103 106 109
24 21 18 17 15 12 9 6

Saigon and Hanoi, Vietnam's two major cities. Ho and his supporters established a government in Hanoi, with ministries assigned to an assortment of officials, not all of whom were Communist. All the French then had to do, if they would, was recognize the Hanoi government.

The decision of the French government in Paris, in all its immediate postwar weakness (there were fifteen cabinets between 1945 and 1954), to reestablish itself in Indochina was one of the major miscalculations of French politics in the twentieth century, and in the memory of that decision, forty and more years later, it seems an almost equal miscalculation of the American government to have permitted the French to return. President Roosevelt at several of the wartime conferences had urged some sort of trusteeship for Indochina, and was strongly against French imperialism, which had given evidence in North Africa and the Middle East of being unable to control colonial peoples except by misgovernment—by terror and brutal police measures.

If the French came back in a vacuum of power, or in forgetfulness, they did not waste time in mulling over their loss of power in Europe and what it meant for Asia. They did not waste time in contemplating the immediate postwar behavior of other European nations, such as Britain in India and Ceylon and Burma, or the Dutch, if belatedly, in Indonesia. The willingness of these European imperial powers, notably Britain, to give up their empires was lost on the French, who decided to keep theirs.

In the tangled history of French political mistakes in Indochina after 1945, it is necessary also to mention another, namely, intrigue. French representatives on the spot, even such personally well-intentioned ones as the priest-admiral, Georges Thierry d'Argenlieu, who was high commissioner in the first postwar months, thought that, local customs being what they were, it might be possible to bribe the Indochinese into cooperation, on the principle that the means might not merely be acceptable locally but would justify the ends of civilized France.

The military measures of the French did not prove successful, and when shot through with intrigue their whole position in Indochina collapsed. At the center of the policy was the former emperor Bao Dai, whom the French sought to make the focus of Vietnamese patriotism, in opposition to Ho Chi Minh's nationalistic Vietminh. Bao Dai was too weak to establish a supportable national government, and managed only to bring all the native fortune-seekers into his government; the more of these supporters the ex-emperor had, the lower he sank in the estimation of his countrymen. When he returned to Saigon under heavy police guard in 1949, after an agreement with the French, he was as dispirited as the populace that watched his arrival.

Ho Chi Minh.

After a few years of battling the Vietminh the French met defeat at an outpost named Dien Bien Phu. The Vietminh undertook to invest and seize this fortress with its sixteen battalions of French Union forces, first ringing the surrounding hills with carefully hidden Chinese artillery pieces, then making the French airstrip at the camp unusable, then tunneling and ditching their way up to the French lines and slowly overwhelming the strong points. In early March 1954, the Vietminh forces, at enormous cost in lives (estimates say 2,500 men entombed themselves in the mud in this initial action), took the strong points Gabrielle and Béatrice, and artillery pounded the third strongpoint into submission. The fortress fell on May 7, 1954.

The background to America's involvement in Vietnam must then include the mistakes of the French. The Geneva Conference of 1954 must be included as well.

Just before the fall of Dien Bien Phu a conference had assembled in Switzerland that had as its nominal purpose an examination of the question of Korea, but its main purpose was to look into the possibility of Vietnamese independence. The plight of France in Vietnam was closely linked to the plight of France in Europe, and it was this fact which at first had so bothered the Americans and helped lead to the Geneva Conference of 1954. So long as the French were maintaining 150,000 troops in Vietnam, their army could not be of much use in Europe. It seemed necessary somehow to give the French a respite in the Far East, so that they could consider quietly their behavior toward the plans which after 1950 were maturing to bring the West German Republic into the defense arrangements of the North Atlantic Treaty Organization. The United States government, in the calling of the Geneva Conference, was not altogether happy with the meeting which would arrange Vietnam, but by that time the pressures of diplomacy in Europe had brought the British and Russians into a willingness to do something for France, if for different reasons, albeit all connected with Europe. The British wanted to help the French get back on their feet and support NATO through the French-originated scheme of the European Defense Community, so strongly championed also by Secretary of State Dulles in 1954. The Russians thought that they saw a chance to defeat EDC, highly unpopular in the French parliament, through helping the French in Indochina as a *quid pro quo*. The Russians apparently were also interested in supporting the French Communist Party, which was the largest Communist party in Europe and was much concerned over the effect of the Indochinese imbroglio upon its political fortunes in France. The European situation, then, at first agitated by the United States, then acted upon by the British and Russians, helped produce the Geneva Conference.

The Chinese Communists likewise were willing to see peace of some sort in Indochina, not to help the French, but to enable the Peking regime to get international recognition. The purposes of Peking have often been obscure, but it does seem probable that in 1954, one year after the end of the war in Korea, the Communists in Peking wished to become more internationally respectable and perhaps get recognition from the European governments if not the American. Cooperation in an arrangement for Indochina would help. Perhaps it even would be possible for the Chinese Communists to join what the Russians in the first post-Stalin months were trumpeting as the Big Five—the wartime Big Three plus France and China. Contrary to American suppositions, then, especially contrary to the thoughts of Secretary Dulles, who felt sure that the Chinese in 1953–1954 were aching to intervene somewhere in Asia now that Korea had quieted down, the Chinese in 1954 actually cooperated with the Russians and British, against the regime of President Ho.

The mechanics of calling the conference were veiled through the convening, at Russian request, of a conference of foreign ministers of the Big Four, held in Berlin in January–February 1954. This conference set up a meeting in Geneva, allegedly to study the Korean situation, but actually as an opportunity to put Indochina on the agenda. The Indochinese item of the agenda came up on May 8, 1954, two weeks or so after the conference opened, a day after the French surrender at Dien Bien Phu. The two Vietnamese sides were present, North and South, as well as Chinese Communist representatives, together with the Big Four.

The resulting agreements were, most of them, not "finalized" in Geneva, and the only documents signed there were by military representatives of France and the Vietminh providing for armistices in Laos, Cambodia, and Vietnam. Subsequent arrangements entered into by the other conferees but not by the United States (which for most of the time had an observer mission), provided for the partitioning of Vietnam at the seventeenth parallel; for no foreign bases in either part of Vietnam, North or South; for neither of the new, supposedly temporary, states to join a military alliance; for countrywide elections leading to unification by July 20, 1956 (two years after the formal conclusion of the Geneva Conference); and for an International Control Commission composed of Canadian, Polish, and Indian representatives, with the Indian representative as chairman. There also was provision for repatriation, within about a year, of refugees.

What precisely was American policy during the Geneva Conference? In the course of these drawn-out conversations at Geneva, the United States faltered and nearly fell, for the conference was not an American idea and the result was not much to the taste of Secretary Dulles, who believed that democratic nations defeated Communists instead of negotiating with them. According to one critic, Dulles was like a global insurance salesman, signing up nations against communism—no man to like Geneva:

> John Foster Dulles [wrote the witty Richard Rovere] raised anti-Communism from ideology to theology. Moreover, he was the first true globalist to become Secretary of State. He did not complain of the lack of specificity in the Truman Doctrine. He wanted us to smite the devil everywhere—or so at least he said—even in those provinces, such as the satellite states of Eastern Europe, where Satan's rule had been a *fait accompli* for several years. He traveled the world like a possessed insurance salesman, offering bargains in American protection to any nation whose leaders would give him their word that they, too, despised Communism.

Dulles therefore played with alternatives to what he considered the Geneva surrender or accommodation (as the British, Russians, and Chinese would have described it). When General Paul Ely, one of the highest-ranking French officers, came to Washington late in March on a special mission to say that he hoped the Americans would give enough support to French forces in Indochina so that the French could hang on somehow until after the Geneva Conference and thereby get better terms at that meeting, Dulles apparently allowed the chairman of the American joint chiefs of staff, Admiral Arthur W. Radford, to propose an American airstrike in support of the garrison at Dien Bien Phu. Anyway, Ely went back to Paris and got consent of the cabinet, and then the American government reneged on its own proposition after Dulles had offered it to a group of congressmen who strongly advised him to consult with the allies and also Congress. An airstrike might have embroiled the United States in Indochina ten years before it did. Dulles's frustration with negotiation of the dispute, rather than a military decision, almost led him up this garden path, but he vacillated and turned another way. American policy thereupon changed from the domino theory, which had a brief popularity (President Eisenhower had announced early in April 1954 that Indochina was like the first in a series of dominoes that could fall to communism in rapid succession), to belief that the division of Indochina into North and South, with the Communists confirmed in possession of the North, would provide a bastion of democracy for the free world in the South and eventually a chance to take the North and return things to where they ought to have been under French rule.

Perturbed by the drift of negotiation, which was out of his hands, Dulles hit on the idea of a security organization for the Far East, which he created in a conference held at Manila. On September 8, 1954, the United States, Britain, France, Australia, New Zealand, the Philippines, Thailand, and Pakistan agreed to a Southeast Asia Treaty Organization (SEATO). Dulles looked upon this new organization as more an enactment of words than a military organization. He preferred the title MANPAC, for Manila Pact, rather that SEATO, which sounded too much like NATO. He said to the conferees at Manila that the pact was not anything like the European analogue, but more of a statement. It specified only consultation among the signatories, and action in accord with their constitutional processes, which could mean much or little. It excluded from its purview the potential "hot spots" of Hong Kong, Taiwan, and all territories to the north, such as the former French Associated States, although a special protocol attached to the treaty included Cambodia, Laos, and South Vietnam by assuring them protection without requiring any obligation, and also specifying that there would be no action except by invitation or consent.

Meanwhile the French government under Premier Pierre Mendès-France had gotten out of Indochina—almost. Mendès-France had asked for the premiership on June 17, 1954, by promising the Chamber that if they chose him he would get the nation out of Indochina by July 20. The Geneva Conference fulfilled his mandate on July 21, backdating the necessary documents to allow him the triumph of his deadline. The idea was that France would grant independence to the three Associated States, and help them toward national survival. The United States government shortly afterward announced to the French that it would deal separately with the Associated States, considering them independent entities available for grants and foreign assistance.

This intelligence persuaded the French government to drop all vestiges of support for the erstwhile colonies, allowing the Americans, who seemed to want the job, to take over.

2. *Sink or Swim with Ngo Dinh Diem*

Bao Dai shortly after the debacle of Dien Bien Phu had appointed the Catholic leader Ngo Dinh Diem as premier, and a year later, having consolidated this office into a position of almost unrivaled power, Diem dumped Bao Dai. South Vietnam became a republic with Diem as president. A new era opened which the *New York Times* correspondent Homer Bigart later would characterize with the unhappy catch phrase "sink or swim . . ."

Diem soon gave some evidence of being a swimmer. As a Catholic he could gain support in the United States and managed good relations with Francis Cardinal Spellman of New York City, one of the nation's most influential clerics. To all appearance he was personally incorruptible. In his first few years of power he consolidated his rule. Helping him in the consolidation were his brother Ngo Dinh Nhu, and his brother's wife, known in the West as Madame Nhu (as Arthur Schlesinger would describe her, "the lovely and serpentine Madame Nhu"). Another brother was the leading bishop of Vietnam. There was still another brother. It was a family enterprise.

One of the points of consolidation about which much has since been written, Diem's refusal to allow elections in his part of Vietnam as stipulated in the Geneva agreement of 1954, deserves some explanation, if only because the United States government backed him in this refusal, and it later became a source of some embarrassment. President Ho of North Vietnam duly invoked the agreement that elections should occur sometime before July 20, 1956. Diem refused, which he technically could do because South Vietnam was not party to the agreement about elections. Should Diem and the United States government have sponsored elections? The result, if honest, might have given the country to Ho. The latter statesman would have received the unanimous support of the people of North Vietnam; Ho would not have allowed a free election there (President Johnson later would ask who had elected Ho president of North Vietnam, pointing out that Ho never had run for election in his life). And Ho would have had a good deal of support in the South, where most of the people had not yet experienced his rule and his name had become a legend because of his opposition to the Japanese and his longtime nationalism. Diem, on his part, could have worked a crooked election, as he had done in 1955 in displacing Bao Dai, but that would have been difficult with foreign observers all over the country. After Diem refused to conduct an election in 1956, the British and Russians, two signatories of the Geneva agreements, issued a halfhearted appeal. The USSR was not anxious for a precedent for East Germany and the other satellites.

As Diem set to work, the prospect economically was not, one should add, poor. At the time of the partition in 1954, the south might have had a better prospect economically than the north. There soon would be a large rice surplus for export. The rubber plantations had not suffered greatly during the First Indochinese War, and rubber could produce foreign exchange. Even if the industry of the country, what little there was of it, was mostly in the north, the south was clearly viable economically.

It was necessary, however, that Diem do something serious about the land problem in the south, and, as we now see, it was a pity that he did not. The south had plenty of land available for distribution among the peasants, for a good deal of land had been abandoned, having gone out of cultivation during the First Indochinese War. The land problem cried out for solution. About 2.5 percent of the landlords in the Mekong delta owned half the cultivated land, and 80 percent of the land was tilled by tenants, with the usual high rents, irrigation fees, uncertain tenure, and scandalously high interest rates for small loans. The large landowners, Vietnamese and French, had supported Diem's predecessors. There were some land successes under his regime, notably a large project sponsored by the Americans to resettle Catholic refugees from the north. But then the land reform began to stagnate, becoming ever more nominal. It did not help when provinces changed hands back and forth from Vietcong (that is, Ho's partisans in the south) to South Vietnamese loyal to the Saigon government. The troops of the latter always seemed to bring along the landlords, whose minds were bent on collecting back rents. Diem also worked out an arrangement to have tenants who bought land pay for it in too few years, such a short time that the cost became a hardship. It would have been better to have given the land away, as the northerners were advocating. There also was a problem of enforcing the laws about the maximum amount of land retainable by South Vietnamese landlords, and of enforcing the maximum rents by tenants as established by the Diem regime at 25 percent of the crops.

The hope of the regime in addition to land reform lay in securing a decent officialdom, but Diem possessed the mandarin feeling that the peasants were stupid—one American said that nowhere had he found a government official who liked the peasants—and refused to send out understanding officials, and instead counted on the grasping type. If an official was honest, Diem and Nhu would tend to distrust him and send him out to an insecure district where the Communists would kill him. The Communists were trying anyway to kill the better officials. This cooperation between Diem and his enemies for different reasons was almost unbeatable as a system to destroy the regime. As it became more and more rotten, reforming the officialdom proved more difficult; because of the rising strength of the Communists in the south, the corrupt officials tended to be the only support the regime had left. When the Americans talked about government reform, Diem smiled and made promises.

The two most important Americans in the early 1960s were Ambassador Frederick E. Nolting, Jr., and General Paul Harkins, and both of these well-meaning men believed that it would be unwise to press Diem. They considered that it might be possible to steer him gently and gradually toward reform, but to press him, they said, would be self-defeating. They seemed to ignore the fact that otherwise Diem would defeat not merely himself but the Americans. The theory of Nolting and Harkins, in retrospect, could hardly have been worse. And so economic and social reform failed, having never really started, and Diem continued to receive a procession of foreign visitors who first heard from subordinates of Diem about the miracle of Vietnam and then listened politely to the president's monologues. The people of Saigon lined the streets and greeted the distinguished foreigners coming and going because Nhu had told them to get out there and wave.

It was in this period that what Arthur Schlesinger aptly has described as the politics of inadvertence occurred—the decision symbolized by the Taylor-Rostow mission of 1961 to increase military assistance. The initial decision to give military aid, taken eleven years before, had seemed entirely sensible. President Truman on June 27, 1950, when everything in Korea was caving in, announced that the United States would increase military assistance "to the forces of France and the Associated States in Indochina," and sent a military mission. Sums jumped from $119,000,000 in Mutual Security program funds in the summer of 1951 to $815,000,000 for fiscal 1954 (July 1, 1953 through June 30, 1954). The numbers of American troops went up slowly. By the end of Eisenhower's presidency there were a mere 800. Then in October 1961 two able advisers of President Kennedy, General Maxwell Taylor and Walt W. Rostow, went out on a mission to Vietnam, and returned to urge enlargement of the military role to include military advisers to improve the level of local action by the South Vietnamese army; American troops in Vietnam increased from 1,364 by the end of 1961 to 15,500 by November 1963 at the time of President Kennedy's death.

As it turned out, November 1963 was a crucial month, as it witnessed the assassinations of Presidents Kennedy and Diem. Cliques of politicians and generals thereafter shuttled in and out of power in Saigon, and President Ho and his partisans began a massive effort to seize all South Vietnam. President Johnson bided his time, and waited until two incidents in August 1964 involved American destroyers in the Gulf of Tonkin. The destroyers had been in the gulf on an intelligence mission, and because their electronic gear was picking up North Vietnamese radio traffic, and because the Americans ingeniously were translating this traffic and knew exactly what the North Vietnamese were doing, there was no large surprise aboard the American vessels when North Vietnamese torpedo boats attacked them. The attacks took place in international waters—the attack of August 2 occurred 28 miles off the coast, and the attack of August 4 occurred 60–65 miles off the coast. The president informed Congress of the attacks and received, in the Gulf of Tonkin resolution, a congressional blank check to use the armed forces to protect the country's national interests.

This, then, together with the precedent of the undeclared Korean War, and the fact that the president even in peacetime is commander in chief of the armed forces, constituted the legal basis of the massive American military intervention in Vietnam, which began in 1965, when Johnson ordered in large contingents of American troops. American army and marine forces in Vietnam rose to 400,000, and then to 540,000, plus supporting troops in Japan and elsewhere, plus supporting air force units in Guam and elsewhere, plus U.S. navy forces in Vietnamese waters. The maximum number of troops committed at any one time by the United States in Korea in 1950–1953 had been 470,000. By the year 1969 the Vietnamese were tying down more than 40 percent of American combat-ready divisions, more than 50 percent of American air power, more than a third of American naval strength.

3. *Ending the War*

Sometimes it is easier to pursue a policy than to change it. Ending the Vietnam War proved extremely difficult. As months and years passed after the escalation of the mid-1960s it seemed as if the Johnson administration had been seized by some kind of resolve that it was not going to stop until victory. Decisions over Vietnam were tightly controlled from the White House, where the president was following Vietnamese campaigns on the tactical level. Within the government as a whole only a few officials had a say-so in Vietnam affairs. They often hesitated to differ from the White House approach because it would seem disloyal. In any event, most of them believed that the might of the government of the United States would force the North Vietnamese to stop the war.

And yet certain military facts gradually became evident and began to overwhelm the tenacity of President Johnson and his assistants. The first of these facts was that military power, of the traditional sort exerted by all great nations on the ground, had not done the trick, had not managed to control the revolutionary situation in South Vietnam.

The second was that air power likewise had not worked as anticipated. Huge amounts of explosives were dumped in Vietnam, with dubious results. It is difficult to be accurate in bombing, flying in with fast-moving planes, for sometimes just a few feet makes the difference. If spotter planes drop smoke rockets, marking the target, the wind may blow the smoke off course before the devastation can arrive. Military objectives were difficult to find, and often it was the same old wooden bridge. The American air force spent billions of dollars to knock out perhaps three or four hundred millions' worth of North Vietnamese industry, most of which was not useful to the North Vietnamese military effort. (The U.S. air force in 1965–1973 dropped on North Vietnam, South Vietnam, Laos, and Cambodia more than three times the amount of explosives dropped by American planes during the Second World War. Total cost of the 7,400,000 tons of bombs was in the neighborhood of $17,000,000,000.) Even if the purpose was to "increase the quotient of pain," it began to be doubtful who was hurting the most.

A third fact was that bombing did not prevent men and supplies from moving increasingly into the south, wherever the North Vietnamese wanted them. The numbers of men passing over the infiltration routes increased from an estimated 12,400 in the years before the bombing to 26,000 in 1965, the year the bombing began, and to 54,800 in 1966. As for supplies, Secretary of Defense Robert McNamara testified that North Vietnam's total imports, of all kinds, were only 5,800 tons a day. Knocking out the docks and piers at Haiphong did not matter much, because the North Vietnamese could bring in 8,400 tons a day by road and rail from China. Of these imports, an estimated 550 tons a day were military supplies. The north required only 85 of these tons in the south. Former assistant secretary of state Roger Hilsman later worked out an equation for the transport necessary to get this material southward: one small steel-hulled coastal trawler, four or five junks, fourteen army-type 6-by-6 trucks, 85 jeeps, 225 elephants, 340 reinforced bicycles, 1,135 quarter-horsepower prime movers (men with packs). The area of interdiction was the size of Connecticut.

A fourth fact was that the north showed no manpower shortage, and hence the business of the kill rate, so much talked about, did not work well. In addition to the insurgents in the south, the Vietcong, President Ho could call on the quarter of a million young men in the north who reached the age of seventeen each year. As for the half million North Vietnamese manning the anti-aircraft defenses, they were no drain on resources, and there were more hundreds of thousands available as "volunteers" from mainland China.

Safe-conduct pass dropped by U.S. pilots over the Vietcong areas. If the Vietcong found any of their men carrying these passes, the men were shot.

A fifth and last fact was that the troops of the Republic of Vietnam, the ARVN forces, were of little help even for holding the cities of their own country. The ARVNs leaned forward in their foxholes and called it a patrol. They were given to siestas and vacations—when the lunar New Year, or Tet, offensive began early in 1968, many ARVN troops were on leave. They had little incentive to fight, as for many of them the army was just a job, or something they had been forced into.

Presented with such a dismal array of facts, what was the richest country of the world to do, since it was being made a fool of by one of the poorest? Some Americans believed their country was readying itself for a fall that would make the fall of Rome seem like a quiet and rather simpleminded thud, compared to our crash. Some citizens recalled the proposed strategy of General MacArthur during the Korean War, that the United States should bomb everything in China, exchanging Chinese lives for American safety. On the other side of the spectrum of opinion about Vietnam was a feeling akin to the pacifism of the 1920s and 1930s, the Kellogg-Briand Pact, a world without war or even evil, and, if war did exist, of turning the other cheek.

In truth, the three possible strategies logically open to the government of the United States seemed fairly clear. They were (1) escalation; (2) a long negotiation accompanied by military forcefulness; (3) immediate withdrawal.

A procession of events early in 1968 at last produced a change in administration policy. Begining on January 30 the North Vietnamese unleashed a surprise and furious offensive which the enemy called the Winter-Spring Campaign and which was focused on the Tet holiday. Major American forces were occupied on the periphery of South Vietnam, half the ARVN was on leave, and suddenly the enemy troops were forcing their way into province and district capitals, most major cities, and airfields. A commando unit of nineteen Vietcong infiltrated the compound of the American embassy in Saigon and made its way into several buildings before the unit was wiped out only after six hours of fighting with embassy guards and reinforcements, including thirty-six U.S. paratroopers landed by helicopter on the embassy roof. Fighting raged throughout South Vietnam, and the result was a bloody military defeat for the Communists, with perhaps fifty thousand killed. But the result also was a psychological disaster for the United States. The American public saw only the lack of control exercised by the more than half million U.S. troops in South Vietnam and the near collapse of native resistance. It appeared as if Vietnam was a military sinkhole.

Shortly thereafter the replacement of Secretary of Defense McNamara, who had been tiring of the war, with Clark Clifford, a Washington lawyer who once had been President Truman's counsel, brought a forceful figure into the center of the administration, and after listening to both sides of what proved to be a developing disagreement within the administration, for and against more escalation, Clifford came down on the side of the so-called doves. General Earle G. Wheeler, the chairman of the joint chiefs of staff, returned early in the morning of February 28 from a quick reconnaissance in Vietnam and carried to a White House breakfast a request for 206,000 additional troops, which amounted to a 40 percent increase in the force already committed. The breakfast, according to a participant, proved to be quite an affair: "It was a hell of a serious breakfast. It was rough as a cob!" Wheeler found that his request was not going to be granted in any automatic way. Within the Pentagon, Clifford began to quiz the military experts to discover, if he could, how many backup troops would be necessary to support a new contingent, if sent. He discovered that the military did not know, and had not included them in the proposed figure of 206,000. The draft would have to be dramatically increased. There was talk of full-scale mobilization.

A psychological defeat in Vietnam and the developing opposition within the Pentagon led by the independent-minded Clifford then joined with other developments to change the calculations of President Johnson. On March 1, 1968, there was a grand upset in the New Hampshire Democratic primary, in which it became evident that Senator Eugene J. McCarthy of Minnesota could prove a formidable challenger to the renomination of Johnson. A run began on the dollar in the European exchanges, out of fear that the administration's Vietnam expenses were passing out of control and would cause inflation. Senator Robert F. Kennedy of New York announced on March 16 that he would seek the Democratic presidential nomination. Meanwhile a presidential speech had been undergoing various amendments as it passed from speechwriters to high officials and as the president himself thought over what he should say. The speech apparently had twelve different versions, the last pointing in the opposite direction from the first, before the president gave it at the end of the month. And a spectacular speech it was, for on the evening of March 31 the president announced a cessation in the bombing of North Vietnamese targets, said he wanted to negotiate in all seriousness, and took himself out of the presidential race.

A decision to end the war had thus been made. A policy had been tried, and reversed. But the war did not end in a hurry. The civil war that had begun in 1946 and then was picked up by the Americans after the fall of Dien Bien Phu and the defeat of the French in 1954 had proved such an ill-starred affair that perhaps it was impossible to stop with one swift diplomatic stroke, getting American troops out, the several hundred American prisoners released, and pulling out of the country.

Washington officials moved slowly. President Johnson made modest efforts at disentangling, but it was not in his makeup to run out of the saloon—he was likely to back out with both guns blazing. In any event, his tenure of office was coming to a close. His successor, President Nixon, at the outset spoke of Vietnamization. In late July 1969 at Guam he told correspondents at a background press conference that the United States would provide military and economic assistance "as appropriate" to a friend threatened by a neighbor, but that "we shall look to the nation directly threatened to assume the primary responsibility of providing the manpower for its defense." A day or two later the White House released this declaration of intent and pronounced it the Nixon Doctrine. In subsequent months and years it would receive all sorts of interpretation, perhaps more than it deserved. Unperturbed, the president went ahead with winding down the war, and in the spring of 1970, when it appeared that the North Vietnamese were using Cambodian territory too openly to supply their forces in South Vietnam, he authorized a large military strike into Cambodia, thereby escalating the war and raising a storm of protest, with marches by college students and a huge demonstration in Washington. During the vociferous reaction to the land invasion of Cambodia the president stood firm. Secret talks in Paris by his assistant for national security affairs, Henry A. Kissinger, seemed to be moving toward some result. Then in the early spring of 1972 the talks were stymied, the president believed, by the deceitful North Vietnamese. Nixon in May announced the mining of North Vietnamese harbors and the "carpet bombing" (a pattern of sheer destruction) of parts of the principal port, Haiphong, and sections of the capital, Hanoi, two cities previously almost exempt from bombing. Again there was a popular uproar, though much less so than two years before during the invasion of Cambodia. Objectors sought to point out that by "interdicting" the use of North Vietnamese ports the United States was blockading North Vietnam, and a blockade was *ipso facto* a declaration of war; the administration kept to its position that interdiction was not blockade, though it did seem like a distinction without a difference. The Nixon administration carried off this new act of belligerence in a surprisingly easy manner. A meeting of the nation's leading Russian experts at Princeton, chaired by George F. Kennan, unanimously agreed that the Russians surely would cancel the president's forthcoming trip to the Soviet Union. The trip came off as planned.

At last, on January 27, 1973, a cease-fire was signed. Shortly before the presidential election in the preceding November, Kissinger announced to a press conference that peace in Vietnam was at hand. The announcement turned out to be premature, and President Nixon's political opponents, the Democrats, were infuriated and believed then and later that they had been upstaged by the president's assistant. Eventually the cease-fire was signed. An involved document, it provided for release of American prisoners of war, and in the next two months 588 men streamed home, greeting their wives, relatives, and countrymen with courageous remarks about their harrowing experiences in prison over the past years. Unfortunately, more than 1,400 Americans, including civilians, were listed as missing, and it was difficult to know what had happened to them. Three missionaries of the Christian and Missionary Alliance had been missing since May 30, 1962—the longest time for any Americans missing or captured in Indochina. During the cease-fire North Vietnamese troops within South Vietnam were allowed to stay put. The Vietcong, the guerrillas, were recognized as a negotiating group. Several nations—Indonesia, Poland, Hungary, Canada—were designated to send observers to enforce the truce provisions. In subsequent weeks a peace conference assembled at Paris, and on March 2 signed an agreement guaranteeing the cease-fire.

The Vietnam War had lasted through the first term of the Nixon administration, until 1973. Vietnam seemed to have cursed the presidencies of recent times, and as it had destroyed the promise of Johnson's "great society" measures, so it proved a tragic inheritance for Nixon. The choice of negotiation rather than a quick exit was, as can now be seen in retrospect, a huge mistake. Here, in the case of the Vietnam War, was an occasion when a swift surgical stroke would have been far better—when of the three choices of policy (escalation, negotiation from strength, immediate withdrawal) the last, a military exit, would have saved much trouble, foreign and domestic. Between January 1969, when Nixon took office, and the signing of the cease-fire in January 1973, during all this time when the war was approaching its end, nearly four million more tons of bombs were dropped; 20,000 more Americans died and over 100,000 were wounded; sev-

"DR. KISSINGER, I PRESUME?"

In the negotiations to stop the war, Kissinger seemed to be everywhere.

eral hundred thousand Asians died, with more wounded; and at least four million people became refugees. Within the United States the constitutional balance between Congress and the presidency had disappeared, overwhelmed by the power of the executive—although President Nixon in his war-making was only following the precedents of the Johnson administration and the Truman administration, both of which had waged war without congressional authority. Wherever one looked, constitutionally speaking, matters were in disarray. When on January 12, 1971, Nixon signed an act of Congress repealing the Tonkin Resolution, he said that the signature made no difference, that it did not in any way diminish his authority as president and commander-in-chief. Somewhat later the Watergate affair demonstrated what could result when the proper constitutional checks and balances were absent.

4. *Aftermath*

This was hardly the end of trouble in what once had been Indochina—the three former French provinces of Vietnam, Laos, and Cambodia. Secretary Kissinger together with the North Vietnamese Politburo member Le Duc Tho received the Nobel Peace Prize for achieving the cease-fire in Vietnam. But in 1975 the North Vietnamese army overwhelmed the troops of South Vietnam and forced a union of the country. Their government commenced a rule in the south that was terribly oppressive, committing enemies to reeducation camps, turning people out of Saigon (renamed Ho Chi Minh City, in honor of the founder of the regime who had died in 1969) into the countryside where existence was barely possible and sometimes not that. Tens of thousands of Vietnamese fled into exile in Thailand or, after harrowing voyages in small boats, to the Philippines and elsewhere. The new rulers of a united Vietnam proved unable to handle the economy of the south, which stagnated at a low level. For this they blamed the United States. In negotiating the release of the American prisoners in North Vietnam President Nixon had proposed a vast economic assistance, which Congress failed to appropriate. This may have persuaded the Vietnamese government to hold back some American prisoners. There is still speculation that American POWs and MIAs remain in Vietnam.

In Laos and Cambodia, a solution proved equally difficult. Both sides, North Vietnamese and American, had violated the neutrality of Laos, contrary to the agreement signed by an international conference in 1962. A cease-fire was arranged for Laos on February 21, 1973. But the situation that had developed in Cambodia was much more difficult, in terms of both the local military situation and what American intervention meant for the provisions of the United States Constitution. The North Vietnamese had used Cambodian territory both as a staging area and a highway—the Ho Chi Minh trail—into South Vietnam. Beginning in 1969 the United States air force had intervened secretly, with massive bombing attacks. President Nixon had known of the attacks, and approved them, well before the ground intervention in Cambodia in 1970, at which time the president announced that the invasion of Cambodian territory was a momentary affair, and that after withdrawal of American troops upon completion of their operation, the United States would continue to seek the preservation of Cambodian neutrality. All the while, of course, the Pentagon was bombing the daylights out of the place. The Defense Department was using a dishonest system of double reporting, so it was called, that kept the attacks secret even from many military officials, not to mention Congress and the public. By chance Congress in 1973 learned of what was going on, and in anger forced the administration to halt the bombing on August 15 of that year.

All the while internal conditions in Cambodia were becoming hellish for the people of that once bucolic province. For years Prince Norodom Sihanouk, a popular ruler, had preserved the neutrality of his kingdom (he himself was variously king, chief of state, prince, and prime minister). But the intrusion of the Vietnam War played havoc with his rule, and he was ousted in March 1970 in a coup led by his prime minister, Lon Nol. Sihanouk went to Peking and courted

Communist support, and the United States threw its support to Lon Nol. There followed a brutal civil war, fought virtually without quarter, and with much physical destruction—one Communist bombardment of Cambodia's capital of Phnom Penh in February 1974 destroyed 10,000 houses. Early in 1975, Lon Nol met defeat and the Khmer Rouge entered the capital, which they immediately emptied by force, sending the population to the countryside without adequate supplies of food and medicine. Between one and three million Cambodians apparently died during the next three years. The Communist government proved almost unbelievably callous, and the neighboring Communist regime in Hanoi rightly described the government of the Cambodian Communist leader Pol Pot as having produced "a land of blood and tears, hell on earth." In 1979 a dissident Khmer Rouge leader, with assistance from Vietnamese forces, defeated Pol Pot. Civil strife continued, and in an effort to suppress the remnants of Pol Pot's army Vietnamese troops poured into Cambodia, increasing between 1979 and 1982 from 60,000 to 200,000.

The aftermath of the Vietnam War, one was forced to conclude, very probably was worse than the war itself. American diplomacy, backed by a military intervention a generation ago, had led to trouble beyond measure.

ADDITIONAL READING

Joseph Buttinger, *Vietnam* (2 vols., New York, 1967), abridged as *A Dragon Defiant* (New York, 1972), is the well-written and generally reliable account of an American insider. A recent and popular book is Stanley Karnow's *Vietnam* (New York, 1983). The best short analysis is by George C. Herring, *America's Longest War* (2d ed., New York, 1986). For their special subjects see Bernard B. Fall, *Hell in a Very Small Place* (Philadelphia, 1966), the fall of Dien Bien Phu; and Robert F. Randle, *Geneva 1954* (Princeton, 1969).

The beginning of the Second Vietnamese War appears in Robert Shaplen, *The Lost Revolution* (rev. ed., New York, 1966). Arthur M. Schlesinger, Jr., took sections from his memoir of President Kennedy and updated and enlarged them into *The Bitter Heritage* (Boston, 1967); Schlesinger's book places no blame on Kennedy, and implicitly considers President Johnson the inventor of the Vietnam disaster, but in many respects is a model of scholarship and understanding, and its judgments have held up remarkably well. Townsend Hoopes, *The Limits of Intervention* (New York, 1969), offered a view from inside the government; Hoopes saw a narrowing circle of presidential advisers, until events and contrary advice penetrated the presidential cranium. Chester L. Cooper, *The Lost Crusade* (New York, 1970), is a witty account by a former official close to Governor Harriman, who followed Indochinese and Vietnamese affairs from the Geneva Conference of 1954 to the denouement of 1968. Henry Graff, *The Tuesday Cabinet* (Englewood Cliffs, N.J., 1970), relates interviews with top American officials. Two popular books, well written, intensely critical, concerned about Vietnam's effect on American life, are Frances FitzGerald, *Fire in the Lake* (Boston, 1972), and David Halberstam, *The Best and the Brightest* (New York, 1972). FitzGerald looks to the life of the people of Vietnam. Halberstam in his title asks how the brightest and best-informed men in American public life in the 1960s, almost without exception, could have favored involvement in such a sinkhole. See also William C. Westmoreland, *A Soldier Reports* (Garden City, N.Y., 1976); Warren I. Cohen, *Dean Rusk* (Totowa, N.J., 1980); Paul M. Kattenburg, *The Vietnam Trauma in American Foreign Policy* (New Brunswick, 1980); Ronald H. Spector, *United States Army in Vietnam: Advice and Support, the Early Years, 1941–1960* (Washington, 1983); and Bruce Palmer, Jr., *The 25-Year War* (Lexington, Ky., 1984).

The Pentagon Papers are available in several versions. *The Pentagon Papers as Published by the New York Times* (New York, 1971) contains the material as sifted and originally published by the reporter Neil Sheehan. *The Pentagon Papers: The Defense Department History of United States Decisionmaking on Vietnam* (5 vols., Boston, 1971–1972) is the material released by Senator Mike Gravel and published by Beacon Press. *United States–Vietnam Relations: 1945–1967* (12 vols., Washington, D.C., 1971) is by the Government Printing Office.

For Cambodia see William Shawcross, *Sideshow: Kissinger, Nixon and the Destruction of Cambodia* (New York, 1979), and the same author's *The Quality of Mercy: Cambodia, Holocaust and the Modern Conscience* (New York, 1984).

☆ 15 ☆

The Seventies: Nixon, Ford, Carter

U.S.-Soviet issues should not be permitted to so dominate our foreign policy that we neglect relationships with our allies and other important issues, as has been the case in the past.

—Cyrus Vance to James E. Carter, 1976

A new foreign policy occupied center stage during the 1970s, under Presidents Nixon, Ford, and Carter. This was a policy known usually by the French word *détente*—a policy of letting the world cool, of attempting to accommodate American interests to those of other nations, even the Soviet Union, in hope that as years passed the heated exchanges that had marked the diplomacy both of the United States and of the Soviet Union, sometimes that of the lesser nations, would come to an end. People everywhere, not merely in the United States, had tired of confrontation.

The policy embraced in the early nuclear age, from 1945 until the end of the Eisenhower administration, had been *deterrence*, which was aimed mainly at the Soviet Union. First during the era of America's nuclear monopoly until 1949, then during a decade and more of nuclear rivalry, the United States sought to maintain sufficient military strength and diplomatic agility to persuade the USSR to refrain from nuclear war, to avoid the unknown but dangerous possibilities even of a limited Soviet-American war, and to maintain the post-1945 arrangement of territory and peoples throughout the world. But by the 1960s, and for two reasons, it began to become clear that deterrence was no longer feasible. One reason was the increasing diffusion of nuclear power: by 1964 the People's Republic of China had joined France, Great Britain, the Soviet Union, and the United States as members of the nuclear club. Before the end of 1967 the mainland Chinese tested a hydrogen bomb as well. By the early 1970s, China had made perhaps fifteen tests, five in the megaton range. The second reason for turning from the policy of deterrence was the increasingly varied nature of the family of nations, which had grown enormously by the 1960s, and was becoming extremely diverse in its interests. The old two-parent domination of the world, obvious in 1945 when two superpowers emerged from the Second World War, had given way to 170 or more assertively independent states, a progeny that was not about to align with either of the erstwhile parents. During the 1960s the Vietnam War preoccupied the makers of American policy, and American foreign policy became in effect Vietnam policy. Under President Johnson the rule seemed to be that whoever was not supporting the United States was against it. The president asked leaders of other nations to sit down and reason with him or Secretary Rusk, but meant that they should sit down and agree, otherwise he would cast them into outer darkness. By the end of the decade, with Vietnam lost and the president readying himself for retirement, a change was possible. Richard Nixon and his national security adviser Henry Kissinger determined to move away from deterrence to détente.

1. *Nixon and Détente*

Within the United States no one was better qualified to change policy than was Richard M. Nixon, whose anti-Communist credentials were impeccable. So were those of his national security adviser, who as a young Harvard professor in the mid-1950s had championed deterrence through emplacement of battlefield nuclear weapons in Western Europe. By 1969, though, circumstances had changed, and Kissinger informed Nixon that the Soviets possessed a "sufficiency" of nuclear arms and carriers and it no longer was possible to maintain American superiority, even though their "throw-weight" might not equal that of the United States. The need for a new direction was clear.

The first of the Nixon moves toward détente was accommodation with the People's Republic of China, a long overdue correction in the policy of his predecessors. Nixon gave up the effort by Truman, Eisenhower, Kennedy, and Johnson to exclude the PRC from the family of nations. It was too large a country, and such a policy was bound to fail, as did the similar effort with Russia after the Bolshevik revolution of 1917. The PRC had not behaved well toward the United States, turning its troops against American forces in Korea in November 1950. This after a long American effort, over many decades, to assist the Chinese people. It had allied with the Soviet Union in

Kissinger at the Great Wall, 1971.

1949, creating a Sino-Soviet bloc. The Chinese broke with the Russians at the end of the 1950s, but they assisted the North Vietnamese during the 1960s. And yet with the end of the latter decade, and the imminent end of the Vietnam War in 1973, it was time for a change. Nixon did not propose to turn policy completely around. He offered only de facto (that is, provisional) recognition. He sought to reduce tension between Washington and Peking, and perhaps let the contentions between Peking and Moscow develop without distraction from Washington. Moreover it was possible that the Soviet Union would pay more attention to the United States because of an American-Chinese rapprochement—the Russians were deathly afraid of the Chinese, and twice during the early 1970s (in July 1970, and during the Nixon-Brezhnev conversations in Washington in June 1973) sought an agreement with the United States on joint military action in case of nuclear attack by China.

The trappings of the 1972 de facto recognition of China (official recognition followed in 1979 during the Carter administration) fascinated the American people. They were treated to accounts of Kissinger's secret flights to the Chinese capital, together with the announcement on television that the president had received and was accepting an invitation to visit China. Nixon duly visited, and met Chairman Mao, and saw the Great Wall, which he said was "great."

Thereafter the Chinese and Americans opened the country to American visitors, and public figures and everyday Americans went to China and brought back their experiences to relate to friends and publish in travel books. Gradually, dealing with citizens of mainland China became a commonplace. By the 1980s the two nations were maintaining fairly close ties, although political, military, and economic cooperation advanced slowly, with a pace that from the Chinese side was probably disappointing. Once more, Americans were learning that China was a huge country and poor; the Chinese people were wonderfully attractive, but their problems would require a long time for solution.

Another reason, apart from China, for moving away from deterrence toward détente was the possibility of a scientific breakthrough in nuclear weapons and their carriers, a chance that deterrence might become almost impossible because of the inventiveness of scientists. American scientists were ahead of the game, developing the weapons and carriers of breakthrough. Nonetheless it was an uneasy situation, and Nixon and Kissinger sensed the danger, and as soon as they could wind down Vietnam they turned to a more careful policy with the Russians.

The initial unsettling scientific possibility to appear over the diplomatic horizon in the latter 1960s was construction by the Soviets or the Americans or both nations of an effective antiballistic missile (ABM) system. Early in the decade there were speculations that the Russians were beginning an ABM system, or completing an important part of it, or had completed all of it. The presumption was that with the Soviet nuclear-weapons delivery system protected by an impenetrable ABM net there would be nothing for the United States to do but surrender. Congressmen conjured up horrible visions of some kind of last stand by the United States against the USSR, perhaps a century after the death of General George A. Custer (d. 1876). Senator Richard B. Russell of Georgia told his fellow senators that if only one man and one woman were to be left on earth, it was his deep desire that they be Americans. The pressure began to rise for the Johnson administration to do something to confront the Russian challenge. The latter was deemed to be twofold: Soviet construction of giant missiles, the SS-9s, carrying warheads of twenty or twenty-five megatons; and appearance of two ground-to-air nets, the beginnings of an ABM system around Moscow together with deployment of a larger and probably anti-bomber, not antimissile, net known as the Tallinn system, across the northwestern part of the Soviet Union.

A series of developments within the United States—a proposal, reactions, and another proposal—led into a great debate in 1969–1970, and then the whole ABM issue disappeared from public view and even from official concern. During the last part of the Johnson presidency Secretary of Defense McNamara, who in earlier years had been against an ABM, came out in favor. In a speech of 1967 he asked for a light ABM net which he said would be a defense against any irrational move by the Chinese. He called his proposed system Sentinel. But Sentinel almost at once came into question, for McNamara's opponents claimed that the proposed light ABM was really designed against the USSR. A light net, they argued, would soon take on weight. Moreover, the defense secretary had said his proposed system was to defend major American cities. By the time the Nixon administration came into office there had been considerable public outcry against the purchase of land by the Defense Department on which to establish components of the projected ABM. The land purchases apparently had to be close to the largest American cities. Opponents began to argue that to set up such hardware so close to areas of heavy population might draw a Russian attack. President Nixon hence reconsidered the proposed Sentinel system, changed its rationale, and renamed it Safeguard. The new purpose was to protect important parts of the Minuteman ICBM force west of the Mississippi; Safeguard was not to have the purpose of withdrawing large portions of the American populace from the balance of terror, which might tip the balance, but was only to make impregnable a sufficient part of the nuclear-weapons delivery system to deter the USSR from attack. A furious debate broke out in Congress in 1969 when President Nixon's supporters presented the appropriations bill for the first part of the light net. The initial appropriation for Safeguard, to begin work on installations to defend two Minuteman sites in Montana and North Dakota, passed the Senate by a single vote. When further appropriations came before the Senate the next year there was another uproar, and the margin of passage rose to five votes. In 1971 the opposition slackened off, and continued deployment of the ABM at the two sites was approved by a vote of 64 to 21 after two hours of relatively moderate debate. Then the issue reached a strange kind of anticlimax during the Strategic Arms Limitation Talks (SALT) between U.S. and USSR technical representatives, which had been alternating between Helsinki and Vienna. Technicians at the talks drew up an ABM treaty which the Soviets signed with President Nixon during the latter's trip to Moscow in 1972. The treaty, which easily passed the Senate, allowed the United States and USSR to have two ABM sites apiece—an installation protecting no more than 100 ICBMs, and an installation protecting a city (the two cities being presumably Washington and Moscow). Since the United States government under the Nixon administration had backed away from protection of cities, and the Russian government never had shown much interest in trying to protect ICBM sites, each nation nicely lost. Fortunately, the threat of emplacement of a new sort of military hardware that might have tipped the nuclear balance disappeared.

Actually the ABM treaty resulted in cessation of the limited American program. The treaty allowed protection of the national capital, but congressmen refused to vote funds for a project that would give themselves protection while leaving their constituents exposed. Then Nixon and Brezhnev, meeting in Moscow in the summer of 1974, agreed that each side would give up one of its proposed ABM sites—which on the American side meant confirming the reluctance of Congress. But the question already had arisen as to whether a one-site program was practical. When the treaty of 1972 stopped construction of the Montana installation, in favor of that in North Dakota, some experts believed that to have only one installation protecting a group of 100 ICBMs might prove useless. The rationale for two ABM installations protecting ICBMs had been that if a large nuclear explosion overhead blacked out the radar of one site, radar tracking could be obtained from another site. Senator Henry M. Jackson of Washington, the Senate's expert in such matters, questioned the practicability of a single site. Meanwhile a large cost overrun on the North Dakota site itself produced questions. It became apparent that this installation would cost about $5,500,000,000—or about $1,500,000,000 more than the original estimate for two sites, and nearly half the original estimate for what in 1969–1970 was envisioned as a twelve-site system. In the autumn of 1974 the Defense Department at last admitted (while it was asking for a final $135,000,000 to complete the Grand Forks installation) that one site was not enough. It told Congress that after completing Grand Forks in 1975 and operating the installation for about six months it planned to close that site down, to put it in mothballs. A few congressmen objected to appropriating $135,000,000, on top of all the preceding costs, only to mothball the result, but the appropriation passed.

At the same time as the expensive North Dakota ABM net was going up, the American government was proceeding with production of multiple, independently targetable reentry vehicles (MIRVs) and was MIRVing its Minuteman missiles and converting the warheads of the missiles aboard most of its fleet of atomic-powered submarines. Here, with MIRV, American technology for several years held a clear lead over the Soviet. The Americans demonstrated their own ability to MIRV a missile warhead in 1968. Not until 1973 did the Soviet Union successfully test a MIRV (the United States government knew this because it could monitor any Soviet tests). Russian inability in this regard appeared implicitly in the terms of the five-year freeze of ICBM forces drawn up during the SALT talks and

Nixon and Kissinger walking in the Kremlin.

signed as an executive agreement by President Nixon during his Moscow trip. The freeze gave the Russians 2,358 launch vehicles as compared to 1,710 for the Americans, the presumption being that the destructive power of the American MIRVed warheads was equal to the "throw-weight" of a larger Soviet missile force. Superficially considered, the MIRV breakthrough had seemed much in favor of the United States. It was an awkward business, though, for the American government had pioneered in a technology which might make future disarmament efforts impossible. Reconnaissance satellites could count missiles, but not what was inside a nose cone. Even ground observers could be hoodwinked five minutes after they left a missile installation. The MIRVing of U.S. missiles also had looked in the direction of breaking the strategic balance. Proponents of MIRV claimed that American science had been forced to move ahead, for the science of the USSR, they said, would surely follow. Skeptics pointed out that for five years, and perhaps more (the United States had announced a successful MIRV test in 1968 but the announcement might have been delayed?), Soviet science had not followed. Was it clever, they argued, for the government of the United States to have gotten out in front in such an obvious way?

Increasing signs appeared in 1974 that to have emplaced MIRV years ahead of the Russians was not a smart policy. The MIRVing of Russian missiles threatened at least some of the Minuteman sites—they could be showered with thousands of warheads in an initial strike.

The Soviets possessed big-thrust missiles such as the SS-9 and each separate vehicle would have a great deal of throw-weight. Talk arose of abandoning the Minutemen, and sending the American deterrent "out to sea," presumably in more submarines. It was an attractive proposal for the sea was a much less populated place than the trans-Mississippi West, a much better locale in case of accident, not to mention war. Still, to scrap a missile bed so recently constructed at enormous cost, complete with its one-site ABM—to announce to the inflation-weary American people that this appallingly expensive, exotic military hardware was now junk and could be used to store potatoes, convert into underground dachas, or provide exciting scenes in futuristic movies—was a delicate, awkward, probably impossible business for administrations as weak as those of Presidents Nixon and Ford, and the temptation was to try to bolster, to reinforce. The Defense Department undertook to increase warhead accuracy, and thinking in terms of a bigger bang it commenced work on larger-thrust missiles. It also announced the possibility of new warheads—MaRVs, for maneuverable reentry vehicles—that would change course, or "wiggle," during the final part of their trajectories as they approached their targets, which meant that they could not be tracked and hence the Soviet ABM would be useless. The prospect of an American first-strike capacity, which the Russians had begun to cancel after huge expenditure, was appearing once more. Was this good for American-Russian relations, or relations with anyone except the angels?

A singularly successful effort at détente during the Nixon years appeared in resolution of the German problem: the problem of a divided Germany and a divided Berlin. German policy had occupied statesmen since the end of the Second World War, but they had made little progress.

For many years an observer might have thought that the German problem was insoluble. Consider the way in which Khrushchev, beginning in 1958, agitated the Berlin question. Supposedly settled a decade before by the success of the Allied airlift vis-à-vis the Russian ground blockade, the issue of Berlin really had not been settled at all, but adjourned. The city lay 110 miles into East Germany, its access routes so susceptible to Russian pressure tactics that it was virtually a hostage for Western good behavior, or so Khrushchev thought. In the autumn of 1958 he suddenly announced that the USSR was going to sign a treaty with the East German puppet regime within six months—by May 1959—and either the Western nations had better prepare to deal with that regime (which previously they had refused to do) or else the regime, backed by Russian might, would deal with them. The prospect was for a facedown in Berlin, where the weak Western garrisons were no more prepared for serious military trouble than they had been a decade before.

In the next months and years Khrushchev turned the Berlin issue off and on as if it were a traffic light. As the prospect of a visit to the United States arose he temporized with his deadline of May 1959, and the deadline came and passed. As events turned out, it coincided with the death, from cancer, of Secretary Dulles, and for that reason alone a Russian move in Berlin would have seemed out of place. Shortly afterward the ebullient Khrushchev was in the United States, touring across the country—holding up an ear of corn in the midst of rural Iowa, arguing vociferously with the mayor of Los Angeles during a public dinner, disappointed like a child when for security reasons he was refused an opportunity to visit Disneyland. The Berlin issue languished until after the U-2 affair, during President Kennedy's visit to Vienna, when Khrushchev rattled Russian military might so fearsomely that the American leader returned to Washington and virtually declared a state of national emergency, calling up reservists, anticipating serious Russian action in the German capital.

The Soviet action, when it came on August 13, 1961, was anticlimactic, and a confession of defeat, though at the time it did not so appear. This was the sudden closing of the border in Berlin between the Eastern and Western sectors of the city, and a tightening of the entire border between East Germany and West Germany. In subsequent weeks the East Germans erected a wall out of concrete blocks, barbed wire, sometimes the sides of knocked-down houses, a wall that ran straight through the heart of the city. Spectacular escapes over or under the wall took place, with East German police sometimes shooting victims in such ways as almost to crucify them atop the wire. The West German police had to look on helplessly, with troops of the Western military contingents stationing themselves discreetly in the background. To Americans and the people of Western Europe the wall looked like a terrible inhumanity. It divided families, members of which were not to see each other for years thereafter. And yet the Soviets had been forced into this move. So many East Germans were escaping over the border, attracted partly by the political freedom but more by the opportunities in the bustling West German economy—a quarter of a million able-bodied East Germans were crossing annually—that the Russians had to do something or else see their East German state bleed to death. The East German regime lost three millions of its population, with sixteen million persons remaining, as compared to West Germany's fifty-three million. Despite the outcry in the West, the barrier was not such a bad proposition in a broader diplomatic sense, for it stabilized what was becoming an impossible situation laden with disaster for European peace.

In the latter 1960s changes in leadership of the Soviet Union, together with a general relaxation of tensions throughout Europe, made possible an international arrangement over the two Germanys that virtually removed them from the confrontations of the United

States and the Soviet Union. In Russia, Khrushchev fell from power in 1964, replaced by Leonid Brezhnev. Rumor had it that Khrushchev had been accused of "adventurism," by which his Kremlin rivals perhaps meant too forceful a position during the Cuban missile crisis. He also had championed the planting of wheat in the more arid regions of the Soviet Union, an experiment that in large part failed. Whatever the reason for his downfall, his successor, perhaps out of the caution of a newcomer, or from the belief that confrontation was not the best international way, chose to play down the Soviet role in Germany and elsewhere, in favor of less tension.

At the same time the East German economy also made strides toward equaling that of West Germany, and unrest in the East zone quieted. The reason for the wall began to disappear. Chancellor Willy Brandt's *Ostpolitik* removed it. His government showed its willingness to arrange a détente not merely with the Soviet Union but with the countries of Eastern Europe, including even East Germany. (Adenauer had begun détente with the USSR years before, when in 1955 he established diplomatic relations in exchange for repatriation of the last remaining German prisoners of war.) Brandt not only signed a treaty with Poland recognizing the boundary of the Western Neisse, which meant the virtually permanent loss to Germany of East Prussia and Silesia, but ended the policy of nonrecognition of East Germany. With the enthusiastic consent of the one-time occupation powers—the United States, the Soviet Union, Britain, and France, which through the years since 1945 always had reserved their rights over any final division of German territory—the West Germans and East Germans got together, concluding treaties, each recognizing the other's regime, providing for visits and travel between the two countries, and applying for admission to the United Nations as separate nations, which was granted in the autumn of 1973.

What with the German problem on the way to a solution it was possible to reconsider the entire matter of European security, and by the summer of 1973 that grand problem was being addressed by a Conference on Security and Cooperation in Europe which assembled in Helsinki. Thirty-five nations—the NATO powers, Warsaw Pact powers, and unaligned countries—sent delegations. The initial work of the conference was not impressive, as it seemed necessary to have speeches from thirty-five foreign ministers, including Secretary of State William P. Rogers of the United States. The purpose of the meeting appeared too large for the taste of Rogers and his British opposite, Sir Alec Douglas-Home. In their speeches both men spoke not of any large result but of an increase in the personal freedoms of the average European, through (as Douglas-Home suggested) linked television discussion programs on foreign affairs, or publication of an international magazine, or circulation everywhere on the Continent of newspapers of each country. The Soviet Union clearly was out for more than this. Having first raised the possibility of such a conference in 1966, the Soviets wanted a general statement of principles foreswearing the use of force in European relations and confirming present boundaries and political systems. Chairman Brezhnev had visited the United States in June to confer with President Nixon, and while in Washington announced that the cold war was over. He said it had done no more for the people of the Soviet Union than for the people of the United States. With those sentiments Americans easily agreed. As to whether such thoughts could be translated into a serious European security treaty, perhaps allowing mutual force reductions by NATO and the Warsaw allies, that was something else. The very fact, however, that a European conference could assemble was a sure sign that Europe's affairs were moving in novel ways.

Perhaps a true détente at long last was in sight, for Europe if not for other parts of the world. The prospect was enticing, attractive, hopeful. Pessimistic observers saw only a mirage, another tactical move in the long, inexorable, rigid attempt of the Soviet Union and its minions to dominate the world. They saw a great state that refused to allow more than a tiny proportion of its disaffected citizens to emigrate. They noticed how Soviet grain buyers had carefully bought up supplies in the United States just before a big price rise, with the American consumer picking up the check for the difference. It was certainly possible to argue that détente was of much greater value to the Russians than to the Americans. It gave the Soviet Union a chance to move in on domestic opposition, the Solzhenitsyns and Sakharovs and Medvedevs and Panovs. It raised a barrier between the United States and China—the Russians were very uneasy about the Sino-American rapprochement that characterized the early 1970s. And it gave more credibility to those many Americans who were becoming weary of the cost of the cold war—of the military establishment, of foreign aid, of all the accouterments of great power which had so increased the cost of the federal government and subtracted, they thought, from what should have been the good life of the past thirty years or so. But whatever the risks of détente, most Americans were inclined to try it, to take a middle position between pessimism and optimism, based on hope and the accumulation, into the long future, of Russian good deeds to accompany the Russian good words.

2. *The Middle East Again*

In the Middle East the troubles of earlier years accumulated, and by the 1970s the Arabs and Israelis were again at the front of American attention. In the early 1970s it was another Arab-Israeli war. In the latter 1970s it was the effort of President James E. Carter and Secretary of State Cyrus Vance to bring the Israelis and Egyptians together, an effort that produced a good result during meetings at the president's retreat at Camp David near Washington.

In earlier years the United States had tried to keep the lid on Middle Eastern politics, adjusting differences and disagreements of the nations of the area short of war. It was heavy going and was not assisted by the little six-day war which the Israelis conducted against Egypt in June 1967, when in a lightning stroke they expelled Egyptian troops from the Gaza Strip and from the straits controlling entrance to the Red Sea port of Eilat. They even chased the Egyptians back to the western side of the Suez Canal and occupied the Sinai Peninsula up to the great ditch itself. They forced Jordanian troops out of Jerusalem, not merely regaining the Wailing Wall but taking the Mosque of Omar. The latter is a very sacred place to Muslims, second only to Mecca, because it contains the rock from which Mohammed, the Prophet of Allah, ascended into heaven (the rock has a footprint on it marking the place where Mohammed was standing before he went on his "night journey" to heaven). The Israelis also occupied a small portion of Syria. Books about this new desert war appeared on American newsstands within a week or two of the event. Newsreels showed millions upon millions of dollars' worth of Russian equipment strewn in the desert sands. The Israelis refurbished some of it and sold some to Western military representatives, who took it home to analyze. The United States introduced a resolution in the United Nations General Assembly, which passed on November 22, 1967, solemnly condemning this war and resolving that the Israelis should evacuate their new imperial holdings. In subsequent years the state of Israel remained in possession, however, and gave no sign of retreat or remorse. In a world in which the two superpowers, Russia and the United States, had their own hostages to public relations, Czechoslovakia (occupied by Warsaw Pact troops in 1968) and Vietnam, there was not much more to say except to deplore the violence which again had inflamed the Arabs, perhaps at a time when they were beginning to forget their humiliations of 1948–1949 and 1956.

Then a fourth Arab-Israeli war broke out in October 1973. As the decade of the 1970s had opened, the troubles in the Middle East had come no closer to solution than in preceding years. The "war of attrition" along the Suez Canal which began in August 1968 ended after mediation by Secretary of State Rogers in August 1970. The Suez Canal remained closed, with several vessels trapped inside, perhaps permanently. President Nasser of Egypt died in September 1970, and two years later his successor, Anwar el-Sadat, expelled the 20,000 Russian technicians who had entered Egypt in 1970 to create modern anti-aircraft defenses of the canal area and help train the Egyptian army in using these and other new Russian weapons. Sadat then arranged for Saudi Arabian money to support a new war against Israel, concerted his strategy with the Syrian government in Damascus, and

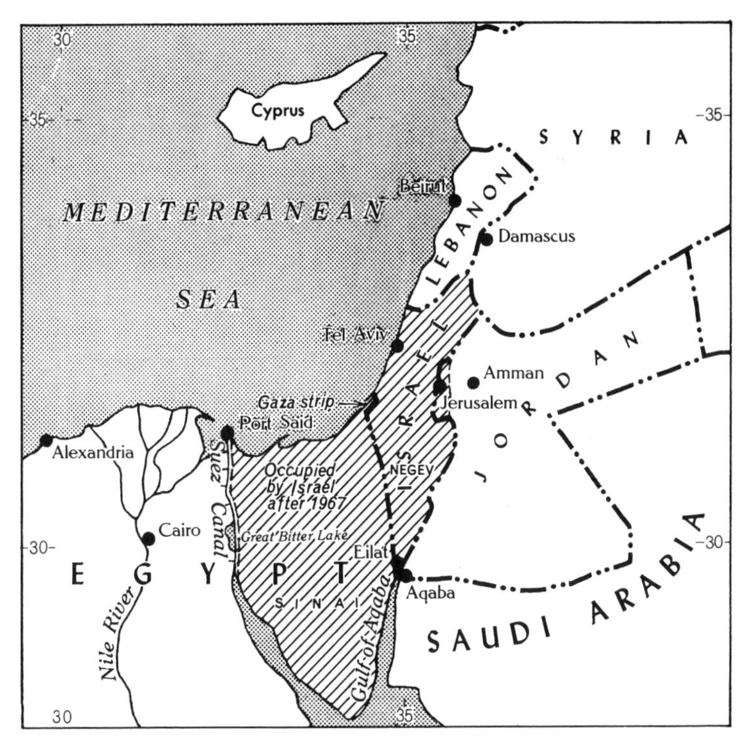

Israel and its neighbors.

suddenly on October 6, 1973, the day of Yom Kippur, launched a tank-led attack across the Suez Canal into Sinai, at the same time the Syrians attacked Israel from the north. Many Israeli tanks and planes were destroyed by Russian-made missiles, adroitly used. Fighting ended on October 22, before the Israelis could complete their counterattack, though they had managed to cross to the west side of the canal and take the city of Suez. They violated the cease-fire to complete the surrounding of an Egyptian corps in Sinai, cutting off its water supply. President Sadat asked for a joint United States–Russian military intervention to enforce the cease-fire. Chairman Brezhnev proposed to President Nixon that the two nations intervene: "I will say it straight, that if you find it impossible to act with us in this matter, we should be faced with the necessity urgently to consider the question of taking appropriate steps unilaterally. Israel cannot be permitted to get away with the violations." Nixon alerted American forces around the world, strongly advised the Russians to use the facilities of the United Nations, and later said that the American government had been involved in the most serious international situation since the Cuban missile crisis of 1962. This was a considerable statement, which the president and Secretary of State Kissinger (he had succeeded Rogers in August) never explained. Congress proved too gentlemanly or too lazy to inquire about details. Affairs meanwhile had wound down when the Israelis allowed the provisioning of the surrounded Egyptians and the UN sent in an emergency force.

As had happened in 1956 when two of America's NATO allies attacked Egypt without informing the United States, so in 1973 the United States failed to inform its NATO allies of the Nixon-Kissinger alert. There was a good deal of hard feeling. Some of the allies felt they could say nothing in support of the United States because the Arabs would retaliate by shutting off their oil; all of the allies, of course, needed Arab oil much more than did the United States. The West German government was angered that the Americans shipped arms to Israel from stores in West Germany, and protested publicly. Secretary Kissinger became embittered and was overheard to say, "I don't care what happens to NATO, I'm so disgusted."

Once again, in what was distinctly becoming a series of occasions, Americans could ask themselves what they should do next. One theory had it that the way to solve things in the Middle East was to conclude a treaty of alliance with Israel, which would give the Israelis the security they needed and allow them to surrender to the Arabs the territories occupied since the Six-Day War of 1967. But this was an awkward arrangement for the American government when so many citizens had tired of the country's forty-odd alliance commitments. Secretary Kissinger set up a talkathon, one might describe it, between the Arabs and Israelis, first to get the cease-fire along the canal and then to bring the Syrians into the arrangements. The secretary's big jet seemed to be zooming across the desert in perpetual motion, between Aswan and Tel Aviv and between Tel Aviv and Damascus. The Egyptians, Syrians, and Israelis finally agreed to quiet down, and to Kissinger's countrymen the result appeared a triumph, though it was a distinctly short-term proposition. Looking to the longer term was an enormous financial assistance to Israel, a credit of $2,200,000,000 for purchase of arms. It was a kindness to Israel, considering that the Israelis had only lost a little over a billion dollars' worth of equipment. It was not an alliance but it surely looked in that direction and was beyond doubt a commitment.

In the latter 1970s it seemed possible that a show of good will by the United States might bring a solution to the Middle East imbroglio, and to this end the Democratic president of the decade's last years, Jimmy Carter, devoted himself with a persistence that brought a peace treaty between Egypt and Israel signed at Camp David in March 1979. If the treaty proved less advantageous than the principals hoped, it was better than nothing, than the grim stalemate of thirty years that had been broken in 1948–1949, 1956, 1967, and 1973 by war.

The Camp David negotiations have now passed out of public memory, obscured by the trouble over Lebanon in the 1980s, and yet they were a signal development at the time. In late 1977, Secretary Vance had begun negotiation, and in September 1978 Israeli prime minister Menachem Begin and Egyptian president Anwar el-Sadat first came to Camp David. The president and secretary of state shuttled between the cabins of the Middle Eastern rivals, trying to get them together. From the outset the Palestinian question dominated: what to do with Jerusalem, where Arabs desired protection; with the West Bank of the Jordan, where Israelis wished to settle; and with the Gaza area, taken by the Israelis in the war of 1967. The result of the initial Camp David meeting was a Framework for Peace, not a treaty but a step-by-step arrangement. The Israelis then made progress difficult by refusing to cease West Bank settlement.

Despite the fate of the Framework for Peace, the Egyptians went ahead with their part of the bargain, which was to conclude a peace treaty with Israel, signed March 26, 1979. But this was the end of American mediation. President Carter was defeated by Ronald Reagan in the 1980 election, and Egypt's President Sadat was assassinated in 1981.

For a short time hope for peace in the Middle East had risen high, but then it disappeared, almost as rapidly as it had arisen. The very idea of an Arab state signing a peace treaty with Israel was exhilarating; it seemed to show that time had healed the animosities of the past. The accord brightened the economic prospects of both Egypt and Israel, for Egypt needed the tourism that peace would provide, and Israeli industries could avail themselves of lucrative local markets. Still, peace did not satisfy the Arab extremists who received encouragement from the Palestinians, Libyans, Syrians, and Iranians, threatened moderates in their midst, and took Sadat's life.

3. *Ford, Carter, and SALT II*

Some observers have viewed the Carter presidency as part of a national response to the debacles of Vietnam and Watergate. The Watergate scandal culminated when President Nixon resigned on August 8, 1974. A tape-recording system he had installed in the Oval Office had revealed his illegal actions to cover up a politically motivated break-in of the offices of the Democratic National Committee in Washington's Watergate apartment complex. For months after the burglars, known jocularly as "plumbers," were discovered and arrested while in the Watergate offices, the president had denied his guilt, and on one occasion said maladroitly that "I am not a crook." When it became evident that he was, Congress moved to impeach him. The threat brought his resignation.

Vice-President Spiro Agnew meanwhile had resigned after admitting that he had accepted so-called kickbacks, and was succeeded by Congressman Gerald R. Ford of Michigan. Upon Nixon's resignation Ford became president. During his brief tenure, until January 1977, there was one diplomatic negotiation of importance. This took place between the new president and Secretary of State Kissinger, on the U.S. side, and Soviet premier Brezhnev, at Vladivostok in Siberia, in November 1974. Here the two sides agreed to a ceiling of 2,400 strategic delivery vehicles for each country's nuclear weapons. The ceiling included not merely missiles but bombers. Each side agreed to a subceiling of 1,320 MIRVed launchers. At Vladivostok the U.S. dropped its insistence on reductions in Soviet large-thrust intercontinental ballistic missiles, set at 308, in return for Soviet agreement to U.S. forward-based systems—nuclear-armed land- and carrier-based aircraft stationed in Western Europe. The Soviets refused to limit the numbers of their Backfire bombers, which they insisted were not strategic weapons, and the U.S. resisted limits on cruise missiles—a delivery vehicle publicly revealed in 1975, jet-powered, terrain-guided, equipped with a nuclear warhead.

When Carter came to office he continued negotiation for what by this time was described as SALT II. Moscow in 1977 accepted a lowering of the Vladivostok vehicle ceiling to 2,250, an American victory, as it required reduction in Soviet but not in U.S. strategic forces. The two sides agreed to a subceiling of 1,200 MIRVed missiles within a ceiling of 1,320 MIRVed launchers; because the Soviet Union was not expected to deploy cruise-armed bombers like the American B-52, the effective MIRV launcher limit was 1,200 for the USSR and 1,320 for the U.S. The sides agreed to a sublimit of 280 MIRVed ICBMs.

Carter and Brezhnev signed the SALT II treaty in Vienna on June 18, 1979. Trouble thereafter appeared, almost from all sides, and eventually the forces against SALT II proved irresistible and the negotiation collapsed. SALT II was the centerpiece of Carter foreign policy, and its defeat a great disappointment to its author, and should have been a great disappointment to the American people who had much to gain from putting a cap on Soviet delivery systems for nuclear weapons.

One problem with SALT II was that during the negotiation President Carter announced the U.S. government's unwillingness to produce a neutron bomb, the anti-personnel weapon favored by the Defense Department in the early 1970s to replace the high-yield battlefield nuclear weapons of the mid-1950s. The neutron bomb's sponsors contended that even smaller nuclear weapons of the usual sort were of little use in crowded Europe, and that the neutron bomb would preserve buildings. Carter rightly saw it as inhuman, and as a possible inspiration for antinuclear protestors. But to his discomfiture his refusal to produce such a weapon persuaded the European NATO allies to ask for cruise missile technology. In the latter 1970s the Soviets did not have cruise missiles, understandably did not desire their distribution to NATO, and said any such arrangement would threaten SALT II.

Another threat to SALT II came from Soviet and Cuban activities in Ethiopia and Angola. The presence of Soviet military advisers in these African countries was bad enough; the presence of Cuban troops was most objectionable. Secretary Kissinger had spoken of "linkage," meaning no negotiation stood by itself, but would be connected to good behavior elsewhere. The United States now began to discuss links between Africa and SALT II.

Difficulties elsewhere in Africa, notably in Rhodesia (present-day Zimbabwe) and Namibia (former German Southwest Africa, a huge area to the northwest of South Africa, administered by the latter), disturbed Americans. The emergence of a black government in Rhodesia, replacing the unrecognized white government of Prime Minister Ian Smith, was fraught with delays and uncertainties, and posed the possibility of another Soviet and Cuban intervention. In Namibia the South Africans were claiming their presence necessary to offset 35,000 Cuban troops in next-door Angola (see below, pp. 396–397.)

President Carter had taken office determined to advance human rights everywhere, believing it was not merely a popular issue in his own country but part of America's revolutionary heritage. His human rights program irritated not merely Central American, Caribbean, and South American governments, but the Russians as well, and made SALT II negotiation more difficult.

SALT II received a setback in the summer of 1979 when revelation of a Soviet force in Cuba of brigade size produced an uproar. It later became evident that the brigade was not undergoing training and had no airlift or sealift capabilities—in other words, it was going nowhere. The Soviets interpreted American objections to the brigade as an effort to extract concessions on SALT II.

After SALT II was reported out of the foreign relations committee by a narrow margin of 9 to 6, in November 1979, an argument arose over verifiability of the treaty. It involved Soviet encryption of missile telemetry. An important way to know whether the Soviets are testing missiles is to monitor flight guidance through remote telemetry. The way to block this information is known as encryption. At Vienna the Soviets had acknowledged that the treaty forbade encryption. But Senator John Glenn of Ohio, the first American astronaut to orbit the earth, warned against Soviet bad faith, and proposed that the USSR allow American aircraft to fly along Soviet borders, and permit monitoring devices inside the Soviet Union.

The prospects for SALT II were not helped by the apathy of the American public. Fewer than two-thirds of Americans polled by the

Roper organization had heard or read about the treaty. Only one-third could identify the parties to the treaty. Still, the treaty might have passed the Senate had it not been for developments in faraway Iran and Afghanistan.

The Iranian situation had been moving toward tragedy ever since the years after the Second World War, when the American government was so busy preserving Western Europe and the Far East that it failed to see what was happening in Iran, where the young monarch, Mohammed Reza Shah, was increasing his power. In 1953, under heavy pressure from the Majlis, the shah had abdicated, but the CIA brought him back. Increasing oil revenues encouraged the shah to adventurism. The rise of oil prices in 1973 persuaded him to transform Iran into the Prussia of the Middle East. The *Spruance*-class destroyers he ordered for his navy were better armed than those the U.S. Navy was receiving. The price of oil dropped momentarily in 1977, and the shah cut the national budget in ways that affected the populace, but continued the purchase of American weapons. Violence began in Iran in the spring of 1978, but American intelligence agencies considered it unimportant and assured Secretary of State Vance that all was well. Suddenly, in 1979, the shah was overcome by the rising tide of Islamic fundamentalism. He departed Iran, lingered some weeks in American hospitals, and months later died in Egypt.

The revolution in Iran was a disaster for SALT II. A bloodbath attended establishment of the fundamentalist Khomeini regime, and the Carter administration sought to wait it out. Then in November 1979 a mob seized the American embassy in Teheran and held its staff members hostage for the next fourteen months. The spectacle mesmerized the American people, who each night on television watched gesticulating Iranians burning the American flag or threatening blindfolded embassy captives. It destroyed Carter's ability to advance any foreign policy.

Meanwhile affairs were heating up in neighboring Afghanistan. A non-Marxist but pro-Soviet regime had governed Afghanistan until 1978, and the USSR exerted a large influence, with 3,500 advisers attached to the Afghan army. That year a Marxist coup ousted the regime, possibly without Soviet support. The Carter administration pursued an accommodationist approach. But foes of the new government seized the American ambassador in Kabul, Adolph Dubs, who died in a shootout with Afghan security forces, in the presence of Soviet advisers. There seems not to have been any intention to kill the ambassador, simply ineptitude by the security forces. All the while the new government clumsily sought to impose Marxist doctrines on the Afghan people, and produced an insurrection. Rebellion grew, and the Soviets increased their advisers by 1,000, to 4,500. Whereupon the president of Afghanistan visited Moscow, and the

The shah in better days: with President Truman in Washington, 1949.

Kremlin leadership apparently advised him to eliminate his doctrinaire prime minister, who perhaps was responsible for the insurrection. The result was another shootout, this time in the People's Palace in Kabul, and the prime minister killed the president. Rumor had it that he also killed a high-level Soviet intelligence official. The result was the Soviet invasion of December 1979, during which the errant prime minister was immediately murdered. The Carter administration seems to have been so diverted by the revolution in Iran that it failed to warn the Soviets against an invasion. On the Soviet side there evidently was insufficient calculation, given the military morass Afghanistan turned into, forcing the USSR to send tens of thousands of troops to maintain a more friendly government.

Afghanistan finished off SALT II. In an appallingly frank television interview Carter confessed that he had erred about the Russians: "My opinion has changed more drastically in the last week than even the previous two and one-half years before that . . . the action of the Soviets has made a more dramatic change in my opinion of what the Soviets' ultimate goals are than anything they've done in the previous time I've been in office." He asked the Senate to delay on the treaty, and followed by curtailing grain shipments to the USSR, forbidding technology transfers, and revoking Soviet fishing privileges in American waters. He waged a campaign to mobilize the United Nations to denounce the Soviet intervention and demand its immediate, unconditional, and total withdrawal.

The president's change of mind, and forceful anti-Soviet measures, proved futile in the extreme. The confession of error over Soviet intentions confirmed in the minds of his countrymen his inability to assess Russian motives. The programs of retaliation all failed. Curtailment of grain shipments took Soviet purchases elsewhere, and precipitated a calamitous drop in prices of grain and farm land. Europeans, Japanese, and others with Western technological knowledge continued to transfer what they knew or possessed to the Soviet Union. There were many fish in the sea, outside American territorial waters. And although the General Assembly voted 104 to 18 on January 14, 1980, in support of Carter's initiative against the invasion, Soviet troops remained.

Not long after the invasion the president attempted a military rescue of the Teheran hostages. The mission aborted, from malfunction of the helicopters landing and taking off in sand at the secret rendezvous on Iranian territory outside Teheran, causing the deaths of several mission members.

Failure of the rescue mission brought into the open what had been fairly well known but not confirmed, namely, the increasingly irreconcilable positions on policy being taken by Secretary of State Vance and the president's national security adviser, Zbigniew Brzezinski. Curiously, as was the case during the Nixon administration, Carter's secretary of state was a Wall Street lawyer, and the adviser a professor, this time from Columbia University rather than Harvard. Brzezinski had disagreed with Vance over various policies, and like Kissinger had not hesitated to undercut the secretary of state. He had urged Carter to undertake the rescue mission. Vance opposed, Carter sided with Brzezinski, and Vance resigned, with the understanding that he would announce his retirement after completion of the mission. Vance's departure after the mission's failure dealt the Carter presidency a severe blow. The secretaryship, however, did not go to Brzezinski, as had happened earlier with Kissinger, but to Senator Edmund S. Muskie of Maine.

Within months the president suffered electoral defeat at the hands of an opponent who promised American voters better leadership. The Soviets and their many friends and fellow travelers, he said, were not to be won over by kindness. Détente, said Ronald Reagan, was no way to deal with an evil empire. The presidential election of 1980 was not fought solely on issues of foreign policy, although Carter's failures in Iran and Afghanistan made him highly vulnerable. The rise in oil prices that came with the Iranian revolution had touched off an inflation that hurt the Carter administration. Reagan won many votes when during a television debate with his Democratic opponent he asked listeners, "Are you better off under the Democrats?" Then, too, voters liked to hear Carter's opponent speak—Reagan knew how to address audiences. Most American presidential elections also have a tendency to straddle issues, to obfuscate, and the differences between the candidates were not always clear. But behind the confusion, the theatrics, and the economics lay the criticism of foreign policy, which had gone wrong, Reagan said, and he proposed to right it.

ADDITIONAL READING

The literature of the 1970s is long on some subjects, short on others, and general treatments of American diplomacy during the decade are on the short side. A glancing essay on problems of the era is James Chace, *A World Elsewhere* (New York, 1973), and a more elaborate description is in Tad Szulc, *The Illusion of Peace* (New York, 1978). See also Coral Bell, *President Carter and Foreign Policy* (Canberra, 1980), and Gaddis Smith, *Morality, Reason and Power: American Diplomacy in the Carter Years* (New York, 1986).

Participants understandably had a head start in writing about the period. Fortunately all three presidents have told their stories—Richard M. Nixon, *RN* (New York, 1978); Gerald R. Ford, *A Time to Heal* (New York, 1979); Jimmy Carter, *Keeping Faith* (New York, 1982). Kissinger has published *White House Years* (Boston, 1979) for 1969–1973 and *Years of Upheaval* (Boston, 1982) for 1973–1974. For the Carter administration see Cyrus Vance, *Hard Choices* (New York, 1983), and Zbigniew Brzezinski, *Power and Principle* (New York, 1983). Interesting biographies of Kissinger are by Marvin and Bernard Kalb, *Kissinger* (New York, 1974), a flattering account; John G. Stoessinger, *Henry Kissinger* (New York, 1976), in the middle; and Roger Morris, *Uncertain Greatness* (New York, 1977), hostile. A later appraisal by an able reporter is Seymour M. Hersh, *The Price of Power* (New York, 1983). David S. McLellan, *Cyrus Vance* (Totowa, N.J., 1985), is Volume 20 in the American Secretaries series.

For their subjects, the four focuses of détente, see John K. Fairbank, *The Great Chinese Revolution* (New York, 1986); John Newhouse, *Cold Dawn* (New York, 1973), on SALT I, together with Strobe Talbott, *Endgame* (New York, 1979), and the same author's *Deadly Gambits* (New York, 1984), on SALT II; Roger Morgan, *The United States and West Germany: 1945–1973* (London, 1974); William B. Quandt, *Decade of Decisions* (Berkeley, 1977), and Jimmy Carter, *The Blood of Abraham* (Boston, 1985), insider accounts of the Arab-Israeli issue.

Iran appears in Richard W. Cottam, *Nationalism in Iran* (Pittsburgh, 1979); Barry Rubin, *Paved with Good Intentions* (New York, 1980); William H. Sullivan, *Mission to Iran* (New York, 1981), by the American ambassador before the revolution; and Gary Sick, *All Fall Down* (New York, 1985), by the NSC expert during the Carter years. For Iran's sequel see Nancy Peabody Newell and Richard S. Newell, *The Struggle for Afghanistan* (Ithaca, N.Y., 1981); Henry S. Bradsher, *Afghanistan and the Soviet Union* (Durham, N.C., 1983); and Thomas Hammond, *Red Flag over Afghanistan* (Boulder, 1983).

☆ 16 ☆

Reagan and the World of Our Time

Lebanon reminded us that we cannot remake society, that we can work for peace but we cannot impose it. It also reminded us that the commitments we undertake must be ones that we as a government and as a people can sustain over time. We did not do well in that regard. Hence the need for both pragmatism and fortitude.

—Assistant Secretary of State Richard W. Murphy, spring 1984

1. *The Views of a Conservative President*

If ever there was a triumph of avowed conservatism in American politics, it was the arrival in the presidency of Ronald Reagan, who had informed the country during his campaign in 1980 that he would solve its problems the conservative way. The question then became what he would do, rather than what he said he would do. Reagan's reputation as a staunch conservative was tempered somewhat by his experience as California governor, when he showed an inclination toward pragmatic compromise. Reagan's bemused observers therefore waited to see what would happen.

It was clear that conservatism, a move toward the right, was what the country wanted after the Carter administration. One cannot be sure that the public realized how connected was Carter's foreign policy with that of his two Republican predecessors. The Nixon-Ford-Carter foreign policy was one of détente, sometimes known as a policy of accommodation, although the latter word smacked of criticism. During his last year in office, in the face of the hostage crisis in Iran and the Soviet invasion of Afghanistan, Carter turned hard-line and did what he could to stand up to the USSR. His enemies within the Democratic party explained his turnabout as the result of persuasion by his national security adviser Zbigniew Brzezinski. His Republican enemies exulted, for he seemed to be confirming their own judgment as to the properly conservative nature of policy toward the Soviet Union. The American public did not seem to understand Carter's turnabout, or his previous closeness in policy to his Republican predecessors, and saw only weakness, which candidate Reagan in 1980 duly and quickly took advantage of.

Coming into office with a mandate to stand up to enemies at home and abroad, the Reagan administration even in the judgment of friendly critics was at the outset too assertive. Its leader was almost preacher-like, and gave the impression that those who were not with him were surely against him. The leaders and intellectuals of the nations of Western Europe were aghast at the appearance of this new Puritan of the West. Few of them could remember his Democratic predecessor of nearly seventy years before, Woodrow Wilson, but the resemblance was fairly close. Wilson, however, had dealt initially with Latin America and the Far East. Reagan at once made pronouncements about European-Soviet relations that offended Western Europe. At a time when his administration was lifting the embargo on Soviet grain shipments he came down hard on the proposed European assistance in construction of a gas pipeline from the Soviet Union into Western Europe. The President seemed to be urging Europeans to make economic sacrifices for policy purposes while Americans abandoned policy for profit. His casual and doubtless un-thought-out references to nuclear war with the Soviet Union seemed downright scary.

At the outset, too, the Reagan administration's chief foreign affairs officers, Secretary of State Alexander M. Haig, recently retired from the U.S. Army, and Secretary of Defense Caspar Weinberger, displayed an almost alarming disposition toward military solutions.

The Reagan administration, led by its popular president, at once proposed a huge military buildup, a measure that had much public support but again worried friends of détente abroad. The plan resulted in military appropriations during Reagan's first term of $800,000,000,000. The reason for the buildup was to toughen the image of the United States abroad, and to make the Soviets willing both to negotiate seriously for arms control agreements and to avoid adventuresome moves such as the Afghanistan invasion.

But how much did the administration improve America's military stance? By the end of the first term there was reason to doubt the effectiveness of the huge appropriations. Very little had been done to reform the armed services, which were plagued by the massively unrealistic inflation of officer numbers and ranks; Representative Les Aspin of Wisconsin pointed out that the U.S. Navy had nearly ten captains for every ship. The services boasted one flag officer, general or admiral, for every 1,000 men and women, as many generals and admirals as during the Second World War when force levels were far higher. And more serious were the statistics of hardware before and after the Reagan appropriations. In conventional weapons the statistics were unimpressive. Tactical aircraft had increased only by 3 percent, although there was a higher percentage of modernized aircraft. The number of ships increased from 479 to 524, but this was not a tremendous rise. In nuclear weapons and carriers the change was modest or marginal. The administration did nothing to reduce the vulnerability of the trans-Mississippi missile beds—the new MX missile, which was to replace the Minuteman, was difficult to base, and one proposal seemed to lead only to another, whereas the small, mobile Midgetman missile so much talked about was a long way from deployment. The administration could take comfort in the deployment of Trident submarines and Trident II missiles, and the new force of cruise missiles. Despite great political difficulties with the European allies, and over the loud protests of the Soviet Union, NATO had deployed Pershing IIs and Tomahawk cruise missiles in Europe. But the Soviets had doubled their lead in medium-range nuclear missiles.

The proposal for the so-called Strategic Defense Initiative, or SDI (widely known, to the administration's chagrin, as the "star wars" plan), perhaps accomplished more harm than good. The cost of SDI was to be high, though not impossible—$25,000,000,000 over eight years. But the talk of "star wars" had generated great confusion. It had attracted right-wing ideologues who much preferred a scientific system of defense, even if it lay in the future, that would avoid human threats and counterthreats and remove everything from the hands of Democratic as well as possibly errant Republican statesmen. Lieutenant-General James A. Abrahamson, head of the SDI research program, did not claim 100 percent efficiency for his system, admitting it was not foolproof or missile-proof, but contended that anything from 50 percent to 99 percent effectiveness would keep the Soviets in confusion, making it impossible for them to plan a first strike with any high degree of confidence. And yet, even if the SDI were to prove technologically feasible, the prospect that one side in the U.S.-USSR nuclear confrontation was more or less safe, while the other was open to attack, was a dangerously awkward possibility in the nuclear age. Moreover, the Soviets surely would manage to catch up, sooner or later, as they had done with earlier American technological feats, and then there would have to be new SDIs, bigger and presumably better, and doubtless more expensive. When the Reagan administration had pushed harder for the MX missile than good judgment seemed to warrant, it had covered its retreat by organizing a commission headed by retired Lieutenant-General Brent Scowcroft, with its membership carefully distributed among both political parties. SDI, it appeared, might have to be covered by another bipartisan commission.

Advocates and critics of Reagan's foreign policy both beheld a movement away from confrontation in the electoral year 1984. As early as February of that year the president told the American Legion's national convention that his administration had managed its two major purposes in taking over from its bankrupt predecessor. It had revived America's economy, and it had vastly strengthened the country's defenses. The time had come, the president said, for proposals for peace. That year the Soviet Union in turn muted its harsh criticism of the president and his assistants. It was difficult to know, however, if the Soviets had made their peace with the likely prospect, soon realized, of a second Reagan term, or were themselves confused and weakened after the death of Brezhnev and the succession of two elderly and ailing leaders, Yuri Andropov and Konstantin Chernenko. On the American side it could have been that three years of standoff had marked only a learning on the job by the members of the Reagan team, including the president himself, and that everyone had discovered by 1984 that to ask impossible things of foreign governments was not productive.

There was an ad hoc aspect to Reagan foreign policy that satisfied the American people but made observers unsure whether Reagan policy was coherent at all. The administration sent U.S. marines to Lebanon, and stationed warships off the Lebanese coast, accompanied by strong pronouncements of the need to keep the Syrians and their allies out of places where they should not be. But when the marines were stationed in a place they should not have been, and the absurdly unprepared building was car-bombed, with huge loss of life, the president made almost no move of retaliation, and after a short wait took all the marines out of Lebanon. He explained that they had achieved their purpose. Two days after the car-bombing, U.S. forces occupied the island of Grenada in the Caribbean, in response to a request from the Organization of Eastern Caribbean States and to rescue 1,000 U.S. medical students attending school there. The operation was over quickly and had a small cost. Again he satisfied the American people, to the consternation of thoughtful observers.

It seemed clear that after the opening Reagan claims to forcefulness in foreign policy, the policy of the preceding decade, although admittedly with rhetorical differences, was returning. As Henry Grunwald, editor in chief of Time, Inc., put the case, the administration was being pushed toward something that, by any other name, was still détente. "As long as it can be protected from the utopian left, which sees it as institutionalized brotherhood, and from the triumphalist right, which sees it as institutionalized surrender, and defined as no more or less than controlled conflict, it remains the inescapable intellectual framework for American policy."

What was also clear was that Reagan possessed a great opportunity to reduce international conflict, through renegotiating SALT II with the Russians and through helping allay problems elsewhere. Enjoying the strong support of the American people, a huge asset to his party (which would allow him to stand against the ideologues of the GOP), benefiting from what Grunwald described as "the Nixon-China syndrome," with anti-Communist credentials at least as good as Nixon's, he could prove a wonder-worker for peace. He was better positioned than Nixon and Carter when they made their breakthroughs on arms control, the Middle East, and in Carter's case the Panama Canal treaties.

The possibility loomed, though, that he would not take risks to achieve diplomatic breakthroughs. To some, Reagan was too protective of his popularity, while others thought he saw breakthroughs as resulting only from a series of small moves. The president's critics charged that he just did not know the basic issues of foreign affairs. A leading member of the House of Representatives foreign affairs establishment, who saw the president fairly often, was heard to say that he never had known so ignorant a president of the United States. Many Americans found such a thing hard to believe. Others thought that a president with sharp political instincts had the basis for making large decisions.

All the while the international economic indicators were uncertain. The United States became a debtor nation for the first time since the First World War, with annual trade deficits running at well over $100,000,000,000 and no sign of letup. What was certain was the continuing arms race. Both sides were working on anti-satellite weapons, anti-submarine warfare, terminal guidance for warheads, space-based defensive systems, and the like. It was becoming increasingly unpleasant to contemplate the late 1990s, not to mention the first decade of the twenty-first century, with such weapons in place and scientists, no doubt, designing even "better" ones.

2. *Central America and South Africa*

Perplexing problems in Central America and South Africa were a continuing challenge to the Reagan administration. In Central America the administration was treated to disorder that verged on revolution. South African racial policies meanwhile threatened chaos in that important part of the world.

The five countries of Central America—Guatemala, El Salvador, Honduras, Nicaragua, and Costa Rica—entered American consciousness in the early 1980s and it seems clear that they will not leave for a while, perhaps until the end of the present century. They

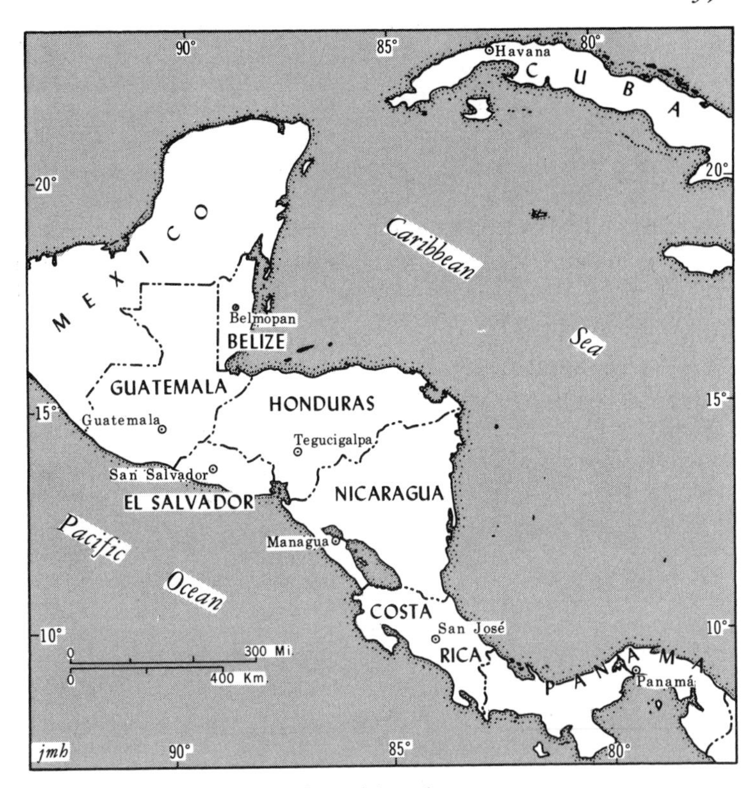

Central America.

had entered the calculations of the State Department before, and once in a while a crisis had developed, only to wind down into total obscurity. But about the time that Ronald Reagan became president of the United States, Central America rose up to what sometimes seemed almost world-shaking importance.

The troubles of Nicaragua had loomed earlier, in the Carter administration. In 1979 the country's dictator, General Anastasio Somoza, had fallen, and left the country for Panama, where he was assassinated. The Somoza family had controlled the country since the early 1930s, when it had arranged the assassination of General Sandino, the man whose name the guerrillas took as their own, the Sandinistas. At the outset the victors who looked back to the Nicaragua of half a century before gave evidence of good behavior, and promised to maintain political pluralism, a mixed economy, and a nonaligned foreign policy. Then they moved to the left, and became not merely Marxist-Leninists but, it sometimes seemed, Stalinists. When Cuban assistance began, United States assistance ended, and soon Nicaragua was facing a revolutionary movement from neighboring Honduras, where the Central Intelligence Agency, the Honduran army, and Argentine officers trained the "contras."

Despite the best efforts of the Reagan administration, nothing seemed to shake the hold of the Sandinistas over Nicaragua. To the north were the contras, attempting to move down from Honduras, but they did not make much headway. Their objectives were part of the difficulty, for they chose not merely to fight the Sandinista army and militia but to destroy cotton and coffee crops, which incurred the enmity of the people they hoped to liberate. Moreover the contra leadership was inept. Much American money may have wound up back in the United States, for "condos for contras." The contras' principal effect may not have been so much military as political, for Managua could emphasize the counterrevolutionary threat from Honduras and Miami to excuse its own austere domestic policies.

Nor did Nicaragua's unfriendly neighbor to the south, Costa Rica, accomplish much toward displacing the Sandinistas, who had staged their revolution against Somoza from Costa Rica. The Costa Ricans had believed that the Sandinistas would bring democracy to Nicaragua. Costa Ricans protested their disappointment loudly, to obtain American money to assist their economy and thereby maintain their democracy. But the Costa Ricans went no further than that.

The continuing rule of the Sandinistas in Nicaragua seemed to be undermining Central American stability, for in a short time guerrilla movements were emerging elsewhere. For its enmity to Nicaragua, Honduras witnessed increased guerrilla activity. With the United States supporting their army, the Hondurans were militarily able to hold their own. Guerrilla activity stirred in Costa Rica too, but the Costa Ricans had the strongest economy and the oldest democracy in the region and were in no immediate danger. Meanwhile guerrilla movements of longer provenance continued in El Salvador and Guatemala, and sometimes received Nicaraguan help. El Salvador managed a stalemate. Guatemala did too, although the human cost was high. In 1982 a born-again Christian, General Efraín Ríos Montt, came to power in Guatemala, and set about ending corruption and controlling rightist "death squads" that had terrorized urban areas. He arranged massacres of selected Indian villages, believed to be supporting guerrillas, and in a matter of six months killed between 3,000 and 5,000 Indians, displaced 250,000, and forced 30,000 to flee into Mexico. El Salvador and Guatemala would no doubt continue to have their troubles.

Critics said that in Central America the Reagan administration's unwavering objective was the departure of leftists from local governments. Under the president's first secretary of state, Alexander Haig, and perhaps only to a slightly lesser extent his successor in 1982, George Shultz, the enemy appeared to be Moscow, Havana, and

Managua. Their point of view was that Central America was one place where the United States could lay down the law.

The essential trouble may have been attributable to the region's economic woes rather than to any Washington policies. For a generation Central America had enjoyed steady economic growth, until about the time of the revolution in Nicaragua. By 1982, a full-scale slump was evident, with negative growth, high inflation, rising unemployment, all caused by the 1979 oil-price increase and a fall in world commodity prices that included cotton and coffee. With the onrush of economic trouble the local governments increased foreign borrowing at high interest rates, private capital fled, and austerity programs became necessary for renegotiation of debts. Four of the five countries, Nicaragua excepted, turned for loans to the International Monetary Fund, and relied increasingly on the World Bank, the Inter-American Development Bank, and the U.S. Agency for International Development.

What was the prospect? To the American people, reading of guerrilla attacks and government repression, Central America was a confusion, a tapestry of disorder in a largely unknown region. Perhaps it was that way to the Reagan administration, which had many other concerns. The *New York Times* published a letter to the editor from a former CIA official relating that Moscow surely rejoiced to see Americans concentrate their energies on a place so far from the bases of international power, a light year removed from the nuclear contentions between Washington and Moscow. The most likely prediction for policy in Central America was that the State Department would involve itself just enough to contain leftist expansion but risk neither economic nor political capital on more fundamental approaches. As the Mexico bureau chief of the *New York Times*, Alan Riding, warned, this left a vacuum of leadership that could be filled by unpleasant surprises.

The second of the perplexing problem areas of the 1980s is South Africa, where a tiny white minority has insisted upon apartness, "apartheid," for the many black South Africans in their midst. And if Central America has been a difficult diplomatic nut to crack, so has been South Africa.

Since the racial mixture in South Africa has developed over centuries, South African racial policies are especially difficult to change. Bantu-speaking peoples who comprise the largest number of blacks in southern Africa began migrating from Central Africa at the beginning of the Christian era. People speaking Afrikaans came after the Dutch East India Company established a supply station in South Africa in 1652; not merely Dutch but French Huguenots and Germans settled in the Cape area, to form the Afrikaner element of the white population. During the Napoleonic wars in the early nineteenth century Great Britain seized the Cape, and subsequent British rule marked the beginning of a long conflict between Afrikaners and English-speaking settlers—a sort of secondary conflict to the larger black-white conflict. The Britons tended to be far more liberal toward blacks than were the Dutch-French-German whites, who were to become known as Afrikaners.

The racial troubles in South Africa rapidly worsened after the Second World War. The Afrikaners dug in their heels in response to unrest, and in 1948 adopted the apartheid policy. In 1961, South Africa withdrew from the British Commonwealth.

For a while, life for blacks in South Africa seemed to improve, despite apartheid. Living standards rose because of impressive economic growth, the conduct of international companies, and trade unions that became legal in 1979. During the 1970s there was a remarkable 63 percent rise in black income per capita outside farming areas and the homelands (areas designated by South African law to be exclusively black, and notorious for their poverty). Blacks attended school in increasing numbers; enrollment in secondary schools went up from 123,000 in 1970 to 615,000 in 1986.

South Africa and its neighbors.

Apartheid is a reality today in South Africa.

Yet segregation was becoming ever more difficult for black South Africans to take. Segregated residential areas, separate public schools through the secondary school levels, and separate hospitals for blacks all remained the rule. The fearful euphemisms remained as well, such as the Group Areas Act, which told people by color where to live; the Reservation of Separate Amenities Act, which told what facilities they might share; and, most important, the Population Registration Act, which tagged racially every South African from cradle to grave. Such minor privileges as the opening of white ("international") restaurants, the legality of a black marrying a white, the possibility of sending a black child to an expensive white school, and being allowed on beaches designated "mixed" as opposed to "exclusive" (a euphemism for white) were impossible for the average poor black South African to attain, and were insults to affluent black South Africans.

The present impasse in South Africa dates from very recent times, essentially from the adoption in 1984 of a new constitution that granted very limited political rights to the country's minorities—Asians (mainly Indians) and so-called Coloreds, the racially mixed populace. The constitution granted no political rights to the vast majority of South Africans who are black. The following population statistics provide a sharp measure of the country's political illness:

Race	Number (millions)	Percentage of the Population
Afrikaners	2.9	9
English-speaking whites	1.9	6
Indians	.8	2
Coloreds	2.8	9
Blacks	24.1	74
Total	32.5	100

Inauguration of the constitution, with its three-chamber legislature—whites, Asians, Coloreds—but no chamber for blacks, opened the floodgates of disorder. Blacks boycotted the schools to protest inferior education, consumers boycotted white merchants, and turmoil in black districts approached anarchy. Thousands of youths wander the streets, intimidating the waverers, the "sellouts" or "system blacks," stoning and burning buses carrying breakers of the school boycott, and forcing people who ignore the consumer boycott to drink the detergent or eat the packets of flour they have just bought from the shops. They have killed several hundred informers. In the past the government controlled dissent by rounding up leaders. Now everything has passed into the hands of the activists, of whom there are many. The street youths have nothing to lose; detentions, police brutality, bannings, killings seem not to bother them. The South African government imposed a state of emergency in mid-1985, and the death rate went up rather than down; it left hundreds of blacks dead, thousands arrested. All this has been reinforced by a sudden economic downturn, with black unemployment increasing and a drop in the rand from $.80 in 1985 to $.39 in 1986.

United States policy toward this political, social, and increasingly economic morass has been to put pressure on the Afrikaner ruling group to move toward peaceful change. The American government has embargoed arms sales since 1963, restricted supplies for police and other apartheid-enforcing agencies, put strict controls on nuclear and computer sales, and prohibited Export-Import Bank and other public financing. The State Department has pushed hard for South African evacuation of Namibia. The South Africans have been pleading the presence of Cuban troops in Angola, but the State

Department has sought a dual evacuation. It has described Namibia as "the last major item on the agenda of African decolonization."

Public opinion in the United States has turned massively against South Africa, and Congress in 1986 passed a bill for economic sanctions, which it enacted over President Reagan's veto. Responding to public pressure, such large U.S. companies as General Motors are moving out of South Africa. The powerful English bank, Barclay's, has also decided to pull out of South Africa.

What has become apparent, however, is that, generally speaking, South Africa is continuing to "make it" economically despite American and other nations' sanctions. Thus far violence has not spread to the whites; fewer than thirty lost their lives in 1985. The imprisoned black leader, Nelson Mandela, is the popular black choice as leader of a democratic South Africa. The sooner he obtains power the better, many observers believe, else communism will enter the scene. The Afrikaners themselves do not know what they should do next about the racial situation, and are inclined to do no more unless they have to. They are split, it appears, between the pragmatic middle right that thus far has supported President P.W. Botha, and the fantasy right that wants to retire behind their wagons and fight it out with the world.

In a thoughtful analysis the *Economist* in 1986 beheld the real possibility of eventual change for the better in South Africa if the Western nations were willing to impose more severe economic sanctions. These would be difficult to enforce, but might well work. Two-thirds of South African trade is with Western Europe and North America, both exports and imports. If this trade were cut off, other countries might well pick it up, either themselves or through middlemen: South Korea, Taiwan, Hong Kong, Israel, Singapore, Sri Lanka, Chile. These countries presently take one-fourteenth of South Africa's exports. To buy more, they would need financing. Of South Africa's present debt of $25,000,000,000, almost all is owed in Europe and North America, and the South Africans would get no more from there. In retaliation they might default on the debt, producing anguish in innumerable places; three American banks—Citibank, Chase Manhattan, and Morgan Guaranty—together with two other banks hold nearly a seventh of the debt. If the South Africans sought financing elsewhere, there is evidence that they might find it in Switzerland and West Germany. In case of severe sanctions the Swiss and West German banks would have to be talked to, and perhaps coerced.

Severe economic sanctions would be difficult for all involved, but the result might be worth the effort. Peace might return to South Africa, redeeming a government that, long past a reasonable time, has resisted the requirements of twentieth-century politics and of humanity.

3. *Economics*

The need for further sanctions against South Africa raises another subject of high—perhaps crucial—importance for the world's nations. For if national economies should ever turn downward, for whatever reason, serious economic trouble could become political trouble, as it did during the Great Depression that began in 1929. Political trouble could bring another national leader like Hitler who in 1933 told his people that he knew how to save them from economic depression.

Three facts of the international marketplace in recent times demonstrate the complexity of the present-day world economy. They show how a shock or change in one place can produce small and then larger waves of shock or change, and drive national economies in ways no one intended. Consider, first, the way in which the collapse of the international monetary system of the industrial countries in the early 1970s has plagued international relations ever since. Second, look at the huge and rapidly mounting national debt of the United States and what it means for the world economy. Third, consider the collapse of raw material prices in recent years, including the recent collapse of oil prices, for it has driven third world economies, and many of the industrializing economies of nations like Mexico and Brazil, to the brink of bankruptcy.

It was in 1971 that then secretary of the treasury John Connally, a forthright Texas politician, announced unilaterally a devaluation of the dollar. There was another in 1973. These moves collapsed the system established at the Bretton Woods Conference of 1944 which had been symbolized by the International Monetary Fund for stabilizing world currencies and the World Bank for lending money to emerging countries.

The treasury, Connally's critics conceded, had good reason to devalue the dollar. The organization of the world economy that came when the United States assumed responsibility at the end of the Second World War and in the immediate postwar years, with Bretton Woods and UNRRA and the Truman Doctrine and Marshall Plan and other large programs of foreign aid, had begun to fray at the edges by the end of the 1960s. But with its replacement by the so-called floating currencies of the major trading nations—the floating dollar, mark, pound, and yen—a large element, perhaps an essential element, of stability went out of the economic organization of the world, and any buffeting from whatsoever source was likely to lead to deep trouble.

Admittedly the Bretton Woods system was too openly American, and perhaps, therefore, it was defective. During the reign of the American dollar from 1945 until 1971, there was a great deal of criticism about how the American government and people had been doing nothing more than looking after the U.S. to the detriment of the other governments and peoples of the world, and there apparently was something egotistical in the United States' making the trade of the world move to the commands of the dollar, rather than to those of the pound sterling as in earlier years. Americans took pride in magazine articles about the American century, the twentieth century, comparing it favorably to the century of Victoria, the nineteenth century. One could trace back the centuries: the eighteenth, when Britain and France fought for trade and dominance; the seventeenth, marked by the enormous power of the Sun King, Louis XIV, the might of France; the sixteenth century, time of the dominance of Charles V and Philip II of Spain. It was pleasant to know, as Americans thought they knew, that their own time marked the worldwide power not merely of their country's currency but of their military power and indeed their very culture. As Americans basked in their own glory, sailing their barques of imagination upon a summer sea, so the Europeans nastily commented on the shortsightedness of the Americans, the lack of culture in the asphalted, interstate-beribboned subcontinent of North America. All the while the Europeans, Americans morosely noticed, were happy to possess as many of the hated dollars as they could get their hands on. They took the dollars and built their own asphalt jungles and highways, their own supermarkets, drugstores, and emporiums for serving Colonel Sanders' Kentucky Fried Chicken.

Whatever the defects of the system, it lasted for a quarter century before it came to an end. For a long time the nation had been running a deficit in foreign trade, inflation was rampant, and it was extremely difficult for the United States to honor its commitment to exchange gold for $35 an ounce. Moreover, America's trading partners needed loans; they did not have the money to pay the now-high cost of the American goods they wanted, so the demand for U.S. products fell compared with foreign products. One of the problems of being the leader in world trade is that one somehow has to support trade deficits—and this had been going on ever since the end of the Second World War—but the deficits were exacerbated by the expenses of the Vietnam War and inflation. It was probably inevitable at this point that the Bretton Woods system (the United States' part of which was to exchange gold at $35 an ounce) should collapse.

From the first American devaluation the other nations, each of which found its currency high or low according to the new American rate, began to jostle each other in attempts to get trade advantages. It all sounded courteous enough: each nation let its currency slip from its announced value according to Bretton Woods and watched while it wobbled up and down as traders brought it to a level where speculation stopped. And, to be sure, there probably was little choice in the matter; the nations, including the United States, had to permit these currency floats, for otherwise the pressure of speculation would have taken the gold covers from all of the high-priced currencies. Still, the American float produced a whole series of floats, the money market reflecting intense uneasiness.

Devaluation was supposed to adjust America's trade balances, and other balances, but it did not work that way. For the remainder of the 1970s international payments were kept moving through a series of bank loans made by European and especially American banks, resulting in huge international debts. The economic dislocations of that time failed to produce immediate chaos. Many countries in the Western Hemisphere, and nations elsewhere, stocked up on the new loans, and covered their budgets that way, assuming the future would take care of itself.

In the 1980s these budgetary chickens began to come home to roost. The Treasury Department found itself in a fix, as it had encouraged private bankers to lend to foreign governments and nationals, and high interest rates abroad had encouraged them. When the bankers could not continue rolling over these loans (according to an old banking maxim, "a rolling loan gathers no loss"), secretaries of the treasury hastily resorted to the World Bank and American lending agencies and hoped that large nations like Mexico and Brazil would not default.

It is an uneasy situation to have the dollar remain as the major world currency, and yet to have payments owed American banks become uncollectible. This raises the possibility of a conservative Republican administration having to bail out the big New York banks to prevent their taking huge losses. What is evidently needed is a combination of the currencies of the United States, Japan, and West Germany, the three strongest Western economies, which together control more than half the world's trade in manufactured goods. But at that point the three would have to subordinate their domestic economies to the stability of the joint international currency, a highly unlikely development.

As if the free float of currencies, especially the dollar, were not enough to unsettle the world economy, there was the mounting national debt of the United States, which some observers likened to a black hole, into which poured the savings of peoples all over the world. Americans, these critics announced, had raised their interest rates to attract dollars from every corner of the universe.

The American national debt was a spectacular monument to deficit spending, and an ironic testimony to Republican spending. It reminded aging Americans of that spendthrift Franklin D. Roosevelt, whose budgets were never in such disarray as those of President Reagan. A few Americans recalled Secretary of the Treasury Andrew W. Mellon, who presided over fiscal policy during the 1920s. Mellon was known as the greatest secretary of the treasury since Alexander Hamilton because from 1921 until 1929 he reduced the national debt from

$24,000,000,000 to $16,000,000,000. Other bygone figures came to mind, such as Speaker Thomas B. (Tsar) Reed, under whose supervision Congress in 1890 appropriated $1,000,000,000, for the first time. Someone asked Reed about the expense, and his retort was, "This is a billion-dollar country." The United States in 1986 threatened to become a $2,000,000,000,000 debtor.

As the deficit accumulated, banks worried that the bond market might collapse. According to classic economic theory, a point arrives when an oversaturated market refuses to take more, and small sales touch off a massive sell-off.

No U.S. bond sell-off has occurred, and all an observer can say is that two forces have been holding up the market, just at the time when the Reagan administration was going deeply into debt. For many years the Japanese have taken an enormous part of the debt; they hold $640,000,000,000 in U.S. government bonds, half the U.S. debt held by foreigners. Compared to other peoples around the world, the Japanese have been huge savers. Their economy has been flat for some time, and savings needed to go elsewhere. The Tokyo government did not want the yen to be an international currency, even a joint international currency, for that would remove its control over the yen. The American interest rate was high, so yen went into dollar bonds. Then another development brought foreign capital to the United States: capital in flight. Huge amounts seem to have been coming from Hong Kong, which is slated to pass to mainland China in 1997. Similarly, the weakening of economies in Latin America has brought large sums to the U.S.

It is true that a comparison of the U.S. national debt to the anticipated gross national product for 1986, $4,200,000,000,000, puts the debt at less than 50 percent of GNP, a percentage easily surpassed forty years earlier at the end of the Second World War. But it is also true that the almost unlimited availability of foreign money had persuaded Congress and the Reagan administration that deficits were less serious than they looked.

If Americans wished to feel good about the debt, there was the fall of the dollar against the yen in 1985–1986. In 1984 the dollar rose against major currencies, and for the first time in years it was possible for some Americans to go to Japan, West Germany, and France, and eat in first-class restaurants, stay in expensive hotels, without worrying about cost. The Reagan administration did not permit this arrangement to last beyond an election year. They began to "talk down" the dollar as against the yen, and the fall was tremendous: in the summer of 1985 the dollar bought 250 yen, and in September 1986, 154. Read another way, Japanese holders of U.S. government bonds lost nearly half their equity. But the precipitate drop did not bring Japanese holders of bonds to sell. The American export market was Japan's largest, taking a third of Japan's exports. The Japanese preferred heavy losses on dollar holdings to domestic unemployment caused by a sharp reduction in that market.

Last in the bewildering developments of the world market was the collapse of raw materials prices beginning in 1977. By early 1986 food, forest products, minerals, and metals were at the lowest levels in recorded history in relation to prices of manufactured goods and services. This was troublesome especially among the poorer nations, which often depend on income from exports of raw materials. As mentioned earlier, one of the reasons for unrest and revolution in Central America has been the fall in world prices for cotton and coffee.

Food was a good illustration of the declining price of raw materials. World agricultural output rose by one-third between 1972 and 1985, reaching an all-time high, and the rise seemed necessary because of the world population increase, from 3 billion in 1960 to 4 billion in 1976 to 5 billion in 1986. But food production increased faster than population, and the glut took prices down. The drop was likely to be permanent. There seemed no way for an agricultural exporter such as the United States to export any additionally large amounts of food. Even Russian needs were not enough to take up the world excess. The starving multitudes in Africa were humanly appalling in their needs, but of only marginal help in ending the glut of food. Some of the increase in food stocks occurred because of new strains of seeds introduced in the 1950s when the population problem was worrying everyone. Some came from better control of the grain produced, as in India, where in the 1950s rats and insects consumed up to 80 percent of harvests; new cement bins and quick hauling to market solved that problem.

As food is now plentiful and cheap—too cheap, farmers in Australia and Iowa are saying—so are forest products, minerals, and metals. The lack of markets for raw materials is not due to lower industrial production, for industries in all large nations produce more each year. The problem has been a steady fall in use. Substitution of cheaper items has reduced demand since the year 1900; by 1986 the industrial nations were using less of the old raw materials—Japan's consumption in 1984 was down to 60 percent of that of 1973. One observer has written that fifty to a hundred pounds of fiberglass cable transmit as many telephone messages as a ton of copper wire; yet to produce the fiberglass cable takes 5 percent of the energy needed to produce a ton of wire. Plastics used in automobile bodies cost less than half of the steel they replace. Like the market for food, the markets for raw materials may never return.

It's easier to understand economic problems than to suggest how nations might respond. One hopes that time will reveal the solutions—for continued economic growth must underlie any chance of world peace.

4. *Toward the Future*

During the Reagan administration, strategy toward the Soviet Union nominally departed from détente, events in Central America and South Africa careened out of control, and economic wisdom faltered in the face of world economic confusion. Still, the major world problem—not just that of the Reagan administration but of all peoples of the world—remained the nuclear arms race. In the absence of serious measures to slow down the race, nuclear war threatened to reduce all the other problems—détente versus deterrence, Central America and South Africa, economic confusion—to insignificance.

It was true that after more than forty years of the nuclear age there had been no nuclear war, and this was encouraging. Perhaps it was the existence of nuclear arms. Churchill had said that the only thing that prevented a third world war was nuclear arms. He described the standoff as the "balance of terror." Whatever the wavering of individuals, the statement-making of diplomats as well as military figures, not to mention the frequent suggestions of publicists that this or that might bring nuclear war, it seemed to be true that sensitivity to what nuclear war could do to the world had prevented the statesmen of Washington and Moscow from resorting to nuclear weapons as a solution to their nations' disagreements.

Certainly the situation in the United States and the Soviet Union was far different from what had obtained in the Europe of the 1930s, when an adventurer had gained control of a great state and precipitated the Second World War. No leader of the superpowers had willed such a result and worked incessantly to produce it. Instead the presidents of the United States and the several premiers of the Soviet Union had proved cautious in the extreme in handling the nuclear hardware that was in their charge. On occasion matters had gone farther than desirable, notably in 1962 during the Cuban missile crisis when Soviet-American disagreement became public, which meant that it became much more difficult to manage, as it involved public opinion. Still, by and large, the statesmen of the past forty years or so, even including Stalin and Khrushchev, were careful about nuclear issues.

The danger of nuclear war remains, though. It stems not so much from the chance of human error or mechanical failure; there are many safeguards that protect against a war triggered in this way. The danger instead is comparable to what happened in 1914, when the First World War broke out not because any nation wanted it, nor because any general staff desired it, nor because of any personal error or mechanical accident. War came when the assassination of the Archduke Francis Ferdinand on June 28, 1914, activated a chain of military and diplomatic reactions that led to confrontation. The alliance system kept the chain reaction going, and soon military mobilizations, which were easier to start than to stop, led to war. It was a relatively slow movement; the Austrians waited a month after the assassination of the archduke before they bombarded Belgrade, the capital of Serbia, and the entrance of the Russians and Germans, and the French and British, required another week. But the sequence of events seemed inexorable.

A similar ratcheting effect, in which events develop their own momentum apart from any person's intention, could lead even careful nations to a nuclear exchange. And considering the power of nuclear weapons, the prospect of controlling a nuclear exchange is slim. As Paul Bracken recently has written, "wartime conditions will impose a radically different information regime on the victim's command system. Because of the destructiveness of nuclear weapons and the vulnerability of communication linkages, a command will be shattered into separated islands of disconnected forces once it is subjected to heavy nuclear attack. Each separated island will then face its own individual assessment problem." At that point, to be sure, the possibility of forestalling a retaliatory nuclear storm would disappear, lost in individual actions.

In recent years statesmen have tried to cut their way out of this thicket, to get their countries out of the military jungle, through strokes of diplomatic sanity. At a meeting in Reykjavik, Iceland, in October 1986, President Reagan and the new Soviet leader Mikhail Gorbachev seemed to approach the disarmament problem emotionally, both of them almost agreeing on a ten-year phase-out of all ballistic missiles. This would not eliminate nuclear weapons but only the least controllable—the swiftest—carriers; airplanes, cruise missiles, and artillery pieces would remain. It would be a first move, and would open the way for others.

Unfortunately a domestic American political confusion ensued that cut the ground from under Reykjavik. It emerged that the Reagan administration had furnished arms to Iran, through the Israelis, in exchange for the use of Iranian influence with the Muslim fundamentalist faction(s) that held several Americans hostage in Lebanon. When this diplomacy came to light it showed the president dealing with the Iranians when both he and Secretary of State Shultz had said there could be no compromise with terrorism. The president tried to stand firm on the Iranian diplomacy. He announced that he would not dismiss his national security adviser, Vice Admiral John M. Poindexter, who had handled the Iranian negotiations. Then the attorney general said that Poindexter's assistant had taken money received from the arms sale and disbursed it to the Nicaraguan Contras who were being denied money by Congress. The president dismissed the assistant, and Poindexter resigned. If the president had known of the diversion of money, he would have acted illegally. In this confusion the President retreated on Reykjavik, retracting what he had said to Gorbachev and giving the impression that he could not trust the Russians. Nuclear armaments remained at their exceedingly dangerous impasse.

ADDITIONAL READING

The Reagan presidency has produced only a small literature thus far, as appraisals necessarily must be tentative and the article and book writers have not had much time anyway. But see Ronnie Dugger, *On Reagan* (New York, 1983), and Robert Dallek, *Ronald Reagan* (Cambridge, Mass., 1984). For foreign policy see Seyom Brown, *The Faces of Power: Constancy and Change in United States Foreign Policy from Truman to Reagan* (New York, 1983), and I. M. Destler, Leslie H. Gelb, and Anthony Lake, *Our Own Worst Enemy* (New York, 1985). Presidential Russian policy is in John Lewis Gaddis, *Strategies of Containment* (New York, 1982), a remarkable effort at synthesis of policy from the Truman era down to its date of publication; and Raymond L. Garthoff, *Détente and Confrontation: American-Soviet Relations from Nixon to Reagan* (Washington, D.C., 1985).

Military policy is in Herbert Scoville, Jr., *MX: Prescription for Disaster* (Cambridge, Mass., 1981); John Edwards, *Superweapon: The Making of MX* (New York, 1982); Lewis A. Dunn, *Controlling the Bomb: Nuclear Proliferation in the 1980s* (New Haven, Conn., 1982); George F. Kennan, *The Nuclear Delusion* (New York, 1982); Paul Bracken, *The Command and Control of Nuclear Forces* (New Haven, Conn., 1983), which believes that in any nuclear war the military's command and control will break down; Edward N. Luttwak, *The Pentagon and the Art of War* (New York, 1984), a slashing attack upon Pentagon bureaucracy; William M. Arkin, "Sleight of Hand with Trident II," *Bulletin of the Atomic Scientists*, Dec. 1984, pp. 5–6, the rapidly increasing accuracy and throw-weight of the new sea-based missiles; Gregg Herken, *Counsels of War* (New York, 1985), rivalries and theories; and Paul B. Stares, *The Militarization of Space* (Ithaca, N.Y., 1985).

The intelligence establishment, on which so much U.S. policy now rests, appears in James Bamford, *The Puzzle Palace* (Boston, 1982), about the National Security Agency, and Stansfield Turner, *Secrecy and Democracy* (Boston, 1985), by a recent CIA director.

For Central America there is Alan Riding, "The Central American Quagmire," *Foreign Affairs*, Vol. 61 (1982–1983): 641–658; Walter LaFeber, *Inevitable Revolutions* (New York, 1983); and Kenneth M. Coleman and George C. Herring, eds., *The Central American Crisis* (Wilmington, Del., 1986).

For Africa a good place to begin is with the several collections edited by Gwendolen M. Carter and Patrick O'Meara: *Southern Africa* (2d ed., Bloomington, Ind., 1982); *International Politics in Southern Africa* (1982); *African Independence* (1986). Also Phyllis M. Martin and Patrick O'Meara, eds., *Africa* (2d ed., Bloomington, Ind., 1986), and J. Gus Liebenow, *African Politics* (Bloomington, Ind., 1986). See also Thomas J. Noer, *Cold War and Black Liberation: The United States and White Rule in Africa, 1948–1968* (Columbia, Mo., 1985), and Joseph Hanlon, *Beggar Your Neighbours: Apartheid Power in Southern Africa* (Bloomington, Ind., 1986).

Economic problems have their appraisals in Barbara Insel, "A World Awash in Grain," *Foreign Affairs*, Vol. 63 (1984–1985):892–911, and Peter F. Drucker, "The Changed World Economy," *Foreign Affairs*, Vol. 64 (1985–1986):768–791. See also the special analyses of Alfred E. Eckes, Jr., in *A Search for Solvency: Bretton Woods and the International Monetary System, 1941–1971* (Austin, 1975) and *The United States and the Global Struggle for Minerals* (Austin, 1975). David P. Calleo looks over policy since the 1960s in *The Imperious Economy* (Cambridge, Mass., 1982).

Index